INVISIBLE

INVISIBLE

The Forgotten Story of
the Black Woman Lawyer
Who Took Down America's
Most Powerful Mobster

STEPHEN L. CARTER

HENRY HOLT AND COMPANY
NEW YORK

Henry Holt and Company
Publishers since 1866
175 Fifth Avenue
New York, New York 10010
www.henryholt.com

Henry Holt® and ⟨image⟩® are registered trademarks of Macmillan Publishing Group, LLC.

Library of Congress Cataloging-in-Publication Data

Names: Carter, Stephen L., 1954– author.
Title: Invisible : the forgotten story of the black woman lawyer who took down America's most
    powerful mobster / Stephen L. Carter.
Description: First edition. | New York, NY : Henry Holt and Company, 2018. | Includes index.
Identifiers: LCCN 2017050088 | ISBN 9781250121974 (hardcover)
Subjects: LCSH: Carter, Stephen L., 1954– —Family. | African American authors—Biography. |
    African American families—Biography. | African American women lawyers—Biography.
Classification: LCC PS3603.A78 Z46 2018 | DDC 813/.6 [B] —dc23
LC record available at https://lccn.loc.gov/2017050088

Our books may be purchased in bulk for promotional, educational, or business use. Please contact
your local bookseller or the Macmillan Corporate and Premium Sales Department at (800) 221-7945,
extension 5442, or by e-mail at MacmillanSpecialMarkets@macmillan.com.

First Edition 2018

Designed by Meryl Sussman Levavi

Printed in the United States of America

10   9   8   7   6   5   4   3   2   1

To Leah Cristina Aird Carter,
without whose dedication, imagination,
research, travel, interviews, love for the subject,
and keen editorial advice the project would
have been impossible.
This book is hers as well as mine.

They wove a spell and took possession of one, yet all the while one was conscious of a certain familiarity.

—Eunice Roberta Hunton,
"Replica" (1924)

CONTENTS

PART II: PASSION

PROLOGUE

THE RAIDS WERE SET FOR NINE P.M.

So secret were the targets that the one hundred sixty New York City police officers involved were not allowed to see their orders until five minutes before the hour. They were told to wait on specified street corners for final instructions. Corruption in the city was that bad. If the cops had known in advance where they were going, the suspects would have been gone long before the raids started. So they waited, stamping their feet against the winter chill. In the frigid night air, their breath formed a faint curling mist. It was February 1, 1936, an icy cold night to be chasing some colored woman lawyer's crazy theory.

At eight fifty-five, the orders were opened. The targets were brothels, eighty in all, some of them fancy townhouses, others no more than tiny back rooms. All were believed to pay tribute to the Mob leaders who ran crime in the city.

The police went in as scheduled. At most addresses they knocked and were admitted. At some they broke down the doors. They found women and men alike in various stages of undress. One woman fled "partly unclad" down a fire escape. Some of the customers climbed out windows. Others slipped past the cops and into the street. This was not difficult, because few of the raids comprised more than two or three officers.

But most of the men were detained. Many were prominent city professionals: lawyers, bankers, civil servants. The orders were to question the men long enough to get evidence that prostitution was taking place, then let them go. The women were handcuffed, taken to the station houses for booking, then transported in taxicabs and whatever else was available to the Woolworth Building, on lower Broadway, at this time still one of the three tallest in the world. They rode the freight elevator to the thirteenth floor. The thirteenth floor was usually unoccupied but tonight was buzzing with activity, for it had been taken over for the next few days by the team of lawyers assembled to work with Thomas Dewey, the special prosecutor for organized crime. One of the lawyers logged and tagged the women as they arrived. Her name was Eunice Carter, and she was both the only woman and the only Negro on the team.

Months earlier she had come up with the theory that the Combination, which controlled prostitution in the city, was run by Lucky Luciano, the most powerful Mafia leader in the country. Dewey had been skeptical but had finally agreed to let her look into it. Eunice had drafted another lawyer to help. Together they had assembled the evidence and badgered Dewey until he yielded. The team had convicted some minor organized crime figures, but Luciano had proved untouchable. There was no way to connect him with the multifarious businesses, legal and illegal, from which he took a cut. Everyone was scared of him. He had risen to the top by ruthlessly eliminating those above him and those who were his equals, including some who had helped him in his climb. No one would testify against him. So Dewey had agreed to try Eunice's idea.

The February raid produced a wealth of witnesses and leads, and as evidence against Luciano mounted, he slipped out of the city. He turned up in Hot Springs, Arkansas, famous at the time both as a place to gamble and as a place for fugitives to hide out. Local authorities kept finding reasons to keep him there rather than let him be extradited. Finally the state attorney general intervened. The mobster offered him a $50,000 bribe. To no avail. The judge told Luciano's lawyers he had no choice but to send him to New York. Three city detectives accompanied him on the train ride northward.

Lucky Luciano—known to his intimates as Charley Lucky—was more than another powerful gangster. He had, in a sense, invented the modern Mafia, arranging for power to be shared among several "families" rather than vested in the traditional *capo di tutti capi*. He had devised the system under which the heads of the families would meet regularly to set policy and settle disputes. And he had, until recently, successfully kept his name out of the headlines. But here he was, under arrest, hauled into court like any other mobster.

Luciano's trial on prostitution charges was held not in the New York criminal court building but in the civil courthouse on Foley Square, on the ironic ground that it was easier to fortify against a possible Mafia assault. There were guards everywhere. Not since the Civil War, the papers clamored, had New York City seen such armament. Forty patrolmen on foot and six on horseback kept back the surging crowds outside the courthouse. Two dozen detectives were posted in the courtroom or just outside. These were in addition to court officers and sheriff's deputies without number. Newsmen and photographers thronged the hallways.

In June, to widespread astonishment, the jury convicted Luciano of compulsory prostitution. Eunice, listening to the verdict in the courtroom, probably kept her usual poker face. But she must have felt a certain satisfaction. She was black and a woman and a lawyer, a graduate of Smith and the granddaughter of three slaves and one free woman of color, as dazzlingly unlikely a combination as one could imagine in New York of the 1930s, and without her work the Mafia boss would never have been convicted. She was an ambitious woman and had plans. She was just shy of her thirty-seventh birthday, and had come a long way from her segregated Atlanta childhood. Hers was the idea that had put away the country's biggest gangster. In the process she had become one of the best-known Negro women in America. She would receive honorary degrees, be featured in *Life* magazine, lecture around the world, be handed medals and plaques from civic organizations everywhere. She would become a prominent and influential figure in the Republican Party. Her professional future seemed to pulse with bright and endless possibility. As she sat there on that fine June afternoon, she must have believed that she had only to reach out her hand and choose a direction.

Eunice Carter was my grandmother. This book is her story.

Eunice died when I was in high school, and I remember her mainly as a stern and intimidating woman of advanced years. She had a younger brother, Alphaeus, who would have been my great-uncle, though I have no memory of having met him. But, as I have learned while at work on this project, he figured prominently in her life. I have never known my forebears as well as I should have. My parents, like so many others in the darker nation, shared the family stories of achievement but omitted the details of racial slights and discrimination, as if the telling were subject to what the historian Jonathan Holloway describes as a "psychologically enduring editor's pencil." So for me, writing this book has been a journey of discovery, both about my own family and about the history of the community that Eunice and Alphaeus, in very different ways, tried to serve. In the process, I have gained a richer understanding of the world that formed my grandmother, and perhaps, as well, a greater sympathy for her habit of holding her grandchildren at a stern distance.

It is the curse of historians, as the estimable Gordon Wood pointed out in gentler language, to judge the past by the norms of the present. Here I will try my best not to do that. If sometimes I slip—if now and then my passion seeps through—the reason is that the experience of reliving my grandmother's story is filled as much with pain as with pride. Her accomplishments were remarkable, but there is tragedy mixed with the triumph. Things did not always work out as neatly as they might have had she been white, or male, or both. The triumph of Eunice's story involves her constant and remarkable reinvention. As ambition drove her ever upward, she would find her path blocked—now by race, now by gender, now by politics. Sometimes she would march through the barriers. Other times she would find a new and different route toward higher ground. The point was to be always in motion while remaining faithful to the values to which she had been raised.

My grandmother's life was far more complex than what we learn of her in books about the Luciano case or even in family legend, and this complexity mirrors that of the black community itself, or of African America, if you like—or, as I prefer to say, of the darker nation. So although what follows is in part the story of an extraordinary individual, it is also the story of an extraordinary people, a community that has survived all the wickedness visited upon it over the past four hundred years—a people, as my wife, Enola, likes to say, who made a way out of no way.

Much of what you are about to read may seem unbelievable. But there really were black people a century ago who did the things that I will describe, who wrote and spoke the way they do here, who accomplished the feats that move this story. True, the people you will encounter in these pages were not all there was to the darker nation. They were a thin slice. African America, then as now, comprised mostly people who lacked both the advantages and the opportunities available to many in this tale. But the struggle to build lives and families in the whitest and harshest days of segregation was their common fate. And yet from within that segregated world emerged remarkable stories of triumph.

In the fall of 2014, two episodes of HBO's *Boardwalk Empire,* which is set during and just after Prohibition, featured a black female lawyer who worked for the New York district attorney. The role was small. She had perhaps two lines. Still, viewers were incredulous. Online comment threads swiftly filled with mockery: Ridiculous. Anachronistic. One post after another insisted that there weren't black lawyers back then—not black women lawyers, anyway. And certainly there were no black female prosecutors. The casting, the skeptics insisted, was just another example of Hollywood political correctness run amok.

But they were wrong. My Nana Eunice was real ... and really did prosecute mobsters ... and lived a life so remarkable that her story should have been told long ago. I am grateful for the opportunity to tell it now.

One word of warning before we begin. The era in which Eunice lived was not politically correct. Neither will this book be. I will use the words to refer to the race that people would have used at the time. To do otherwise would be an insult to a proud people and a prouder history. The darker nation has survived worse than a few uncomfortable words. For there is a secret our forefathers and foremothers knew that we nowadays too readily forget: if you let them know that their words are getting to you, they will never stop repeating them.

PART I

INHERITANCE

A child has a right to the inheritance of the very best of body and soul its parents can bestow. If these are not granted, the child is defrauded of its birth-right.

—ADDIE HUNTON,
"A Pure Motherhood the Basis
of Racial Integrity" (1902)

CHAPTER 1

THE BURNING

ATLANTA WAS BURNING. THROUGHOUT THE FOURTH WARD, HOUSES and businesses were aflame. Ordinarily the neighborhood bustled with life—lunch counters and banks, doctors and dentists, stores and churches, saloons and back alleys, all thick with the burgeoning middle class of the darker nation. But on this violent night, colored families huddled in back rooms behind drawn shades. Lamps were doused. Pistols and hunting rifles were solemnly distributed among wives and children, because at any minute the angry white mob might break down the door. Rumors flew from house to house: Negroes pulled from the streetcars on the bridge and beaten to death on the tracks below. Negroes shot to death while trying to protect their property. Most of the rumors were true. It was late September of 1906, and the complacency of black Atlanta had been shattered.

Among those waiting for the mob to come were William and Addie Hunton, along with their two young children. Eunice was seven years old. William Junior had just turned three. The family's home at 418 Houston Street was several blocks from the epicenter of the violence, but the Huntons were as frightened as everyone else. What Addie would later call the "pent-up hate and envy of a dominant group" had burst whatever shaky norms of civility and decorum had previously managed to hold it in check. The riot had taken everyone by surprise. The commercial classes of black and white Atlanta were deeply intertwined through networks of loans, services, and trade goods. Slavery had been dead for four decades. Civic leaders touted the city as an example of what the South could be. To be sure, just two years earlier Atlanta had accepted the Supreme Court's invitation in *Plessy v. Ferguson* and imposed racial segregation on its streetcars. To be sure, the local papers had for several days run screaming headlines about nonexistent assaults by Negro men on white women. To be sure, rival Democratic candidates for governor were competing over whose program would more thoroughly disenfranchise the darker nation. To be sure, a white neighbor had recently told Addie that she was very sorry but their children couldn't play together anymore: people were beginning to talk. In short, all black Atlanta must surely have felt something wicked brewing. But nobody knew it would be as bad as this.

The violence continued for two days. The mob has been estimated variously from the middle hundreds to the middle thousands. Negroes were beaten. Many were killed. The precise number is disputed because nobody in those days kept careful count of dead Negroes, least of all in the South. The deaths may have numbered over a hundred.

Yet the main target was not people. The main target was property. The riot began on lower Peachtree Street, at that time the heart of the Negro business district. Black-owned banks and insurance companies, barbershops and restaurants, real estate agents and newspapers, all had premises there. Many subsisted heavily on business with white customers. The mob did not care who the customers were. The mob cared who the owners were. For years worried whites had been exchanging whispered half-truths: The Negro middle class was taking over Atlanta. Negro workers were taking white people's jobs. And at lower wages. The politicians refused to act, so the rioters took matters into their own hands. The Fourth Ward was where the well-to-do of the city's black community lived; the Fourth Ward, therefore, would be the target.

Family legend holds that the rioters stopped one house away from the Hunton residence at 418 Houston Street. Possibly the tale is even true. The block on which my great-grandparents lived was half black and half white, neatly segregated down the middle, and their house sat precisely on the border. (In case the mob wondered which homes to attack, the city directory helpfully appended next to the name of each colored family the symbol "(c).") A white neighbor had offered to hide the Huntons should they be driven from their home, but they chose to stay and guard the house. There is no family story on whether William and Addie armed themselves against the mob, but they might well have. At this time, owning a firearm was still a signal of manhood, and despite efforts to restrict gun possession among Negroes, most colored households would have had weapons of some kind. The guns, as it turned out, were needed. When the rioters grew bored of burning and killing in the environs of Peachtree Street, they tried to leave the business district and swarm into the residential areas, spilling onto the tree-lined lanes amongst the stout houses, searching for fresh targets. They were greeted with a hail of gunfire as Negro families protected their own.

The mob fled.

I have little trouble imagining the family's relief.

Of course the police eventually arrived, followed the next day by the state militia, which made several hundred arrests. And in a mighty show of egalitarianism, a handful of those locked up were even white. But most of those arrested were black men with guns, trying to protect their homes and businesses. In the Brownsville neighborhood, near the city's great Negro colleges and universities, a combination of mob and militiamen went door to door, searching for weapons. Men who resisted were shot dead. Many of the rest were dragged off to Atlanta's dreaded stockade. Nobody was surprised. Negroes were constantly being arrested in the city, for crimes they committed and for crimes they did not, for rudeness or talking back or looking at a white woman, for being in the wrong neighborhood or being suspected of being in the vicinity of the wrong neighborhood. Upon conviction, many of these men were, in the words of one historian, "literally sold to the highest bidders." Convicts were much in demand as workers, and the state, not the convict, got the wage.

After the wave of arrests, local newspapers assured their white readers that the city was now safe from marauding Negroes with guns. The newspapers, of course, had the facts backward, probably on purpose.

Atlanta's black middle class realized that its tranquil existence in the midst of Jim Crow was a lie. The riot had shaken the general sense of security. Among those shaken were the Huntons. William's work took him away frequently. He was an international secretary for the Young Men's Christian Association, and his duties led him all over the world. He had lunched at Buckingham Palace. In a few weeks he was scheduled to give a speech in Tokyo. Addie, too, was frequently out of town. She was a popular writer and speaker on issues of race and womanhood. She lectured all over the North. She taught part-time at a Negro college in Alabama. When both parents were away, a maid or a friend looked after the children. Now that seemed inadequate protection. William and Addie made their decision. Atlanta was no longer safe. They would take their children and move north.

The Huntons were not alone. The emigrants numbered in the thousands. Black and white leaders alike begged the Negro middle class to stay, and begged those who had left to return. Scant weeks after the riot, President John Bowen of Gammon Theological Seminary would write an essay assuring those who had fled that order had been restored and the community was safe. Booker T. Washington himself wrote to the *New York Age*, an influential Negro paper, urging students at Atlanta's several black colleges to head back to the city, where "the dangerous period, I am sure, has passed." But the exodus continued.

The migration frightened Dixie. The South was losing both cheap labor and skilled professionals. Hoping to keep Negroes put or lure them back, Southern states began running newspaper advertisements in the North touting their virtues. The ads spoke of wonderful colored schools and plentiful land for cultivation, available at low prices. Some counties bragged that they had never had a lynching. A few states even sent commissions to Northern cities to make the case for return face-to-face. Few of the emigrants listened—and William and Addie Hunton were not among the few. "With the Huntons' departure," one historian has written, "black Atlanta lost two of its most influential black activists."

Actually the family's life in Atlanta had been rounded by violence. Their arrival in the spring of 1899 happened to coincide with the lynching of Sam Hose, a particularly brutal murder that made worldwide headlines, not least because for the next few days you could buy pieces of the mutilated Negro in the city's shops. After the lynching, the Huntons considered leaving but decided that duty required them to stay. The themes of duty and hard sacrifice, learned at her parents' feet, would become a constant of their daughter's life.

When the family arrived in Atlanta, Addie was pregnant. Two earlier children, Bernice and William, had died in infancy, probably of tuberculosis. The third pregnancy proved difficult. The Huntons worried. So cautious were they that William did not so much as mention Addie's pregnancy to his protégé and close friend Jesse Moorland until June. Before that, William had only dropped hints. "Have lots to tell you," he had written in April. "But must wait." When their third child, a girl, arrived on July 16, 1899, her parents did not give her a name. Not at first. They wanted to make sure that she would survive. As late as August 8, in a letter to Moorland, William would refer to his daughter only as "Sugar."

Two weeks later, Sugar finally had a name. On August 22, William wrote to Moorland from Atlanta: "Wife, Eunice Roberta and I are well and send regards to Mrs. Moorland. Our house is going up nicely."

She had a name. She had a house. "Eunice came and bound our love more closely," her mother would write years later.

In October of 1899, when Eunice was three months old, the family took possession of "their handsome new home" at 418 Houston Street—an event recorded in a popular *Atlanta Constitution* column called "What the Negro Is Doing." The house no longer stands, and no images have survived, but photographs of other dwellings from the neighborhood in that era show gabled Victorians with wide, ornate porches. The Hunton home is usually described as "modest." This should not be taken to mean that it was small. Thirty years later, Eunice would recall that the family "lived quite comfortably, in a 12-room house staffed by a cook and a maid and a man to tend the furnace and garden."

The property lay at the less expensive end of Houston Street. Farther west were the larger and more impressive homes of the truly well-off of the darker nation. It is a peculiar irony of our history that it cost less to build nearer to the white precincts of the Fourth Ward. Down at the better end of Houston Street lived the Whites, George and Madeline, whose son Walter would grow up to become the revered head of the National Association for the Advancement of Colored People. The Whites and the Huntons were friends. Their children knew each other. George White was a mailman. Federal jobs like his were precious and highly sought after. On the night of the riot, the White home was specifically targeted by the rioters. They tried to burn the house, shouting, "It's too nice for a nigger to live in!" But the Whites were among those who returned fire, driving the mob away.

Just beyond the White home lay Peachtree Street, with its increasing number of Negro businesses. One popular destination was the Gate City Drug Store, a black-owned pharmacy and lunch counter that "served as a busy gathering place for working- and middle-class black Atlantans." (One of the grievances of the mob, later, was the transfer of the store from white to black ownership.) Gate City proudly advertised its soda fountain as "the most costly one in the south." Nearby was the Freedman's Bank. At 66 Peachtree Street was the "elegant and palatial" barbershop owned by the legendary Alonzo Herndon, at that time the city's preeminent barber, whose employees were all black and whose clientele was exclusively white. The neighborhood where the Huntons built their house was home to many of the great institutions of colored Atlanta. The family worshipped at First Congregational Church, led by the Reverend Henry Hugh Proctor, at that time perhaps the most prominent Negro preacher in America. And just around the corner from the Huntons' home was the most revered institution in the Fourth Ward—the Houston Street School, the place where their precious Eunice began her formal education.

The Houston Street School, properly known as the Gate City Colored Public School or the Fourth Ward Grammar School, was located at 399 Houston. It was one of only three schools for colored children in the entire city, and, when it opened, the only one staffed by black teachers and run by a black principal. "[T]he colored people insisted on having persons of their own race teach their children," noted the head of the school board in apparent perplexity. The school was the pride of the community. In the midst of the Fourth Ward, the middle classes of the darker nation were creating a world in the teeth of a system that, to say the least, had other plans for Negro education. The Houston Street School, by all accounts, represented exactly what the segregationists feared. It was a place where the darker nation could raise its own children to its own values. Its commitment to excellence would be lauded for decades in the memoirs of leaders of the race. Assuming the Huntons followed the same model as other parents in the Fourth Ward, Eunice most likely enrolled in 1904, just after her fifth birthday.

By this time, the family had a fourth member. William Alphaeus Hunton Jr. was born in September of 1903. He was named after his father, of course, but also after the brother who had died in infancy. To avoid confusion, William Junior soon became known as plain Alphaeus. Both children struggled with bouts of illness. So did their mother. William sometimes described Addie as sickly, and perhaps she passed on this trait to her children.

Despite the cook and the maid, Eunice's family was far from wealthy. Her father William, born in Canada, was the only black international secretary for the Young Men's Christian Association. The YMCA of the early 1900s had not yet been reduced to running health clubs and providing inexpensive accommodations; the association of that day was a rich and powerful organization with chapters around the globe. Her father's constant travel was in service of the organization's goal of building strong and virtuous Christian men. William was responsible for creating almost from scratch the network of colored YMCA branches in the United States, a necessity at a time when the Christian warriors who ran the group countenanced the widespread racial segregation by the local branches. (A branch in Norfolk, Virginia, still bears his name.) And because the International Board was headquartered in Switzerland and held conferences all over the world, William was frequently abroad.

He built the house on Houston Street for the family he and his wife hoped to have. The couple moved from Virginia to Atlanta, Addie would later write, because William considered the city "a very desirable center for the supervision of student work to which he then hoped to devote the major part of his time."

Addie had attended a prestigious Boston high school. In Atlanta

Eunice's mother, Addie Waites Hunton, in the early 1900s. Addie was an activist and clubwoman, and famous throughout the community for her views on Negro motherhood.
HUNTON FAMILY PHOTOGRAPH

Eunice's father, William Alphaeus Hunton Sr., an international secretary of the Young Men's Christian Association.
HUNTON FAMILY PHOTOGRAPH

she taught penmanship and shorthand to girls. Sometimes she taught them at the local colored branch of the Young Women's Christian Association. Sometimes she taught them in her home. At one point William complained to his friend Jesse Moorland that her students had started to overwhelm the household.

The Huntons moved comfortably in Negro society. The family's comings and goings featured regularly in the pages of the black press. Their future in Atlanta, in those halcyon days at the dawn of the century, seemed summery and bright.

William was a stern and often distant man, but he delighted in his playful and precocious daughter. In August of 1900, just after her first birthday, the ink was smudged in one of William's letters to Moorland, his confidant. "Eunice caused the blots above," he wrote indulgently. "She is into everything in a minute." Two months later we find this: "Eunice is as sweet as sugar & it will be hard to pull away Monday for a two months trip." Early the following year: "My stenographer [Addie] has gone to the Club. And this baby girl is a case. Anyway, she is a joy forever." In February he urged Moorland to bring his wife to Atlanta: "She [won't] believe how smart Eunice is, even when you tell her. She must come [&] see for herself." There are more letters in the same vein. And this outpouring of delight is unique in William's letters. On other topics he is either serious or grimly humorous. Nowhere else does he allow this simple joy to come to the surface. Plainly his daughter touched something in him that the rest of the family did not.

William was very much a man's man. When he had worries, he shared them not with his wife but with Jesse Moorland. Moorland, an Ohioan with a divinity degree, had become the association's second colored international secretary. The two men were the same age and had similar tastes and philosophies. Both were fired by a determination to build the YMCA within the darker nation even as they challenged its determination to maintain racially segregated branches. William's many letters to Moorland are full of emotion. At home with his wife, however, he was a stoic presence. Addie occasionally grew frustrated by his preternatural calm. She would rage at him, and in response he would quote Japanese philosophy. She loved her husband but now and then must have felt a degree of relief when he went on the road.

Addie also traveled, even if not as often as William. She served for a time as principal of the Commercial Department at Alabama's Agricultural and Mechanical College for Negroes (now the Alabama Agricultural and Mechanical University), in the town of Normal. There, too, she taught secretarial skills. Sometimes at her many speaking engagements Addie would be referred to as Mrs. Hunton of Normal, Alabama, rather than Mrs. Hunton of Atlanta, Georgia. In his two decades of correspondence with Moorland, William, too, always referred to his wife as Mrs. Hunton. But little Eunice, the apple of his eye, he called Sugar.

The Huntons moved to Brooklyn early in 1907. As it happened, in May of the same year, Antonio and Rosalia Lucania arrived in New York City from Palermo, joining tens of thousands of immigrants from Italy who that year spread themselves among the rows upon rows of tenements on the Lower East Side of Manhattan. Salvatore, their third son, was nine years old. His parents enrolled the boy at P.S. 19, where he somehow picked up the nickname Charley. Soon he would begin playing hooky to run the streets with a wild and violent bunch.

The Lucania family arrived just in time to endure the New York garbage strike of 1907, which began when cart drivers on the Lower East Side walked off their jobs in late June. Within two days, most of the drivers in the city were on strike. The great heaps of refuse and the baking summer heat transformed the busy streets into a fetid, steaming mess. Residents began setting the garbage ablaze, creating huge noxious bonfires. New Yorkers walked the streets with scarves and handkerchiefs covering mouths and noses.

A principal cause of the labor strife was the corruption in the city Sanitation Department. Supervisors routinely used their authority to penalize drivers who supported the wrong political candidates. Drivers who annoyed their bosses were sometimes fired illegally, and had no recourse. Most of the drivers were Italian Americans. The city sent out strikebreakers to collect the garbage. Armed groups of men scattered them. Police guards were set up. They fought pitched battles with angry mobs. The police used their revolvers. In response, bombs were tossed from rooftops. The mob found ways to evade the police and get at the drivers. The police presence was strengthened. In Harlem, where colored cart drivers were also on strike, a riot broke out. The police clubbed Negro men and women indiscriminately. Officers accused the women of grabbing them so the men could attack. The public, by now, was in open revolt. People just wanted the garbage collected. With the city under pressure, the strike was soon settled. Both wages and conditions for the drivers were improved. Charley Lucania may have still been a boy, but these men were his family's neighbors. He must have heard their stories. And he would surely have been impressed by the realization that city officials had no more integrity than anyone else. It was clear that there was money to be made from corruption, and in the decades to come he would make a great deal of it.

Across the East River, the black woman who would become his nemesis was also in grade school. Eunice was a year and a half Charley's junior. And although she was smart and ambitious and would grow up to be a lawyer, there was nothing in the inauspicious beginning of her career to suggest that when, later on, the boy grew up to be Lucky Luciano, the most powerful Mafia leader in history, she would be the one to take him down.

CHAPTER 2

THE LEGACY

THE CHARACTER TRAITS EUNICE WOULD REQUIRE FOR THE pursuit of Luciano ran deep in her family. Her parents were once sitting in a whites-only coach on a railroad train in the South. This was in the 1890s, right around the time the United States Supreme Court decided in *Plessy v. Ferguson* that railway segregation did not violate the Constitution. The conductor came along and ordered them to move. I can see him looming over them, prim and officious in his uniform with brass buttons and tie and billed cap, expecting the colored couple to comply at once. And following his orders would surely have been the wiser and easier response. But that did not happen. William talked the conductor into letting them stay where they were. William never so much as lost his temper. Instead, he reasoned the conductor around to his point of view.

Had the conductor not backed down, William would have faced arrest. But here the story has an intriguing coda. In Addie's telling, her husband, a man who devoted his life to battling unfair treatment of Negroes, undertook this courageous act not as a matter of egalitarian principle but so that his wife would not be discommoded. He was a great traditionalist, and would not see her embarrassed in such a fashion.

Actually William came by this fortitude naturally. We see the same determined calm in his father, Stanton Hunton, the grandfather Eunice never met but greatly admired. Born around 1809, Stanton was enslaved in Fauquier County, Virginia, where he was owned by a man named Thomas Hunton, who had been a general in two of the country's wars. The name of Stanton Hunton's father is unrecorded, although the historian Christine Lutz speculates (I am skeptical) that he might have been Thomas's brother William. Stanton's mother was probably a woman named Betty, owned by one Gustavus Horner of Fauquier County. In any case, his mother was surely enslaved; and so the act that led to Stanton's conception we might call less than voluntary. Like the forebears of so many African Americans, Stanton was a child of rape.

The Hunton family was a prominent one. Thomas's nephew Eppa Hunton II was a Confederate general in the Civil War and later a successful lawyer. The third Eppa, known as Eppa Hunton Jr., was a founder of what is today the powerhouse international law firm of Hunton & Williams. So if Lutz is correct that William Hunton was Stanton's father, then Eppa II was Stanton's cousin, and Eppa Jr., who founded the law firm, was his first cousin once removed.

Thomas died around 1829, and Stanton (known in those days as "Staunton") was one of fourteen slaves who passed into the hands of his wife, Mathilda, or "Mitilda" as she was called in her husband's will. Stanton was a skilled laborer, most likely a carpenter, although he has also been described as a blacksmith. According to family legend, Stanton escaped not once, not twice, but three times. On his third try, he reached Erie, Pennsylvania, a terminus of the Underground Railroad, where, so close to freedom, he was snared by the slave catchers and dragged back to Virginia. Another story holds that he was taught to read by the "kindhearted" woman who owned him (if we can consider "kindhearted" a human being who owns another). Kindhearted or not, during the agricultural depression that struck the South during the 1830s, Mathilda Hunton began selling off slaves. She finally sold Stanton to William C. Gaines, a notorious negrophobe. Gaines thought the presence of free Negroes constituted a dire threat to the Commonwealth and regularly lobbied for their forcible removal. And yet, probably with considerable reluctance, he allowed Stanton to purchase his freedom. Either Gaines, too, was experiencing liquidity problems or

Stanton had managed to earn so much money that the bargain was too good to refuse.

Stanton Hunton's deed of emancipation—again, in the document he is "Staunton"—is dated January 24, 1837. It was filed in the courthouse the following day, at which point, in the eyes of the law, he became a free man. After purchasing his freedom from Gaines, Stanton remained for a time in Virginia. The state law requiring freedmen to leave the Commonwealth within six months allowed exceptions by court order. Many former slaves remained longer. In 1840, about 10 percent of Virginia's black population was free. Neighbors rarely turned in freedmen who overstayed the legal limit, and the authorities, even if informed that a free Negro was living in Virginia illegally, almost never took formal action. So Stanton, had he wished, could probably have stayed without penalty. But he decided to ask formal permission. Perhaps this was prudence, but one observer has suggested that Stanton was trying to show himself to be "a loyal and dutiful person attempting to live within the law." Whatever Stanton's motive, in early July of 1837—just short of the six-month grace period—he filed a formal petition at the Fauquier County courthouse asking for an extension. The petition was joined by two other former slaves, one of whom was also filing on behalf of her children. Apparently no one objected.

Stanton eventually left Virginia and—again, according to family legend—crossed the Potomac into Washington, D.C., where for a time he made his home. Nothing is known of his years there. Presumably he worked at his trade, saving money with which to continue his journey. Yet even in freedom Stanton would have been in danger. The city at this time was full of freedmen and runaways alike. A Negro might be stopped by the authorities at any moment. The officers would demand to see his manumission papers. If he could not produce them, he could be arrested on the spot and sold back into enslavement. Probably Stanton did not stay in Washington an instant longer than he had to.

By 1843, Stanton had crossed the Canadian border and found his way to Chatham, Ontario, a town in Kent County that had become a haven for the formerly enslaved. There Stanton prospered. A street of businesses in buildings he constructed was known as the Hunton Block.

In 1846, now formally known as Stanton, he traveled to Natchez, Mississippi, to purchase the freedom of his brother Benjamin. Free black men in Mississippi—the state was notorious for this—were often arrested and sold back into slavery, and this fate was more likely to befall free Negroes in and around Natchez than in the rest of the state. Stanton went anyway, made a deal with the man who owned Benjamin, and brought his brother back.

In 1858, the abolitionist John Brown arrived in Chatham. Brown was recruiting for his planned raid on Harpers Ferry, a murderous attack that has gone down in history as a precipitating cause of the Civil War. Brown hoped to provoke a slave rebellion. A large public meeting of Chatham men cheered him. But the pending raid was a secret vouchsafed only to a few. Stanton was among the few. A family story holds that the attack was largely planned at the Hunton kitchen table. The story is likely an exaggeration, but Stanton was certainly involved. He was nearly fifty, but Brown's vision enthralled him. He even wanted to accompany the raiders. His family talked him out of it.

Brown launched his assault in October of 1859. He had guns ready to be distributed to the slaves he assumed would flock to his banner. But the word never got out. The townspeople fought back. Two were killed. A contingent of federal troops arrived, under the command of Colonel Robert E. Lee. Brown and his men were cornered. Several died in a firefight. The rest were captured. Brown was tried and hanged. Had Stanton gone, he would doubtless have been hanged alongside him, as was the one Chathamite who had joined the band. When the names found on documents in Brown's possession at the time of his arrest were published in the newspapers, "S. Hunton" was among them. With cries for the arrest and execution of all of Brown's co-conspirators echoing in the North as well as the South, Stanton never returned to the nation of his birth.

By this time Stanton was married to a woman named Mary Ann Conyer, of whom little is known except that she was from Cincinnati and had been born free. Together they had nine children. The eldest was named Benjamin, after Stanton's brother, who had died not long after his rescue from enslavement. William Alphaeus Hunton was the couple's seventh child, arriving in October 1863. He was born, wrote

Addie later, "into a free and intelligent atmosphere" and was blessed with "a large and happy family." His mother died four years later, after giving birth to two more children. After that, his sister took over the household, with the assistance, for a time, of Mary's "stern but devoted" mother.

As a boy, William was known to friends as "Billie," a nickname Addie tells us she refused to use even though her husband urged her to. William's upbringing was strict and traditionalist. His father was of the view that "boys should be systematically industrious." Therefore, he loaded down his sons with chores: cutting and cleaning, running errands, and even managing his various businesses. Stanton believed that hands should never be idle. When his sons ran out of chores, he would send them out back, where he stored the bricks he used in his construction business, and have them move the heavy piles from one corner to the other. If the workday was still not done, he would instruct them to do the same in reverse.

The strictness of William's raising would color his entire life. Nothing was as important as duty. He excelled at Chatham's Wilberforce Academy, a private school on whose board his father served, and afterward found employment with the Canadian government in Ottawa. But he soon accepted a position with the YMCA, where he was swiftly named secretary of the colored branch in Norfolk, Virginia. Ranking officials of the association wondered whether it was wise to send a black Canadian into the United States—worse, into the South—where the racial norms would be very different from those to which he had been raised. But they had not reckoned with the Hunton fortitude. William, unruffled, made a considerable success of the Norfolk branch, not least because of his success in persuading local white merchants to open their wallets. Soon, aided by his wife, Addie, he began to expand his YMCA operation across the region.

Addie was born, probably in June 1866, into a prosperous Norfolk family. Her parents, Jessie Waits and Adelina Lawton, had both been enslaved. Her mother was probably born in South Carolina, her father in either Virginia or North Carolina. Like her mother, Addie was christened Adelina. The name came from the white daughter of the family that had owned her parents; she had opposed secession and was disinherited. Jessie and Adelina Waits had four children, three daughters and a son. Addie was the eldest. Her mother died in 1882. Afterward, Jessie sent Addie to Boston, where she lived with an aunt and attended the prestigious Boston Latin School, believed today to be the oldest school in America still in operation, having been founded a year before Harvard. Among her classmates was James A. Gallivan, who would go on to serve eight terms in Congress. After graduation Addie taught briefly in Fort Valley, Georgia, although this period of her life remains largely unaccounted for. But certainly she showed no reluctance to travel on her own around the South. Around 1890, she returned to Norfolk, where she met William, then serving as secretary of the city's colored YMCA. They married three years later and moved first to Richmond and then, in 1899, to Atlanta.

In addition to her teaching, Addie worked as her husband's secretary and helped edit the magazine he founded for the YMCA's colored branches. She also wrote for *Voice of the Negro*, a popular national magazine edited by Max Barber and John Wesley Bowen. Despite her frequent illnesses, she was constantly looking for things to do. In the late 1890s, she had even enrolled in business college in Philadelphia. But it is not clear whether she ever completed her degree. Late in 1898, still in Philadelphia, she fell ill once more—so ill that William canceled his travels and hastened to her bedside. What they thought was illness was actually pregnancy: she was carrying Eunice.

By the time the riot drove the family from the city, eight years after their daughter's birth, Addie had attained prominence not only as a clubwoman (she was involved in the founding of several of the most important organizations of colored women) but also as an activist, particularly on behalf of Negro women. She lectured frequently, including to all-male audiences, about the betrayal of the race that occurred when men mistreated the women in their lives—an unpopular subject at a time when most Negro men cared only about the barriers created by color. Questions of gender were as relevant to their concerns as the phases of the moon. Her most famous address, delivered in August of 1902 in Atlanta to the Young People's Christian and Educational Congress, was titled "A Pure Motherhood the Basis of Racial Integrity."

In the speech, which is still being reprinted today, Addie argued that the most important duty of colored women—she never said "Negro"—was to tend to the family. The home was where the children of the race were born and raised, nurtured and taught. And there the problem lay: "As a general rule, the highest and most blessed duty of the family is totally disregarded." She drove home the point:

> A child has a right to the inheritance of the very best of body
> and soul its parents can bestow. If these are not granted, the
> child is defrauded of its birth-right.

Her conclusion fit perfectly the class prejudices that by then had taken hold among the more educated of the darker nation. Many among the black middle class had come to believe that the behavior of the less educated colored folk was holding back the progress of the race. Certainly William shared this view. In 1899, he had joined with other prominent colored men of Atlanta in endorsing a literacy test for voting, as long as it was applied, without distinction, to white and colored alike.

This position was consistent with William's view of life. His philosophy did not demand sweeping changes in the social order. He believed in self-improvement. He held that the Negro race could accomplish wondrous things if the white race would only leave it alone. His YMCA work among colored men was fired by his determination that the race must better itself by education, hard work, and Christian virtue. The riot that drove the family from the state only strengthened his conviction that the fate of the race lay in its own hands.

Within months of the Atlanta riot, the Hunton family headed northward, stopping briefly in Washington, D.C., before arriving in Brooklyn, most likely in early 1907. Addie and the children boarded with friends on Decatur Street while she searched for a place of their own; William spent most of his time traveling. At first the Huntons intended the sojourn in the North to be a temporary one while William traveled. But the family never returned to Atlanta. They would raise their children in Brooklyn.

* * *

The move north changed the family's life, and not for the better. At first, with William still in Asia, cash was tight. Addie was being lauded by the Negro press as "one of the greatest women of our race." Even the mainstream papers took note of her organizing activities. But accolades did not pay the bills. She penned a plaintive note to Moorland: "When Mr. Hunton left, he told me you would send me some money in March. I would not need it but for the constant sickness in my family." She explained that Eunice was recovering from tonsillitis and Alphaeus "has been wrestling with typhoid for seven weeks." She had to pay both a doctor and a nurse. A scribbled note at the end asks Moorland to please send a money order. (What Addie did not say, probably because she worried that Moorland would tell her husband, was that she, too, had been ill.) A few days later, chagrined by whatever response she received, Addie sent a hasty qualification: "I did not mean that you should send me of your own purse." And yet she did not entirely retreat. She made clear that she still needed help. She made no mention of Eunice, but told Moorland that Alphaeus, although now recovering, was "still confined to the room." She also confessed that she herself had now fallen ill.

At last enough was enough. With her husband away and little money coming in, Addie realized that she would have to earn her own living. In the spring of 1907, she found full-time employment with the national office of the Young Women's Christian Association at the salary of forty dollars per month. She was hired as a "special worker," tasked with evaluating potential colored branches. At first the post was intended to last only through the summer, but somehow her tenure was extended, and later that year she "embarked on a five-month tour of the South and Southwest" to prepare a report on Negro women and the YWCA—the first of many journeys that would take her away from home for extended periods. Meanwhile, she continued to be invited to address the meetings and conferences that marked the club life of the black middle class.

Still Addie remained dissatisfied. Money remained short. She began to grow depressed. She had swiftly tired of Brooklyn, which was so crowded and dirty in comparison with the South that she loved and still described as her home. She had tired, too, of William's long absences, for although by the summer he had returned to the United

States, he was practically living in Atlanta and Washington, leaving her alone with the children. And she had tired, probably, of her husband's condescension, for he was very much a man's man. Although he would sacrifice much for his wife, he rarely confided his concerns, or even shared his emotions. He had been raised to believe that the problems of men were not to become the worries of women. When upset or fearful, William would write another letter to Jesse Moorland. Some of the letters gently belittled his wife.

And so in the fall of 1908, two years after the riot, Addie decided to act. Under a pretext, she inquired of her friend Mary Church Terrell, who had spent two years in Europe, how much it might cost to live abroad. Then, her mind made up, Addie carried out her plan. She took the children and decamped for Germany. Eunice was nine; Alphaeus was five. Their destination was Strasbourg, at that time still part of the German Empire. It was an entirely different world. Addie enrolled at Kaiser Wilhelm University, where she began a course in German and philology. The children attended a private German-language school. Back home, William continued his work as though nothing had changed. He was now living chiefly in Washington, home of the Colored Department of the YMCA, which he ran. The only difference was that his wife no longer visited from Brooklyn, and he no longer went north to see the family.

The sojourn in Europe was something new for Addie and the children. William was a world traveler. His YMCA work had taken him everywhere: Switzerland, Japan, Korea, England. No one else in the family had previously visited Europe. Now Addie and the children lived in Germany and traveled to Belgium and Holland and France. They vacationed in Switzerland, where they saw "most of its far-famed mountains and lakes from Rigi to Mt. Blanc." This was a time when Americans rarely traveled abroad, and those who did were heavily white and rich. Yet the darker nation fascinated Europeans. The *Times* of London wrote in an editorial that "in respect both of physical refinement and intellectual capacity, the American negro shows a marked superiority over the African." Back home, leaders of the race eagerly credited press reports that "at the various courts of Europe, . . . the prejudices so prevalent in this country concerning the dusky-hued brother are not only unknown but likewise unintelligible." And the family's stay in Europe coincided with the very moment when for the intellectual classes of the continent (even in Germany) an appreciation of jazz was becoming a symbol of one's engagement with the avant-garde.

Eunice and Alphaeus would each later describe their European excursion in terms suggesting that the family was happy there. Both children developed an excellent facility with the German language. Addie wrote to her husband every week. William's letters to her, she tells us, were "boyishly joyous" about how well his work was going. Somehow the distance seemed to strengthen their relationship, "despite the ocean between." Moreover, her own ambition was at last being truly satisfied: she was working toward the university degree she craved, and from a school in Europe no less. Yet after a year and a half, Addie returned to the United States, her course unfinished. She was concerned about her husband. William, she feared, was working too hard and might relapse, for he had long been troubled by an unexplained but serious respiratory malady. Other sources say that William was already quite ill, and Addie was worried that this time he might not recover.

The family's return from Europe occasioned a moment of unexpected racialist theater. On June 6, 1910, Addie and the two children arrived in New York on the *Nieuw Amsterdam*, which had left Rotterdam on May 28. Eunice was a month shy of her eleventh birthday. Alphaeus was almost seven. The three were briefly detained as they disembarked. The stated reason was "LPC"—meaning "likely to become a public charge." This category was for aliens who, in the judgment of the immigration officer, would be unable to support themselves; it was applied with some frequency to foreign women traveling with children but no husband. The officer was, of course, mistaken in assuming that they were aliens. All were American-born. But because her husband was Canadian, Addie was traveling on a British passport. A Negro woman traveling with two children, no husband, and no American passport—an immigration officer's racial nightmare.

Yet even though the files to this day record Addie as "LPC," the classification turned out to be only an excuse for detaining her. The true reason was different. Addie and the children had taken ship with a young German woman named Marie Rodenbeck, a fellow student in Strasbourg, whose lifelong dream was to go to America. As the white press gleefully reported, however, Rodenbeck's friends back home had become concerned. She was traveling to the United States in the company of a colored family and even shared the same second-class suite—some said as their maid—and, as a result, "might be ostracized by white Americans." The papers loved the man-bites-dog aspects of the story: the detention of a white woman for consorting with Negroes. Rodenbeck, wrote the Baltimore *Sun*, "did not know there was any feeling here about a mingling of the races." Her friends therefore arranged for an official of the German consulate to meet her at the dock and have her held at Ellis Island while he tried to persuade her to return home. According to the press, Addie and the children were also held so that she could testify at Rodenbeck's hearing.

Rodenbeck was released the next day, after she admitted to immigration officials that she "was not aware of the color line in this country" or, in the words of the *New York Times*, "the difficulties she might encounter with the negress on arriving here." As for Addie, she and the children had already been freed the previous day. She told the *Tribune* that the entire episode had been "a great mistake" and that Rodenbeck, whom she described as "a cultured woman of considerable means," had certainly not accompanied the family "as a servant." Rather, the two women had simply been traveling together as a convenience. A few weeks later, Addie told the *New York Age* that she had received an apology from immigration authorities. As for Rodenbeck, she moved to Michigan, where she married a year later and, as far as is known, passed out of the family's life.

William Hunton, who met his wife and children dockside, accompanied them throughout the ordeal. Despite his illness, he went along to Ellis Island and was with them when they were at last set free at four o'clock in the afternoon on the day the ship docked. Often such cases could stretch out for a week or more. I like to think that what explains officialdom's change of heart is that Addie, following the example of her husband with the railway conductor, talked the immigration officials out of their racialist instinct that something was amiss. Like William before her, Addie displayed a remarkable capacity for channeling fortitude and indignation into calm and persuasive conversation.

* * *

Eunice and her younger brother Alphaeus, around 1913. She was vivacious and charming. He was quiet and bookish.
Hunton family photograph

And so the family abandoned Europe and settled once more in Brooklyn. For a time Addie cared for her husband. In the fall of 1910, scant months after Addie's return, William had two minor operations. He seemed to recover, but was left with "a chronic coughing" that never really went away. Over the next few years, William and the disease would be in a constant battle. But as William recovered his strength, he went back on the road. Soon he was essentially living in Washington, headquarters of his beloved Colored Department. As for Addie, she was off again, this time under the auspices of the YWCA, which had hired her once more, this time to prepare a study of its colored branches. She joined the boards of various Negro institutions. The press of the darker nation continued to laud her. She even made the mainstream papers again, this time when she was to be a guest for tea at the home of Professor and Mrs. John Dewey to hear her friend Mary Church Terrell speak about women's suffrage. The tea was canceled after the landlord threatened an injunction against the interracial gathering.

These years must have been confusing for Eunice and Alphaeus. In Atlanta their father had been constantly on the road, and half the time their mother was, too. For a year and a half in Germany, they had been with their mother without seeing their father. After Addie brought them back stateside in 1910, the children once more boarded with the Hairstons in Brooklyn, even as their father purchased a lovely townhouse at 922 S Street, N.W., in Washington, close to his place of work. Addie began shuttling back and forth between the two cities but was soon spending more time with her husband than with her children. Documents from the period refer to both Addie and William as residents of Washington. Eunice and Alphaeus, on the other hand, never moved down from Brooklyn.

At Thanksgiving of 1913, anticipating their father's return to Brooklyn, Eunice and Alphaeus were "dancing for joy." But William wrote from Georgia to say that he would not be coming home after all. Addie worried that her husband's health had taken another bad turn but said nothing to the children. He finally arrived in Brooklyn shortly before Christmas, and the whole family could see that he was ill. Yet as soon as he felt better, he went back on the road. The cycle of work and illness continued. William refused to stop his travels. In April of 1914, as he sat with his wife in the parlor of their townhouse at 922 S Street, he collapsed. Soon he was coughing up blood. He was diagnosed with an advanced case of tuberculosis, the same illness that had claimed the life of at least one and possibly both of the first two Hunton children. At first William was cared for in Washington. Addie made frequent visits to see the children but each time quickly returned to her husband, leaving them behind. Soon William returned to Brooklyn, where by now the family had a place of their own at 575 Greene Avenue.

William's sojourn in the city was brief. He and Addie moved on to Saranac Lake, New York, famous at the time for its tuberculosis sanitarium and the "cure cottages" that dotted the landscape, where sufferers could breathe clear mountain air. Alphaeus came up to Saranac Lake to stay with his parents. Eunice remained in Brooklyn, attending

Girls High School, probably still boarding with the Hairstons. In the fall of 1914, William was still seriously ill but looked forward to Christmas, when Eunice would come up to Saranac Lake to visit. For the next two years, William and Addie shuttled back and forth between Brooklyn and Saranac Lake, depending on his health. Addie still went occasionally on the road to lecture. In the summer of 1916, she was one of the few women to attend the Amenia Conference, arranged by W. E. B. Du Bois and Joel Spingarn. The participants, representing most of the major organizations of the darker nation, tasked themselves with dividing responsibility for the movement for equality following the death of Booker T. Washington, whose widow was a dear friend of Addie's. The outcome of the meeting mattered. Washington's views were controversial, but even his critics conceded his dominance of the activism of the darker nation. With his passing, many feared that rivalries would rend the movement asunder. The organizers hoped that his more traditionalist followers and younger, more radical activists might find a way to make common cause. If by some chance Addie dithered about whether to attend, I suspect that her husband, stoic in illness as in health, encouraged her to go.

In October of that year, William told his wife that he knew he was failing and wanted to go home to Brooklyn. On Wednesday, November 29, the day before Thanksgiving, he died. The pain and coughing had become so severe that he had been kept heavily medicated for some while. But early that same morning, in a lucid moment, he had asked for some time with the children, and prayed for them, hands on their heads. Shortly after they left for school, the last rites were administered. Years later, Addie described her husband's passing:

> It was all so beautiful, so quiet, and yet with such a full and thrilling sweep from time into eternity that my sorrow was stilled and I could wail no monody. My desolate hour must wait. This had been Mr. Hunton's triumphant hour—the consummation of all his devotion to service and to God.

Expressions of sympathy poured in from around the globe. On the college campuses where William had tirelessly pushed YMCA work, young colored men held prayer meetings and vigils and memorial services. This was a spontaneous response, not a centrally organized activity. The young men loved him. It was really that simple. Addie was admired and feted and could draw cheering crowds, but William was loved. When William and Addie boarded that first train to Saranac Lake, two students who knew him happened to be on board. They attended to his every need, even getting off the train to fetch fresh milk. When the two young men reached their stop and detrained, they stood on the platform and removed their hats in respect.

Addie's own grief was private. Although she was touched by the many letters of support, she seemed to think she should hide her feelings from the world. Three months after her husband was buried, she would construct her own memorial. She would dry her eyes and get back to work, going back on tour for the causes she and William believed in.

CHAPTER 3

THE STUDENT

THE CHILDREN COPED AS BEST THEY COULD. EUNICE HAD ALWAYS been the more vivacious, the charmer, their father's favorite. She was outgoing and openly ambitious. Back in the summer of 1907, the family had vacationed in Sea Isle, New Jersey. On the beach one day, eight-year-old Eunice told a playmate that when she grew up she wanted to be a lawyer. When he asked why, she explained that she wanted to make sure the bad people went to jail. Perhaps she had been infected with her parents' belief in the importance of working for justice. Perhaps she was just remembering the violence of that September night and the family's flight from Atlanta. In school she worked hard. She was always an excellent student, a favorite of her teachers. According to family stories, the teenaged Eunice was bright and charming, respectful to her elders, but to her peers a bit of a show-off, rarely worried about whom she might wound with her sharp, clever tongue.

During her father's illness, Eunice had grown somewhat distant from the family. It was her younger brother, Alphaeus, who accompanied his parents up to Saranac Lake during the last year of William's life; Eunice by contrast was only an occasional visitor. When William died, the daughter he called Sugar was a senior at Girls High School in

Brooklyn. The following fall, she would enroll at Smith College, in Northampton, Massachusetts.

Toward the end of William's life, he spent much more time with Alphaeus than with Eunice. When William had the energy, father and son would walk the beautiful mountains surrounding Saranac Lake. Together, they would sit up late on the porch, having quiet conversations. William also helped his son with homework, although I suspect that his son rarely needed much assistance. Alphaeus had always been bookish. As a child, he "would read all night if he were not found out." He preferred to keep his own company and think his own thoughts. In the fall of 1917, a year after William's passing, Alphaeus entered Boys High School in Brooklyn, where he not only excelled academically but became something of a leader. During the first term of his first year, he won a medal for the best essay on the Liberty Bond, tops among the six hundred boys in his class. His favorite activity was the debate team. But he could not be content with academic achievement alone. He hungered for knowledge. The November 1921 issue of the *Crisis* celebrated an unusual achievement: "Colored high school students in Brooklyn, N.Y., have organized the *Alpha Chi Sigma* Fraternity in the interest of higher scholarship. William A. Hunton, Jr., is the secretary."

Left alone, Alphaeus would surely have devoted all of his time to scholarly pursuits. That choice, however, was not available. After William's death, the family fell on hard times. Addie and William Sr. might have been celebrated by the darker nation, but their work was not of a kind that promised financial security. High school summers found Alphaeus working as a Red Cap at New York's Pennsylvania Station, saving money for college. A few years later, Addie and her son would even resume boarding with the Hairstons. Probably Alphaeus obtained the job at Penn Station through the good offices of Harry Hairston. Harry was a Pullman porter and worked on the trains. Alphaeus, as a Red Cap, carried bags in and out of the station.

According to Dorothy Hunton, Alphaeus's third wife, who would later write his biography, "The bags he carried were so heavy that they caused his right shoulder to droop, and made one arm two inches longer than the other." But he could not quit because "the hard work

Addie with black American soldiers in France, around 1917–18.
She became well known for her work with the YMCA during World War I.
KAUTZ FAMILY YMCA ARCHIVES, UNIVERSITY OF MINNESOTA

supplied the means to continue school." More accurately, he was earning the means to begin, because it would be four tough years before he
was able to start college.

As for Addie, she emerged from her mourning invigorated, and the
children bore uneasy witness to another of their mother's several rein-
ventions. In April 1917, the United States entered the First World War.
A few months later, with eighteen-year-old Eunice away at college,

Addie made arrangements for Alphaeus, then fourteen, to board with friends in Philadelphia and attend school there. She then took a startling step: she arranged for the appointment of a legal guardian for each child. With that matter settled, Addie took ship for France alongside the tens of thousands of colored troops heading for the war—one of only three Negro women to do so. Their duties essentially involved morale. Under the auspices of the YMCA, they showed movies, worked in canteens, helped the soldiers write letters, shopped for soldiers who lacked time, taught the soldiers how to look after their cash, offered educational and religious services. Of course they were not the only women who went, but they were the only Negroes. There was an irony here: the racial segregation within the association that William had spent his days combating continued and even intensified in the theater of war. Thus, there were white YMCA workers to serve white troops and colored YMCA workers to serve colored troops.

Addie was away for a year and a half.

Although the ostensible purpose of the journey was service, in practice the women documented both the Negro soldiers' heroism in battle and their wretched treatment at the hands of their fellow Americans. Upon arriving in Europe, the women were for a brief time shunted away from the front. They found colored soldiers digging ditches and working as stevedores rather than fighting. As later historians have documented, the army's view at the time was that black draftees were probably too stupid for combat. Instead, they "would serve in the military equivalent of chain gangs." But needs must. War is war, and when at last the colored troops of the 92nd Division finally marched off to battle, the women went with them. They endured the same rigors of camp and combat as the men. In July of 1919, the *New York Age* published on its front page a photograph of Addie, "showing a determined woman in a greatcoat, in rugged snow-covered terrain alongside a young soldier."

Upon Addie's return the following month, she was welcomed at the pier by "a delegation of ladies from Brooklyn." A year later, together with Kathryn Magnolia Johnson, who accompanied her to Europe, Addie would publish *Two Colored Women with the American Expeditionary Forces*, a popular account of her time with the troops. The book, which is relied upon by historians of World War I to this day, cataloged the discriminations, large and small and often dangerous, that the United States Army imposed upon its Negro troops.

Two Colored Women is a brisk and mesmerizing read. The scenes the authors describe are by turns inspiring and depressing. Many of them involve feats of heroism by members of a race widely viewed at the time as cowardly. But many more serve as profound reminders of the intensity of anti-black feeling among whites of the era. The authors write of the time General Pershing arrived at Le Mans after the armistice to review the troops. An order was posted: "All troops possible, except *colored*, to be under arms." And the time a unit of the 92nd Division was sent over a hill to be slaughtered, because the proper armament was reserved for the whites. Then there is the fact that colored troops were not allowed to march in the victory parade in Paris. When officers discovered that the French entertained the troops in their homes, orders were issued forbidding the 92nd Division—and only the 92nd Division—from "addressing or holding conversation with the women inhabitants of the town." The Negro soldiers were also prohibited "from entering any building" other than their own billets or certain public places—that is, they could not go into private homes.

The examples go on and on. Yet most of the book is dedicated not to recording the slights against the Negro soldiers but to celebrating their heroism in battle. A part of Addie's purpose in the book was to make clear to readers that everything their prejudices told them about the inferiority of the colored troops was false. The authors argue toward the end that the brave showing of the 92nd in combat against Germany was just more evidence, should any have been needed, of the fitness of the Negro for full equality back home.

The book was widely applauded, at least within the darker nation. Addie had left home an admired widow of a beloved man, and returned a year and a half later as a celebrated activist in her own right.

The story of Addie's trip to France also has a bizarre side note. Before she could depart, she had to apply for a passport. To obtain it, she of course had to disclose her age—a fact about which she was, to say the least, cagey. She offered a different answer every time she was asked. The lies were not even consistent. She would change her birth date by a decade or more. Of course untruths to make one seem younger are not uncommon. But Addie raised the matter to an art form so rarefied that we do not actually know for sure when she was born.

The 1918 passport application gives her date of birth as June 11, 1871. But in 1930, Addie told a census taker that she was fifty-one years old, meaning that she would have been born around 1879. The 1920 census gives her age as forty-eight, which is at least consistent with the 1871 birth date. The 1940 census gives her age as sixty-six, meaning that she would have been born around 1874. Her headstone states that she was born on June 11, 1875, suggesting that her children considered this the accurate date. Their source must have been their mother. *But all of these dates are wrong.* Addie's true age was probably the one given either on her original British passport (June 11, 1866) or on her marriage license (June 11, 1867). On this subject the truth became, for Addie, a well-hidden secret. As we shall see, she did not lie only to children, census takers, and the State Department. She also lied to a court while under oath. Yes, she always preached integrity. But rules have their little exceptions—especially when applied to the rulemaker.

Yet the sin, if sin there was, was surely venial. Addie was devoted to her children, and the more so after William died. To make ends meet, she cobbled together two or three jobs at a time. Money was scarce. In 1917, when Eunice matriculated at Smith College, in Northampton, Massachusetts, tuition ran to about $200 a year. Room and board cost $400, with a higher charge for those who lived in suites. These sums may sound small, but the school was actually quite expensive for the era. One must bear in mind that the median household income was around $1,300—and we can be certain that Addie was either below or not far above the median. Where the family got the money for Eunice's expenses remains a mystery. A scholarship would have been widely and delightedly reported in the Negro press, but no such report appears. And although after William's death, the YMCA had briefly continued to pay a portion of his salary, that period had ended. By 1917, without William's income, Addie and the children no longer had a place of their own in Brooklyn, but were boarding again with the Hairston family at 372 Grand Avenue. Addie scrounged what money she could. Shortly before Eunice left Brooklyn for Northampton, Addie accepted a position as "northern secretary" for the Fort Valley School in Georgia. But the job was only part-time, and little money was likely involved. Besides, Addie would soon depart for France and the war, leaving the job behind.

Probably someone else paid for Eunice's education at Smith—most likely, Mary White Ovington. Ovington, a Smith graduate who lived in Northampton, was a wealthy suffragist and Socialist, and a generous supporter of many reform movements. Racial justice was a passion of hers, and she was a founder of and major donor to the NAACP. By the time Eunice began her freshman year, Ovington and Addie had been close friends for a decade. They first met in 1906 in Atlanta, a few months before the riots, when Ovington came to dinner at the Hunton home at 418 Houston Street—at a time when a white woman dining with a colored family was a considerable social sin, made worse because a Negro man escorted her. Her description of Addie on this occasion of their first meeting is vivid: "deep brown in color with a finely molded mouth, and large unfathomable eyes." She admired her hostess both for her militance and because she was "nobly beautiful." She also enjoyed the children: "Eunice and Alpheus [sic], little tots then, entertained us while their mother prepared supper."

In time, the friendship between the two women would come to transcend race. Their common bond was gender. Fifteen years after that dinner, while suffering discrimination as the only female field secretary for the NAACP, Addie would write to Ovington, in something like despair, "How I miss you when I come in from the field. . . . [N]obody understands a woman's point of view like a woman." Nothing would have been more natural than for Ovington to steer her dear friend's daughter toward her own alma mater and, of course, to help with the expense: a salutary lesson for young Eunice in the importance of having friends everywhere.

Mary White Ovington maintained a summer home in the Berkshires that she often lent to various liberal and even radical organizations for conferences and meetings. She was the chair of the board of the NAACP, and the cottage was often used for the group's retreats. Ovington gave

Eunice the run of her house, and Eunice often spent her weekends and vacations there; Ovington apparently used the house only rarely.

And yet Eunice seemed more comfortable with male than female mentors. At Smith, where she majored in government, the faculty included a significant number of women, but her principal influence was Professor Everett Kimball, a veteran progressive and reformer, a passionate advocate for women's suffrage and racial equality. It was Kimball who introduced her to Calvin Coolidge, at that time the governor of Massachusetts, who maintained a house in Northampton, at 19–21 Massasoit Street. The future President became, in Eunice's own words, her "friend and advisor." She afterward spent a great deal of time at Coolidge's simple clapboard house, seeking his advice when he was in residence, partaking of his magnificent library when he was away.

The press would later describe Eunice as popular among her classmates, but it is difficult to imagine that there was no snubbing of the smart, sassy Negro. Still, she did well. She made the honor roll. She joined the debate society and served as one of the hostesses when Marie Curie visited the campus, but judging from the yearbook Eunice did not participate in many clubs.

As it happened, Eunice's undergraduate years coincided with an unusual cultural moment. She arrived in Northampton right on the cusp of what has been called the "dress reform" movement, which seems to have started at Smith, and was actually not so much a movement as a pitched battle. The battle pitted traditionalist women at Smith against those who wanted to adopt newer, freer (some would say more sexually assertive) forms of dress. Similarly, she arrived at the very moment in history when large numbers of Smith women began dieting in earnest. Some were so concerned about losing weight that they would write letters home, asking their families to send less food. For Eunice, this would not have been a problem: years later, reporters still marveled over how little she ate.

Ironically, while Smith College was roiling over whether to discard the traditions to which Eunice had been raised, her mother, Addie, the great traditionalist, was wearying of pleas for gradual reform. Her book about the experience of black soldiers, published in 1920, was angry. But even before then, the apostle of Negro motherhood had been increasingly attracted to radical solutions. She was invited by Jane Addams to join the Women's International League for Peace and Freedom, where she immediately became enmeshed in a nasty controversy over charges that the WILPF segregated its colored members. Like many disillusioned black intellectuals, Addie became fascinated with nationalism. She addressed the 1919 Pan-African Congress in Paris, but reported unhappily that the group had no interest in issues of gender.

Although gender was for Addie an issue of increasing salience, she never entirely abandoned her commitment to the cause of virtuous womanhood as the basis of racial advancement. Like many early feminists, she saw the issues as deeply related. Thus in October 1919, at an interracial forum on lynching, as one speaker after another reminded the audience of the horrors wrought upon Negro men, Addie sought to broaden the conversation. "While white men have been preserving the sanctity of white women," she pointed out in her remarks, "the colored woman has had to preserve her own sanctity." The proposition harked back to the Atlanta address that had made her famous. There, too, she had warned her astonished audience that although racial oppression posed a threat to the virtue of the colored woman, so did the attitude of the colored man.

Two years later, in 1921, Addie traveled to London for the Second Pan-African Congress. In between she corresponded with Du Bois on the subject. (A few years later, she would become one of the handful of women on the congress's advisory board.) By the time of the 1923 congress, the movement was mainstream. On behalf of the National Association of Colored Women, Nannie Helen Burroughs wrote to Addie inquiring whether Margaret Washington—the widow of Booker T. Washington—might find a place as either vice president or a member of the executive council. Addie's role in the Pan-Africanist movement led to frequent correspondence with prominent colored activists. By this time, her growing radicalism had brought her to the attention of the United States government. American military intelligence kept a sharp eye on the conferences, and some of the delegates were informants.

Eunice declined to follow her mother into the maelstrom of the

Eunice's yearbook photograph from Smith College, where she graduated in 1921, having completed both her bachelor's and master's degrees in four years.
Smith College Press Board, College Archives, Smith College (Northampton, Massachusetts)

nation's suddenly stormy racial politics. To be sure, both would remain lifelong Republicans. Political parties in those days willingly embraced members with a wide spectrum of opinions on almost every issue, and Addie's views would increasingly diverge from her daughter's. But by this time they had different interests. Addie was the activist, moving further and further to the left. Eunice, by contrast, was determined to advance in the larger white world. Smith College was simply the first step on her ladder.

In the spring of 1921, Eunice was graduated from Smith *cum laude*. She was only the second woman in the history of the college to receive both a bachelor's and a master's degree in four years, an achievement noted in the Negro papers and almost as widely in the mainstream press. Her mother and her brother were present in Northampton to cheer her on. In the fall, Alphaeus would enroll as a freshman at Howard University, in Washington, D.C. Unlike his older sister, he would have no wealthy philanthropist to pay his way. Here, perhaps, we see the germ of the resentment that he would come to direct against the values that Addie preached. Alphaeus, bookish and intellectually intense, won prizes at the mostly white Boys High in Brooklyn, and was written up in the Negro press. But unlike Eunice, he had to work to put tuition money aside. As a Red Cap, he would spend the long summers before college carrying other people's bags for low pay and insignificant tips. It is hard to imagine that he felt no anger toward his older sister and her wealthy benefactor.

Besides, Eunice had always been their father's favorite. So says family lore, and William's correspondence with his friend Jesse Moorland bears this out. Even when he lay dying at Saranac Lake, William was always excited when it was time for Eunice to visit. In the fall of 1914, Alphaeus was with his parents, attending school nearby. Eunice, however, was boarding in Brooklyn, still enrolled at Girls High. Here is Addie's account of the ensuing holidays:

> After the formal observance of Thanksgiving, which Mr. Hunton freely shared, we began looking forward to the coming of Christmas, which would bring Eunice to join us. She was always the most animated member of our family and kept her father cheerful. It was an unforgettable holiday.

True, Addie makes a point of telling us how much William enjoyed helping Alphaeus with his homework, and how father and son enjoyed the beauty of the lake and mountain vistas. And all of that is important. Yet one cannot come away from the scene without the sense that as much time as William may have spent with his son, in his heart he was waiting excitedly for his daughter to arrive. Eunice brought out the smiles, both in Addie's memory and in William's correspondence. It would be odd indeed for Alphaeus not to have noticed the difference.*

Quite apart from reminding him of where he stood in relation to his vivacious sister, those months carrying bags at Pennsylvania Station also marked Alphaeus in another way: they taught him keenly how the world works. The Red Caps, most of them colored, labored long, sweaty

---

* Another possibility bears mention. Alphaeus's full name was William Alphaeus Hunton Jr.— the same name as the earlier son who died. A traditionalist like William would surely have wanted a male heir. William likely felt an occasional pain when he looked at the living son and remembered the dead one of the same name. A paternal flinch, even a small one, would have driven a further small, albeit unspoken, fissure between father and son. (I am grateful to Leah Carter for suggesting this possibility.)

hours in the summer heat and were poorly paid. Tips were unreliable. Several of the men got together and tried to organize a job action, seeking higher wages. Management's solution was simple and swift: those who walked off their posts were fired and replaced. The resistance collapsed.

Alphaeus had not joined the job action. But he had seen first-hand the power of the owners. Others in his position might have sworn to own the railroad one day. For Eunice's younger brother, a different dream began. By the time he started college, he was already searching for radical solutions to the problem of capital.

CHAPTER 4

THE CZARINAS

THEN AS NOW, AN IMPORTANT REASON TO ATTEND A SELECTIVE college was to come to know those who might help you later, and many young women of the day chose Smith with just that goal in mind. Eunice, however, made little effort to stay in touch with her classmates: a year after graduation, the college bulletin listed her among those whose whereabouts were unknown. Actually she was in Baton Rouge, spending an unhappy year teaching at Southern University. It was the surroundings, not the school, that made Eunice miserable. She enjoyed the teaching. But she had left the South as a child a decade and a half earlier, and she found no particular joy in being back. "Digression," an autobiographical short story Eunice would publish the next year, constituted a remembrance of her miserable time in Baton Rouge. "Christmas isn't Christmas," she wrote, "when you're marooned in a boarding school in the far South in Louisiana." Even the planned distribution of baskets to the poor left the nameless narrator depressed: "The anticipation of this evoked no particular pleasure and I fell asleep with visions of sugar cane stalks, muddy roads, draughty cabins and Christmas baskets chasing each other through my head."

Eunice could not escape fast enough. But her desire to flee the South did not imply a desire to remain under Addie's roof. Although Eunice would later say that she spent her first couple of years after college caring for Addie, this does not appear to be the case. Upon her return to Brooklyn in the summer of 1922, Eunice left immediately on a motoring trip to the Midwest, where she stayed for at least a month. And no sooner did Eunice get back from vacation than her mother embarked on a seven-week tour of the Northeast and Midwest on behalf of the YWCA. Addie was away until just before Thanksgiving. Early in 1923, Addie would go on the road once more, this time in the interest of the NAACP, undertaking a courageous and inspiring journey through dangerous, Klan-dominated territory.

These journeys put Addie at risk, but they were her job. The year 1921, for instance, had found Addie in Indiana, where the Republican Party, in most of the country still the party of the darker nation, had effectively been taken over by the Klan. And not just the Republican Party: the Klan essentially ran the state. There were calls for an investigation. The group insisted that it had nothing to hide. Ministers defended the Klan from the pulpit. Addie was undeterred. She spoke bravely "in the interest of the NAACP" and put the local branch back on its feet.

Her 1923 Southern swing was very much in the same spirit. And the spirit was evidently contagious. When news spread that Addie Hunton was coming to town, large crowds would turn out. Her visits reassured and inspired worried Negroes around the country. The NAACP *did* care about them. Its leaders *were* willing to place their bodies in harm's way. And each time Addie emerged from another appearance unscathed, her legend grew.

The excited anticipation of Addie's visit to Columbia, South Carolina, in January of 1923 was typical. The *Southern Indicator*, the local black newspaper, reported that she was coming to town to speak. "Hear Mrs. Hunton," the paper urged on page 2, not identifying her beyond the fact that she was an NAACP field secretary. On page 3, the paper again reminded readers that she would be in town the following week, this time informing them that she "is renouned [sic] as a public speaker" and "has an international reputation as a club woman and a Y.W.C.A. worker." The piece concluded: "Don't fail to hear her."

Perhaps the most fabled of Addie's 1923 journeys was her visit to

Birmingham, Alabama, which boasted one of the largest Klan memberships in the country and where three years of racist violence had intimidated the population and thrown the local NAACP branch into disarray. Attacks on Negroes were frequent. They were snatched off the street, dragged into the woods, and beaten. A black man was flogged for supposedly having committed "miscegenation" with a woman he had never met. For balance, the Klansmen flogged the woman, too. She was by no means the only white victim. A Catholic druggist had his jaw fractured and his teeth knocked out by attackers who ordered him to sell his store and leave town. A Catholic priest was shot dead for officiating at a wedding between a white woman and a Puerto Rican man. The killer was the bride's father, who testified in open court that he had done it because the priest married his daughter to a "Negro." He was acquitted. Later that year, a Klan rally in the city would draw fifty thousand cheering supporters. One local resident told the NAACP that Birmingham was under a "reign of terror," a description Addie dutifully passed on to headquarters. She made the trip anyway—as usual, alone. In the official report on her journey, she would calmly dismiss any concern: "I had no idea of the apprehension for my safety until I left."

Nobody questioned Addie's courage. But she was taking chances with her health. By this time, her peripatetic life was exacting a toll on her body. Upon her return to Brooklyn in 1923, she spent three days in the hospital. Her children kept a worried vigil. Soon Addie was up and about and, like her husband before her, could scarcely wait to get back on the road.

Meanwhile, Eunice searched for ways to fill her time. She did substitute teaching in the Brooklyn public schools. One report has her leading gymnastics classes at the YWCA. She did some social work. Casting about for mental stimulation, she joined the Professional Women's Luncheon Club, which sponsored a speakers' series "for the purpose of blending intellectual thought and creating an interest in international affairs." And she began to write. A lot. She published a string of short stories and book reviews, most of them in the magazine *Opportunity*. True, some of the stories were ordinary, but most were excellent, and one of them—"Replica," a vaguely Pan-Africanist tale published in 1924—was brilliant. As for Eunice's reviews, they were usually erudite and cool but at times could be scathing. Her savaging of Wallace Thurman's controversial novel *The Blacker the Berry* on what we might today label feminist grounds is anthologized and dissected to this day. On the other hand, she may have been the only colored reviewer of note who was impressed by Waldo Frank's anti-lynching novel *Holiday*, a volume that aroused considerable antipathy because Frank was white.

Eunice plainly enjoyed writing. Her sharp eye and acerbic wit combined with a fluent yet fancy style common among black intellectuals of her day. And her talent was recognized. People began to talk about her as a leading light of what Alain Locke would shortly label the Negro Renaissance, and would be known to history as the Harlem Renaissance. In the spring of 1924, Charles S. Johnson, who ran *Opportunity*, organized a gala dinner where the older generation of Negro intellectuals would in effect pass the torch to the younger. Present as distinguished elders were James Weldon Johnson and W. E. B. Du Bois. Alain Locke was the master of ceremonies. Famous white editors attended. And among the small group of young black writers whom the group feted was Eunice Roberta Hunton. Her work was included in a special issue of the popular magazine *Survey Graphic* that included contributions from most of the big Negro writers of the day. There was Eunice, alongside Countee Cullen, Du Bois, Langston Hughes, Jean Toomer, Alain Locke, and all the rest.

Then, in the fall of 1925, Eunice received the greatest honor of all: she was formally inducted into the fabled Writers Guild, the small coterie of intellectuals at the apex of the Renaissance.* Sources differ on whether the formation of the Writers Guild was a consequence or a cause of the *Opportunity* dinner. Either way, the group's ten members as of 1924 included Alain Locke, Langston Hughes, Harold Jackman, Countee Cullen, Jessie Fauset, and Gwendolyn Bennett. Eunice's approval was not without controversy. She and Zora Neale Hurston joined at the

---

* The group founded at the peak of the Harlem Renaissance should not be confused with the Negro Writers' Guild, formed in the 1930s; the Harlem Writers Guild, later formed by Benjamin Davis of the Communist Party; or the currently existing organization of the same name.

*Mae Walker (granddaughter of the great Madam C. J. Walker) with her bridesmaids
at her 1923 wedding, the social event of the year in Harlem. Eunice (back row, second
from right) was included because of her family's social position.*
A'LELIA BUNDLES/MADAM WALKER FAMILY ARCHIVES

same time, leading a disgusted Gwendolyn Bennett to write to Harold
Jackman, "I didn't vote on them!!!!"

Given the charm for which she was uniformly applauded, Eunice
likely moved smoothly and stylishly within the group. Had her ambitions pointed in that direction, she probably could have continued as
one of the leading lights of the Harlem Renaissance. But although much
of her social life would always involve writers, artists, and musicians,
Eunice swiftly realized that a career as a writer would not satisfy her
gnawing ambitions.

Addie, the apostle of colored motherhood, must have been wondering by now when her daughter would get started on her responsibility
to marry and bear the young people who would be the future of the

race. Eunice was apparently still living at home on Bedford Avenue, and one can imagine the arguments that must have raged between these two strong-willed women. Probably the tension only grew worse when Eunice served as a bridesmaid in the darker nation's wedding of the year—we might as well say of the decade. November of 1923 brought the wedding of Mae Walker, the daughter of A'Lelia Walker, the wealthiest woman in Harlem. Eunice's service in Mae's bridal party was likely a matter of social standing, not friendship. "Most of us had never met before," one of the bridesmaids recalled years later, "but our parents knew each other since we were among America's small percentage of relatively affluent Negroes."

The wedding made headlines all over the country. The mother of the bride wanted the celebration to be on the most lavish scale, "to prove to the world that a Negro, with all his many handicaps, could rise to a position of both wealth and social standing." Published estimates of the cost of the wedding run from $42,000 to $62,000—the equivalent of $600,000 to $900,000 today. The Negro papers called the event the "most elaborate social function ever occurring among the colored citizens of New York City." The mainstream press was astonished: "9,000 Guests Invited to a Colored Wedding," ran the headline in the *New York Times.* "'Cullud 400' on Edge as Miss Mae Walker Awaits Wedding Gong," chortled a Pennsylvania paper. Story after story marveled at the pomp. Because as far as the mainstream papers were concerned, families like these did not exist. Negroes were domestic servants and elevator operators and laborers. If they were educated, they were schoolteachers. The only ones with real money were the singers and sports stars. By the racialist logic of the era, Eunice's world was an impossibility.

As it turned out, 1923 was an auspicious year for Eunice, for she came to the attention of Harry Hopkins, then heading the New York Tuberculosis and Health Association, who would later gain prominence as Franklin Roosevelt's top aide. Hopkins tasked the young social worker with leading the effort to create Harlem's first free dental clinic. Eunice took on the challenge with enthusiasm. She persuaded financiers to open their wallets. She recruited dentists, placated bureaucrats, negoti-

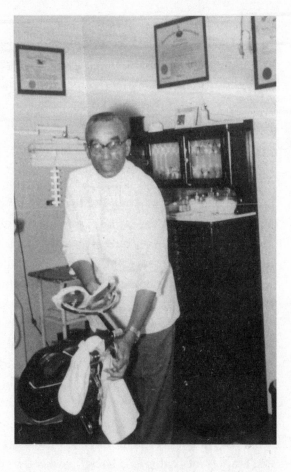

Lisle Sr. in his Harlem dental office, 1950s. The photograph is of low quality, but it was the only one to survive a fire that destroyed nearly all the family pictures and keepsakes.

<small>CARTER FAMILY PHOTOGRAPH</small>

ated with community leaders. The clinic opened its doors a year later and proved an enormous success. In the course of the work, she met Lisle Carleton Carter, a Barbadian immigrant who had first partnered in and now owned Harlem's most lucrative dental practice. He had arrived in the city around 1915. For a time, he had worked as an elevator operator and "hall man" while boarding with his older brother Cecil and Cecil's wife Ophelia at 368 Lenox Avenue. Lisle enlisted in 1918 and apparently spent the entire war in dental school, at government expense, at the College of Dental and Oral Surgery of New York, now known as Columbia Dental School. He was discharged after the war ended in 1919 and received his degree in 1921. He was an outstanding student. His academic achievements were featured in the *Crisis*, which reported that the young man had "won the Faculty Gold Medal for having the highest average in operative dentistry" and was also "one of ten men to receive the highest general average in the final examination of the graduating class." He was also quite the raconteur. Alongside his yearbook photograph we find this encomium: "He looks forward to the day when his silvery tongue shall hold spellbound some huge audience. What greater ambition could one possess?"

In the summer of 1923, Eunice asked Lisle to take on the burden of enlisting his fellow Harlem dentists to volunteer their time at the clinic. Given that the two did not travel in the same social circles, this was probably their first meeting. But they hit it off and were soon engaged. The match likely pleased the Czarinas, as Adam Clayton Powell Jr. memorably dubbed the "queenly, sometimes portly, and nearly always light-skinned" women who "presided over the Harlem upper class." Although some Harlemites still harbored a mistrust of West Indians, that prejudice had mostly faded. Certainly Addie would have been an enthusiast for the match. Lisle was a traditionalist of the old school, a fact that would have pleased her, and he would also be a great provider. Eunice would have many of the advantages Addie had enjoyed in her own marriage to the upright William without suffering either of the principal disadvantages: the family would never be short of money, and because Lisle was a dentist, he would travel rarely.

This is not to say that Eunice herself was struggling financially. She made a decent living as a social worker—so decent that she loaned money to friends, including W. E. B. Du Bois. She was paid for her short stories and book reviews. Probably she could have supported herself indefinitely. But Addie, although she had earned money throughout her marriage, hewed to the traditional view—not that the wife should not have a job, but that the husband should remain the principal supporter of the family. This role she was confident her prospective son-in-law would play.

Lisle and Eunice wed on Wednesday, November 26, 1924, at St. Augustine's Episcopal Church in Brooklyn. The bride was given away by her brother Alphaeus. Her maid of honor was Mrs. Dorothy Tuck Parsons, whose son Archibald Jr. would later become the first Negro reporter at the *New York Herald Tribune* and one of Eunice's son's lifelong friends. The celebrant was the Reverend George Frazier

Miller, who at the time had been the rector of St. Augustine's for better than a quarter century. Miller was the family pastor, and had administered the last rites to Addie's husband, William, just hours before his death. Afterward he had conducted the funeral.

The wedding was not large. At a time when the custom in colored "sassiety" (another Powell coinage) demanded the listing of the entire wedding party, press accounts mentioned only the maid of honor and the best man. The *Chicago Defender*, in a cleverly backhanded compliment, referred to the "very impressive ceremony" as having been "attended by family and intimate friends." The leading Negro families of the era traditionally splurged on large celebrations. Perhaps Addie would have frowned on ostentation in any case, but the truth is that her preference made no difference. Money was scarce. The family was barely making ends meet. Nevertheless, the Huntons were admired, and the marriage was no small news. "Both the bride and groom are widely known," the *Defender* continued breathlessly, "and the wedding is the topic of discussion among society folk."

Perhaps what society folk were discussing was the way Eunice's wedding had nearly been overshadowed by her mother's scandalous divorce—which put an end to a marriage so scandalous that it has all but vanished from the historical record.

In May of 1923—a year and a half before Eunice's nuptials—Addie, without warning, had wed a certain James W. Floyd, often called Sea Captain Floyd because he had made his name (and, some said, his fortune) decades before by running guns into Cuba during the Spanish-American War. The couple met in January of 1923 when Addie spoke in Floyd's hometown of Jacksonville, at that time trembling in the grip of the Ku Klux Klan. She was in the city as part of the tour upon which she had embarked a few months after her daughter's return from Baton Rouge. On behalf of the NAACP, Addie was visiting Southern towns where Klan activity was intimidating the local branches. She was unaccompanied on these journeys, and her courage as much as her renown drew large crowds. Her job was to let local colored activists know that the national office had not, as they feared, forgotten them, and to inspire them to continue the fight. She spoke in small towns in

Georgia and Alabama and South Carolina. She was cheered everywhere. That was how she met Sea Captain Floyd. He was impressed by her and courted her, sending telegrams and flowers to her as she continued her tour. Finally Addie yielded.

Captain Floyd was not entirely unknown to sassiety. A decade earlier, his daughter Nora had married J. Rosamond Johnson, brother of James Weldon Johnson and lyricist of "Lift Every Voice and Sing." After several years in London, the couple was now a Harlem fixture. Moreover, in his home state of Florida, Floyd was a considerable activist for the NAACP. A ruggedly attractive man, by all accounts, and all that money too. But still—a *sea* captain! To marry Addie Hunton, whose life and achievements to that point already qualified her in the minds of many for something close to sainthood. One has to recall the esteem in which she was held in the community. The widow of the adored William A. Hunton Sr. The defender of Negro womanhood. The essayist, activist, lecturer, and indefatigable NAACP field secretary. The ardent fighter for the rights of the race and of women alike.

How the tongues must have wagged.

Eunice appears to have been the only family member to attend the hastily arranged wedding in Fort Valley, Georgia. She must have been terribly unhappy about the whole thing. Eunice had worshipped her late father, and now here was her mother, the apostle of virtuous womanhood, proposing to bring into the household a man she had met scant months earlier. After the wedding, Floyd went back to Florida and Addie resumed her tour. Come summer, they lived together in Brooklyn for about a month before the captain went home. As matters turned out, each party had fooled the other: Sea Captain Floyd was not nearly as wealthy as he had led Addie to believe, and Addie was not nearly as young as she had led Floyd to believe. Their divorce was bitter, and the battle twice reached the Florida Supreme Court, which finally ruled in Floyd's favor. Addie had independent means to support herself and had refused to live with her husband. She was owed no alimony.

The marriage had been a moment of madness, and Addie was happy to get it behind her. So thoroughly has the tale been airbrushed from history that the only remaining bits are the two opinions of the Florida court and a handful of old news stories and NAACP reports referring to Addie as "Hunton-Floyd." There seem to be no family legends, extant writings, or history books that preserve the strange and simple fact that Eunice and Alphaeus, for a period of about three years from "I do" to divorce decree, had a stepfather.

When news of the marriage had first hit New York, the Czarinas had been scandalized. ("Their protocol," in the words of Adam Clayton Powell Jr., "was more rigid than that of the Court of St. James.") But the divorce was a bigger scandal still. The colored papers had a field day. "It is said that the 'wealth' of the captain is not what it was reported to be," cackled the *Pittsburgh Courier*. The family was reduced to refusing to comment when reporters knocked on their doors. Worst of all, the news of the divorce proceedings broke just as Eunice's own wedding was being announced. The Sea Captain was the plaintiff. He charged his bride with desertion for refusing to live in Jacksonville. The papers, by reporting dolefully that the scandal might overshadow Eunice's nuptials, committed that selfsame act of overshadowing.

Still, it was surely best that the divorce precede Eunice's wedding. At least this way she could ensure that the Sea Captain would be nowhere near the ceremony—and, for that matter, nowhere near her married life. Had his marriage to her mother lasted, Floyd might have been Eunice's stepfather for a very long time. (Certainly the Sea Captain kept coming to Harlem to visit his daughter Nora Johnson for many years after.) But it is difficult to imagine that he would ever have become a mentor to Eunice, or that their relationship would ever have been anything but distant and correct. Observing her prim mother's humiliation solidified in Eunice an absolute determination to hold fast to the values to which she had been raised.

Alphaeus, meanwhile, continued to learn the opposite lesson.

When Alphaeus gave his sister away at her wedding in November of 1924, he was taking time away from his just-begun studies for a master's degree in English at Harvard, where he had enrolled after having graduated from Howard in only three years. And Harvard, too, had been for Alphaeus the site of a further bit of racialist theater—an experience that doubtless shaped his view of the world. In the first place, he arrived in

Alphaeus, Addie (r.), and another woman in the Berkshires, 1927.
HUNTON FAMILY PHOTOGRAPH

Cambridge immediately after a huge campus brouhaha over whether Negro freshmen would be allowed to live in the newly constructed dormitories. (The president of the university believed that they would not be comfortable there; after a public fight, the board overruled him.) As a graduate student, Alphaeus would not have been directly affected by the outcome of the very public struggle; but the segregationist tint would surely color his experience.

In the second place, Alphaeus himself arrived under a racial cloud. The usual time in residence for a master's degree at the time was one year, but Alphaeus was informed in September of 1924 that he would have to spend two. Only early the next year did the school make plain the reason: students from Howard, Alphaeus was told, had proved to require extra time to complete their work. Others could receive the degree in one year; for Howard students, the rule was two. Nobody told him that the burden had anything to do with skin color; nobody had to. Everyone who graduated from Howard at the time was black. He could hardly escape being scarred by such open and obvious a discrimination.

Alphaeus petitioned for an exemption. He "would be most glad to spend another year at Harvard," he wrote, but he simply did not have enough money. George W. Robinson, the longtime dean of the graduate program, responded that as of the midyear, his grades did not warrant an exception. Alphaeus then asked whether Robinson might help him get a fellowship or scholarship to support a second year in residence. "If your record improves," was the cool reply.

As it happens, Alphaeus's record did improve. He even won an A-minus from the fabled John Livingston Lowes, an expert on Chaucer and Coleridge and a notoriously tough grader who just the year before had given an examination on which no one received anything higher than a B. Lowes was important for another reason. His theory of literature was very much dialectical. He saw the development of poetry over time as a constant battle between the forces of revolution and the forces of reaction. The reactionary forces always strike back, Lowes wrote, but then the revolution would launch its "inevitable counter-offensive" and regain whatever territory it had lost.

Marx and Engels could not have put it better. Alphaeus, by then already a budding Communist, must have been enraptured. He would not be the only one of Lowe's students who credited the great scholar with his radicalization. Alphaeus was still in his early twenties, but already an ideological gulf separated him from his more conservative sister. Within a few years, the gulf would become an unbridgeable chasm—with disastrous results for both.

CHAPTER 5

THE ESCAPE

SHORTLY BEFORE CHRISTMAS OF 1924, EUNICE AND LISLE RETURNED to Harlem from their extended honeymoon. They moved into an apartment at 90 Edgecombe Avenue, a low-rise sandstone building at the corner of 139th Street, where their neighbors included her Atlanta friend Walter White and his wife, Gladys. White was already a rising star at the NAACP, although it would be some years yet before he came to run the organization. The Whites hosted a fabulous salon at their apartment, where famous actors, singers, and intellectuals, black and white, could usually be found. The Carters were there often. Still, life for Eunice could not have been easy. In the 1925 New York state census, Lisle's occupation was listed as "Dentist." Eunice—likely to her chagrin—was recorded as "Housewife." Moreover, apart from the Whites, their neighbors at 90 Edgecombe were mostly working-class. Seamstresses, porters, lady's maids, housekeepers, and waiters surrounded them on all sides. It was honest work, but in her secret heart Eunice must have chafed at her situation. She craved intellectual stimulation. Just yesterday, she had been hobnobbing with Calvin Coolidge and Mary White Ovington, winning accolades at college graduation. Now she was a Harlem Czarina in training.

It was not with this future in mind that she had earned two degrees in four years at Smith.

On November 18, 1925, Eunice gave birth to the couple's first and only child. They named him Lisle Jr.* In the Negro press, the boy's arrival made the society columns. Marriage. A child. Eunice now had the opportunity to live the life Addie preached, as wife and mother, working in the home for the future of the race. But although sassiety never quite lost its hold on her, domesticity did. Eunice was restless. She was ambitious and driven, charismatic and smart. She did not want to live for cute stories in the Negro press, like the one in June of 1926 about how "Mrs. Eunice Hunton-Carter [sic] and little junior are visiting friends in Washington, D.C."

While Eunice moldered in her Harlem apartment, her mother was traveling to Haiti under the auspices of the Women's International League for Peace and Freedom, and returning to co-author a scathing report on the wrongs committed by occupying United States troops. Addie was suddenly a well-known peace activist. Haiti had radicalized her. She spoke at mass meetings against American militarism and hob-nobbed with the likes of the suffragist Carrie Chapman Catt and the future Nobel laureate Jane Addams. The Carnegie Endowment for International Peace sent Addie to Mexico. She and Addams would shortly travel to Prague for a peace conference. She would lecture at a "peace school" in Budapest. In an address to the Alpha Kappa Alpha sorority (of which she was an honorary national member), she argued that women must not confine their activism to their communities or even their country, but should try to improve the entire world.

Addie dragged her daughter into the periphery of the movement. Eunice served for a time as assistant secretary of the Circle for Peace and Foreign Relations, a pacifist and Pan-Africanist organization essentially run by her mother. In 1927 she helped Addie organize the Fourth Pan-Africanist Congress. But the last thing Eunice wanted was to become her mother's dogsbody. Her ambition was to lead her own life.

---

* Lisle Jr. was also Addie's only grandchild. Although Alphaeus married three times, he never had children.

And it was not only Addie whom Eunice wanted to escape. She was determined to be free of the twinned roles of housewife and clubwoman into which the Czarinas hoped to welcome her.

This was a time in America when Egypt was all the rage, and Harlem was caught up in the fervor. Everyone claimed to be descended from the great pharaohs. The finer apartments were decorated in wallpaper sporting faux-Egyptian hieroglyphs. Popular books about the Great Pyramid of Giza sold briskly: its hidden prophecies, its secret treasures, its magical powers. In the darker nation, people were particularly interested in claims that the Great Pyramid was constructed according to hidden arithmetical codes; unraveled, the codes might lead to picking a winner in the numbers game. Pyramidal images began showing up everywhere—in symbols of fraternal organizations, on jewelry, in store windows, on stationery. And that was what middle-class Harlem was becoming, too: a Great Social Pyramid that clubwomen fought each other to scale. The climb was treacherous. The sides were rocky and steep. There were false chambers and dead ends and other assorted traps. The mightiest Czarina could put a foot wrong and tumble from the apex; there were always eager newcomers ready to scramble over the fallen in their ascent toward the top.

Eunice knew already that the competition was not for her; the climbing she wanted to do was elsewhere. She had satisfied Addie's rules: she was a wife and a mother. But not even Addie had spent her life raising children for the race, as she had long counseled other women to do. Nor would Eunice. Mulling her options, she involved herself in local activism, joining a committee aimed at pressing Harlem stores to hire Negroes. She took a couple of night classes at Columbia University. She continued publishing stories and reviews, building her reputation as a writer. But even the literary world would soon prove too small. She wanted more. What she had not realized was that there was a deadline.

In June of 1927, when Lisle Jr. was one and a half, the *Pittsburgh Courier* published a list of Harlem's "society matrons" and "junior matrons," for the purpose of demonstrating that, for the first time, more were from the North than from the South. Eunice's name was on the list. There was her future, laid bare before her in black and white, decades to be spent scrambling up the side of the Great Social Pyramid, then trying to maintain her tenuous hold on the slippery surface. One can imagine her studying the article again and again. But unlike many young Harlem women, Eunice did not gaze at the page with pride. What she probably felt was terror. If she did not find a way to escape the prison of domesticity immediately, she might be stuck on that list forever.

In the fall of 1927, Eunice settled on an escape plan. She enrolled at Fordham Law School. Years later, she tried to explain her decision to an interviewer. Studying law, she said, had long been her "hidden desire." She added that it was something she "always had intended to do." She did not, this time, mention how at age eight she had told a little boy on the beach that she wanted to be a lawyer and put bad people in jail. But perhaps that is what she meant by "always."

Eunice chose a challenging moment to begin the study of law. Many American law schools—perhaps most—still maintained an informal color bar. The New York Bar Association would not admit a Negro lawyer until 1929. The American Bar Association, which had imposed a ban on black lawyers in 1912 after inadvertently admitting three, removed the requirement that an applicant disclose his race only in 1943, and did not actually admit another member of the darker nation until 1950. And Fordham itself was struggling to resist new aggressive policies in Connecticut and New York that placed heavy barriers in the path of part-time students—of which the school had many—who wished to sit for the bar. (The policies were aimed heavily at immigrants, in particular Jews and Catholics.) Yet Eunice was also preparing to join a flood of Negro professionals: between 1920 and 1930, their numbers increased by 69 percent.

Fordham's admission policies were relatively progressive for the era. Part of this was determined by its mission. As a law school attached to a Catholic university, Fordham became by necessity a place "most of whose students were targets of exclusion by legal elites." With minor exceptions, the Catholic law schools arose in urban areas and served largely immigrant urban populations. Fordham Law had opened its doors to women ten years earlier—that is, in the midst of World War I, when, like other institutions, it was scrambling to fill the seats. The first Negro students arrived at Fordham only in the 1920s. When Eunice began her studies, the numbers of both were still small. Fordham Law School enrolled some 535 students the year Eunice entered, most of them from Catholic colleges. Only seven women graduated three years later, in 1930—compared to 364 men.

At this time, the school was mostly located on the twenty-eighth floor of the Woolworth Building at 233 Broadway, and used the magnificent views from its windows as a selling point. As a full-time first-year student in the evening division, Eunice would have had classes every weeknight beginning at either six or six-thirty. Among her first-year classmates were Thomas F. Murphy, later a distinguished federal judge, and Adrian Burke, who would serve nearly two decades on New York's highest court. A year behind were Irving R. Kaufman, who as a federal judge would preside over the Rosenberg trial, and future state court judges Max Bloom and Vincent A. Lupiano. And the moment was in other ways a propitious one for the school. Ignatius Wilkinson, recently appointed as dean, had worked hard to raise academic standards, and Eunice's was the first class to bear the full brunt of the new rules. Wilkinson established a proctoring system to ensure attendance at lectures, with "penalties for excessive absences."

The academic atmosphere was tough and challenging. William R. Meagher, a 1927 graduate who later would co-found the law firm Skadden, Arps, Slate, Meagher & Flom, recalled what classes were like:

> Students were required to occupy assigned seats, and absences—unoccupied seats—were recorded. Three unexcused absences from a course caused failure in that course. The case system was ritually followed throughout the three-year program. The student stood and stated the facts and principles of the case; class discussion followed and ended with the professor's statement of the law, generally and in New York. This, of course, took time—a case book was rarely completed—and a course ended with lectures on uncovered material.

When Eunice received her degree, in 1932, the dean reported with evident pride that the "rigorous academic policies" were having their intended effect: fully one-third of the class failed to finish.

Wilkinson modernized the law school in a number of ways. By the time of Eunice's arrival, he had embarked upon a campaign to replace the school's "old and dilapidated" furniture. During her years at Fordham, Wilkinson established the placement office to help graduates find jobs. Prodded by the organized bar, he hired more full-time professors in place of the practitioners who had traditionally carried most of the teaching load. And Eunice could no doubt be grateful that Wilkinson built the school's first women's lavatory.

In remarks to a meeting of Catholic men's societies toward the end of Eunice's first year, Wilkinson tried to explain what made Fordham different from other law schools: "By sending forth students who are taught that the minds of men differ but in degrees of brutishness, selfishness is encouraged and a philosophy of materialism propagated. We Catholics represent a philosophy diametrically opposed—one that thinks in terms of eternity." He added, "You can't train the mind alone without creating a lopsided man who will be a menace to society."

By her own account, Eunice found the law fascinating. She loved the intellectual challenge. The study of law brought to her powerful mind a necessary discipline. Still, one must wonder how she might have responded if asked in her Contracts course to stand and recite *Gunning v. Royal*, an 1881 Mississippi case that features a cart driven by "an inexperienced negro boy" who ignores a warning that he is heading in the wrong direction, and whose stupid mistake causes the death of a valuable horse. Or perhaps she was asked to give the facts in *Boone v. Eyre*, an eighteenth-century British decision that casually discusses the status of "negroes" as property. For like most law school texts of the day, her Contracts casebook, by Wormser, Loughran, and Keener, included many an offensive case with entire indifference to the racial sensibilities of readers. Most likely Eunice would have handled the opportunity with the same sharp precision she brought to the rest of her work. It remains striking, nevertheless, that even at the law school that represented her escape from the daily pressure of the scramble up the Great

Pyramid of Harlem, her studies provided no escape from the wicked persistence of the lie of black inferiority.

Although Eunice enrolled at Fordham in the fall of 1927 for what should have been a three-year course, she did not finish until the summer of 1932. The school's records tell us that she was excused in February 1928 because of illness. She would tell interviewers later, however, that it was her son, Lisle Jr., who had fallen ill, and she was forced to take off a year and a half to care for him. Her grades were not the issue. When Eunice withdrew, she had completed two half-year courses (all the others were full-year) with marks of 84 and 86—this at a time when the median was somewhere in the low 70s.

Ill or not, Eunice found plenty to keep her busy during her time away from Fordham. In the fall of 1928, twenty-nine-year-old Eunice, scant months after her withdrawal from law school, was working for the Bamberger Fund, supervising its work among Negro residents of Newark, New Jersey. She also was running the Harlem branch of Women for Hoover, with an office at 139 West 135th Street. This was her first serious foray into electoral politics, though she would have seen Addie crisscrossing the country on behalf of Coolidge in 1924. Like most of the darker nation of the era, the family had been Republicans all their lives. This time around, too, Eunice's mother was on the campaign trail. "[E]verything that we have had since the dawn of freedom," Addie told a colored audience in upstate New York, "has come through the Republican Party."

Although this attitude must nowadays seem quaint, in the context of the era it was by no means unreasonable. Addie's parents had been enslaved. The Republican Party had fought the war that freed them. The Republican Party had enacted the Thirteenth, Fourteenth, and Fifteenth Amendments. Her entire life experience had been of a Democratic Party in implacable opposition to the rights of her people. In national elections, the Democrats still counted on the electoral votes of the Solid South, where few colored people could vote. This was the common experience of the entire darker nation of the era. One might suppose that by the late 1920s, with the growing political power of relatively progressive Democratic Party machines in the cities of the North, this perception would have changed. But one would be wrong, as Eunice was about to learn.

Painfully.

Imagine a parade of white men in blackface, chanting as they march along a suburban street on a bright afternoon during an election campaign where one of the candidates is a Negro. Their only and obvious purpose is to remind the voters of this fact. Place the display in the midst of a racially charged era in American politics, and you can understand the fate of Hubert Delany, the Negro lawyer who was the GOP candidate in the November 1929 special election for Harlem's seat in the House of Representatives. The marchers were sent by the Democratic machine known as Tammany Hall, and their display constituted only one of several dirty tricks that were deployed during the campaign. Dirty or not, the tricks were all directed at a pair of objectives: to drive white voters to the polls in large numbers, and to persuade them to vote against the black man when they got there.

Eunice witnessed all of this firsthand, for she was heavily involved in Delany's campaign. He was a graduate of New York University Law School and an assistant United States Attorney who specialized in prosecuting what nowadays would be known as white-collar crime. Earlier that year he had helped convict the fraudsters who had brought down the Clarke Brothers private bank, a catastrophe that helped lead to closer supervision of the state's banking industry. His sister Bessie had a dental practice in the building next door to Lisle Sr.'s offices. (Years later, Bessie and her sister Sadie would pen the bestselling memoir *Having Our Say*.) Leading white Republicans endorsed him. Charles H. Tuttle, the United States Attorney who would later run for governor, was his honorary campaign chairman. The president of Columbia University came out enthusiastically for Delany. Fiorello La Guardia, at that time a member of Congress, was running for mayor. His district overlapped black Harlem, and he stumped for Delany all over the neighborhood. "Don't vote for me if you can't vote for Delany," he pleaded. At another campaign appearance, La Guardia argued that Tammany

Hall's resistance to Delany proved that the Democrats didn't have "the interest of the Negro at heart." (Eunice campaigned hard for La Guardia too.)

Other big Republican guns lent support. The popular Hamilton Fish Jr., a power in the House of Representatives, came to town. "You've got to stop depending on white people to do for you," he urged. This was a paean to the virtues not of self-help but of voting Republican: "Why should not 12,000,000 free, colored citizens not [sic] have more than one representative in Congress?" In Harlem, at least, the answer would depend on turnout. Eunice joined with other influential sassiety wives to create the Women's Political Council to increase voter registration.

True, the major newspapers were at first confused. In its initial article on Delany's nomination, the *New York Times* called him "Hobart." Some voters were bewildered too, including a racially integrated group that showed up at a Harlem townhouse expecting to meet a spiritualist, only to discover, to their dismay, that the speaker was Delany—a political candidate. Overall, however, the campaign ran smoothly. Observers considered Delany the favorite. His supporters were confident. Just days before the vote, Eunice and her husband attended a "victory celebration" in his honor.

The Tammany Democrats fought back hard—and they knew exactly where to punch. They hired young white men to march through the streets of the still segregated parts of the district with blackened faces, bearing signs that read, "DO YOU WANT A NEGRO CONGRESSMAN?" White voters "accidentally" received leaflets, purportedly from the Republican Party, urging colored voters in incendiary terms to vote for Delany. The GOP claimed that the flyers were a Tammany trick to discredit their candidate, and the United States Attorney (who, as we've seen, was honorary chairman of Delany's campaign) promised an investigation.

The point of all this race-baiting was that Delany could not win with Negro votes alone. Like all of Harlem's electoral districts, the congressional district in which he was running remained mostly white. La Guardia, at a campaign appearance, made an impassioned plea to black voters, arguing that Delany could hardly ask for white votes if his own people did not back him heavily.

And back him they did. On Election Day, the black precincts went for Delany by a margin of four to one.

He lost anyway. The white precincts went against him by a margin of six to one, but at this time they constituted only about 30 percent of Harlem. Nevertheless, the incumbent, Joseph Gavagan, won by a huge margin. Plainly, white turnout must have been much higher than black turnout. Why so high? After his defeat, Delany accused his opponent of "sending out spurious literature to stir up race prejudice in my district." Harlemites complained of being unable to vote because of machines that malfunctioned and polling places that closed early. No doubt the Negro-baiting and Tammany trickery played a role. But there were other reasons for the outcome. The stock market crashed just days before the election, ushering in the era that would later be called the Great Depression. New York was crushed by a Democratic wave. La Guardia lost the mayoralty race by a plurality of half a million votes. Nevertheless, connections were made and alliances were remembered. When La Guardia finally achieved the mayoralty, in 1934, he would quickly find posts for both Delany and Eunice.

Something else happened, too. Eunice had always despised the Democratic Party. Her antipathy had been nurtured in her Atlanta childhood and reinforced by her mother's partisanship. The Delany experience seared the loathing into her soul. Whatever weaknesses the GOP might have possessed, Eunice believed to the end of her days that the Democrats were the party of racism and hate.

In February of 1930, Eunice returned to Fordham. This time things went smoothly. Her sharp, quick mind was fully on display. If not perhaps the top-ranked student in her class, she was nevertheless impressive, maintaining a solid B average at a time when a C was considered a reasonable grade. She earned A-pluses in Contracts and Suretyship, and an A in Quasi-Contracts. Most of her other grades were B's. Her academic standing could have been higher still but for a single uncharacteristic lapse in her usual rigor. In the spring of 1932, at the end of her third year, Eunice inexplicably failed to pass the final examination in Mortgages, and had to repeat the class over the summer.

Or perhaps the result was not so inexplicable. Eunice was still an evening student, still working full-time. By 1932, she had become a supervisor in the Harlem division of the Emergency Unemployment Relief Committee, a job that surely added another pressure to her highly pressured life. The committee was actually an umbrella organization for several fund-raising entities, and was known as the Gibson Fund, after its chairman.* The Harlem division allocated clothing and food to those who were out of work. It made constant appeals for more funds. Eunice joined a public campaign through which sassiety wives asked every Harlemite to donate 1 percent of his or her income to the fund. Nearly a year later, the Negro papers were still urging those who still had jobs "to share their earnings with less fortunate brethren." Harlem would receive "a more respectful hearing" in its plea for relief "if it can be shown that the Harlem community made a generous response." The committee faced an impossible task. Employees drove themselves to exhaustion. Eunice was likely among the exhausted.

And yet her reinvention was a success. Five years earlier, she had dreaded the future she saw looming before her like a prison sentence. It was not that she did not love her husband. And although once she resumed law school she sent Lisle Jr. to stay with her husband's relatives in New Jersey, she loved her son too. But she was not prepared to spend her life as another Harlem matron. She needed more.

Eunice was not yet ready to compete with her mother, who, between her peace trips abroad, found time for tea with Mrs. John D. Rockefeller. But she was more than ready to strike out on her own. The reinvented Eunice was not rejecting Addie's teachings about the primacy of motherhood and home life for the Negro woman. She was reinterpreting them according to Addie's example. The great apostle of the virtuous home life had spent Eunice's childhood on the road, fighting for the causes in which she believed. She had gone off to the Amenia Conference when her husband was near death. After William died, she had left her children behind for nearly two years to go to war with the colored troops. Eunice, too, had ambitions beyond raising a family. The pursuit of those ambitions had led her to law school, and would carry

---

* Eunice had also worked for the predecessor organization, beginning in 1929 or 1930.

her, just three years after graduation, to Tom Dewey and the investigation of Lucky Luciano.

At around this time, Eunice's brother became what she herself worked energetically to avoid: a source of scandal to the family. More to the point, he had already scandalized the family back at Christmas of 1927, offending his mother and angering his sister, and chose 1931 as the year in which to make things worse. In the middle of Eunice's first year of law school, her younger brother—by now an English professor at Howard—had stunned Harlem by making a sudden marriage even more unsuitable by the standards of sassiety than Addie's of a few years earlier. "Howard Professor Weds Stage Girl," ran the headline in January of 1928. Just after Christmas, Alphaeus had married Ethelyn Boyd, a "popular stage beauty," whom he had apparently known when they were children together in Brooklyn. "The young folks have been the cynosure of all eyes at the various and many social functions which were held during the holiday period." The son of the sainted William Hunton had married a showgirl: that was bad enough. Worse, she had "run off" from a Broadway play to be with her beau—that was how the colored press put it—and the couple had apparently been cohabiting before the wedding in Alphaeus's apartment at 654 Girard Street, on the edge of the Howard University campus, a building known as Howard Manor. The Czarinas were suitably appalled. Addie, the papers said, "disapproved" of the match. A more accurate summation would likely be that she was both shamed and infuriated. Eunice, who had made a traditional marriage, must have felt exactly the same.

Still, the family made a stab at accepting Ethelyn, and she was even seen out and about in society, in both Washington and New York. In 1930, Eunice visited the couple at Thanksgiving. As for Alphaeus, wed to a chorus girl or not, he was still the son of William and Addie Hunton, and the Czarinas could not entirely freeze him out. At the fabulous Harlem wedding of Countee Cullen and W. E. B. Du Bois's daughter, Yolande, a ceremony attended by thousands, Alphaeus served as a groomsman, alongside such notables as Langston Hughes and Arna Bontemps. The wedding, in the words of Du Bois biographer David Levering Lewis, "was the Harlem social event of the decade." Some

twelve hundred guests were invited to the ceremony, but a crowd estimated at three thousand squeezed into Salem Methodist Episcopal
Church to witness the event. So vast was the crowd that keeping order
required the services of extra patrolmen from the nearby Fourteenth
Precinct. Despite the turnout at the ceremony, the reception, held at
Madam Walker's studios, was limited to three hundred carefully
selected guests—a process to which Du Bois referred as "separating
the sheep from the goats." Neither Eunice nor Addie made it onto the
short list—but Alphaeus and Ethelyn did.

As Eunice probably expected, the unsuitable marriage could not
last. By 1931, Ethelyn was living in New York once more, complaining
that life as the wife of a college professor was a bore. For the family, the
scandal deepened. It seemed that Alphaeus had lately been keeping
company, to use the polite euphemism of the day, with another woman.
He and his new sweetheart had been spotted at the beach in Atlantic
City. They seemed not to care who knew they were together. The columns
could not get enough of the story. Huntons were not supposed to divorce.
Certainly they were not supposed to flaunt relationships outside of marriage. Sassiety was stunned. But the rebel in Alphaeus enjoyed shocking
the Czarinas.

First Addie had been caught up in scandal, over both marriage to
and divorce from Sea Captain Floyd. Now Alphaeus had joined her,
first in marrying Ethelyn, then in leaving her behind to cavort with
another woman at the seashore. Eunice, her father's favorite, was left as
the only member of the family whose standing in sassiety was untar-
nished. The pressure to maintain that reputation would prove to be
almost more than she could bear.

In fairness, little of Harlem's attention in the summer of 1931 was likely
on the society pages. The colored papers were full of news about the
gang war that had erupted over control of the illegal numbers business.
The Harlem rackets, particularly the numbers, were by far the most
lucrative in the city, yielding millions of dollars a year. They had traditionally been run by Negro gangsters, known colloquially as Black
Kings and Black Queens. The best known of these were Bumpy Johnson and Stephanie St. Clair. Various white ethnic gangs had footholds

in Harlem, but policy banking (as the numbers racket was some-times called) remained largely in Negro hands. All of that began to change in 1931. Acting on behalf of a syndicate of several gangs, the city's best-known mobster, Dutch Schultz, made a move to seize con-trol of Harlem's numbers game. The Black Kings and Black Queens were tough, organized, and capable. But when the Dutchman decided to take over the Harlem numbers, his organization arrived with a well-deserved reputation for savagery. In the ensuing battle, Schultz mostly won and the Black Kings and Black Queens mostly lost.

The press covered what it described as a "bloodless" war as if it were a sports match, telling eager readers who was winning and who was losing. The claim that the struggle was bloodless was not entirely true. The initial incursion by the white mob (let's call it the Mob, with a cap-ital *M*) evidently was managed without anyone being killed. Indeed, Schultz first presented himself as a savior, for a number of the Negro policy banks had become all but insolvent at Thanksgiving, when an especially popular number "hit." But not everyone acquiesced in the coup. Joe Ison, who managed one of the biggest banks in Harlem, was taken for a ride by a pair of Schultz gunmen until he saw the light. There were threats and beatings galore—the war turned out not to be so bloodless—and, as later testimony made clear, the police largely stood aside and let Schultz's gang have its way.

By 1932, Schultz was the clear winner. A year later, when the black gangsters tried to fight back, the battle became bloodier still. Martin L. Harris, a banker and strong-arm man rumored to be affiliated with Stephanie St. Clair's operation, was ambushed and killed. Bankers tried to band together and refuse to pay tribute to the Mob. Several of them disappeared. Still, it remains unclear how much actual violence occurred. For the most part, the threat alone was sufficient. St. Clair openly appealed to the mayor for police protection—essentially asking for official help running her numbers racket in the face of Schultz's onslaught. In September, she promised publicly to kill Schultz before he could kill her, and openly pondered picketing his Harlem numbers drops. Then she went into hiding.

Until the Mob began to move in, the colored press had hardly cov-ered the numbers at all. Everybody played, everybody talked about whether they won or lost, but nobody wrote about it. Some of the major Negro policy bankers managed to keep their names out of the papers until the war for control itself became news. Now there were stories galore about this black numbers runner or that one fleeing, often to the Caribbean, where many were from. A few Negro gangsters, like St. Clair, did what they could to run much-reduced operations from hiding. Others who survived the onslaught either retired or found themselves suddenly mid-level functionaries in a larger white-controlled criminal enterprise. Later on, the *Amsterdam News* would editorialize about the battle, "It is ironical but true that Negroes build things only to have them taken away and successfully exploited by the white man."

By the time Eunice finished law school, the Mob owned Harlem.

CHAPTER 6

THE CANDIDATE

IN OCTOBER OF 1932, TO CELEBRATE HER GRADUATION FROM LAW school, Eunice was given a party by her friends William and Regina Andrews, who lived at 405 Edgecombe Avenue. The guest list confirmed the esteem in which her family was held. Attendees included, among many others, Mr. and Mrs. Walter White, Mr. and Mrs. Aaron Douglas, and Mr. and Mrs. Roy Wilkins. (Minnie Wilkins was a co-host of the event.) The new Eunice had arrived. Addie's ambitious daughter had completed her transition from Czarina in training to literary lioness to lawyer. On the surface she was full of energy. She was still, as they used to say, seen about. She brought a party of guests to the Hampton-Howard football game. She served actively on the board of the Harlem Experimental Theatre, the successor to the Krigwa Players. And she gave a "forceful" speech to "a rousing mass meeting" of New Jersey Republicans on the eve of the election that would sweep Democrat Franklin Roosevelt into the White House.

But Eunice did not plunge immediately into law practice. In fact, by her own account, she did not plunge immediately into anything. All through law school, Eunice had been a regular in the society pages, swirling through glittering round after glittering round of cocktail receptions and dinners. There seemed to be two of her. One was the law student who had classes every weekday evening and was subject to Fordham Law School's mandatory attendance rules. The other was present at just about every important event of Harlem sassiety, not a few of which she actually hosted. How she managed this feat of legerdemain we will never know. What we can say is that once she graduated and had more time, Eunice was suddenly in the columns a good deal less. She did not vanish entirely, of course, but the pace at which she whirled through sassiety slowed noticeably. Several years later, an admiring profile in the *Boston Daily Globe* would dance around what happened:

> Getting the degree seemed to snap something in her. She doesn't understand yet what happened, but it was six months before she could get out of bed and two years before she could undertake what she regards as a full program.

Was it really likely that Eunice, looking back, did not understand what was plaguing her? Perhaps she was protecting her privacy. We know from the public record that Eunice, like her mother, suffered from unexplained bouts of exhaustion and listlessness. According to the recollections of her son, she spent much of her life fighting depression.

She also had trouble with the bar examination. Her second try came in March of 1933, and in May she was declared to have passed. At some point later that year, she hung out her shingle at 2145 Seventh Avenue, not far from her husband's dental office, and began the practice of law. Her early clients were not such as would make a lawyer rich. She drafted a few wills, handled a few misdemeanor cases, and waited for business to improve. She remained optimistic. She took the view that eventually she, as a woman, would have a "real opportunity," not because there were few women lawyers but because there were few "really good" lawyers.

In the midst of her reinvention, however, Eunice faced a fresh challenge. In May, not long after she received word that she had passed the bar, her mother fell ill. Addie was hospitalized at a Harlem sanitarium. Alphaeus came to stay with Eunice and her husband for several days at their new apartment at 103 West 141st Street, and the siblings visited their mother. Addie was always sickly, but this time she never fully recovered. Although she would survive another decade, Addie grew steadily weaker, and within a few years would begin to curtail her public appearances.

Then, in the autumn of 1933, it was Eunice's turn. The press, without quite saying why, reported that her doctors had put her on a strict regimen of bed rest. But rest turned out not to be enough. In early December she was hospitalized and underwent emergency surgery. Her operation made the papers, including several outside of New York. "At press time," the *Amsterdam News* solemnly informed its readers, "Attorney Carter's condition was fair." The public was never told what the surgery was for, but her son, Lisle Jr., would later say that his mother had undergone a hysterectomy. She may well have been expecting. A difficult pregnancy would explain the ordered bed rest; a lost baby might have led to the surgery.

Following the operation, Eunice was again ordered to stay in bed. But Eunice, being Eunice, grew tired of confinement. She was accustomed to being up and about, and if she stayed home for the usual six or eight weeks, she would have been out of circulation for far too long. So she got up. In February of 1934, an event was held at the Nicholas Roerich Museum at 310 Riverside Drive, to present nine members of the Philomathians, a group of Baltimoreans "who are patrons of the arts." Mrs. Addie Hunton chose the venue and, as hostess, presided over the reception. The cream of Negro society was invited:

> The eighty-five socialites were received in the corridor by Harold Jackman, Augustus Granville Dill, Edward Coates, Dr. Lisle Carter, Mr. Latimer, Alpheus [sic] Hunton and Robert Jackson and directed to the room, where a 2:30 program was offered.

We are further told: "Mrs. Eunice Hunton Carter, daughter of the hostess, presented the arrivals to the receiving line."

Probably she rose from her bed too soon; certainly she needed further recuperation. Soon Eunice and eight-year-old Lisle Jr. were on the train to Florida, where they would live for a while with Mary McLeod

Bethune while Eunice recovered. Bethune, the renowned educator, was a great friend of Addie's. The two had long worked together in various organizations of the women of the darker nation. They had co-founded a women's organization in Haiti. They had even protested together, walking out of a music festival sponsored by the International Council of Women because audience members were seated according to race. Presumably it was through Addie that the arrangements for Eunice's stay in Florida were made.

In the years to come, Lisle Jr. would remember the long train ride alone with Eunice as the happiest time the two of them ever spent together. It was just the two of them, he would remember fondly; best of all, his mother was not doing any work. As her son told the story later, Eunice was, for once, giving him all of her attention.

The Negro press, which covered all the goings and comings of even the junior Czarinas, differed on whether their readers should be allowed to know that Eunice Carter was showing any weakness after the reception. The *Chicago Defender* was frank: "Mrs. Carter has been ill this winter, and is going to Florida to complete her convalescence." Other papers disguised the purpose of the trip. The Baltimore *Afro-American* made the journey sound like a lark:

> Mrs. Eunice Hunton Carter[,] wife of Dr. Lisle Carter, has
> gone with other fashionable Fith [sic] Avenue folk to Florida.
> She will be the guest of Mrs. Bethune.

Who the fashionable folk might have been we are not told. Possibly Eunice had friends along initially. But only Eunice and Lisle Jr. stayed.

For Eunice, the two months she spent with Mrs. Bethune provided a remarkable opportunity. Bethune, who in 1904 had founded a school for Negro girls in Daytona, had just recently engineered the merger that created Bethune-Cookman College, and she was constantly busy, raising money and inviting prominent people to the campus to speak or even to teach for a while. By the early 1930s, she was one of the best-known Negro women in the country. She had also become deeply involved in civil rights activism, in ways that clubwomen of her generation tended to avoid. I can see the two of them sitting up at night, the house and the campus silent, as Eunice partakes of the older woman's wisdom. They forged a lasting bond. When, the following year, Bethune founded the National Council of Negro Women, Eunice was present at the creation. She would remain close to Bethune for many years, and would hold high office in the Council for most of her life. The weeks with Mrs. Bethune affected Eunice in a more personal way as well, for it was during her recuperation in Florida that Eunice finally discovered a direction for the seething ambition that had led her from one career into the next.

In May, she and her son returned home, once more by train. This time the papers told the world that she had been in Florida recovering from surgery. So the secret was out. But Eunice hardly cared. Because she now knew exactly what she wanted to do next.

The year 1934 was one of the hottest on record. Throughout the summer, most of the nation baked in triple-digit temperatures. In the continental United States, some five hundred people died from the heat. But politics continued apace. In Harlem, the Republican Party of New York needed a warm body to run for the state assembly from the Nineteenth District against the incumbent James E. Stephens, a Democrat who was the only colored member of the state assembly. The Republican candidate was expected to be something of a sacrificial lamb. Since the Civil War, the darker nation had staunchly supported the GOP, but times were changing, especially in the cities. To keep its hold on colored votes, the party had begun running Negro candidates in urban districts where whites were a minority. Four years earlier, the Republican Oscar De Priest of Chicago had become the first black congressman of the twentieth century, and the first ever elected from outside of the South.

De Priest was unusual only in that he won. The Republicans had been furiously recruiting Negro candidates in cities all over the country, for offices high and low. The unsuccessful congressional campaign of Hubert Delany in 1929—the one seared into Eunice's memory after Tammany sent out the marchers in blackface—had been a part of the GOP strategy. The congressional district that encompassed most of Harlem was at this time still mainly white. The state assembly district, however, was mostly black. Although the Democrats had won the seat several years running, the Republicans believed that an attractive Negro candidate could make inroads against the Tammany Hall machine that ruled New York politics, even in Harlem. Whoever was chosen would enter the race as the underdog, but should the nominee happen to prevail, there would be a reasonable shot at a congressional seat a few years down the road.

The party found its attractive candidate in Eunice Hunton Carter. She was a graduate of Smith College and Fordham Law School. She was married to the most prominent Negro dentist in the city. She was known and liked along Harlem's boisterous streets, yet moved easily in colored sassiety. She came from a revered family. Besides name recognition and her own résumé, Eunice had other appealing qualities. She had a smooth, resonant voice that made audiences sit up and listen. She had a fine command of the language. And although she could sometimes be chilly and even censorious to those who crossed her, she was by all accounts enormously charming when she chose to be. She was also tall and slender, and generally considered quite attractive.

Perhaps most important, she was smart and ambitious, and unafraid to speak her mind. Like her mother, Eunice was a committed Republican but not a yes-woman. She had all of Addie's feistiness. During the 1928 presidential campaign, for example, even as she'd worked passionately for Hoover, Eunice had stood up during a mass meeting at the Women's National Republican Club to warn a flabbergasted member of the GOP's national committee that the party was losing Negro votes due to its alliance with lily-white Republican organizations in the South.

In 1934, Eunice's interest and the party's converged. The GOP looked at Eunice Carter and saw a candidate with a bright political future: black and female, conservative and brilliant, charming and charismatic. She had campaigned for La Guardia. She had campaigned for Republican nominee Charles Tuttle in his unsuccessful run for governor. Yes, she was likely to prove a sacrificial lamb, but the party was delighted to have her on board.

Eunice faced an uphill battle. Like the darker nation generally, the Nineteenth District had turned increasingly Democratic. Harlem suffered badly during the Depression. Between 1929 and 1932, the median income of skilled workers in Harlem fell by an astonishing 50 percent. The income of less skilled workers fell by more than 40 percent. Half of the city's Negroes received public relief at some point during the Depression. At Christmas, the Cotton Club handed out three thousand holiday baskets of food. Families behind in their rent were daily being put out on the street with their belongings. Parents dug through garbage to feed their children. But none of this would necessarily help Eunice's candidacy. The darker nation blamed the GOP for the catastrophe. Although Franklin Roosevelt had not won the Negro vote in 1932—his landslide was very much a white landslide—he was increasingly popular within the darker nation, particularly in the cities. Harlem's once-dominant black Republican clubs were now dwarfed by their Democratic counterparts.

James Stephens, moreover, was the incumbent. To Harlemites, his was the familiar face. But the GOP saw him as vulnerable. He had close connections with the Tammany Hall machine, at that time still powerful but in disrepute. Over the summer he had been investigated on allegations that he had accepted a bribe to help a postal worker keep his job. In response to the charges, Stephens said what every candidate caught in a scandal says: "The whole thing is a political plot hatched by my enemies to handicap me in my campaign for re-election." He survived the threat but, despite his incumbency, was now regarded as a weak candidate. His time in Albany had up to that point resulted in no legislative accomplishments of note. The Democratic leadership tried and failed to replace him on the ticket. Well into the fall, the Negro press was rife with rumors that the party might yank its support for him.

Eunice established a campaign headquarters on Seventh Avenue between 131st and 132nd Streets, a few blocks north of her law office. The location placed her staff very much in the center of things. Just nearby stood Connie's Inn, the Harlem nightspot that had first brought Louis Armstrong to New York. Originally closed to Negroes unless they were performers or waiters, Connie's soon became known for its integrated audiences. Next to Connie's was the grand marquee of the Lafayette Theatre, known as the headquarters of "colored vaudeville." Up the street was the Yeah Man (properly the "Yeah Man?"), a popular Italian American restaurant that drew diners from all around the city. Around the corner from Eunice's headquarters was "Jungle Alley," where the adventuresome could crowd into establishments like Basement Brownies, perhaps the greatest of the late-night jazz clubs, or Monette's, where just the previous year a teenaged sensation named Billie Holiday had been discovered. And—ironically, given the future course of Eunice's career—every one of these nightspots paid tribute to the Mob.

The location of her headquarters was also close to emblems of Harlem that had nothing to do with entertainment. A bit to the north stood a physical reminder of the hard times that had befallen the darker nation during the Depression: the empty shell of the International, a black-owned private hospital recently forced by economic conditions to close its doors. And a few short blocks away was 351 Lenox Avenue, the unassuming storefront of the Ritzy Beauty salon, which all Harlem knew to be a major "office" for the illegal numbers operation run by Dutch Schultz. But players didn't have to stop by the office to bet. By one estimate, numbers could be bought at two-thirds of all the cigar and stationery stores in Harlem.

By the fall of 1934, when Eunice ran for state assembly, the Mob's control over Harlem was firmly established. Newspapers ran sensational stories of black resistance, but along the streets there was mostly black acceptance. Certainly nobody was prepared to stop buying the numbers just because the purchase would enrich white rather than colored gangsters. Just about everyone who went into a Harlem store was paying tribute to the Mob. A thirty-five-year-old colored lawyer seeking her first political office—and a woman, no less—was hardly in a position to take on organized crime.

Not yet.

The GOP cleared Eunice's path to the nomination. Local Republicans had been notoriously divided, but now, wrote the press, they were "smoking the pipe of peace." So Eunice was unopposed, unlike Stephens, who faced a primary challenge. As the general election approached, she ran a determined campaign, and although there were no formal polls, she was soon considered the favorite. The Negro press was on her side. She earned the endorsement of both the liberal but staunchly Republican *Amsterdam News* and the staunchly conservative and equally Republican *New York Age*. The *News* argued that the time had come to send Tammany a message by voting a straight GOP ticket. The local Democratic leader, an editorial noted, "has defeated every attempt to change the leadership because Negroes have helped him." The principal helper was Stephens, derided by the *News* as "his candidate." Eunice, on the other hand, was described as "the militant, intelligent young attorney." By voting for her, Harlem would "elect perhaps the first Negro woman to any legislature."

The *Age*, the more traditionalist of New York's major Negro papers, labeled Eunice "exceptionally well qualified." The paper predicted "with certainty" that she would win. *Age* columnist Ebenezer Ray offered three reasons:

> First, her platform is practical; secondly, it would give her the distinction of being the first Negro woman to attain such a position, and, lastly, SHE CAN'T DO LESS THAN THE MEN.

The column added: "Here is an opportunity for women voters to be 'clannish' to one of their own sex."

Nor were the New York papers alone. The pre-election roundup of the Baltimore *Afro-American*, while not taking sides, gave Eunice more coverage than any other New York candidate. The paper went out of its way to describe her as "college-bred and unruffled, but intelligent, both in looks and actually." The article, published on the eve of the election, told readers that Eunice "has no skeletons to fear" and added,

> Mrs. Carter is also the only one of the colored candidates who has been given the unqualified endorsement of the Citizens Union, the non-partisan, highly respected body which every year rates candidates for office.

Her connections mattered, too. She was, in the words of the *Crisis*, a "member of an old, well-known family." To the educated classes of the darker nation at this time, the "oldness" of a family was measured in part by its middle-class credentials, and in part by its generations out of enslavement. In effect, the magazine was assuring its readers that she was a member of the elite.

In her campaign, however, Eunice emphasized her connections with Harlem itself:

> For myself I make no plea. I live here, I have lived here. I am going to continue living here. I am one of you and I want many things for Harlem. I have an eight-year-old son whom I hope will live and whom I expect to work here. You have known me for the better part of half of my life that I have lived right here with you. I need say no more as to my interest in this community, than the fact that I will put the community first.

Not all of this was precisely true. For example, Eunice, by this time, had lived in Harlem for just ten of her thirty-five years. Moreover, as events would shortly prove, there is reason to believe that she had no intention of seeing Lisle Jr. raised in Harlem. But politics is politics, and what mattered was her emphasis on connections to the community. Her words constituted a subtle thrust at her opponent without mentioning his name, for there were many who believed that Stephens was too much a party man and had done too much for himself and too little for Harlem. Wherever Eunice went, she drew cheering crowds. She had every reason to be confident.

Harlem of the 1930s still evokes a magical warmth in our collective imagination, and to some extent the imagined Harlem was real. The avenues were loud and boisterous. Street-corner preachers stood on soapboxes or stepladders. Ice vendors and knife sharpeners still rolled their wagons along the avenues, hawking their wares. Loudspeakers mounted on cars blared political messages. A brand-new movie theater had recently opened. There were social clubs and fraternal organizations everywhere. Many of these owned ornate buildings on the facades of which obscure symbols had been scrawled. Women wore fancy hats. Men wore colorful suits. Lapels were wide. Shoulders were padded. Baggy pants had come into style. Church groups held huge parades, the women marching all in white. Everybody played the numbers. The Negro gangsters wore diamond stickpins. Social clubs and dance halls and saloons stayed open long into the night, defying law and custom alike. Many of their customers were whites who'd fled uptown because the rules were better enforced below 125th Street. In the clubs, jazz combos played. The whole neighborhood seemed to shimmy to their rhythm. Within this segregated world, the rising black bourgeoisie flourished.

Eunice crisscrossed Harlem. She spoke from "the dais of any number of churches, St. Mark's, Mother Zion, Abyssinian, Salem, . . . and in dozens of political and civic clubs." Unlike white political clubs of the day, the Harlem party organizations were dominated by women, particularly at the street level. It was the female vote, therefore, that the Republicans needed to engage. And those atop the Great Social Pyramid approved. Middle-class black women found Eunice a particularly admirable candidate. A Eunice Carter Club was formed by some of the most prominent women in Harlem. Among the founders were J. Ida Jiggetts, a fellow social worker and graduate of Columbia, and the prominent suffragist Wenonah Bond Logan. Unsurprisingly, their candidate tirelessly pressed the message that gender mattered, noting, "A woman would have a keener insight into the needs of the community from a social point of view." The *Chicago Defender* wrote that the candidate was "much in demand especially before women's organizations."

No Hunton had ever run for office, and Eunice's mother probably found the idea of stumping for votes undignified. But the Negro papers constantly reminded readers that the candidate was the daughter of the famous Addie. And whatever her mother thought, Eunice took to politics quite naturally. She enjoyed herself on the stump. Her audiences were enthusiastic. The press called her "a convincing speaker—not thunderous, but impressive." As the record-shattering heat wave wore on, she continued to draw enormous crowds, including an estimated five thousand for an event at the Mother AME Zion Church on West 137th Street. The party worked hard for her election. Prominent white reformers often joined her on the dais.

Eunice's platform was like any other politician's: long on promises and short on the practical means for attaining them. She promised to ease the qualifications for what were then known as old-age pensions (Social Security did not yet exist); to improve unemployment insurance (the Depression was at its height); to lower electric, gas, and telephone rates; to bring about "immediate action on slum clearance"; to make it harder for companies that sold to Harlemites on credit to garnish wages and repossess furniture; and to redraw the lines of congressional districts to make it easier to elect a Negro to represent Harlem in Washington. Familiar goals all—yet Eunice was able to make people believe she could pull them off.

Mostly Eunice spoke to mass meetings, but her campaign found clever ways to turn out single-issue crowds, too. An October advertisement in the *Amsterdam News* promoted one of her appearances with this message: "Attention, Hairdressers and Operators! Come and Hear What Is About to Happen to the Hairdressers Profession!" It is not clear to what looming threat the advertisement referred. But the cosmetologists of the darker nation suffered greatly during the Depression, as struggling Negro families spent less on beauty and hair products. No large scare would have been required to turn them out in droves.

Scant days before the election, Eunice even found time to practice her craft, heading to Magistrate's Court to represent two Harlem voters charged with registering illegally. The men were alleged to have given business rather than home addresses when signing up to vote. They did not deny the charges. Instead, Eunice persuaded the magistrate that using a business address was permitted by the relevant section of the election law. The case was dismissed. The press loved it. Taking and winning the case so late in the campaign, wrote the *Amsterdam News*, "enhanced her chances for success in next Tuesday's election."

All the signs seemed to be running her way. There was every reason to believe in her imminent victory. The GOP was delighted with its new star. First the state assembly, then the Congress—and after that, who could say?

On Election Day, the heat wave finally broke. November or not, temperatures the day before had reached seventy degrees. But as Harlemites streamed to the polls on Tuesday, November 6, the mercury topped out in the mid-fifties. The day was clear and fine, and turnout was expected to be high. Eunice remained the odds-on favorite, and her team was brimming with confidence.

When the votes were counted, however, she had lost. Some observers, pointing to the margin of about 1,600 votes, described the race as close. It wasn't. Stephens received 7,582 votes, Eunice 6,005.* Percentagewise, he won 56–44. A landslide. In the words of the *Amsterdam News*, "the voters turned deaf ears to the pleas of supporters . . . that she was highly qualified for a seat in the Legislature." The Baltimore *Afro-American* called her defeat election night's "greatest surprise." The paper told readers that even as Eunice gave a conciliatory concession speech, she "looked as if her faith in humanity had been shaken."

What went wrong?

Although she ran a spirited campaign, Eunice faced significant obstacles. For one thing, Stephens, in addition to being a known quantity, was the Tammany Hall candidate, so it is likely that significant patronage was being handed around. In addition, although the impact would not be obvious for another decade, the segment of the community Eunice was seen to represent—tradition-bound, clannish, respectably middle-class—was losing its stranglehold on the politics of the darker nation. And, of course, at this time a substantial portion of the Negro and white electorate alike remained skeptical or perhaps even hostile toward female candidates.

Perhaps most important, however, was the simple fact that the darker nation was undergoing a partisan transformation. When Hubert Delany ran in 1929, African America still trended Republican. By 1934, Harlem was voting Democratic—the party won every contest in the neighborhood that year—and the same partisan tide that defeated Eunice was sweeping the darker nation in election precincts around the country. In Chicago, for instance, the "virtually invulnerable" Oscar De Priest, a black civil rights stalwart thrice elected to Congress on the Republican line, was crushed by newcomer Arthur W. Mitchell, who had just that year switched to the Democratic Party and would go on to serve four terms. Two years later, Jane Bolin, another prominent

---

* Harlem's other legislative race, for the Twenty-first District, was won by William T. Andrews. He and his wife were close friends with Eunice and her husband, Lisle.

Negro lawyer, would run as the Republican candidate for the same seat that Eunice had contested . . . and be soundly thrashed.

A few days after her unexpected defeat, Eunice decided to head down to Washington for a rest. At Penn Station she encountered Maurice Dancer, the sharp-tongued gossip columnist for the *Pittsburgh Courier*. Probably he made a disparaging comment of the sort for which he was famous. In any case, he and Eunice apparently had a heated argument. Dancer told his side of the story in his column:

> I know she will love to cut our columnistic throat when we tell you the entrancing and brutally attractive defender was on her way to the Nation's playground for a much needed rest following a break-down when the veteran Assemblyman James A. Stevens [sic] came out on top.

According to Dancer, Eunice "upbraided" him for divulging "her fight for a seat with Mayor La Guardia and Park Commissioner Moses on the platform during the 'Tree of Hope' dedication." A week earlier, Dancer had reported that despite "[l]ovely Eunice Carter's campaign manager's effort," she had been "refused . . . a seat on the dedication platform." The Tree of Hope, the second of its name, had been planted just before the election on Seventh Avenue between 131st and 132nd Streets—that is, right next to Eunice's campaign headquarters. The old one had been cut down, to the distress of many Negro actors and singers, who claimed it brought them luck. So did thousands of the jobless, who touched the tree in the hope that their fortunes would improve. There is an extant photograph of the planting of the new one, the ceremony Dancer described. Mayor La Guardia is crouching in the foreground, trowel in hand. Directly behind him is Eunice. She does not look crowded out.

Well, Dancer had a job to do, entertaining his readers with half-truths and innuendo. Yet it may be that there was a scintilla of accuracy behind the silliness. Certainly Eunice must have been stunned by the outcome of a race she'd thought she was winning. Whether or not she had a breakdown, she may well have needed a rest. She had suffered from mysterious ailments in the past, and had started her candidacy after spending several months recuperating from a difficult surgery. The grueling campaign must have worn her out.

In any case, the vacation did not last long. By December, Eunice was back in Harlem, once again clambering up the Social Pyramid. The columns listed Eunice and her husband as attending a Christmas night party where the guest list read, as one columnist put it, "like a Who's Who of the Coal Bin"—"Coal Bin" being one of many aphorisms of the day for the families at the top of sassiety. The columnist ranked the Carters second among "the social cliques" who were present, just behind the Dick Kennards and just ahead of the Reverend and Mrs. Adam Clayton Powell.

Despite what Maurice Dancer wrote about their Penn Station encounter, Eunice held no grudge against him. Within weeks of the election, the young lawyer was defending her tormentor in court. In early January of 1935, the gossip columnist was arrested in Harlem on charges of having failed to make support payments for his daughter, who was living in Detroit with his first wife. Although the amount was only five dollars per week, the arrears stretched back to 1925, and were now in excess of two thousand dollars. In the darker nation, the case was front-page news. Dancer was the brother of the prominent bandleader Earl Dancer, the discoverer and former "husband" of Ethel Waters. (According to her biographer, they were never actually married.) Maurice was a colorful and controversial personality. His columns could be scathing. He had a dance studio on Seventh Avenue in Harlem. He had been in trouble before, arrested the previous year for allegedly playing games with money raised for what was then known as the NAACP National Defense Fund. The previous spring, with much fanfare, he had announced a benefit show for the group in Pittsburgh. All of Negro society attended a preliminary gala at Harlem's Apollo Theatre—including the Roy Wilkinses, the Walter Whites, the Bill (Bojangles) Robinsons, and Mrs. Cab Calloway. Eunice also attended, escorted not by her husband but by her brother, Alphaeus. The press crowed over the glittering event:

It is safe to say, up to the present in the annals of social events in New York the affair has never been surpassed. . . . There were the lovely young debs of the Social Set wearing evening gowns, who acted as hostesses, and others who sold flowers— all to help the cause. The uniformed ushers wore white mess coats with evening trousers, and a tiny page was all dressed up in his brass buttons, and looked as though he had never been up quite so late.

Dancer, in short, did a masterful job of arranging beautiful fundraising events. The question was what happened to the cash. The tawdry story involved allegations of infidelity leveled by his third wife and checks written by famous Negro entertainers, including Stepin Fetchit and Waters herself. The Negro papers warned sternly that the NAACP should exercise more control over those who raised its money. The charges were ultimately dropped for lack of evidence. The magistrate, in releasing Dancer, lectured the police commissioner for allowing so flimsy an arrest.* His editors at the *Pittsburgh Courier* explained, unpersuasively, that they had arranged his arrest to protect him from "foul play" at the hands of mobsters who were hoping to steal the money. Nevertheless, the *Chicago Defender*, the *Courier*'s longtime rival, reported that despite Dancer's release, something "big" was about to break.

Perhaps the *Defender* was making up a story from whole cloth. Or perhaps the paper had some inkling of the coming probe. Eunice got involved after Dancer was nabbed in New York, through the ruse of inviting him to the telegraph office to collect money supposedly wired. His estranged second wife, Myrtle Passon, retained Eunice to fight Dancer's extradition to Michigan. Myrtle was from a prominent Negro family. A registered nurse who had previously worked in the home of Woodrow Wilson's friend and adviser Edward Mandell House, she had also cared for the wife of Socialist leader Norman Thomas. And

---

* Dancer was represented by the prominent Harlem attorney Vernon C. Riddick, who would later have a distinguished career on the bench. It is not clear why he switched lawyers when fighting arraignment, although given Dancer's looseness with money, it is plausible that he failed to pay Riddick.

she had nursed Eunice through one of her convalescences, although it remains unclear exactly when. This may have been how the two first met. Certainly they were close friends. In December of 1935, Eunice would be among the guests at Myrtle's birthday party "at her palatial home" at 1855 Seventh Avenue.

Eunice managed to get Dancer's extradition hearing postponed three times. She pressed the intriguing legal argument that the Michigan courts lacked jurisdiction because Dancer's first wife, the complainant, was no longer a resident of that state. Alas, the law was (and still is) to the contrary. At the end of January, the magistrate rejected Eunice's plea and turned her client over to Detroit detectives. Back in Michigan, Dancer's counsel would borrow Eunice's argument, to no avail. Dancer was ordered to pay all the back alimony, beginning with an immediate lump sum of $300, or else go to jail. Evidently he could not put together the cash. Which is how in the end, despite Eunice's efforts, the once wildly popular columnist found himself behind bars.

Although Dancer wound up in jail, representing him put Eunice on the map as a lawyer. Her name was in the papers. Even the society pages suddenly began referring to her as "attorney" rather than just "Mrs." She even gained a full name: "Mrs. Lisle C. Carter" became, then and for decades to come, "Eunice Hunton Carter." And yet she had trouble building a law practice of her own. Despite her sudden prominence, she simply could not get enough clients to make ends meet. Some of this was, of course, anti-black prejudice, but by this time there were any number of black male lawyers in America, and not a few earned a substantial living, particularly in Harlem. Also at work, therefore, was a bias against women. The early generations of female attorneys—and black female attorneys, in particular—wound up working mainly for the government, because there was no other arena where their talents were valued. Eunice could scarcely be unaware of this unhappy tradition. She was determined not to go that route.

But she did not have enough private cases to occupy her full-time. At some point, she took a post as a part-time "volunteer assistant" in the Women's Courts, working for the magistrates, helping clear a backlog of cases. This was much like the modern position of a law clerk, except that it was unpaid. By accepting the post, Eunice became part of a vast social experiment. New York's version of the Women's Courts, established formally between 1908 and 1910, was part of a movement that swept the nation during the Progressive Era. Municipal reformers had argued for years that investigation and prosecution of women should proceed in a clean, comfortable, and hygienic setting. The Women's Courts, of which New York's provided the first example, were the result. The reformers, ironically, echoed the same concerns as Addie: that the purity of womanhood was crucial to society. At the time, few found these arguments peculiar. Certainly Eunice did not.

The Women's Courts handled mainly prostitution cases, although in some jurisdictions they dealt with failure to pay child support and even adultery and fornication. They were the place where nearly all of the handful of female prosecutors in America at the time had begun their careers. Most never emerged. (There is a myth, common to much writing about Eunice, that she herself was at this time a prosecutor in the Women's Courts. This is false.)

Eunice took up her position at a time when prostitution cases (often euphemized in the newspapers as "vice prosecutions") were rising sharply. Supporters insisted that the Women's Courts nevertheless represented a major reform, in large part on the ground that the judges showed mercy in sentencing, usually imposing only probation or a fine. Despite the dreams of the reformers, however, the courtrooms themselves were often crowded and dingy. Conditions were considered so poor that one judge threatened to resign from the bench unless he was reassigned. Other judges were accused of corruption. By the 1930s, when Eunice arrived as a legal assistant, the Women's Courts as an institution had a tawdry reputation.

That was where Eunice found herself: stuck in a tawdry professional graveyard from which few female lawyers returned. But she had little choice. Despite publicity from the Dancer case, she could not support herself in a private practice. She could not find a paying lawyer's job. Perhaps she had made a mistake eight years ago when she had decided to surrender the dream of becoming a great writer in order to pursue the more quixotic dream of becoming a great lawyer.

And yet Eunice would not wander in the wilderness for long.

CHAPTER 7

THE COMMISSION

On March 19, 1935, a riot erupted in Harlem. The proximate cause was almost mundane. A teenager was caught shoplifting a penknife at the W. H. Kress store on 125th Street. He was black and Puerto Rican. He fled the store. The staff chased him and caught him. The boy struggled as they manhandled him back inside. The police arrived and placed him under arrest. By this time, a crowd had gathered outside the store. The police decided, for the sake of prudence, to take their suspect out through the back door. To get to the back door they had to go down into the basement. A girl of about fifteen saw them hustling the boy away and misunderstood what was going on. She shouted that they were going to beat him up, maybe kill him. The crowd grew angry, swarmed inside, and began knocking over counters and smashing merchandise. They insisted that the police produce the boy, an act that was quite impossible as he was already gone. Rumors spread that the boy had been so badly beaten that he might not live. None of the rumors were true, but untruth as well as truth can move a people to action. Within hours, many hundreds of protestors had gathered outside the store. A large fraction—perhaps a majority—were white. Many were activists sent by various radical groups. The crowd chanted against brutality. They demanded to see the boy. During the speeches, a demonstrator tossed a rock through the store window. The police then moved in to force an end to the protest.

The crowd by now numbered in the thousands. The police were at first unable to contain the surging rage. Store windows were broken up and down 125th Street. The police stood back until the group's anger seemed to have burned itself out. The mob began to disperse. Then a hearse drove up. Its arrival meant nothing. The hearse pulled into the alley behind the store. There was a funeral home next door, and this was simply where the hearse usually parked. But the crowd did not know that and probably would not have believed it if told. The sight of the hearse persuaded the protesters that the boy must be dead. Fury spread through the crowd like a wild live energy. The riot could no longer be contained. Stores were looted and burned as far north as 138th Street. The police made a constant stream of arrests, but it was many hours before Harlem was able to experience anything approaching calm.

By the time the riot was brought under control, three Negroes were dead. Many more were hospitalized. Hundreds were under arrest. The mob's attacks had been aimed at white-owned stores. Most black-owned businesses were spared. The care with which the targets seemed to have been selected led to a widespread belief that the Communists must have organized the whole thing. Harlem's Negroes could not possibly have worked out the distinction for themselves.

And all of this time, the accused shoplifter was perfectly fine. In fact, he had already been released. The *Times* nevertheless was unable to resist calling him the "boy who caused the riot," even as it published a photograph of him, healthy and smiling, beside a Negro police lieutenant, also smiling, who had an arm around his shoulders.

The flame of violence had been waiting to be kindled. Harlem had been smoldering for some while. The Depression continued to weigh heavily on the darker nation. The prospects for recovery seemed bleak. Both major parties were openly courting Southern segregationists. Even in New York, discrimination was rampant. Many Harlem stores refused to hire Negroes. By the time of the riot, a boycott campaign was well under way. One could hardly stroll down 125th Street, the heart of Harlem's retail district, without encountering angry protesters carrying signs saying, "DON'T BUY WHERE YOU CAN'T WORK!" The mantra was everywhere. Preachers thundered it from the pulpits. Activists handed out flyers. Popular fury was rising, and a particular target was the department stores. So the outbreak of violence, when it came, was not entirely unexpected. The Harlem riot was bound to happen. It had only been, in the words of David Levering Lewis, "awaiting its immediate cause."

Eunice must have experienced a strange déjà vécu. As a child she had lived through the Atlanta riot, which everyone claimed (wrongly) that nobody could have foreseen. Now she had lived through the Harlem riot, which everyone claimed (wrongly) that nobody could have foreseen. What Eunice could not know was that like the Atlanta riot, the Harlem riot would change her life—as it happened, forever.

People respond variously to unrest. Some Harlem merchants pleaded with the governor for "military assistance," due to fears that if continuing protests once more turned violent, the police might be overwhelmed. (The request was denied.) Others demanded that the city pay for the damages. After all, even if identified and successfully sued, the rioters themselves could hardly put together the necessary recompense. (Lawyers call this being judgment-proof.) For the city's liberals, the riot was uncomplicated. "These people feel that justice cannot be theirs until the public becomes conscious of their plight," a reader wrote to the *Times*. "Give a people a chance to earn a livelihood and there will be found a spirit of contentment." For the Red hunters, however, the riot illustrated their point—that Negro unrest was being fomented by the Communists. And it is true that the Communist Party bore some of the blame. The demonstrations outside the Kress store on 125th Street had been organized in part by the Young Liberators, a Communist offshoot. And the Young Liberators had stirred up the crowd with their claims that the shoplifter had been brutalized. There was also, however, a different truth. The same Communists had pleaded with the rioters to stop the destruction, to refrain from anti-white rhetoric, and at all costs to avoid provoking the police into violence. But these details were lost in the welter of accusation.

Mayor Fiorello La Guardia decided to kick the question of fault down the road. On the day following the riot, he appointed a commission to study the causes, made up of six Negroes and five whites. No one had ever seen such a thing. His Commission on Conditions in Harlem was touted as the first municipal body of any kind in the nation's history where the majority of members were black. The intellectual firepower was impressive. The membership read like a who's who of both races. And it tilted left. The whites included the crusading liberal journalist Oswald Garrison Villard and the lawyers Arthur Garfield Hays and Morris Ernst, cofounders of the American Civil Liberties Union. The six Negro members were Hubert T. Delany, on whose congressional campaign Eunice had worked, now city tax commissioner; the young poet Countee Cullen, at whose fabulous Harlem wedding Alphaeus had been a grooms-man; A. Philip Randolph, a radical Socialist who was founder and head of the Brotherhood of Sleeping Car Porters; Charles E. Toney, a judge and a close friend of Eunice's; Charles H. Roberts, a prominent Harlem dentist and a good friend of Lisle Sr.'s; and Eunice herself, described in the press as a lawyer and social worker.

For Eunice, the appointment to the commission came at just the right moment. Her career was becalmed. This is not to say that she was hurting for money. Her husband's dental practice thrived. Eunice enjoyed a comfortable life. She wore tasteful, expensive clothes and took pricey vacations. She was constantly busy. She went yachting. She went to New Jersey to watch Joe Louis train. She gave public addresses on the status of Negroes in America and judged acting competitions. She bought tickets to glittering benefits. Her apartment at 103 West 141st Street was large and beautifully furnished, and in the Harlem of the 1930s both were important, because even those Czarinas who held down full-time jobs were expected to entertain frequently and lavishly. Which she did.

Her circle of friends included the cream of Harlem sassiety: the Walter Whites, the Roy Wilkinses, the Henry Lee Moons, the Aaron Douglases. She hosted such prominent out-of-towners as Edith Sampson, a Negro lawyer with a practice in Chicago, with whom she would later cross swords. She hosted Idalee Thornton McGill, who was on her way to Europe following a spectacular divorce from Nathan McGill, the wealthy lawyer who had represented Sea Captain Floyd in his suit against Addie and now managed the *Chicago Defender*.

Eunice's acquaintances spanned the generations. Through her mother, she was on familiar terms with such luminaries as W. E. B. Du Bois, Mrs. Booker T. Washington, and Mary McLeod Bethune. Eunice and Bethune had grown particularly close during those weeks when Eunice recuperated at Bethune's Florida home—so close that when Bethune founded the National Council of Negro Women in 1935, the year of the riot, Eunice was one of the first women she invited to join. Addie, too, attended that initial meeting, and in fact "made the motion . . . that brought the National Council of Negro Women into existence." Her early and enthusiastic endorsement helped the Council gather steam. But it was Eunice who would become, for over a decade, Bethune's most trusted and reliable associate.

Addie herself, who still lived in Brooklyn, was a frequent visitor to her daughter's apartment. By this point she had resigned as field secretary for the NAACP, which for years had sent her into badlands throughout the country: Alabama, Mississippi, Georgia, Ohio, Indiana, Florida, South Carolina—everywhere the Ku Klux Klan was active and the black community intimidated. Addie made these trips by herself, without escort or guard, and spoke at mass meetings that local white supremacists often threatened to but never did disrupt. But she had not left the association because she was worried about her safety; she quit, she told friends, because she felt badly treated due to her gender. Even that, however, was not the whole truth. Addie was exhausted. She continued her activism for another decade, lecturing around the world, but by the time Eunice joined the riot commission in 1934, her mother had worn herself out and entered what would prove a long period of decline. From the mid-1930s on, Addie hardly ever ventured far from her home on Bainbridge Street in Brooklyn. She would continue to entertain—Eunice would later refer to her mother in this era as "a famous hostess and an excellent cook"—but Addie would henceforth remain mostly in New York City and its environs.

Alphaeus, by now a full professor at Howard University, also paid regular visits to Eunice's apartment. He had finished his master's degree at Harvard and was working on a doctorate at New York University. Alphaeus continued to spend his life in rebellion against the traditionalism that Addie preached and Eunice strived to live by. In fact, he had only recently managed to return to his sister's good graces after the scandalous collapse of his first marriage. In December 1934, a month after Eunice's electoral defeat, her brother had made his last compromise with the norms of racial respectability as preached by his mother and lived by his sister. He had finally married Margaret Reynolds, the woman with whom he had been keeping company now for well over three years. Margaret was from what Addie would have called a "good family": her parents were well-to-do Negroes from Chicago, and her formidable mother had helped run Republican presidential campaigns in the Midwest. Margaret herself held university degrees and would later be the first black librarian hired by the Library of Congress.* Although Alphaeus made an ostentatious point of not caring about the Great Social Pyramid, Margaret was the sort who would have little trouble, if she cared to, scaling those slippery walls.

The siblings continued to travel back and forth to see each other—flying visits, they called these trips—and their shared worry about their mother kept them close. Their father had been dead for almost two decades, and now Addie was ailing. Although she still very much thought of herself as an activist, the truth was that traveling to Manhattan to spend time with her daughter was already a chore. Certainly there were no more visits to Paris and Budapest and London and Prague.

Probably Mayor La Guardia chose Eunice for the riot commission in part as a payoff for her agreement to run for the state assembly the previous year. New York's Republican-Fusion machine had a reputation for finding places to stash its defeated candidates. If they were lawyers, they often went to the district attorney's office, but the man who now held the post, elected just the previous year, was a Democrat named William Copeland Dodge, a hack who would not blow his nose without Tammany's blessing. Nevertheless, the party owed her. Eunice's appointment, however, was not just politics. La Guardia was personally grateful to Eunice, who, like Delany, had campaigned hard for him in Democratic Harlem. Once elected, he had found Delany a judgeship, then

---

* Technically, she would be one of two, as another black woman was hired on the same day.

the post as tax commissioner. Now Eunice too would have her reward: a seat on the commission that would dominate city news for the next year.

Within days of the riot, and before holding a single hearing, the commission issued a brief statement to the effect that the riots "were merely symbols and symptoms." The statement blamed "economic and social conditions which the depression has intensified." The mayor must have been astonished. Plainly his hope had been to gain time, months or even a year, while the members did their work. Now here was his handpicked group, in existence for less than a week, advertising the avenues the investigation was likely to explore. The commission, meanwhile, was busy choosing its officers. Roberts, the Negro dentist, was the chair. The vice chair was Villard, the white journalist. Eunice, the only woman, was elected secretary.

Politics then were like politics now. Even before the commission was able to hold its first hearing, the membership was already under attack. Some critics worried that the group included too many radical leftists. Others insisted that the members had no experience of life on the streets. Harlem ministers pointed out that there were no clergymen on the commission. Community groups complained that Mayor La Guardia had refused to meet with them before choosing the members. The Consolidated Tenants' League singled out the Negro members, who, with the single exception of A. Philip Randolph, were deemed to have "political and other affiliations" that were bound to affect their objectivity. The commission, said the critics, was the mayor's "smoke-screen" and would never discuss the true underlying causes of the violence. Then there were the skeptics who called the membership too "high-toned." At the time and in this context, the term would have been a slur, suggesting that the members—Eunice included—were light-skinned and therefore in some indescribable way inauthentic. In short words, they were not real Negroes.

Caught in the ideological crossfire was Eunice, because as the secretary she was on the front lines. The commission, in its wisdom, invited anyone with suggestions or information to contact her. And they did, deluging the courthouse that was the group's mailing address with letters of complaint, letters of advice, letters of anger. They wrote about problems with landlords and problems with street gangs, problems with their children's teachers and problems collecting alimony. Worried Harlemites stopped Eunice on the street to pour out their woes. Yet she met the challenge with aplomb. She was by all accounts both gracious and warm in her role as secretary. Her reputation grew. Her political skills strengthened. Indeed, had she served in this post a year earlier, she might well have won her race for the state assembly, and would now be dreaming of higher office.

Meanwhile, pressure mounted from another front. William Dodge, the Tammany-controlled district attorney, was not about to wait for the commission to finish its work. Dodge had no interest in structural problems, in poor schools, in substandard housing, in unemployment. He knew that Communists were responsible for whipping things up, and he was determined to respond aggressively. Immediately after the riot, Dodge began the search for what the papers called a "Red plot." He announced "a city-wide grand jury investigation of radical agitators," and a tame grand jury swiftly indicted a dozen "rioters and radicals." Other officials agreed: if bad blood existed between Harlemites and the police, the Reds must be responsible. The Hearst newspapers echoed the charge. James H. Hubert, head of the New York Urban League, was the most prominent black leader to agree that the Communists bore part of the blame for the riot. But other Negroes were skeptical. A columnist for Baltimore's *Afro-American* went so far as to assert that where conditions in Harlem were concerned, the Communists were "the only persons who seriously work toward a cure." The *Amsterdam News* published a sampler of local opinion. None of those quoted thought the Party bore any significant responsibility for the riot.

Dodge, however, remained certain that unnamed radicals were the problem. He was always chasing radicals. According to his critics, he was far more interested in prosecuting left-wingers than in putting racketeers behind bars. He took the same approach to the riots. His grand jury kept handing down indictments of accused Communists. At the same time, in a refrain as familiar then as today, no police officers were punished. But the Harlem teenager who had shouted the false news that the shoplifter was being beaten by cops was arrested and hauled before a judge. The judge found that her screams had provoked the riot and offered her the choice of paying a ten-dollar fine or spending three days in the workhouse.

La Guardia's commission took a different approach. Over a period of two months, April and May, the group held a series of hearings, mostly in Harlem, mostly on weekends to allow working people to attend. Each was devoted to a specific topic, such as housing or education or crime. Many took place in courtrooms. The venues were packed. The proceedings were often tense. At a hearing on criminal justice, the Harlem audience loudly jeered the police, including a Negro lieutenant who happened to be in the room. At another, an unruly Negro witness refused to leave until ejected by a white court officer. When the witness's friends intervened, the officer shouted, "I'll shoot you full of holes." A chaotic melee ensued.

Many city officials, including the police and hospital commissioners, pointedly refused to cooperate with the commission. La Guardia's endorsement of the group's work meant nothing to them. The reason may have been that the mayor's support turned out to be somewhat equivocal. The commission was poorly funded, the staff was constantly being whittled down, and the salary paid to E. Franklin Frazier, the rising black sociologist who was the group's director of research, always arrived late. The only reason Frazier's check ever arrived was that Eunice wrote to the mayor's office every two weeks with a reminder.

Most of the major Negro organizations also declined to participate in the hearings. Eunice's friend Walter White of the NAACP later admitted that this strategy was a major mistake. The Communist Party, by contrast, had a major presence, presenting detailed information about social and economic conditions in Harlem, on occasion cross-examining city officials and even organizing demonstrations in the hearing room. Among the frequent attendees was Benjamin Davis Jr., a rising star in the Party, who had been a childhood friend of Eunice and Alphaeus's in Atlanta, where his father edited the *Atlanta Independent*, a Bookerite newspaper with a huge nationwide readership.

Eunice's role as secretary was not meant to be a full-time job. Members of the commission were volunteers. She kept her law practice open and probably did some social work on the side to bring in additional income. Nevertheless, the prestige of serving on the commission reinvigorated her. The election defeat had cost her some part of her sense of self-worth. Now she had her confidence back. In June, she even spoke at a testimonial dinner for Stephens, the candidate who had so soundly defeated her, and his fellow Harlem assemblyman William T. Andrews, whose wife was her close friend. Later that evening, disagreement erupted after another speaker, Guy R. Brewer, contended that it was time for Negro rather than white leadership in the local Democratic Party. There was shouting. There were near fistfights. Eunice, who never forgot Tammany's race-baiting campaign against Hubert Delany, surely smiled.

The commission's final report would go through two major rewrites. The first draft, written by Frazier, was considered by other members too radical. Eunice wrote to fellow commission member Arthur Garfield Hays that more work was needed:

> I heartily agree with you in your opinion that Dr. Frazier's opening chapters contain misstatements as to the finding of the commission and creates [sic] a totally incorrect impression of the results of the Communist activities in the events of March 19.

She suggested a meeting of the full commission to "discuss the matter more fully" and "take definite action on the subject." (The Communist Party was presumably unaware of Eunice's note; after the report was finally delivered to La Guardia, it praised her as among "the most progressive leaders in Harlem.") After the mayor rejected a second draft as also too radical—he never saw the first—the final report would finally emerge in June of 1936. Although the drafting is credited quite properly to Frazier, Eunice is thought to have had a major hand in the rewriting.

Maybe "emerged" is not the right word. The mayor's office never released the commission's report for publication. Small wonder. Even after being toned down, the final draft was unsparingly critical of the municipal government. "The first and most fundamental problem of the Negro citizens of Harlem is the economic problem," the commission concluded. That problem, in turn, arose from "social factors which keep the Negro worker in the ranks of unskilled laborers and in a state of perpetual dependency." First among these "social factors" was racial discrimination.

The problem, the commissioners explained, was systemic. For example, the report noted, a recent $120 million building project to improve the city's schools included only $400,000 for Harlem—an almost meaningless sum, given the state of dilapidation of the neighborhood's educational and recreational facilities. But no other result could be expected, given that Harlemites were "powerless" and the city officials "indifferent."

Moreover, the increased police patrols in Harlem since the riots were, in the judgment of the commissioners, not a solution to the problem but a symbol of it: "[T]his show of force simply signifies that property will be protected at any cost, but it offers no assurance that the legitimate demands of the citizens of the community for work and decent living conditions will be heeded." In fact, the police presence made the underlying problems "more irritating" to Harlemites.

Like the commission's conclusions, its recommendations have a familiar ring to the modern ear: better protection against employment discrimination, improvements in housing and education, and so forth. There is something terrifying in the realization that the needs of the darker nation in the 1930s were little different from the needs of the darker nation now. But it is nevertheless a fact.

La Guardia remained steadfast in his refusal to release the commission's report, but the text was leaked to the press. Presumably the leak originated with one of the Negro commissioners, given that the document first showed up in the *Amsterdam News*. Liberals praised the report. And not liberals alone. Even the conservative *Herald Tribune* conceded that there might be something to the group's conclusions. But there were those who disagreed. The police, for instance. And those who thought the job of every government committee was to track down Reds. Nor were the Harlem merchants happy. The Uptown Chamber of Commerce argued that nothing but "flimsy evidence" supported the notion "that every innocent colored man stands in constant fear of being assaulted by an officer."

Eunice's service on the commission once again placed her squarely in the public eye. Long before the final report was delivered, she had left behind her old life as a struggling lawyer. In a remarkable act of reinvention, she would parlay her public moment on the commission into the position that would make her, for a decade, one of the most famous Negroes in America.

CHAPTER 8

THE PROSECUTOR

As a schoolboy at P.S. 19 in lower Manhattan, Salvatore Lucania had a single ambition: to grow up to be a rich American. By 1936, he had succeeded beyond his wildest dreams. Now known as Salvatore Luciano, he had become perhaps the most feared Mafia leader in in America. Charley Lucky, they called him. Some said he had earned the nickname after his seemingly miraculous escape from a hit by rival mobsters that should have killed him. Others insisted that the sobriquet reflected the fact that despite being arrested dozens of times, he had not been convicted of anything since his youth. Still others claimed that it stemmed from the preternatural sense of danger that had enabled him to kill the most powerful Mafia leaders in New York before they could get to him first. In April 1931, he had betrayed his boss, Joe Masseria, whose murder ended the Castellammarese War. The killing was carried out under a deal between Luciano and Salvatore Maranzano, Masseria's rival for primacy. In return, Luciano was given control of what later became known as the Genovese crime family. Maranzano was now the so-called boss of bosses. Seven months later, having learned that Maranzano had put out a contract on him, Lucky killed him first.

Now Charley Lucky was the most powerful crime lord in the country.

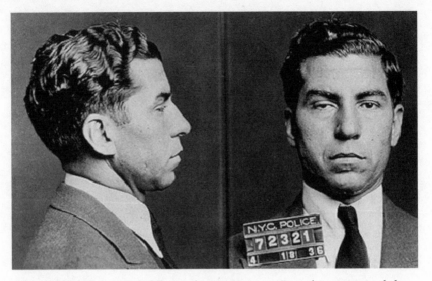

Lucky Luciano's mug shot, following his arrest in 1936. Eunice's investigation led to his conviction for compulsory prostitution, the only crime ever proved against him once he rose to prominence.
<small>ALAMY STOCK PHOTO</small>

But he learned a lesson from the animosity Maranzano had generated by his insistence on standing above the other bosses: No single person should be in charge. Instead, Luciano organized what became known as the Commission, where—in theory—every Mafia family had an equal say. Of course everyone knew that as a practical matter Luciano stood alone, first among equals. Estimates of his annual income range from $10 million to $25 million—hundreds of millions of dollars today—and even if those figures seem improbably high, no one disputes that Luciano was fabulously wealthy. It was widely known that he ran organized crime in the city; and yet he had proved untouchable.

A year earlier, the public had barely heard of him. In 1935, the focus was on Dutch Schultz, believed to control organized crime in the city— the same Dutch Schultz who had defeated the Black Kings and Black Queens for control of the Harlem rackets. The press had been predicting his downfall for years. His looming trial on federal tax-evasion charges got big play, but, as cynics pointed out, there were plenty more mobsters where the Dutchman had come from. Civic reformers and newspaper editorials had spent the past decade screaming for a serious investigation of New York's rackets. Mayor La Guardia took a tough line against the Mob, but his handpicked police commissioner preferred arresting strikers and subversives. Similarly, William Copeland Dodge, the Tammany-controlled New York district attorney, kept promising to go after organized crime. But he, too, proved more interested in pursuing suspected radicals. Dodge did empanel a grand jury to look into illegal gambling, but the eleven-month investigation, led by junior assistants from his office, resulted in only a tiny handful of indictments, all of low-level crime figures. A second grand jury, convened in March of 1934, soon complained to the judge that the prosecutor was not taking the probe seriously.

Thus began what the press called New York's "runaway" grand jury. The twenty-seven members refused to consider any more of the minor cases Dodge's office kept bringing before them. Instead, they demanded a serious investigation into the rackets. What about Dutch Schultz? What about his rivals for control of organized crime in the city? That was where the jurors thought the prosecutor should be spending his efforts: at the top. In May, the grand jurors became so frustrated with Dodge's lackadaisical approach that they kicked an assistant district attorney out of the room. They told the judge they no longer trusted Dodge or anyone from his office and asked whether some sort of independent investigator could be brought in.

The jurors took an even more extraordinary step. The foreman, real estate broker Lee Thompson Smith, met personally with Herbert Lehman, the governor of New York. They sat together in the governor's apartment on Park Avenue. Lehman was a Democrat but not a Tammany Democrat. He was a reformer and a New Dealer. He had a round face and heavy eyebrows. He had been a partner in Lehman Brothers and was personally wealthy. He was wildly popular in the state and would serve four terms before heading to Washington as part of the war effort. Foreman Smith told the governor that racketeering in the city was out of control. Nobody was prosecuting the mobsters. The office of the district attorney, said Smith, was "useless." Lehman heard him out patiently. Then he asked to see the grand jury minutes. In what was surely an unprecedented breach of protocol (and, probably, a violation of law), Smith handed them over. The governor promised to consider the matter.

Dodge might have ignored the runaway grand jury and simply empaneled a new one, but by then the newspapers had wind of the story. Pressure began to build. Rumor had it that the Dutchman had ears in Dodge's office. At last Dodge yielded—or appeared to. With great fanfare, he announced that he was appointing a lawyer named Harold H. Corbin as a deputy assistant district attorney to look into the rackets. He told the press that Corbin had the grand jury's endorsement. The runaway jurors hit the ceiling. They had agreed to nothing of the kind. Corbin was another Tammany man, and not at all what they'd had in mind. Dodge insisted that he was not going to budge, but Corbin had the good sense to back out. The papers were stunned. Tammany did not lose such battles. New York political observers speculated that the old Democratic machine was finished. Just as troubling, their city was becoming a laughingstock. All over the country, editorialists were poking fun. Finally, Governor Lehman stepped in with an ultimatum. He gave Dodge a simple choice: He must agree to select a special prosecutor from four names provided by the governor, all of them Republicans. He must further agree that the grand jury would henceforth be presided over by Supreme Court Justice Philip J. McCook, a prominent Republican jurist.* If Dodge refused to do either of these things, the state attorney general would open an investigation.

Dodge surrendered. He agreed to choose from the governor's list. But all four men promptly declined to serve. Evidently they wanted nothing to do with Dodge, who would still be the nominal superior of whoever was appointed. Their refusal left the path open for a new candidate: Thomas E. Dewey, a former federal prosecutor who, at age thirty-three, had recently left government service for the private practice of law. Ironically, Dewey had been the first choice of the reformists at the New York bar. The bar president had even submitted his name to the governor for the post. But Dewey's was not among the four names on Lehman's list. The reason for his omission has always been a puzzle. Newspapers at the time suggested that the governor thought Dewey lacked sufficient experience for the post. More recent speculation holds

---

* In New York, the "Supreme Court" is the trial court, what in most jurisdictions is called the Superior Court or the District Court.

Thomas E. Dewey, the special prosecutor, with New York mayor Fiorello La Guardia. Both men advanced Eunice's career. Dewey in particular was her mentor for more than a decade.
HERITAGE IMAGE PARTNERSHIP LTD/ALAMY STOCK PHOTO

that Lehman had no interest in awarding the post to a politically ambitious young lawyer who might become a political rival.

Backed into a corner, Dodge offered Dewey the job.

And Dewey, after specifying certain conditions, said yes.

At this time, New York had no statutory provision for an independent prosecutor. Technically, therefore, Dewey would be merely another deputy assistant district attorney, subject in the chain of command to Dodge. Dewey would have none of that. Before accepting, he negotiated several concessions. He would operate independently of Dodge. He would have a separate budget that he alone would control. Perhaps most important, he would have the right to hire his own staff, from lawyers right down to accountants, secretaries, and messengers. And his offices would be nowhere near Dodge's fiefdom of corruption.

Dewey got everything he asked for. True, his salary of a bit less than $17,000 a year would be barely 10 percent of what he could have earned in private practice. But Dewey did not consider this much of a sacrifice. He was ambitious, and the task nobody else wanted—prosecuting the

Mob—was exactly the way to come to public notice. On top of which he genuinely believed that he could pull it off.

Expectations were low. The Mob was too powerful, the city government too corrupt. And yet everybody seemed to want in. Dewey decided early to take no one who had worked for Dodge. He wanted lawyers who were young and unspoiled. At 120 Broadway, where Dewey conducted his private law practice, the line of applicants stretched down the corridor. According to Dewey biographer Richard Norton Smith, "Three thousand lawyers—one sixth of the profession in New York—wanted to work for him." The positions paid very little compared to what most lawyers could earn elsewhere, but the prestige of landing a post was enormous. One's career would be made. A few of his wealthier hires turned out to be willing to earn only a dollar a year for the honor of being able to say that they worked for Dewey. And of course the Depression was still on. Many New York lawyers had no jobs at all.

The interviews were described as brutal, even terrifying. Dewey conducted each one himself. He wanted people he could trust. He was careful. The process was slow and deliberate. Applicants under serious consideration endured rigorous screening. The press reported that potential hires were being "tracked back to the cradle" in order to ensure their integrity. In the end, Dewey hired twenty lawyers. Nineteen were white males. The twentieth was Eunice Hunton Carter.

Eunice's appointment was announced on August 5, 1935. In actual sequence, she was the tenth lawyer Dewey hired. Hers was also the selection that made the biggest splash in the papers.

A remarkable mythos has come to surround Eunice's hiring. Most writers about the Luciano case tell us that Dewey plucked her from the Women's Courts, where she was prosecuting cases for the egregious William Dodge. In this oft-repeated tale, Eunice realized that prostitution cases were being fixed and took the evidence to Dodge, who refused to do anything about it. So she presented her theory to Dewey, who hired her on the spot.

But none of this is true. Eunice never worked for Dodge. She had never been a prosecutor until Dewey hired her, and if she had been, he would not have chosen her. She did not earn the job by bringing evidence of corruption to his attention. During her brief period of private practice, Eunice might well have tried a handful of cases in the Women's Courts, but her principal experience there stemmed from her time as a legal assistant to the magistrates. When Dewey was appointed special prosecutor, Eunice was just one among the thousands of job seekers. If her application received special attention, the likely reason was a combination of the high profile she had achieved because of her work on the riot commission and the political pressure to hire someone from Harlem. Mayor La Guardia might also have pointed Dewey in her direction. Eunice had campaigned for him, and he was determined to push her career. And then there was the party machine's tradition of finding places for candidates willing to run in tough races against incumbents, as Eunice had the previous year. Just weeks after her selection, an article from the Associated Negro Press was explicit: "Republicans feel that in appointing Eunice Hunton Carter to the law staff of Special Prosecutor Thomas E. Dewey, they have discharged their obligation to that lady for her defeat at the hands of William Andrews [sic; James Stephens was her opponent] for the Assembly two years ago."

Moreover, when Eunice was hired by Dewey, the news accounts had her in private law practice and working as secretary of the Commission on Conditions in Harlem. None mentioned any work as a prosecutor. Had Eunice at some point prior to August of 1935 been hired as a deputy assistant district attorney, the news would surely have made the Negro papers, which kept Janus-like eyes on even the minor doings of prominent Harlemites. And not the Negro papers alone. As we learn from what happened after her appointment was announced, the hiring of a black woman prosecutor would be big news everywhere.

The *New York Times* put the story of Eunice's hiring on page 3, informing readers that Dewey had added a "Negro lawyer" to his staff—an indication, said the paper, that he intended to target "Harlem's policy racket," at that time run by Dutch Schultz. (The "policy racket" was a reference to illegal numbers games.) The *Herald Tribune* conjectured that Dewey would "rely to a great extent on her knowledge of persons and conditions in Harlem." Both newspapers ran photographs of Eunice on page 3. None of Dewey's other hires were pictured anywhere. Out-of-town papers carried similar stories.

And the Negro press, of course, was even more obliging. Eunice's appointment was lauded everywhere. "Orchids to Mrs. Carter," gushed a columnist for Norfolk's *New Journal and Guide*. "The race is justly proud of her!" "She'll Fight Policy Racket," headlined the Baltimore *Afro-American*. Eunice was one of the tiny handful "culled from 3,000 applicants," bragged the *Philadelphia Tribune*. Only her local paper, the *Amsterdam News*, pointed out dourly that Eunice seemed likely to be the only person of color not just among Dewey's lawyers but on his entire staff.

The journalist Hickman Powell, in his 1939 book about the Luciano case, had a simple explanation for Eunice's hiring. "Mrs. Carter was a girl who knew her way around town," he wrote, adding that she "knew how to make things happen." According to Dewey's biographer Richard Norton Smith, Eunice was chosen for "her command of Harlem poolhalls as well as Albany committee rooms." The newspapers apparently felt the same way—after a fashion. They ran stories to the effect that by putting her on his staff, Dewey was signaling an intent to attack the rackets in Harlem, too. The papers said nothing about any other relevant experience she might have had. Eunice was a Negro; they knew why she must be there. The truth was rather different. The new deputy assistant district attorney was far more comfortable playing bridge in the parlor than sitting in a pool hall; quite possibly, Addie's daughter had never been inside a pool hall in her life.

In an interview four years later, Dewey himself told the story differently. In his version, his selection of Eunice reflected less his determination to investigate Harlem than his unprejudiced eye for talent:

> I hired Mrs. Carter the first day I met her. Shortly after I was appointed, a prominent judge, who knew that I was looking for a woman assistant, told me he knew a wonderful colored woman lawyer. I told him to send her over, was impressed, and retained her. She has made good, and commands the respect of the bench of the city.

In applauding Eunice for making good, Dewey here is of course actually applauding his own ability to spot talented people. Probably the skill is one he genuinely possessed. After all, his original twenty assistants included any number of future judges and superstar lawyers, as well as a man who would later serve in the cabinets of two Presidents of the United States, one as attorney general and the other as secretary of state.

As for Eunice, even prior to the appointment, her summer had been busy, a mix of work for the riot commission, her own law practice, and the continuing social whirl. In July she helped organize a testimonial dinner for Jesse Owens. She addressed the national conference of the National Business and Professional Women's Clubs, an organization her mother, Addie, had helped found. She again had as a houseguest Edith Sampson, the black Chicago lawyer who would become a close friend—and then a bitter rival. The week before her appointment to Dewey's staff was announced, Eunice took a few days to relax with a clutch of girlfriends at the Parker Lodge in Montrose, New York. It would be her last vacation for some while.

Eunice had landed the job every young lawyer wanted. Luck may have played a role, but mostly it was the result of hard work and smarts and perseverance. Though her brief legal career had been marked by setbacks, she had always continued to push onward. Illness in law school, the dearth of paying clients, the barriers of race and gender, the surgery that put her out of commission for months, the election defeat, the taunting by Maurice Dancer, the criticism on the street that she was not black enough—none of these had vanquished her. From the inauspicious beginnings of Eunice's career, a combination of talent, determination, and fortitude had combined to carry her from the lower rungs of the legal profession to a position quite near the top.

It is difficult to say exactly what Dewey expected of Eunice when she first joined his team. Certainly there were whispers in the press that she was a mere token, although nobody dared use the word. Instead the newspapers wrote about her hiring as a payoff to Harlem's Negroes— as if Dewey had hired nineteen white men on merit and one black woman because he had to.

Dewey himself always insisted that he offered Eunice a place because of her excellence, and perhaps that was the truth. From Eunice's point of view, however, the motivation behind her hiring was irrelevant. Even if the rumors were true, she was hardly the sort to allow herself to be shunted aside and then trotted out from time to time for public display. A calm determination formed part of her inheritance. The family in which she had been forged was notable for its fortitude. Her enslaved grandfather had escaped not once, not twice, but three times, then persuaded his vicious owner to set him free. Her father had stood up to a white railway conductor at the height of Jim Crow. Her mother had traveled alone through Klan country. The family was conservative and traditionalist, but these traits did not lead to passivity or acceptance. Huntons fought back. They did not tolerate either insult or offense, but believed that both could be met successfully by perseverance and persuasion. They believed that the darker nation could do fine on its own if whites would just get out of their way.

This is the tradition that Eunice tried her best to embody; and it is a tradition in which one can detect an uneasy undercurrent of resentment. The demand to be left alone implies a willingness to take a stand when one is not. A short story that Eunice published in the March 1924 issue of the journal *Opportunity* nicely illustrates the resentment that even the well-off among the darker nation continued to feel toward even whites who purported to like them. In phrases that would have done credit to Fitzgerald, she described the nighttime view from the window of a lovely Harlem apartment:

> Motor cars whizzed by carrying throngs of pleasure seekers, aliens many of them, in search of novelty and thrill, come to the black city for something new. And in the small morning hours they went back to their homes in Westchester and the Bronx, on Park Avenue and Riverside Drive, back to their haunts on Broadway and thereabouts, serene in the belief that in Harlem cabarets they had found something new, that in black and tan replicas of downtown cabarets, roofs and supper clubs, promoted by quacks of every race, they had seen life in the black city.

The implication is that these nighttime visitors to Harlem know nothing of the "black city" through which they whirl. Nor will the race kowtow to them merely because they are white. Eunice channeled her family's ideology through the lens of what was being called "the New Negro"—an educated, reflective, and sober race that stood up and demanded rather than cringing in the face of white authority. She had been raised on tales of the family's achievement, and its defiance of the nation's racial norms. Now an accomplished black woman in her mid-thirties, she had come too far to serve as window dressing.

All of which is to say that when Thomas Dewey, the special prosecutor, hired Eunice as one of his twenty young lawyers in the summer of 1935, he may not have known what he was getting into. He might well have imagined himself simply checking off a pair of boxes against potential criticism—*Yes, I have a Negro; yes, I have a woman*—but if he thought that Eunice would be content to be shunted aside, he was in for a rude awakening.

CHAPTER 9

THE PREMISE

TWENTY LAWYERS, THEN. THAT IS WHAT DEWEY HIMSELF WOULD title his bestselling memoir thirty years later: *Twenty Against the Underworld*. Although nineteen were white males, the team was in other ways quite diverse for the era. Six of the lawyers were Democrats, seven were Republicans, and the rest were political independents. One was a former journalist. Although Dewey himself had attended Columbia Law School, only a handful of his deputies had attended Ivy League law schools. And at a time when employment at the major New York law firms was still reserved for Protestants and the very occasional Catholic, 90 percent of his team was Jewish. Dewey called them "the ablest group of lawyers in the country."

The team took offices on the fourteenth floor of the Woolworth Building at 233 Broadway—coincidentally, the same building where Eunice had attended law school a dozen or so floors higher up. Dewey was concerned about security. He rebuilt the suite into what the press later called "a labyrinth of solid doors and opaque glass." The work was expensive, but the city denied him nothing. He found detectives who were "familiar with underworld characters" and posted them in the lobby in case some mobster might try to slip in. Frosted panes separated the assistants, each of whom had a private waiting room so that potential witnesses would not see each other. Venetian blinds kept outsiders from using binoculars to see who was being interviewed. To avoid unauthorized listeners, the telephone lines went directly to the company rather than through a switchboard or exchange. No outgoing calls were allowed unless authorized by one of the attorneys. The suite was guarded day and night because Dewey worried that mobsters might try to break in and steal the team's records.

Eunice was not given a particularly prestigious office. Nor was she near the center of things. Dewey and his principal deputy, William Herlands, had a suite at the end of a private guarded alcove. Other assistants were ranged along a separate intersecting hallway. Eunice's cubicle was "far down at the end of the corridor, next to the room where the cops hung out."

But small cubicle or not, she was part of what had swiftly become the most famous team of prosecutors in the country. Long before a single witness had been presented to the no-longer-runaway grand jury, the names and backgrounds of Dewey's assistants were emblazoned in newspapers and magazines from coast to coast—Eunice's in particular. The public was fascinated. Just how this magical effect came to be is not quite clear. Expectations remained low, and only got lower when the office's first prosecution was of a teenager who might possibly have been a hanger-on at the outer edges of the Mob but who counted as nobody at all when set against the targets Dewey had been brought on board to investigate.

From the start, the team focused on Dutch Schultz, at the time still the city's best-known mobster, who by that time had beaten the tax evasion charges. On top of his other businesses the Dutchman still ran most of the rackets north of 125th Street. (Actually, Schultz ran these rackets on behalf of a larger syndicate, but the press possessed at best a dim awareness of this fact.) Again and again, Dewey told the press that Schultz was his principal target. A perhaps overly enthusiastic Mayor La Guardia took up the refrain, pledging that the gangster was not welcome in New York City and would no longer be considered a resident. (Answered Schultz: "Well, I'm going there.") From early on, Dewey made clear that he would not be investigating the Dutchman for anything as trivial as tax evasion. He wanted to prove what he considered a real crime: that Schultz ran the numbers racket, for instance, or perhaps that he had paid for political protection. In the effort to bring down Schultz, Dewey gave his staff a loose rein. His people ran wiretaps. They pressured petty criminals. An informant outlined the Dutchman's connection to Jimmy Hines, the Tammany leader who controlled Dodge. Dewey liked the idea of going after Hines too. But he continued to believe they would pick up the trail north of 125th Street. In October he sent Eunice and Victor Herwitz, another member of his team, up to Harlem to nose around. As the two sat in a bar, they met a police inspector who was leaving the next day for Europe. Mistaking them for a couple, he invited them to a lavish going-away party on the ocean liner that would carry him across the Atlantic. With Dewey's permission, the two lawyers attended. They found gangsters handing out gifts, including alcohol by the case and tickets to Joe Louis's next fight. Dewey told them to keep the presents: "Let them think you've been bought."

But that bit of personal investigation represented an aberration. The hard truth is that while the rest of the office, in the effort to snare the Dutchman, looked into the policy rackets or protection schemes or bribery of public officials, Eunice, in her tiny cubicle at the far end of the hall, spent most of her time stuck looking into prostitution. Why "stuck"? Because at this time nobody took the practice seriously as an organized crime problem. Brothels were a moral problem. Dewey (or the Chief, as his staff had taken to calling him) made clear to his team that he had not taken the job to join a crusade against vice. He was there to go after gangsters who caused mayhem. Besides, the brothels were not organized. Unlike, say, the illegal numbers, there was no syndicate in control. Everybody knew that. The brothels sprang up like weeds, and when the vice squad yanked one up, two more would sprout around the corner. No matter what story Dewey might have told about why he hired Eunice, the truth was that in assigning his lone female assistant to the prostitution angle, he was as much as telling her that she would do no important work.

So why was there a prostitution angle at all? Why did the office have even one lawyer working on an issue that the special prosecutor was determined to stay away from? The problem had been caused by Dewey himself. Shortly after taking the reins, he had gone on the radio and asked the public for help. Speaking simultaneously on stations WABC, WOR, and WMCA, he warned the city that the Mob was everywhere:

> There is today scarcely a business in New York which does not somehow pay its tribute to the underworld—a tribute levied by force and collected by fear. There is certainly not a family in the city which does not pay its share of tribute to the underworld every day it lives and with every meal it eats. This huge unofficial sales tax is collected from the ultimate consumer in the price he pays for everything he buys.

Chilling words, perhaps. But Dewey offered the solution: his investigation. He was not after organized labor, he assured his listeners. He was not after publicity: "The object of this investigation is to rid this city of racketeers." He promised to keep secret the names of his targets and not to respond to rumors. The work would take some while, he said, and would proceed in secrecy.

Dewey made a special plea to union members who had seen their locals taken over by the Mob:

> If you will come to my offices in the Woolworth Building you will be seen by a responsible member of my staff. He will welcome your help. He will respect your confidence. He will protect you. You will not read your testimony in the newspapers, nor will the heads of your union learn you have been to the office.

He offered the same opportunity to the public at large: "Your cooperation is essential. Your confidence will be respected. Your help will be kept secret and your persons protected."

The assurance of anonymity seemed to break a logjam. New Yorkers in droves accepted Dewey's invitation. Some called. Many wrote letters. And they showed up at the Woolworth Building, dozens upon dozens, one angry citizen following another. Now and then one of these irate citizens might even possess a tiny snippet of information about

Eunice in her office during her time as a prosecutor.

drugs or numbers or the protection rackets. It quickly became clear, however, that most of the drop-ins wanted the special prosecutor to do something about brothels and streetwalkers, about madams and paid-off cops. Dewey did not want to touch prostitution with a ten-foot pole. But the offices were being deluged. Furious New Yorkers kept on coming. Somebody had to hold their hands and listen to their stories and answer their letters, to let them know their complaints were being taken seriously. That somebody was Eunice. And with the rest of the team focused on how to go after the city's best-known gangsters, Eunice was pushed into this work almost entirely by herself. The letters and calls were routed to her. Even people who showed up off the street without appointments wound up at her desk.

The point is not that Eunice did no other work. As early as September we find her as one of the few assistants presenting witnesses to the grand jury. She was heavily involved in the prosecution of eighteen-year-old Salvatore Marrone, accused along with a friend of kidnapping and assaulting a teenaged girl in Central Park. But in the main she stuck to her assigned area of inquiry, and her assignment was at the distant margins of the case the Chief hoped to prepare. She might be called upon to help out on other aspects of the investigation when help was needed. Otherwise, her job was to sit in her office, make sympathetic noises for angry citizens, and pretend that Dewey planned to do something about the brothels.

One has to understand the situation of female prosecutors in America at this time. There were not many, of course—perhaps a couple of dozen in the entire country, of whom only one or two were Negroes. And nearly all of them, from one coast to the other, whatever the color of their skin, were consigned to the Women's Courts or their equivalent, the places where prostitution and abandonment and abuse cases were heard. These were not the grand courtrooms of *Law and Order: Special Victims Unit*, peopled by wise judges and expensive lawyers, warm social workers and attentive judicial personnel. The Women's Courts were dark, fetid, grim chambers, loud and disorderly and presided over by bored time-serving magistrates, many of whom—as an investigative commission led by retired appellate judge Samuel Seabury had recently established—were thoroughly corrupt. Except when touched by scandal, the Women's Courts were never in the news. They heard no high-profile cases. And deputy assistant district attorneys who found themselves assigned there were rarely promoted out. Across the country, Women's Courts were a graveyard from which the careers of female prosecutors never recovered.

Let us be clear: contrary to myth, Eunice was not a Women's Courts prosecutor. But Dewey and Herlands, by assigning her to look into prostitution, were carrying on the same gendered tradition. While the nineteen white men in the office investigated corruption of the sort that made the front page of the papers, Eunice was sent into the wilderness, consigned to what prosecutors of the era considered women's work. On the other hand, had she not been exiled to the seamy world of what the papers still called vice, Luciano might never have been convicted. For it is a matter of record that from the moment of her assignment to this dreary and thankless corner of the investigation, Eunice went over to the attack.

*   *   *

Eunice's attack rested on a simple premise: Dewey was wrong. In particular, he was wrong in his certainty that no central syndicate controlled the business of prostitution in New York City. Part of the rationale was a straightforward exercise of logic: the Mob demanded tribute from every other large-scale illegal business, and there was no reason that the lucrative business of selling sex should be left out.

But there was more. Aside from her ambition, experience, and intellect, Eunice had at her disposal another weapon: the thankless tasks she had been assigned around the office. In the first place, she was the one who listened to the parade of angry New Yorkers who took the elevator to the fourteenth floor to share tales of how the police never did anything about the bawdy houses in their neighborhoods. One of the most detailed statements came from a man named John Romano, who dropped in to complain that the dwelling next to his was a brothel. He had called the police, who had conducted a raid, but the arrested women were quickly released, and the madam was right back in business. Romano accused the police of protecting the house.

Romano was hardly unique. Hordes of New Yorkers wrote to Dewey, and those who mentioned prostitution had their letters answered by Eunice. One such letter was from a soap salesman named William Bernard. Eunice invited him to come down for a chat. He gave her the name of one Leo Markowitz, who used to sell chinaware to clubs and hotels but now, under the name Lee Markey, was "engaged in the business of supplying girls," whom he imported from Florida. On the side, Markey was in the business of blackmail. Bernard also supplied the names or positions of six individuals who he said were witnesses. Eunice wrote a detailed memorandum and sent it up the chain of command. She received no response. This pattern repeated itself. Eunice interviewed the angry and frightened, and filed one memorandum after another. Of course she could not listen to every irate New Yorker who stopped by 233 Broadway to complain about prostitution. There were too many. The other assistants and the non-lawyers alike did their best to avoid this duty, but when the sheer weight of numbers required them to take part, they immediately fired off memoranda to Eunice, essentially leaving further action up to her.

Eunice referred case after case. She gathered reports from the police Complaint Bureau, particularly about Harlem. No action was forthcoming. She began to add spice to her memos, no doubt to make sure that the recipients understood that some witnesses were in fear of the Mob. A woman named Frances Kleinman, a parolee, told Eunice that she had tried repeatedly to get the police to act on information she had supplied about a violent gang that sold narcotics and procured women. Writing up the case for the files, Eunice pointed out that Kleinman seemed as frightened of the police as of the gang, and was worried that if she were known to have informed she would be incarcerated once more. Surely this tale of actual police malfeasance would . . . but no. No response. She wrote about a Harlem landlady who alleged that the police collected twice-weekly payoffs in exchange for ignoring complaints about a building near hers. No response. It made no difference what facts she presented. Eunice interviewed and wrote and interviewed and wrote. No responses to her memoranda appear in the files.

This was not simple rudeness. Given the subsequent course of events, it was not simple bias either. Dewey did not disbelieve the stories. Rather, as we have seen, he was not prepared to undertake a crusade against the brothels. He was well aware of how badly the United States Attorney's office had been embarrassed by its inability to convict Dutch Schultz of tax-evasion charges. He thought that organized crime figures should be tried for the sorts of things that made them rich and powerful: murder and extortion, loan-sharking and drugs. To try big-time mobsters for prostitution was to invite ridicule.

Only Eunice saw the larger picture. Whatever others might have thought, she realized early that there were simply too many similarities in the stories told by those complaining citizens who kept winding up in her cubicle. Madams operating their houses with impunity, the police paid off, competitors driven away. How could every brothel in the city be protected? There was a consistency about the whole thing, the same tale told again and again. A pattern.

So that was the first weapon in Eunice's attack: she mined the stacks of citizens' complaints that others ignored, and she found gold.

Second, Eunice remembered an oddity from her time as a volunteer assistant in the Women's Courts. A lawyer named Abe Karp often showed up on behalf of girls who had been arrested for prostitution—that was what they were called, girls—and could not possibly have had enough money to pay him. Every time Karp showed up, the defendant seemed to go free. Sometimes the arresting officer had a sudden case of memory loss, and was unable on the stand to recall important facts. Other times the judge simply announced that he believed the girl's story (often, that the whole thing was a mix-up and she had only been at the madam's house to attend a party—another pattern). All of Karp's cases ended the same way. The charges were dismissed or the sentence was suspended. Eunice could scarcely believe what she was thinking. Her memory must be playing her false. But when she reviewed the records, she was right. Karp's clients always went free.

Fixed cases. Forgetful cops. Bribed judges. Crooked lawyers. Untouchable madams. Invulnerable brothels. This was not small-time corruption—not with the vice cops and the magistrates both on the take. This was someone large, and organized, and well financed.

This was a syndicate.

Which meant the Mob.

Eunice knew she had the makings of a case. The question was whether anyone would believe her.

CHAPTER 10

THE RAIDERS

IN LATE OCTOBER, DEWEY LOST HIS NUMBER ONE TARGET. DUTCH Schultz and three associates were gunned down during a meal at an Italian restaurant late on the night of October 23. The Dutchman, clinging to life, was rushed to the hospital. That same day, two of his fiercest lieutenants were brutally murdered. A little more than a day after being shot, after muttering a few nonsense words in his delirium, Dutch Schultz died. The police investigated a pair of "cryptic" telegrams delivered to the hospital as the Dutchman lay dying. The first was bizarre: "Keep the white elephant busy. We are all with you." It turned out to be from a woman in upstate New York who had met Schultz and wanted to lift his spirits. She collected white elephants and had given him one for luck. The second telegram was simpler: "Don't be yellow. As ye sow, so shall ye reap." The *Times* amusingly identified the writer as "Stephanie Sinclair." Of course this second message was in fact a final taunt from Stephanie St. Clair, who would later claim that the gang war had cost her "a total of 820 days in jail and three-quarters of a million dollars."

Although no one was ever charged with killing Schultz, nobody doubts that his murder was orchestrated by his fellow gangsters. The continuing investigation into his rackets had caused the Dutchman to become so frightened and unstable that he had become determined to kill the probe by killing Dewey. He had arranged to have Dewey followed, charted out his daily routine, learned exactly where and how he was separated briefly from the bodyguards who accompanied him everywhere. Other top mobsters saw what Schultz did not, that assassinating the special prosecutor would do nothing to turn down the heat. On the contrary, the murder would only fan the flames of public anger. There would be more pressure than ever, as even police and judges who were on their payroll had no choice but to turn against them.

The risk was too great. Schultz was out of control. Therefore his associates—particularly Luciano and Frank Costello—arranged to put him out of the way. Among the top mobsters, only Meyer Lansky thought that getting rid of the Dutchman was a mistake. Lansky noticed how Schultz drew the ire of the public and the prosecutor even as most of the actual power slipped into the hands of Luciano. "If Dutch is eliminated," he supposedly warned Charley Lucky, "you're gonna stand out like a naked guy who just lost his clothes."

But with Schultz gone, Dewey had a dilemma. Who should be his number one target now? The answer depended on who appeared to have taken over the rackets. And it quickly became clear that the answer was Luciano. In fact, so swift was Charley Lucky's rise to the top that some believed he had been there all along, perhaps even pulling the Dutchman's strings. Others had a more plausible suggestion: Luciano had gone along with the hit not because Schultz had become erratic but because he coveted the illegal businesses the Dutchman controlled.

The change in focus did not mean that Dewey's twenty prosecutors needed to change their responsibilities. They would follow the same leads, but now with Luciano rather than Schultz in the crosshairs. The assistants who had been looking at corruption in the bakery industry would keep looking at corruption in the bakery industry. The assistants who had been looking at the policy racket would keep looking at the policy racket. The assistants who had been looking at the unions would keep looking at the unions. And at the wrong end of the corridor, Eunice continued her lonely labors, studying the all-but-forgotten prostitution angle. In the little cubicle far from the center of things, she was developing the theory that would bring Charley Lucky down.

By this time Eunice had an additional weapon at her disposal—one that was forced upon her more or less unwillingly: the records of the Committee of Fourteen.

Here we have to work backward. The Committee of Fourteen was founded by a group of prominent New Yorkers early in the twentieth century, and spent the years until 1932 compiling evidence about the existence of houses of prostitution at various addresses. It was a successor to the Committee of Fifteen, which, during the final years of the nineteenth century, had tried to clean up vice in the city. The Committee of Fourteen was typical of the Simon Pure reform groups of its day, which tended to be funded by the well-heeled with an eye toward cleaning up municipal corruption—in most cases, Democratic corruption. The committee's supporters were mostly anti-Tammany progressive Republicans. The membership included local clergymen and businessmen. Among the committee's leading lights was William H. Baldwin III, whose father, the industrialist and philanthropist William H. Baldwin Jr., had been involved with both committees. Baldwin Jr. had also given enormous sums for Negro education and sat on the board of Tuskegee Institute.

The infamous lists kept by the Committee of Fourteen included hotels, bars, nightclubs, and private apartments that hosted activities the groups considered immoral. Also meticulously recorded were the names of young women believed to be prostitutes. The members were influential. To wind up on a list was to find that your suppliers suddenly would no longer deliver what you needed to run a business. Needless to say, the committee was controversial. Its methods soon led to blistering criticism. In particular, the group was hit by allegations that its investigators coerced witnesses and smeared the innocent. Of course its Simon Pure members proclaimed their innocence at every turn. But the damage was done. The committee's funding, much of it from John D. Rockefeller III and his foundation, began to dry up. In 1932, the group closed its offices. But not before cataloging and storing its vast collection of file cards, each with the reason prostitution was suspected at this saloon or that hotel.

All of which brings us to William Baldwin III. Although by now retired from his battles against the brothels, he saw in Dewey's appointment an opportunity. As Baldwin himself described what happened, in August he happened to be playing tennis with a friend, and they agreed that Dewey should take a look at the committee's records. At this point, the old boy network swung into action. Baldwin got in touch with one of his "lawyer friends" at the firm of Sullivan and Cromwell. The lawyer friend spoke to someone else at the firm, and the someone else apparently had a way to get to Dewey, because shortly thereafter Baldwin had a call from William Herlands, Dewey's top assistant. Baldwin, acting as though this whole thing were somehow Dewey's idea, told Herlands that he should be in touch with the committee's former secretary, George Worthington of Washington, D.C., who could tell him about the records.

Neither Worthington nor Herlands seemed enthusiastic, but Baldwin made a pest of himself. Finally Dewey's chief investigator, Wayne Merrick, had one of his assistants meet Worthington at the New York Public Library, where the records turned out to be stored. In mid-October, Merrick dutifully reported back that the records "are very voluminous" and consisted largely of card files with information about women suspected of prostitution or premises believed to be brothels. Merrick told Herlands, almost in so many words, that someone would have to go through all the cards. Herlands knew at once which someone to assign. He dropped the matter in Eunice's lap with a hastily scribbled note informing her that she would be "practically the only assistant working on this record."

As if she could not have guessed that for herself.

After a rather prim exchange of correspondence, arrangements were made for Eunice to visit the library and study the records. They were every bit as voluminous as described, but they yielded precious information: lists upon lists of addresses at which houses of prostitution were believed to be located. These could be combined with the citizen complaints to create a reasonably complete index of where New York's brothels might be found.

As it happened, Eunice's initial examination of the records occurred on October 24, the same day Dutch Schultz succumbed to his wounds. Shortly thereafter, she was ready to present her theory to the Chief.

Eunice did not go to Dewey's office alone. At some point she had confided her conclusions to Murray Gurfein, one of Dewey's top assistants, who would later become a distinguished federal judge. Gurfein was initially no more enthusiastic than anyone else in the office about going after low-level vice. But Eunice laid out the fruits of her researches, and persuaded him that the prostitution angle should be investigated. And so the two of them together took her suspicions to Dewey.

Who greeted her theory with skepticism.

He had two reasons. In the first place, he told her once again that he simply did not believe that prostitution in the city could possibly be under any sort of central control. There were too many brothels, too many madams and girls in the business—no syndicate could possibly be running them all. Second, he worried that if he investigated the Mob for prostitution, the public would think of him not as a gangbuster but as some sort of morality warrior. Given Dewey's political ambitions, that was the very last thing he wanted. So his initial answer was no. But Gurfein helped persuade him to let Eunice pursue the lead.

Liberty magazine, which at this time had the second-highest circulation in the country, would later run a series of behind-the-scenes articles on the Luciano prosecution, based on interviews with some of the participants. In the *Liberty* account, Gurfein tells Dewey that he, too, was skeptical at first.* But he had been persuaded by Eunice's "exhaustive studies" of city prostitution. "She has interviewed and listened to the complaints of a number of girl prostitutes. She has made reports of what she has uncovered and turned those reports in to me. I have studied them carefully," he concludes. "As a result, I'm inclined to agree with her." The evidence, he says, suggests "that the whole business of prostitution in the city is being fundamentally revised so that its control

---

* Although I will refer several times to the *Liberty* series, the references must be taken with a grain of salt. Direct quotations, in particular, are rough reconstructions by the magazine's writers, based on documents and interviews.

rests in the hands of a few men who are under the domination of one top-flight racketeer."

None of the prostitutes, Gurfein says, know the identity of the man in charge. They refer to him only as "the Boss."

Gurfein is followed by Eunice, identified by the magazine as "a brilliant young Negro woman." She lays out for Dewey the way prostitution in the city has changed over the past two years. Formerly it was a trade that women plied alone or as part of a group, usually run by a madam who paid each girl a salary. The rise of the bookers (the term with which the pimps glorified their sordid ranks) then brought a degree of organization to the trade. A booker might work with a hundred girls or more. He would spread them around, moving them from house to house because "customers like variety." The girls would pay part of their earnings to the madam and part of their earnings to the booker.

Then things changed, says Eunice:

> That was the way prostitution worked until the summer of 1933. Then the combination stepped in. Each girl now, in addition to her other expenses, must pay ten dollars each week as a bonding fee.

That was the point that emerged from her interviews: a trade that had originally been run by small illegal businessmen and businesswomen was now, as of just two years ago, being taxed by this "combination." The understanding of how prostitution worked that had led Dewey to his adamant insistence that he would not go after the practice was now obsolete. As a result of her lonely labors with the complaints nobody in the office wanted to handle, Eunice was the only New Yorker on the right side of the law who had figured out that the trade was now centrally controlled.

She continues:

> For this, the combination guarantees that if she is arrested she will not go to jail. And that guaranty is made good. Mr. Gurfein and I have checked back over court records. One lawyer who represents these bonded girls has not lost a case in three months.

Unless action is taken, says Eunice, prostitution "will become a source of continual revenue for criminals who, by terror and violence, appropriate the earnings of these women." She assures the Chief that her theory will not require going after the madams, the girls, or the bookers—the voices on the telephone who told the girls each day where their services were required. They should go after the syndicate. The "combination."

Dewey tells them to go ahead, as long as they concentrate on the people at the top.

"I trusted their judgment," Dewey would write decades later in his memoir, "but I had no enthusiasm for the investigation they proposed." Although he told Eunice and Gurfein to proceed, the rein on which they were kept was tight. Dewey was still nervous about appearing to be a vice warrior. He kept most of the office on other projects. He assigned two additional assistants to the prostitution angle, but both had other work, and their names appear rarely in the record of that fall's investigation. And even Gurfein, who enthusiastically supported Eunice, was burdened with "an investigation of major industrial rackets."

This was likely the same October conversation in which Dewey reluctantly granted Eunice permission to ask Justice McCook for permission to wiretap the offices of the Mob bondsmen.* Here, too, she and Gurfein were to work together. But Gurfein still had other responsibilities, entirely independent of the prostitution angle. So as the transcripts began to trickle in, Eunice continued to pull the laboring oar.

At first the wiretaps were inconclusive. From listening to calls at the bonding office, they learned that Abe Karp, the Mob fixer, was still doing business, even though he had lost his law license. The taps on the bookers had been going on longer. They yielded information aplenty about prostitution, but nothing to tie the business with the Mob. And Dewey was very clear. He was not going to prosecute the madams or their girls. He would not move unless evidence tied the madams and the bookers to higher-ups—preferably, to people with direct access to Luciano.

---

* The sources differ on exactly when the wiretaps began, and the original request does not seem to have been preserved.

Once more Eunice took up her lonely labors. She still heard citizen complaints. She still wrote up her interviews. She tallied addresses. She continued to build a picture of prostitution in New York. She could not show who was behind it, but the evidence suggested that somebody was. She had come to understand that most of the girls were not permanently attached to any one brothel but were "booked"—that is, assigned to different madams on different days. An operation of this size, with just a handful of bookers deciding the day-to-day whereabouts of hundreds or thousands of girls, meant a central organization. Yet once again, she found her theories largely ignored. Eunice was working so hard that she all but vanished from the society pages, even as the holidays approached. New Year's Day found her not at home entertaining or out making the rounds of friends' homes, but in her office at the Woolworth Building.

Feeling isolated.

On January 1, 1936, frustrated and ignored, Eunice sat down in her cubicle, took out a few sheets of official letterhead, and scribbled a memorandum to Dewey. "Dear Boss," the handwritten message begins. "It would seem that I can never see you." The three-page memorandum was apparently intended to catch Dewey up on her work. She added at the end that she would be in late the next day, because she would be attending the opening of the women's wing of Harlem Hospital, a task she described as "part of my official duties with that Mayor's Committee." But the main point of the memorandum was probably that plaintive first sentence: "It would seem that I can never see you."

Again the files record no answering note from Dewey. But within days things began to change. The wiretaps suddenly began to yield fruit. First, by early January the recorded conversations made clear that the circle was even tighter than thought, that the bookers knew each other, worked together, traded girls back and forth. The police had assumed that bookers worked independently. Now they learned that the bookers acted as more or less a single entity. A part of Eunice's theory had been confirmed.

Then, on January 13, one of the taps picked up one mobster telling another to have a third call Tommy Bull. Tommy Bull was Thomas

Pennochio—part of Luciano's inner circle. As if everyone involved had grown careless at once, more names began to be heard on the telephones. More names of people close to Luciano, all mentioned in connection with prostitution. True, the name Luciano was never mentioned. But the team was getting closer. Based on the wiretap evidence, Dewey assigned more members of the team to work the prostitution angle. The extra manpower, however, did not free Eunice of her responsibility to listen to irate citizens who dropped by.

By this time, Luciano himself had left New York. At first he had gone about his business as if unconcerned. The equanimity was feigned. Charley Lucky had more than once discussed with associates the possibility of getting out of the prostitution business. The amount his syndicate earned was too small to justify the risk. His aides kept talking him into waiting a bit little longer. They assured him that no one who knew anything would ever turn against him. True, Luciano's name was frequently in the papers. But never with respect to prostitution, and hardly ever in connection with Dewey's investigation.

In late December, shortly before Eunice sent her "Dear Boss" memorandum, everything had changed. William Randolph Hearst's *New York Evening Journal* published details of what Dewey's team had learned: the bookers received ten dollars a week from each of the girls, and paid the Mob bondsmen, whose job was to protect the brothels and keep the girls out of jail; if the girls got in trouble, they went to the bonding office to be told (often by Abe Karp) what to say to the police. By this time Eunice, with help from Murray Gurfein, had developed a comprehensive model of how the syndicate ran prostitution. She must have been stunned to read all of these details in the paper. There had to be a leak somewhere.

And because there was a leak, Luciano knew how far they had come. For that was the other thing the article said—that the prosecutors expected soon to arrest "the head of the mob." Actually, Dewey's people were still not sure who the head was. But Charley Lucky, by leaving town, told them what they needed to know.

So now the team knew whom they were chasing. The question was whether they could build a case from the bottom up. Their launching point had to be Eunice's theory. She had pointed out from the start that many of the girls, when arrested, had the same lawyer. They shared bail bondsmen, even girls who possessed no apparent means to pay. Dewey had always considered this evidence thin. But now, as a result of the wiretaps authorized by Judge McCook, Dewey's people came to understand that the bookers constituted a major operation all by themselves. They knew each other. They coordinated their efforts. They passed girls back and forth. And they shared a single overlord: the Combination. That was the name one particularly angry girl had been overheard hurling at a lawyer who was late bailing her out: "Some combination," she had sneered.

Thanks to Eunice, the team could establish that the Combination ran prostitution in the city. Now the challenge was to give the Combination a face.

They would have to peel back the layers protecting Luciano one at a time. The girls could give them the madams. The madams could give them the bookers. The bookers could give them Luciano's inner circle. And the inner circle would give them the Boss himself.

It sounded so simple. It was anything but.

Eunice and Murray Gurfein came up with the idea of raiding all the brothels on her list simultaneously. No one would be able to warn anyone else. They would drag in all the madams and all the girls, and see who might be prepared to turn against the syndicate. Dewey went along with the plan, but cautioned them again that he was not interested in being a vice crusader. He was not about to waste precious time building cases against the street-level offenders. They could be arrested and charged, but only as a means of pressuring them to tell what they knew.

The raids were scheduled for the first weekend in February, but there was talk of postponing them. Over the previous weekend, a burglar had gotten loose in the Woolworth Building and ransacked several suites, including the offices of a law firm. A night watchman who surprised him on the seventh floor was shot and wounded. A rumor that the burglar had been through Dewey's files turned out not to be true. But he seemed to know what he was looking for. He had apparently stolen some three dozen keys from the building superintendent's office and could have been inside any room the keys happened to open. The burglar was sophisticated. Not only did he know where the keys were stored, but he wore the familiar denim of the building's engineers. The manhunt turned 233 Broadway into what the press called "a besieged castle." Police speculated that the burglar had slipped in on Saturday night "and slept like a hermit" before emerging on Sunday morning, when the building was all but empty.

The mysterious burglar was never found. Given his level of preparation and the fact that he seemed to have taken nothing of value from the offices he ransacked, it is likely that Dewey's suite was indeed the target. But with guards on duty twenty-four hours a day and the team working late into the night even on weekends, the plan could not be carried out.

The raids went ahead as scheduled on the night of Saturday, February 1. The day before, the police had very quietly arrested as many of the bookers and fixers as they could find. They knew the others would go into hiding. The madams and their girls were accustomed to being bailed out immediately by the Mob bondsman should they be arrested. That was the point of the bonding fee. But this time would be different. This time no one would be available to get them out.

Still, secrecy was essential. Apart from Eunice and Murray Gurfein, only one or two of Dewey's own "twenty against the underworld" were informed in advance about the raids. Nevertheless, the rest must have known something big was about to happen. They were all called in on Saturday and told to stay late at the office.

The air was frigid that night. The United States was enduring one of the coldest winters on record. Rivers were frozen as far south as Virginia. In New York, a biting wind swept across the city. But the raids could not be postponed. The planning had advanced too far. Events were in motion. The bookers were behind bars. Waiting another day might mean losing the element of surprise. Indeed, the day before the raids, one of Luciano's lieutenants apparently felt the heat. He suggested that perhaps they should step out of the prostitution game until things died down. In other words, time was very short. On the other hand, the Combination might have been deceived into believing, as the newspapers did, that Dewey's major focus was elsewhere.

Eunice and Murray Gurfein had actual charge of the raids. Eunice briefed Deputy Chief Inspector David J. McAuliffe, who sent the actual instructions to the teams on the ground. The instruction sheets were detailed—the detectives were to arrest the prostitutes and madams but let the johns go after taking their particulars—and included warnings not to discuss the arrests with anyone and not to allow the suspects "to make or receive any telephone calls to anyone under any pretext whatsoever." Dewey had the idea of excluding the vice squads from the raids, since they were assumed to be corrupt. In addition, the officers who participated were assigned unfamiliar partners. The sealed envelopes that contained information on the targets also included instructions not to question any of the women, and to keep McAuliffe posted on their progress. McAuliffe, in turn, would keep Eunice up to date.

A decade later, Eunice would tell an interviewer that between a quarter to eight on the morning of January 31 until seven at night on February 2, "she never had a single moment of rest or sleep." Small wonder:

> The Woolworth Building's freight elevator was busy for hours, disgorging young women in evening gowns and nothing else, in loud silks and satins, reeking of smoke and cheap perfume. Eunice Carter tagged each, then offered coffee and the hospitality of the special prosecutor's office.

The hospitality involved interrogation, but Dewey was determined that his staff should be gentle: "Treat them decently, speak to them respectfully. Say 'please' and 'miss' to them." Anticipating high numbers of arrests, the team had set aside the unoccupied thirteenth floor for detention. It was not enough: "By midnight a hundred suspects jammed every cubicle, every hallway and reception area on both floors." The rooms, said one lawyer, "were crawling with them." A detained madam wrote later that looking around she felt "as though all the racket people in N.Y. were in." Nor would the ladies of the evening be bailed out—not this evening, anyway: "The customary angels of mercy were themselves lying helpless in jail cells or scared off for fear of their own capture." Not only that: Justice McCook himself had come down to the Woolworth Building in the middle of the night to set bail for the arrestees.

McCook declared the women material witnesses and set high bail. Nobody was getting out tonight.

The raids were front-page news. "Vice Raids Smash '$12,000,000' Ring," wrote the *Times*. "New York Vice Raiders Break City-Wide Gang," enthused the *Chicago Daily Tribune*. It is commonly reported that the police raided eighty brothels that night. This is untrue. Yes, eighty were targeted, but somehow raids were carried out on only forty-one. The reason that nearly half were missed is lost to history. Most likely, despite all Dewey's precautions, there was a leak somewhere. He chose not to launch an investigation. The obvious candidate was the police force, which denied any culpability, despite having allowed the brothels to operate for years. Pressed to explain why so many of the targeted premises had escaped the raids, the best the embattled police commissioner could come up with was that the brothels moved around a lot.

But although half the targeted premises had been missed, more than a hundred suspects were being detained down on the thirteenth floor. The question was how long it would take them to turn.

CHAPTER 11

THE PREPARATION

NOW HALF THE OFFICE WAS WORKING THE CASE. DEWEY PULLED assistants off other assignments to share in the task of interviewing the madams and their girls and trying to get them to talk. Gurfein drafted a memorandum explaining to the rest of the team what the girls should be interrogated about. Arresting the bondsmen and fixers had been a clever move. Without the bondsmen, the prostitutes had no one to post their bail. Without the fixers, they had no one to bribe the judges or the police. Nevertheless, the women initially stuck to their stories. They had been "schooled in perjury." They were tourists. They were models. They were housewives and artists and telephone operators. These were the tactics that had worked before: stall and stall until the bondsmen and fixers showed. Slowly the girls got it through their heads that this time they were staying inside. Eunice took several of the interviews herself.

Since October, for instance, she had been on the trail of a madam named Sally Kaplan (known as Red Sadie), who sent women to fifteen separate brothels. Surveillance showed that Kaplan's operation was protected by officers from the local precinct, who shut down any competition. Prodded by Eunice, Red Sadie was able to connect two men, Dave Miller and Jimmy Fredericks, to prostitution. Miller—real name

David Marcus—would later turn state's evidence. Fredericks was a top Luciano aide. Of course, other witnesses, too, would show the involvement of Charley Lucky's top men in the Combination, which ran the sex trade. Many of them were young women Eunice had cultivated since last summer. Most were caught up in the February 1 raids and finally started talking when they tired of sitting behind bars. Mildred Harris (also known as Mildred Balitzer) later described the process through which she slowly agreed to turn state's evidence. At first Mildred assumed she would be bailed out. Then she thought that nobody else would talk about the Combination, and if nobody talked, they would all be released. But as the days inside became weeks, the questions she was being asked became more knowledgeable, and she realized that some of the girls must be cooperating. Still Mildred remained steadfast, sticking to the code. The prosecutors threatened her with up to fifteen years in prison for compulsory prostitution. She refused to say a word. Eventually one of the prosecutors showed her a photograph of Lucky Luciano and asked if she recognized him. She was terrified. She denied knowing him: "I knew that anyone who mentioned his name was as good as dead," she said later.

But by now Dewey's team had arrested Mildred's common-law husband, Pete Balitzer, who was one of the bookers. He, too, faced charges. The prosecutors urged her to try to get him to talk. Eventually, Pete turned. So did Mildred. And her testimony would prove crucial at trial. At this time, however, the trial was still months away. She had plenty of time to back out. After Mildred testified in the grand jury, a mobster she knew came up to her on the street and whispered that her husband was talking, and that unless she "refuted" whatever he said, she would be killed. (Yes, Mildred had police protection after she turned state's evidence, but when she saw the mobster heading toward her, she asked the detective escorting her to step aside so that they would not be seen together.) By now Mildred was living in a guarded apartment rather than the jailhouse, but she was so frightened she could hardly sleep. This, of course, was Luciano's great advantage: every witness was going to be afraid of him.

* * *

From all that appeared, Charley Lucky had no reason to worry. Although the Combination, which controlled the bookers and to which they paid tribute, could not have operated without his permission, he was so well insulated from the day-to-day business of prostitution that he seemed unlikely ever to be implicated. Yet he had made a series of minute errors, chief among them talking business to some of his partners in the presence of their girlfriends, some of whom were now under arrest. In ordinary times this would not have been a problem, but Dewey also had under lock and key the bookers who could usually be counted on to bail the girls out.

Actually, the team did not know what they had. They did not know that Luciano had been indiscreet around some of the girls. In fact, even after the raids, Dewey himself was still not persuaded that Charley Lucky was the mastermind they were looking for. Some of the men who had been named on the wiretaps were major racketeers: murderers, extortion artists, stickup men, loan sharks. Any one of them, even all of them together, could have run the prostitution enterprise without the need for Luciano's involvement. Or so the argument ran. So when the first witness to turn—as it happens, David Marcus, the pimp named by Red Sadie—insisted that he had heard people say Luciano was the big boss, Dewey did not really believe him. In fact, Dewey thought at the time that the Combination was being run by a former Capone aide named Little Davie Betillo. Betillo usually gave the orders to the bookers. It was easy to believe that he was the man at the top.

Yet over the first weeks after the raids, the evidence began to pile up. Some of it (like Marcus's claim) was hearsay. Some of it was potentially more solid. And when the girls who had overheard Luciano talking business with their boyfriends began to speak up, Dewey knew that he had enough to go to the special grand jury that had been empaneled to hear evidence against the rackets boss. Eunice had been proved right. The model she had constructed of how the syndicate worked was accurate. She had hypothesized a big boss at the top, and she had been right about that too. At the same time, Eunice was helping to pin down the means through which some of Luciano's top people earned their other off-the-books income. The means included taking over soda fountains and small stores and skimming the profits.

True, there were problems with the case. First among them was that so far, the only witnesses who claimed to have overheard Luciano discussing prostitution were themselves prostitutes. And, like others in their trade, they had problems. One was a drug addict. Another was an alcoholic. Dewey and his team believed them. Whether a jury would was another question. Still, time was running out. Luciano might slip away to Sicily at any moment. So Dewey decided to go ahead and seek an indictment.

As it happened, Luciano was in New York. He had returned to the city after his brief absence in late December. For a year now, in a grand show of confidence, the Mob boss had been living in suite 3102 of the Barbizon-Plaza Hotel, at 101 West Fifty-eighth Street, under the assumed name Charles Ross. (During his time at the Barbizon, as Eunice learned in an interview, he also used the alias Charles Lane.) Assumed name or not, Luciano made little effort to mask his trail. He scoffed at the possibility that he might go to jail. But as the noose tightened, he suddenly decided not to stick his neck out any further. At the end of March, somebody tipped him that he was about to be indicted. Luciano vanished from New York. The crime lord was on the lam.

But not for long. A police detective followed him to Hot Springs. And after the comedy mentioned in the prologue, and the threatened arrest of local officers, Luciano was at last in custody, on the train headed back to the city, guarded by three detectives. Claims by Luciano's people that their boss had been kidnapped were ridiculed by the papers. When the train arrived at Grand Central Station, some thirty-five detectives were on hand to escort the crime boss to police headquarters. He was whisked to the courthouse, where bail was set at $350,000—equivalent to a bit over $6 million in 2017—and, at the time, the highest in the state's history. According to the press, at his arraignment the Mafia leader was "surly, annoyed and dazed." The reason for his annoyance was that he had been arrested on "such a messy charge." But the charges were anything but messy. Thanks to Eunice's meticulous work, the evidence was crystal clear.

* * *

Now the same press that had been so skeptical of the investigation was unstinting in its praise for Dewey. A *Times* columnist was almost lyrical: "Prosecutor Dewey, working with a mere handful of anonymous investigators, wormed out the secrets of the alleged Luciano prostitution monopoly and when all was set, hauled in the ends of the net." At 233 Broadway, the work grew frenzied. With Luciano in custody, the priority became preparation for trial. Eunice no doubt expected a major role. Unlike most of Dewey's young assistants, she was an experienced trial lawyer. She was the one who had noticed the peculiar goings-on in the Women's Courts. She was the one who had listened to the streams of ordinary citizens objecting to houses of prostitution next door. She was the one who had combed the reports of the Committee of Fourteen. The idea that the Combination had gained control of New York prostitution had been all hers. Dewey had been the skeptic. Eunice had done the spadework and the footwork both. She had persuaded Gurfein. The two of them had arranged the raids. Eunice had briefed Inspector McAuliffe in preparation for the raid and had stayed up all night tagging and sorting the arrestees as they arrived at the thirteenth floor of the Woolworth Building.

But when the time arrived to choose who would try the case, Dewey looked elsewhere. He did not limit himself to people who had worked the brothel angle. Barent Ten Eyck—like Eunice, a deputy assistant— had been investigating racketeering in the bakery industry. Unlike Eunice, he had been Dewey's law school classmate at Columbia, as well as his chief assistant at the United States Attorney's office. Dewey asked him, Ten Eyck later recalled, to drop the bakeries and "take general charge of preparing for trial the testimony of the prostitutes and madams in the organized vice case." Ten Eyck chose four deputy assistants to assist in the preparation of witnesses. Eunice was not among them. (Neither was Gurfein.)

Nevertheless, by her own description, in the run-up to the trial, Eunice worked pretty much every night "way into the early hours of the morning." Part of the evidence to be offered against Luciano and his co-defendants would consist of charts showing what had happened as various prostitution cases came to court. The idea was to present a pattern of cases being dismissed or defendants in other ways receiving unusually lenient treatment. In order to admit the charts, the prosecution would first have to show that they accurately reflected the court files and docket books of the Women's Courts. Eunice, as the one lawyer in the office with experience there, was assigned the task of preparing a memorandum that would set forth the practices of those courts, presumably in order to admit the files and books into evidence under what is known as the public records exception to the hearsay rule.

Eunice dutifully assembled the exhibits. In the files is an undated five-page memorandum explaining how the charts are constructed, including the standards by which Women's Courts cases were selected for the exhibits, how the foundation should be laid for their introduction, and the basics of what is included in a Magistrate's Court case file. Who wrote the memorandum isn't clear. A subsection divides among the assistants working the case the task of developing witness testimony. This is perhaps the most important part of trial work. The greatest courtroom performer in the world will not avoid disaster if faced with a witness who has not been prepared. Among the assignments we find this: "Mrs. Carter will develop, along the lines indicated, the testimony of Pete Harris, Jo-Jo, Al Weiner, Dave and Ruth Marcus, Chris Redmond, Bingie Curcio and Abe Karp." All were key witnesses in the case. The work of developing testimony "of the madams and girls" is assigned in the memorandum to Frank Hogan and Barent Ten Eyck.

But when the actual responsibility for prepping the key witnesses was parceled out, Eunice, the originator of the theory, was assigned only one. The others on the list of eight went to other deputy assistants—five to Charles Breitel, two to Sol Gelb. The one left for Eunice, Anthony "Binge" Curcio, had played a crucial but minor role in the Combination, sitting in an office between eight and twelve o'clock every night and answering a telephone. Curcio would not necessarily know who was on the other end. After each shift, he would meet Jimmy Fredericks in a restaurant and give him the messages. The messages were from bookers. Curcio's testimony therefore mattered, and Eunice was entirely professional about the whole matter. She prepared an excellent memorandum summarizing his testimony. No doubt it was of enormous assistance to Dewey, who would wind up trying the case alone. But Eunice had endeavored, in the run-up to trial of the case she had created, to secure for herself a significant slice of the behind-the-scenes preparation of witnesses.

And been told no.

Which brings us to the girls. Family history holds that Eunice was the only member of Dewey's staff in whom the prostitutes felt comfortable confiding. Perhaps the legend rests on the early part of the investigation, when no one else from the team was likely to be talking to the girls at all. But once things began to move, the notion that Eunice alone interviewed the prostitutes does not quite jibe with the record. True, there are certain sad stories that Eunice alone discovered. But once Dewey decided to go with her theory, the task of interviewing the girls was spread around the office, and Eunice by no means undertook the lion's share. One later writer suggests that Dewey made an explicit decision to keep Eunice away from the interviews because the prostitutes preferred to talk to handsome men. The record does not remotely bear this out, either. Still, there is no question that as the office focused more and more on following the trail Eunice had blazed in such solitude, her function was diminished.

Nevertheless, she continued to work with the girls and, once the trial commenced, was responsible for their well-being and protection. But even during the preparatory work, her role is pretty clear. There is, for example, no other way to interpret a phrase that recurs in the memoranda summarizing the development of evidence:

> Informant told Mrs. Carter, Tommy Bull had obtained permission to conduct the business of prostitution with Lucky Luciano.

The man known as Tommy Bull or Tommy the Bull, a former bootlegger and ranking mobster, would ultimately be convicted alongside the boss. The claim, if true, would connect Luciano to the Combination.

In another memorandum, we have this:

> Informant told Mrs. Carter that Jimmy Fredericks had obtained permission to operate from Charley Luciano. Certain madams mention Luciano, also, as the boss.

Jimmy Fredericks was James Federico, another mobster close to Luci-ano. Fredericks was a scowling, foulmouthed enforcer who had once beaten a homicide rap when multiple eyewitnesses who had been coop-erating with the prosecution suddenly decided not to testify.

The memoranda in question were part of trial preparation, setting forth all the evidence against each defendant. The informants' statements Eunice had elicited were crucial in Dewey's construction of the line of responsibility from the street to the top. Without Eunice's informants, there would be plenty of evidence, but little of it would touch Luciano.

Who were the informants? They must have been some of the girls. We have only incomplete and inconsistent records on who interviewed whom. But Eunice had been talking and listening to the girls since Dewey first handed her the vice angle, way back in August of 1935. She may not have been formally responsible for all of those who turned; but she was clearly responsible for some.

Another witness the prosecution hoped to flip was Ralph Liguori, one of the principal enforcers for the syndicate. When independent broth-els refused to pay tribute, it was Liguori who was sent to hold them up. Literally. His job was to take their money, by whatever means neces-sary, whether they wanted to turn it over or not. Liguori had been arrested more than once before, and back in 1934 he had been beaten by police while in custody. But he always refused to talk at all, much less to implicate Luciano. In April of 1936, after Liguori was picked up again, Dewey's team decided to hold him. As they were unable at this time to charge the holdup man with a crime, Eunice was dispatched to persuade Justice McCook that Liguori should be detained as a material witness. She asked that bail be set at $25,000—an enormous amount for the time.

McCook turned to Liguori:

> Do you understand what the lawyer is saying? This lady is a
> lawyer with Mr. Dewey's office. Do you understand what she
> is saying about you? . . . [T]hat you are likely to get into trou-
> ble, if you are not taken care of for your own protection . . .
> that you may be intimidated or perhaps harmed by somebody
> unless you are locked up . . . ?

Liguori at first made no response. Pressed by the court, he finally gave the answer all the mobsters used to give: "Judge, I have nothing to say. I don't know anything about it."

Still perturbed, McCook turned back to Eunice. He noted the size of the bail request. "I have only fixed one bail, I think, as high as this for a material witness, haven't [I]?"

Eunice politely corrected the judge. He had twice awarded the sum, she said, once for $25,000, once for $25,200. She then gave her reasons: "This man, I think I can safely say, is acquainted with all the members of the ring against whom we now have indictments and has been closely associated." She added that although "he is now being detained as a material witness, . . . it is very possible that he may become a defendant."

Which is exactly what happened. Liguori was indicted and his bail was raised to $50,000. In their efforts to get him to talk, the prosecutors threatened prison for his girlfriend, a prostitute named Nancy Presser. Presser told Liguori that if he turned on the boss, Dewey would send them on a European vacation.* If he stayed silent, he would face a long prison term. None of the pressure made any difference. Liguori refused to testify, and would ultimately be convicted of compulsory prostitution and sentenced to seven and a half to fifteen years at hard labor.

As a matter of fact, none of the men closest to Luciano betrayed him. But their silence would make no difference, as long as Dewey could count on the girls.

---

* It is not clear whether such a promise was actually made. If made, it would have been highly improper. After the trial, Presser and a friend did go to Europe. She claimed that the prosecutor had indeed paid for the trip. But when her claim was brought to the attention of the trial judge the following year, he dismissed the notion that there had been any quid pro quo. Presser would later write a book attacking Dewey and insisting that the charges against Luciano had been trumped up.

CHAPTER 12

THE TRIAL

THANKS TO A LAW DEWEY HAD SUCCESSFULLY URGED UPON THE legislature, all the defendants could be tried together, even though not every one of them was alleged to have undertaken all the same illegal acts. They were charged with working in concert, and that was enough to get them all into one courtroom. Luciano's counsel tried repeatedly to get his client's trial severed from the rest, but Justice McCook was having none of it.

The courthouse was a circus. Reporters were everywhere. Worried police guards had stashed machine guns and other weapons around the building in case of a rescue attempt. The indictment originally named thirteen defendants, but three of the bookers, faced with long prison sentences, pleaded guilty at the start of trial and turned state's evidence. The prosecution knew that this bombshell was about to fall, but the defense was taken by surprise. Again Luciano's lawyer demanded that his client be tried separately from the others. Again Justice McCook refused. The lawyers for the defense were excoriated by the press. "[P]rotecting rights is one thing," sneered an editorial in the *New York World-Telegram*. "Deliberately maneuvering and scheming to turn loose a guilty criminal is another."

The first big battle involved the composition of the jury. Defense counsel as a group had twenty peremptory challenges. The prosecution had ten. Because of extensive pretrial publicity, the defendants had to burn several of their challenges excluding people who believed that Luciano would not have fought so hard against extradition if he were innocent. The several defense lawyers argued that with so many men being tried together, twenty challenges were not enough. But the judge stood his ground.

Dewey excluded among others potential jurors who questioned the credibility of pimps and prostitutes—two groups that dominated the prosecution's witness list. Finally a jury was seated and the trial began. Dewey made an opening statement. All of the defense lawyers declined to do so, with the exception of George Morton Levy, Luciano's counsel, whose fee for the case was rumored to be $100,000—nearly $1.8 million today.

The trial opened on May 13, 1936, and would run until June 8. Dewey had never wanted to try a vice case, but given that Eunice, alone among his assistants, had come up with a theory that linked Lucky Luciano to an actual crime for which there was actual evidence, a vice trial was what he was stuck with. The charge, therefore, was compulsory prostitution, a legal term of art that means only making money from someone else's exchange of sex for money. Dewey promised the jury that he would present more than one hundred witnesses. In the event, he offered sixty-eight. (Some backed out at the last minute.) The case against most of the defendants would be easy to make, but the press was not crowding the hallways to learn the fate of a handful of bookers and bondsmen. The reporters wanted to find out whether the popular young prosecutor could convict Charley Lucky Luciano.

As for Eunice, she was not entirely sidelined; but during the investigation she had held center stage, and now she was closer to the wings. Of course she had always known that Dewey would try the case himself. They all had. Still, she might have hoped for what is known as entering an appearance—that is, showing up in the transcript as a counsel of record, meaning that she most likely would have been sitting at one of the long tables up in the front of the courtroom. Instead, on those occasions when she was present, she evidently sat with the spectators. The other assistants, except those few involved in the trial, would have been sitting there, too; but New York's most important prosecution in decades was being tried according to her theory, and although Eunice was known for her poker face, she would not have been human had she not chafed at her exclusion.

The prosecution went first. Dewey easily established that the Combination existed, and he was able to show how protection money was extorted from madams and prostitutes alike. Proving the guilt of the bookers presented no challenge. Similarly, there was plenty of evidence against the bondsmen and accountants. On the witness stand, the girls told stories of kidnapping, violence, and rape. Many of them had been forced into the business as teenagers. Some of them were teenagers now. The press was suitably fascinated. No doubt the jury was, too. The challenge for the prosecution was tying any of this to Luciano.

Over the trial's first few days, prosecution witnesses outlined exactly how the prostitution business worked under the Combination— the bookers assigning girls to different madams during different weeks, the bondsmen keeping the girls out of jail—all largely as Eunice had laid it out for the Chief six months ago. The witnesses told jurors that until two or three years ago, the madams had been independents who kept the lion's share of the money their girls earned. Now madams and girls alike had to kick a chunk of the cash to the Combination. In effect, the brothels found themselves in the same situation as many New York businesses, paying protection money to the Mob. David Marcus, the booker Dewey had doubted when he'd first named Luciano, testified that when he'd asked Jimmy Fredericks who ran the Combination, Jimmy had named himself, two others, and someone called "Charley." Similarly, Pete Balitzer testified that when he'd expressed uneasiness about the Combination's finances, one of the defendants had said to him, "Charley Lucky's behind it." These were tenuous connections indeed, neither of them spoken by Luciano himself. The identifications were also inadmissible hearsay—witnesses testifying to what others had said about Luciano—unless the prosecution could prove that Luciano and those who purported to speak for him were part of the same illegal enterprise.

To carry this burden, Dewey settled upon the conspiracy theory— exactly the approach Eunice had advocated months before. At this time, the law of conspiracy in New York State was not fully developed. Because of that difficulty, no conspiracy had been explicitly charged in the indictment. But the conspiracy was charged implicitly, as the appellate courts would later rule. Therefore, Dewey needed to prove only that Luciano was a co-conspirator. The obvious route was to show that Luciano had ordered any one of the overt acts undertaken by other members of the conspiracy or had received funds from their illegal activities.

This approach proved tricky. Although several members of the syndicate testified for the prosecution, none of Luciano's key lieutenants turned against the man they called the Boss. So, for example, Al Weiner, one of the original defendants who had turned state's evidence, told the jury about a meeting in which Little Davie Betillo threatened holdout bookers—those who refused to pay tribute to the Combination. Betillo was believed to be Luciano's top associate, but Weiner could tie the threats only to Little Davie—not to Luciano himself. Similarly, the several madams who testified for the prosecution were able to tell lurid and at times horrifying stories about how they had been mistreated and abused. They laid out the system through which the girls were assigned and paid and, if necessary, bailed out of jail. But they could implicate directly only bondsmen and the bookers.

The key witnesses implicating Luciano himself were a trio of prostitutes, Mildred Harris, Nancy Presser, and Florence Brown (also known as Cokey Flo). All three women testified to having been present during meetings in which Luciano and his senior associates discussed the business affairs of the Combination. This testimony, if credited by the jury, was sufficient to create the needed link between the boss and the activities of the prostitution syndicate.

Mildred Harris, who had both run and worked in brothels, had previously lived with Pete Balitzer, a booker who had turned state's evidence. She testified that she had overheard Luciano offering to pay a man forty dollars a week to collect from the brothels. She also told the court that Little Davie Betillo—who, as Eunice suspected from the wiretaps, largely ran the prostitution syndicate day to day—had introduced Luciano to her as "my boss." Mildred also related a touching story about how she had gone to Charley Lucky in an effort to get

Balitzer out of the business, but Luciano had told her that Balitzer could not quit until he worked off a debt he owed Betillo.

Nancy Presser, the girlfriend who had tried to get Liguori to squeal on his boss, claimed to have been present when Luciano ordered his senior associates to put pressure on brothels that were resisting appeals to join the Combination. She testified to having heard Luciano discuss prostitution with Little Davie Betillo, and that she had heard Luciano wondering aloud whether he should take the "thing" away from Betillo and run it himself. She also told the jury that she had visited Luciano privately at two hotels where he had lived, and that he had personally arranged bookings for a girl named Betty Cook. (This last part seems fanciful. Luciano would have no reason to be involved as a booker. But in his world, anything was possible.)

Cokey Flo Brown was a particularly damaging witness, and the one who most fascinated the press. She testified to having been present in 1934 when Luciano, dining with some of his associates in a restaurant, wondered aloud whether he should get out of the prostitution business, given the small profits. On another occasion, in October of 1935, she overheard him complaining to his lieutenants that his name was being mentioned too much in public. He told them that Dewey's investigation was getting too close, and suggested that the operation "ought to fold up for a while." Both times he allowed himself to be talked into waiting longer. Perhaps most important, she testified to being a passenger in a car when Jimmy Fredericks warned that some of the bookers were "holding out"—to which Luciano replied, "Well, have them all come down and we will straighten the matter out."

The trial pivoted on the testimony of the three prostitutes, because only one other of the sixty-eight prosecution witnesses could place Luciano anywhere near the Combination.* Naturally, the attorneys for

---

* The other witness who implicated Luciano directly was Joe Bendix, a professional burglar, who testified that Luciano offered him a job at forty dollars a week to collect from the brothels. "I will tell Little Davie to put you on," Luciano supposedly said. Contrary to the claims of Luciano's defenders, it is entirely plausible that the mobster might on rare occasions let a few words slip when relaxing with his associates, whose girlfriends would have been all but invisible to him. But it at least mildly strains credulity to suppose that he would have negotiated directly with a small-time hood who would operate with many layers of insulation between himself and the boss. We have no way of knowing whether the jury found Bendix credible; and the answer makes no difference, as long as the jurors believed at least one from among Brown, Presser, and Harris.

Luciano and his co-defendants went after the women hard. Under cross-examination, the three admitted that the prosecution had threatened prison if they refused to testify about Luciano. Nevertheless, all denied having manufactured their stories.

Mildred Harris would later describe the day of her testimony. At eight in the morning, Eunice called the guarded apartment where Mildred was hidden to tell her to be ready to go to court. A patrolman escorted Mildred to the courthouse. Eunice was waiting for her. Mildred knew that she was safe, but when her name was called, she was still terrified: "I know how a condemned person feels when they walk the last mile." On the witness stand, she saw the glares of the defendants and knew they considered her "[a] rat and a squealer." She made it through her direct testimony, and through a brutal cross-examination, where many of the questions were "so crude" that she was reluctant to answer in public.

Cokey Flo Brown faced an especially tough cross-examination. At one point the defense lawyers asked that she be tested for drugs. Brown was an admitted user—hence the nickname "Cokey"—and she conceded that she had shot heroin just two months before the trial. She was obviously in a bad way, shivering in the courtroom from withdrawal. So strong were Brown's jitters that three times during her testimony the judge allowed her a sip of brandy to steady her nerves. Counsel demanded that Brown prove that she was not high while on the witness stand. Remarkably, the judge went along. Physicians were sent for. The witness was taken into another room to be examined. Apart from the two doctors, no males could be present, so Eunice, who had escorted Brown into the courtroom, went along to observe the examination. The physicians declared Brown drug-free.

"She did a thoroughgoing job and enjoyed herself," the *Times* chortled in its report on Brown's appearance. "Before she was done, Lucania [sic] had flung down his pencil in disgust and was glaring at her." Over at the *Herald Tribune*, the editors crafted a lurid headline: "Luciano Named Vice Ring Head by Drug Addict: Florence Brown Testifies, Fortified by Brandy, That He Directed Syndicate." But for all the mockery, Cokey Flo Brown, like Harris and Presser, had done what other witnesses could not: placed Luciano at meetings where the business of prostitution was discussed. As matter of law, his actions were now intertwined with those of the bookers and others whose guilt had been well established. If the jury believed even one of the three women's testimony, Dewey had his conspiracy.

The prosecution presented additional witnesses—dozens of them—but the trio of women mattered most. The others established the existence of the conspiracy; the girlfriends linked it to Luciano.

The defense case was brief but passionate. Luciano took the stand, a bold act that may have been a mistake. He denied any connection to vice, and even denied knowing all but one of his co-defendants. This was legally irrelevant: one can be convicted of a conspiracy without knowing all of one's co-conspirators. During a four-hour cross-examination described by the *New York Times* as a "battering," Dewey forced Luciano to admit to previous crimes and acknowledge that he had lied under oath—not once but many times. According to the press, the mobster was left "stuttering." But Dewey was unable to shake Luciano's denials of involvement with prostitution.

The bulk of the defense case was, naturally, devoted to attacking the credibility of Nancy Presser, Flo Brown, and Mildred Harris, the principal witnesses through whom the prosecution had tied Luciano to the Combination. The star witness for Luciano was George Heidt, a police officer who had helped guard the prostitutes during Dewey's investigation. Heidt, a twenty-one-year veteran of the New York force, testified that Mildred Harris was often inebriated while in his care. He claimed that "once or twice" he had delivered her sober to the Woolworth Building, and she had emerged in the wee hours of the morning "slightly intoxicated." Heidt also testified that he had often taken Mildred out to eat, and that she sometimes consumed twelve to fourteen drinks, mainly brandy. One night during trial preparation, said Heidt, they were accompanied out on the town by Sol Gelb, a prosecutor from Dewey's team. The three of them went to a pair of nightclubs, where Mildred had several drinks.*

---

* The testimony, if true, also implicated Eunice. She was responsible for the welfare of the prostitutes who testified and certainly was tasked with keeping an eye on Mildred Harris. Therefore,

Dewey presented himself as a paragon of integrity. Corruption was for the bad guys. No hint that his team had acted improperly could be allowed to linger in the courtroom. On cross-examination, therefore, it was crucial that Dewey blunt the force of Heidt's story. "You were instructed to take all these women out periodically, were you not?" Dewey asked. Officer Heidt conceded that this was so. He further admitted to being told to take the women out three times a day to eat and, specifically, not to leave them cooped up in the apartment. As for Gelb's role, Dewey turned Heidt's testimony back on him:

> Q. Isn't it a fact that Mr. Gelb on a number of occasions rebuked
>   you for letting Mildred drink as many drinks as she did?
> A. He did.
> Q. Bawled you out pretty hard, didn't he?
> A. He bawled me out.

But Dewey never challenged Heidt's testimony that Mildred had been delivered to the Woolworth Building sober and had emerged intoxicated. Whatever may or may not have happened on those occasions, exploring them further could only have helped the defense, whose case was built around the notion that the prostitutes who tied Luciano to the Combination were not reliable witnesses. Still, as Dewey emphasized in his closing argument, the women were frightened of the gangsters who ran the Combination. Not to testify would surely have been their easier way out.

Sol Gelb later offered his own version of the night he and Heidt had taken Mildred out to the clubs. In the car headed back to her apartment, said Gelb, she had begged for a drink. He had agreed, hoping the alcohol would calm her down, but was surprised when Heidt took them not to a bar but to two fancy nightclubs. He was more surprised when the issue arose in court. How, he wondered, did the defense even know to ask? Heidt must have told them, he concluded; the officer "was a real wise guy who knew everybody on the wrong side."

The defense put on other witnesses, including prostitutes who chal-

---

although the prosecutor who accompanied Harris and Heidt to the nightclubs was Gelb, Eunice would likely have borne partial responsibility had scandal ensued.

lenged the credibility of the prostitutes who had testified for the prosecution. Finally the defense rested. A day was devoted to closing arguments on behalf of each of the ten defendants. George Morton Levy, Luciano's lawyer, dedicated most of his lengthy peroration to attacking the credibility of the three prostitutes who had tied his client directly to the vice ring. He went meticulously through their testimony. Typical was his comment on Nancy Presser, whom he called "definitely unworthy of belief," adding that "to save her own skin, she had concocted that story." Levy did not accuse the prosecutors of suborning perjured testimony. He accused them of being credulous. So determined were they to get Luciano, Levy argued, that they believed whatever they heard.

Dewey's own closing argument the following day took five and a half hours. Justice McCook's jury charge occupied another two and a half hours. By the time the case was left in their hands, the jurors must have been exhausted. The *Herald Tribune*, meanwhile, sympathized with their plight for a different reason. The jurors had a difficult task, the paper told its readers, because both sides in the case had relied "primarily upon the sworn words of narcotics addicts, prostitutes and even lower degenerates." Sensitive to this problem, Justice McCook warned the jurors that while questions of credibility were entirely for them to decide, a woman should not be presumed to be lying just because she was a prostitute.

Dewey, too, was exhausted after that final day in court. Rather than return to 233 Broadway, he went upstairs to the dining room reserved for the judges. The chamber was empty, so he lowered his head down and went to sleep.

Everybody settled down to wait.

On June 7, the jury found Luciano and his nine co-defendants guilty on nearly all counts. He was, at the time, the most senior organized crime figure ever convicted in an American court. At a press conference after the verdicts were announced, Eunice was one of the handful of assistants Dewey made a point of publicly thanking by name. Eleven days later, still protesting his innocence, Luciano was sentenced to thirty to fifty years in prison. He and his co-defendants were taken back to the

Tombs (the Manhattan House of Detention), then transported by van to Grand Central Terminal, where a horde of reporters and photographers waited. On the train to Ossining, the convicted men were guarded by more than a dozen sheriffs and detectives. During Luciano's intake interview at Sing Sing, he listed his profession as barber. He also checked $199.40 in cash at the prison office—the largest amount the staff recalled any inmate to have been carrying upon arrival. He gave as his address the Waldorf Hotel.

Eunice was outside the courtroom immediately after the verdict when she was stopped by Luciano's brother. She steeled herself. But no threat was forthcoming. Instead, he offered his congratulations for her work on the case. Still, it's possible that he was implying something more ominous. Not long after, Tony Luciano would be named as the man who approached a key prosecution witness on the street, promising her money if she would recant her testimony.

Did Lucky Luciano have a spy inside Dewey's handpicked team? Probably. Nothing else can explain how he knew about Mildred Harris's wild night on the town; or when to flee to Hot Springs just ahead of indictment. The most likely candidate is Patrolman George Heidt, the defense witness who had testified to Mildred Harris's frequent inebriation—and a man with whom Eunice worked regularly. Following the trial, the police commissioner relieved Heidt of all duties, pending a departmental investigation.

Ten days after the verdict, a former prostitute named Thelma Jordan, who had testified for the prosecution, told Justice McCook under oath that Heidt had been taking payoffs from the Combination. Later, during a hearing to investigate charges that Dewey's witnesses had been coerced, Mildred Harris would testify that Heidt had earlier taken money from the gangster Owney Madden. An internal police department investigation found that Heidt was living in a penthouse apartment well beyond his limited means. Investigators discovered that during the previous ten years, Heidt had banked over $83,000, on a salary that never exceeded $3,200 annually. His explanation was that he won the money in illegal gambling games. After a September departmental hearing, Heidt was fired. The following year, a court would throw out the results of the hearing on the ground that the evidence was insufficient. Heidt's rein-statement would provide the press with the opportunity to rehash his Luciano testimony. But the patrolman would retire for good in 1940. A decade later, he would be linked to Mob bookmaker Frank Erickson. He would also turn up as an employee of an illegal casino run by the gangster Meyer Lansky. Heidt might have denied being the spy, but the Mob took awfully good care of him.

In films and literature, Luciano is often romanticized. The reality was different. Luciano was brutally and violently ambitious. Even as a young up-and-comer he was, in the words of one biographer, "a killer, a gun-man whose dirty deeds were undertaken in darkness." As the boss, he was ruthless.

Over the years, a number of observers, particularly those clinging to a romantic view of the Mob, have contended that Dewey's prosecu-tion was a setup. In his memoir, onetime Mafia boss Joseph Bonanno insists that Luciano would not have been connected to prostitution. Another Luciano defender is the novelist Jack Higgins, whose 1981 thriller *Luciano's Luck* paints an oddly admiring portrait of the brutal mobster. Higgins's fictionalized Luciano insists that although he was "boss of the rackets," he "had an interest in most things, but never girls." He goes on to explain that the prostitution charges were trumped up because "Tom Dewey tried every damn way he could to get me and failed." When Henry Carter of British intelligence tells the warden of the prison where the crime boss is incarcerated that prostitution is "the one thing that doesn't seem to fit," the warden doesn't disagree with him but adds that he is state-appointed, implying that he doesn't want to risk his job by suggesting that Luciano is innocent. Then there is the common theme, echoed in skeptical accounts published not long after the events, that Dewey's case "was based on the word of fright-ened, ignorant prostitutes, many of them alcoholics and drug addicts." The idea behind this line of attack is that Luciano may have been a big racketeer but, like Vito Corleone in *The Godfather*, would have consid-ered profiting from prostitution beneath his dignity.

Such arguments as these misapprehend what the trial was about. Apart from Nancy Presser's claim that Luciano personally arranged bookings for one particular girl, the picture painted by the witnesses was not that Luciano was involved in the day-to-day management of New York's prostitution racket. Nobody argued that. The case against him was that the Combination, the organization that ran the bookings day to day, existed only by his sufferance, and paid a fee for its right to do business. Luciano need not have approved of or been "involved" in prostitution in order to profit from it, any more than the federal government must approve of or be "involved" with Big Tobacco in order to tax it. Sometimes you take money because you can. And a showing of profit, however small, would be sufficient for conviction.

This was the entire point of Eunice's theory. Luciano taxed every major illegal operation in the city. Bookmakers and loan sharks, stickup artists and con men, all paid tribute to his organization. So did gambling dens. So did drug dealers. So did the extortionists who sold protection to shopkeepers. It was absurd to think—so Eunice argued—that an activity as widespread and profitable as prostitution would somehow escape the net that Luciano's people spread over all the other criminal activities in New York. They didn't need to approve of a business in order to demand a cut; they only needed to be greedy.

Yes, the key witnesses against Luciano and his co-defendants were prostitutes. But as Justice McCook told the jury, their station in life was not by itself a reason to reject their testimony. Eunice had worked closely with the women. She had believed their stories when nobody else did. She had comforted them, reassured them, encouraged them, and done her best to see that they were cared for. To Eunice, the vehement attacks by defense counsel on the credibility of women she had persuaded to get involved in the case came as a personal affront. No doubt she was pleased to see the end of George Heidt.

The following year, the defense would move for a new trial on the ground that prosecution witnesses had been coerced. The motion would be accompanied by affidavits from the very women Eunice had worked with, recanting their trial testimony. A hearing on the matter was set for April of 1937. At last acknowledging Eunice's role in the successful trial, Dewey named her one of just two lawyers—Sol Gelb was the other—who would go with him to court to rebut the defense argument.

But that would all come later. After the trial, many of the assistants took well-earned vacations. Eunice was among them. First, however, she went off to Smith for her fifteenth college reunion, which began on June 11, scant days after the trial. She had not attended her fifth or tenth. Like so many graduates, she seemed unready to return until she felt she had something to brag about. At the class dinner during the reunion, Eunice spoke about her work for Dewey. According to the alumnae magazine, her remarks were one of "the meaty parts of the meal."

Eunice had finally returned to Northampton, and in triumph, but at about the same time, her beloved Republican Party, on the eve of its presidential nominating convention, was suffering a public embarrassment . . . over race. In an early June battle over whether Southern states would be represented by integrated or lily-white delegations, the GOP sided with the lily-whites. Although the Democrats seated segregated Southern delegations all the time, it was the Republicans who each election cycle sought colored votes by reminding everyone that they were the "party of Lincoln." But this year, perhaps seeking to take advantage of the GOP's racial skirmishing, the Democrats seated Negro delegates for the first time. (As recently as 1928, Negro alternates at the Democratic convention had been forced to sit behind chicken wire.) All of this bears mention because 1936 would mark the first time since her graduation from Smith that Eunice did not go out on the hustings to campaign for the Republican ticket. Most likely, she decided to skip this year's contest because she was too busy in the prosecutor's office, not because she had any doubts about the GOP. But given the racial controversy at the Republican convention, Eunice was probably happy that she went to her reunion instead.

After returning from Northampton, Eunice had to perform her final duty for the Harlem riot commission. On June 30, she joined the other members to brief Mayor La Guardia on their findings. A few days later, she boarded ship for Barbados, by way of the Virgin Islands. She was on her way to visit family—specifically, her son, Lisle Jr.

She had not seen him in over a year.

CHAPTER 13

THE VISITOR

THERE IS A TALE TOLD TO THIS DAY AROUND THE OFFICES OF THE New York County District Attorney that Eunice, once ensconced on Dewey's staff, sent her nine-year-old son, Lisle Jr., to Barbados for his own safety. After the Mob investigations began in earnest, Dewey warned his prosecutors to beware of pressure from Luciano and his associates. Several are said to have packed wives and children off to stay with relatives. In arranging for her son to leave the country, Eunice would simply have been exercising a sensible prudence.

The account has a surface plausibility. Dewey's prosecutors were indeed subject to both offers of bribes and subtle threats. "[E]verybody is capable of being your enemy," he told his team. The offices were guarded by the police night and day. Special locks were fixed to the filing cabinets. Unneeded papers were collected daily for burning. Dewey himself moved about town with two bodyguards, but Dutch Schultz still plotted his murder. The team worried about the safety of witnesses. As for Lisle Jr., he did indeed travel to Barbados in 1935, and would remain there, living with his father's parents, for the next five years.

But here is where the story breaks down: Lisle Jr. left for Barbados in February, and Eunice was not hired by Dewey until August. When she sent her son to Barbados, she had not even joined the riot commission, and Dewey had not yet been appointed. In early 1935, Eunice was still trying to make her private law practice work, while serving as an unpaid legal assistant in the Women's Courts. Nothing about this role would have demanded that Eunice smuggle her son out of the country to protect him from the wrath of the Mob.

Nevertheless, send him to Barbados she did. He left on February 14, aboard the S.S. *Fort St. George* of the Bermuda and West Indies Steamship Company, a division of the Furness Withy cruise line. The twin-screw, fourteen-thousand-ton displacement ship was advertised as offering "every luxury and comfort of a modern hotel." The journey took a little over a week, including an intermediate stop in St. Croix. Lisle Jr. traveled in first class, accompanied by a relative. He was nine years and three months old. Except for a pair of brief summer trips back home, he would live away from his parents for the next five and a half years.

And yet for Lisle Jr. the experience of being separated from his mother and father was nothing new. Already he had been spending much of his time at the New Jersey home of his Uncle John, his father's brother, because his parents were too busy to care for him. A cousin remembered years later that Eunice just showed up one day and whisked him away, sending him off to the West Indies. More likely there was a gap. Lisle Jr. probably stayed with his aunt and uncle while Eunice was a law student, doing social work all day and going to classes at night. After graduation she whisked him back to Harlem, only to send him on to Barbados a couple of years later.

The more intriguing question is why she sent him at all. Lisle Jr. often said later that he went to the islands for his health—he had terrible childhood pneumonia—and Eunice regularly confirmed this version to reporters. Sometimes, however, her son told a different story: that he was sent to Barbados because he had been misbehaving. He skipped school frequently, preferring to wander the neighborhood alone. He would spend hours sitting near the elevated railroad tracks where they passed through Harlem. He would count the cars on the trains. He was in other small ways disobedient, even rebellious against authority. In this version of the tale, Eunice and Lisle Sr. sent their son away to Barbados to put some steel into his soul.

And yet just months before Lisle Jr.'s departure, there was no public hint that he was leaving. A puff piece during Eunice's campaign for state assembly the previous autumn included this nugget: "Mrs. Carter is also a mother, and takes time out to listen to her eight-year-old son, Lisle C. Carter, Jr., whom she has never neglected despite her active years of social and civic interest." No mention of the time he had spent living at the home of his cousin in New Jersey; or of her own plans to send him to Barbados.

There is also another, grimmer version of the story, also passed down in the family. In this version, Eunice sent her son to Barbados because she simply did not know what to do with him. She had borne a son for her husband's sake, and perhaps for Addie's. She had done what tradition required. But now she was busy pursuing her ambitions. She had little time for a child and (family members would whisper) little interest in him. So when her son's health provided an excuse to send him away, Eunice jumped at it. Late in life, Lisle Jr. was occasionally heard to say that he felt as if his mother just wanted to get rid of him.

To be sure, this last version, emotionally charged as it may be, does not explain why Eunice could not simply have hired a nanny to raise her son, or perhaps taken him back to her brother-in-law's house in New Jersey. According to the census, there was already a maid living full-time in the apartment. Eunice and her husband could have afforded a nanny. Had she really wanted to, Eunice would have found a way to keep Lisle Jr. at home.

However the decision to send him to Barbados was actually made, it's striking that Lisle Jr. always blamed his mother. He always remembered his father with great affection. On weekends, Lisle Sr. took his son on walks around the neighborhood, telling him stories from the classics or from the history of the darker nation. Along the way, Lisle Sr. would introduce his son to friends, shopkeepers, and business associates. Usually father and son would end their peregrinations with a big breakfast at a favorite local restaurant. Later there might be a quiz on the names of people he had met. Sometimes the boy would be criticized for not speaking up or failing to show proper respect to his elders. Yet Lisle Jr. never minded; by his own telling, he loved these excursions.

And although he experienced the time in Barbados as an exile, he always considered the whole thing his mother's doing.

Whatever the truth of the matter, by the time Eunice went to work for Dewey in the summer of 1935, Lisle Jr. was no longer an issue. He was in the Caribbean, living with her in-laws, and Eunice was free to pursue her career without impediment.

Lisle Jr. would later say that his mother never visited him in Barbados. Here his memory played him false. She vacationed with her in-laws after the trial. In July of 1936, a Virgin Islands newspaper reported that Eunice Carter had passed through on an ocean liner, on her way to "a short visit to Barbados to her family." Only Lisle Jr. could have been meant. A month later almost to the day, the same newspaper published a lengthy profile of Eunice, perhaps signaling that she had stopped in St. Thomas again on her way home. How the articles were planted is a mystery we will likely never solve. The more striking element is that Eunice's accomplishments were considered sufficiently impressive that the paper published both stories on the front page. The initial article described her, in glowing if somewhat creepy terms, as "highly representative of the better type of American Negro," a woman "devoid of affectation." Added the unnamed reporter: "Her poise reflects culture and her simplicity intelligence."

Eunice was away for three weeks (of which two were likely occupied by travel). Upon her return to Harlem, another presumably planted item sprang up on the society page of the *Amsterdam News*:

> Aty. [sic] Eunice Hunton Carter, 103 West 141st Street, returned to the city on Monday, July 27, from Barbados, B.W.I., where she visited her son, Lisle Carter, Jr., who is living temporarily with his paternal grandmother, Mrs. Louise Carter. The youngster, according to his mother, is as happy as a child can be. Mrs. Carter is a member of Dewey's racket investigating commission.

Was Lisle Jr. indeed "as happy as a child can be" during those years in Barbados? In late age, he would tell family members that although he had been happy living with his grandparents, he was never again happy around the mother who had sent him away.

Yet Eunice was only living as she had been taught. She, too, had been raised by strangers. Lisle Jr. might have chafed at what he later called his "exile" to Barbados, but in her own life her father's return from a long trip abroad or her visits to Saranac Lake during school holidays were treated as occasions for family celebration. Even had Eunice realized that her son was unhappy, she would have had trouble comprehending why. They were not the sort of family that discussed problems. Both Eunice and her husband had been raised to a certain mannered reserve. Although it is of course a cliché, her son would say later that the household was one in which he was expected to be seen and not heard. It is unlikely, therefore, that Lisle Jr. ever spoke up.

So when Eunice's vacation ended and she boarded the ship that would take her away from her son and home to New York once more, the chances are that she genuinely believed the boy was doing just fine down in Barbados. Separation from his mother was no great thing. After all, Eunice herself had emerged successfully from a childhood where she saw her parents only intermittently, with no permanent damage done.

Or so she thought.

Back in New York, Eunice had a full plate. After the Luciano trial, she was suddenly a big deal. Journalists speculated on what she planned to do next. She brushed aside the questions, insisting that she was too busy. *Liberty* magazine helped build her reputation with its multipart semi-fictionalized account of the trial. (As I mentioned earlier, *Liberty* was the second most widely read periodical in the country.) So vivid was the magazine's storytelling that some historians even today treat the many verbatim quotations as facts. But even if some of her lines were made up, *Liberty* was right in painting Eunice as a central player in the story.

Approval thundered down, too, from the summit of the Great Social Pyramid. Every Harlem Czarina wanted Eunice to adorn every Harlem party. In truth, at the unusually young age of thirty-seven, she was now something of a senior Czarina herself. She had not followed the usual course. The climb up the slippery sides was supposed to take years, with plenty of pratfalls along the way. She had not struggled up the slope by attending the right teas and entertaining the right guests; and although she was involved in a handful of the traditional organizations of sassiety, she had nothing like the full plate of meetings and conferences expected of those who aspired to the wondrous existence atop the Pyramid. Eunice had chosen another path—achievement in the larger world. This was something not entirely unheard of, but also not entirely familiar. No matter. All the darker nation knew that this was the woman who had put Lucky Luciano behind bars. They might not be able to recite the details of the prosecution, but they understood that there had been a tectonic shift at the peak.

The fall of 1936 brought a presidential contest, but for the first time in over a decade Eunice was too busy to get involved. A divided Republican Party had nominated Kansas Governor Alf Landon, and Roosevelt rolled over him in what was at the time the biggest electoral landslide in history. No doubt Eunice voted for the GOP ticket, as usual. Apart from that, however, she scarcely broke stride. She was too busy planning another raid.

In January of 1937, a team of sixty patrolmen launched a surprise raid on four policy banks and several apartments, in an effort to take down the biggest numbers gang in Harlem, run by Alexander Pompez and Joe Ison. The day was unusually warm for winter, with highs over sixty degrees. In such fair weather, Harlemites were taken by surprise as legions of patrolmen and detectives pulled up at the suspected addresses. According to Dewey's public estimate, the numbers game grossed $50 million a year. The *New York Times* put the Pompez-Ison bank's share of the total at 10 percent, or $5 million. A big chunk—no one knows how much—went to the Mob, which still had its tentacles in policy banking despite the murder of Schultz and the imprisonment of Luciano. This was Dewey, and so, once more, the raids were national news.

The headquarters for the raids was the Claremont Inn, a restaurant owned by the city and conveniently closed for the season. Located on the Hudson River just north of Grant's Tomb, the Claremont had once hosted Presidents of the United States and the city's social elite. Now it was run-down, a sprawling, crenellated structure with Carpenter's Gothic touches on the street side. Inside, Dewey and Eunice waited for the results of an operation that was in some ways more spectacular than the brothel raids a year ago. Those raids had been intended only to catch the madams and the girls, none of whom could be expected to put up resistance. This time, the police would be up against seasoned mobsters, some of whom were known to go armed. Intent once more on concealing his purposes from his targets, Dewey had assembled a raid force comprising almost entirely rookies, who appeared at the Claremont thinking they were going to have a tour of Grant's Tomb.

Planning the raids had occupied most of Eunice's time. Along with her colleague Charles P. Grimes, she'd spent months preparing the case against the policy bankers and lining up the targets. Afterward, she was named in the *New York Times* as one of the architects of the raids. Again the Negro press sang her praises. "Eunice Carter's Sleuthing Lands Two Racketeers," headlined the *Pittsburgh Courier* in January of 1937. (She was now sufficiently well known in the darker nation that there was no need to identify her in the headline beyond her name.) The article began breathlessly: "Clever detective work on the part of Eunice Hunton Carter, special assistant on the staff of Rackets Prosecutor Thomas E. Dewey, resulted last week in a series of well-planned raids and the capture of two of the city's biggest numbers barons." Some eager journalists reported that part of the evidence had been gathered when she went undercover, posing as a numbers player. But Dewey denied this, and, as the press noted, since all Harlem knew that Eunice was a member of his staff, "numbers folk had suspected her every move as one of a sleuth."

The numbers game was popular north of 125th Street. Tens if not hundreds of thousands of Harlemites played regularly. (A file captured at just one of the banks listed 75,000 frequent players.) Though numbers were by then played all over the city, Harlem remained the most lucrative territory. The policy banks were also by some estimates Harlem's biggest employers, with literally thousands of men and women on their payrolls. Unsurprisingly, not everyone in the neighborhood was happy about the raids. Dewey tried to calm the popular anger by insisting that the bankers cheated, using an elaborate scheme to arrange things so that the most popular numbers never won.

Pompez lived at 409 Edgecombe Avenue, the fanciest apartment building in Harlem. Eunice knew him socially. Twelve years before the raid, almost to the day, Eunice had been a guest at a glittering banquet at Smalls Paradise, the fancy Harlem nightclub, to celebrate the decision of the National Association of Negro Baseball Clubs to award Pompez a franchise. Harlem adored his team, the New York Cubans. Eunice occasionally attended Negro League games at the Polo Grounds. As a matter of fact, so did Tom Dewey. A photograph from October of 1937 shows Eunice sitting beside Dewey in the front row, with Lisle Sr. and another member of Dewey's staff seated just behind.

Pompez was popular on the streets. Nobody wanted him to go to prison. Most of his thousands of employees doubtless considered themselves law-abiding. A Negro journalist captured Harlem's general view when he described the operations as illegal but not immoral. Pompez was known as a generous philanthropist, and his ownership of the beloved New York Cubans only burnished his image. When the initial raid yielded Joe Ison and Moe Weintraub (said to be a lawyer for the Mob) but missed Pompez, the Negro press reported that the fugitive had "made a virtually impregnable fortress of his third floor apartment on Edgecombe Avenue." Prosecutors, however, believed that he had fled to Florida and planned to leave the country. A search began up and down the coast. Pompez turned out to be in Mexico, from which he would soon be extradited. The Negro papers reported with evident glee that the policy banks operated by Pompez's organization were still up and running. Harlem was rooting for the fugitive—and against those who were chasing him.

As for Eunice, she was suddenly a betrayer. After the raids, Dewey chose her as part of the small group of assistants who would develop the evidence for trial. People grew angrier still. Harlem had celebrated her appointment to Dewey's staff. Harlem had cheered her for helping convict Luciano. But now that the prosecutor's office had turned its attention to Negro policy bankers, Eunice was hit with accusations of being a turncoat or worse. The whispers heard along the streets were the same ones passed around back when she was on the riot commission: she did not understand Harlem. Her critics seemed to think she should give crime north of 125th Street a pass. But the *Amsterdam News*, always quick to support Eunice, editorialized in her defense: "When are Negroes going to grow up?" The paper added: "If a Negro is selected for a responsible position he is expected to perform the duties that go with the job." Those duties did not include "covering up" crimes within the darker nation.

Addie's daughter bore all the criticism along the streets with her usual stoicism. She was busy once more with Lucky Luciano, whose case refused to die.

The bookers who had testified against Luciano all received reduced sentences. But they still went to prison. For their own protection, they were segregated from the general population. Nevertheless, they felt under threat. One of them warned prosecutors that the men who had turned state's evidence were being referred to as "Dewey rats"—not only by fellow inmates but by guards. Promises of cash were in the air. Pete Balitzer had already decided to recant his trial testimony, and he urged the others to do the same. More important, all three of the women who had explicitly tied Luciano to the Combination—Nancy Presser, Mildred Harris, and Cokey Flo Brown—had now changed their stories. When Luciano's motion for a new trial was argued before Justice McCook in April of 1937, the defense lawyers were armed with a lengthy affidavit from each, recanting her trial testimony.

Dewey chose Eunice as one of the two lawyers from the office who would appear with him to contest the charges. At the hearing, the legal skirmishing was fierce. Luciano's lawyers pointed to the affidavits as evidence that the prosecutors had pressured the witnesses to implicate Charley Lucky. Dewey, furious, called the affidavits "perjurious from beginning to end." He waved them in the air. "Fear screams from every page," he told the judge. "Money screams from every page." But Dewey's rhetoric was less important than his evidence. He was ready with affidavits of his own, sworn before McCook himself immediately after the trial, in which the witnesses insisted that they had told the truth. The sworn statements made closer to the events, he insisted, were more reliable. "The moving papers," he told the court, "reek with perjury." Luciano's counsel tried to get McCook to recuse himself on grounds of bias. The judge refused. One of Luciano's lawyers threatened, perhaps tongue-in-cheek, to ask the governor to have the special grand jury look into the conduct of the trial.

Dewey argued that the recanting witnesses had been pressured. Clearly he was correct: someone had intimidated the three women. McCook's task was to decide whether Luciano or Dewey had done the intimidating. The easiest way to resolve the conflict would have been to hear live testimony from the witnesses themselves. But the women had vanished. Luciano's counsel finally admitted that two of them had recently been in Hartford, Connecticut, being watched over by a hired security guard. A search was mounted, but the girls could not be found. The papers loved it. Another rumor had it that the pair had last been seen at a sanitarium in the nearby town of Enfield. The papers loved that story too.

Justice McCook handed down his decision in early May. To no one's surprise, he sided, entirely, with the prosecution. No new trial. There was not even any need, he concluded, to hear what the recanting witnesses had to say. The judge had interviewed them after the trial and satisfied himself at the time that their testimony was truthful. He saw no reason to change his mind. "The hypothesis of a victimized, 'framed' Luciano is utterly destroyed," the judge wrote after reviewing the evidence presented by both sides. The allegations of the defense affidavits were "poisonously false." (The press also loved that line.) This seems correct. Nancy Presser, one of the witnesses who recanted, told another witness who stood by her story that by changing their testimony, "we would get plenty of money, and after Lucky went free, we could always get anything from him we wanted." But once the request for a new trial was denied, the Mob's payments to the women stopped cold.

With the post-trial motions dispensed with, there remained only the tricky matter of Luciano's appeal, which dragged on for another year. In the end his conviction was affirmed, first by the Appellate Division and then a year later by the Court of Appeals, New York's highest bench. Eunice's work on the case was finally done.

By that time, she had a new job.

CHAPTER 14

THE POLITICO

IN THE FALL OF 1937, DEWEY RAN FOR DISTRICT ATTORNEY OF NEW York County, the post held by his titular superior, William Dodge. Before announcing his campaign, Dewey dithered for a time, and his biographer suggests that perhaps he wanted to be wooed harder than the kingmakers were wooing him. But once he decided to throw his hat into the ring, he ran hard. Dodge glanced at the handwriting on the wall and hastily stepped aside. Dewey was the most popular lawyer in New York and one of the most famous men in the country. Already there was talk that he would be a leading contender for the Republican presidential nomination in 1940. Being elected Manhattan's district attorney would represent but a stepping-stone.

Having hitched her wagon to Dewey's star, Eunice saw no reason to unhitch now. She campaigned energetically on his behalf. The pair made frequent appearances together. From the start, Dewey understood the importance of the black vote. Eunice featured prominently in his campaign film, *Smashing Crime with Dewey*. According to the papers, he never went to Harlem without Eunice beside him—and he went to Harlem a lot. When he spoke at Harlem's Renaissance Casino, he managed a lovely grace note that showed his great respect for his protégée. As he strode toward the platform, he saw that she had fallen behind, perhaps intending to remain in the audience. At that point, according to press reports, Dewey "stopped and motioned to her to accompany her down the aisle to the rostrum." They proceeded to the stage, where they took adjoining seats.

After Dewey's easy victory, the Negro press predicted big things for Eunice. When he took office on January 1, however, he did not reward her with a major post. True, she was named a deputy assistant district attorney, a post no woman in New York had ever held. Actually she was one of two Negroes Dewey appointed to his staff. The other was Francis Rivers, who initially received the same title, albeit with a different set of duties. That the city suddenly had not one but two Negro deputy assistant district attorneys was another headline.

Dewey assigned Eunice to the Women's Courts and the Abandonment Bureau—dim graveyards where the careers of female prosecutors went to die. In addition, he promised vaguely that she would perform "special work in special sessions." Her new annual salary was $5,500, princely for the era—but twelve white men equally new to the office were receiving more. Of those assistants whose places Dewey announced his first day on the job, one would be earning the same as Eunice and only four would be earning less. Another potential hire turned down the same salary, on the ground that it was insulting. Nevertheless, after two years spent struggling to get clients, Eunice had become at a stroke "one of the highest paid black lawyers in the nation."

Eunice threw herself into the job and, by all accounts, proved excellent at trial work. She might have been trying prostitution cases, but she tried them well. She kept busy enough to acquire an assistant of her own. As the Negro press gleefully pointed out, the assistant was a white woman named Florence Kelley, whose father and mother were both well connected. Kelley was apparently the only female legal assistant in the office. And Eunice needed the help, for her multiple assignments generated plenty of work.

Dewey was serious about attacking the Harlem numbers game, but the policy bank raids Eunice had coordinated were also part of a larger strategy: he was determined to take down Tammany Democratic leader Jimmy Hines. Dewey set out to prove a point: that organized crime cannot exist without political protection. And there could be no more valuable protector than Hines. For over a decade, he had been the most powerful politician in the city. In the bureaucracy, in the police department, and in many a courtroom, his word was law. Everybody knew that Hines was corrupt, but at the height of his influence no one had dared cross him. Samuel Battle, the city's first Negro police lieutenant (and a friend of Eunice's), nearly had his career destroyed after he led a raid on Wilkins's Exclusive Club, where backroom gambling was protected by Hines.

From the start, Dewey had believed that Hines did more than run the hapless William Dodge. Informants had said that Hines was in cahoots with Dutch Schultz. The Tammany leader had taken Mob money, and a lot of it. Given that the biggest source of syndicate income was the numbers, it stood to reason that numbers runners would know about the arrangement with Hines. And so, as he had done in going after Luciano, Dewey conducted raids in order to arrest people he had no intention of prosecuting—the fear of being seen as a morality crusader was never far away—with the hope of turning the arrestees against higher-ups.

Hines was indicted in July. The public was astonished. Going after the Mob was one thing, but Hines's name was magic. He practically ran the city. The press coverage was lavish. The indictment detailed his involvement with Dutch Schultz, who had paid him $750 a week (just over $13,000 today). With the Dutchman gone, however, witnesses who in the past might have been afraid to testify against the Tammany boss were no longer as fearful. There was evidence aplenty, and once again the investigation largely belonged to Eunice. Her approach to the Luciano case had brought down New York's biggest gangster. Now her sleuthing was about to bring down the city's most powerful Democrat. Yet, once again, when it came time to try the case, Dewey chose only white men to assist. Among them was Charles P. Grimes, with whom Eunice had shared the task of guiding the investigation and developing the evidence. The two had done the same work; in fact, she had done more. But Eunice was shut out. The white man was chosen and the black woman was not. Harlem noticed—and even complained.

To no avail.

* * *

The trial began in August 1938. Once more, the coverage was nation-wide. The press drew analogies with the Luciano case. The papers were enthralled by Hines's swift and sudden fall from power, and often published verbatim transcripts of the proceedings. The mood in the courtroom was raucous and combative, but the evidence was overwhelming. To prove that Hines had taken payoffs from Schultz and other mobsters, the prosecution called numerous witnesses; what most fascinated the newspapers was the testimony of the numbers kings, even though by this time hardly anyone called them that: henceforth they were racketeers. Pompez was finally brought back from Mexico for the trial, having negotiated an agreement under which he would testify against Hines and in return receive a suspended sentence. Ison made the same deal. Bold headlines told readers that Schultz's mob had docked the accounts of the policy bankers some $125 a week for payments to Hines, and had taken out more for contributions to the Democratic Party—money that was used to help elect Dewey's predecessor, William Dodge, who had been so infamously reluctant to go after the city rackets.

The numbers kings were not the only gangsters to show up on the witness stand. Some of the most damaging testimony came from the colorful lawyer and mobster Dixie Davis. Ordinarily he would have kept silent, but Davis believed that Hines had betrayed him. After he was imprisoned in the wake of the raid, Davis had expected the Tammany leader to arrange a reduction in his crushingly high bail. He was furious when instead he remained behind bars. He had failed to realize that Hines no longer had that sort of clout around the courthouse.

Despite all the evidence against Hines, the prosecution ended in a mistrial. The decision was front-page news around the country. How could such a thing have happened? The fault was Dewey's. He made a fatal courtroom mistake, asking a witness a question that mentioned facts that the jury was not supposed to hear, linking the defendant to a crime not charged in the indictment. After the defense objected, the judge took the weekend to ponder his ruling. Finally he decided he had no choice. He threw out the case. It was the sort of thing that was supposed to happen to a tyro, not to Thomas E. Dewey. Years later, in his memoir, he would still insist that the question was proper. In court he

Eunice in 1938 after receiving an honorary degree from Smith College, her alma mater. At the same time she was being honored, Tammany Hall leader Jimmy Hines was facing trial back in New York City. Eunice's work had been crucial to the investigation but she was allowed no role in the courtroom.
COLLEGE ARCHIVES, SMITH COLLEGE (NORTHAMPTON, MASSACHUSETTS)

insisted that his staff had vetted the question. Actually, the team thought he was mistaken. And the team was right. (I say this as one who teaches the law of evidence.) Not every judge would have ended the prosecution, but despite Dewey's complaint, a mistrial was not an unreasonable outcome. Certainly the question should never have been asked.

Perhaps he'd picked the wrong lawyers to help him try the case.

And where was Eunice while Dewey tried and failed to send Jimmy Hines to prison? Out of town. As often as possible. After all, she had her self-respect. She had no intention of hanging around the office while, for the second time, a major case she had prepared was being tried without her.

In April of 1938, during the angry pretrial skirmishing, Eunice went off to Pittsburgh for the inaugural meeting of a new club of socialites, the Swelegants, after which she attended a dinner in her honor. June found her at the Smith College commencement. She returned to her alma mater to receive the honorary degree of doctor of laws. Eunice was the first black woman ever to receive such an honor from the school, and the event was widely reported in both the black and white press. The *Times* was sufficiently impressed to put her name in the headline. She drove up to Northampton in the company of her mother, her husband, and her brother. Alphaeus must have been at least a little bit uncomfortable; the commencement address was delivered by George Lyman Kittredge, a Harvard professor with whom Alphaeus had had difficulties while pursuing his master's.

In his remarks to the graduates, Professor Kittredge singled out Eunice for special praise, hailing what he called her seventeen years of devoted public service. The citation for the degree lauded Eunice's "brilliant abilities," which "have brought high credit to her college and her race." The colored press cheered the award as "an example of what Negro people can do if they have the brains and the intestinal fortitude." Editorials praised the college for bestowing "its greatest gift upon a young colored woman whose ancestors less than a century ago were held in bondage."

As the Hines trial began, Eunice was addressing the annual convention of the National Bar Association in Durham, North Carolina. After that, she took a vacation, a four-week motoring trip through Canada and the Midwest with her friend Regina Andrews. Eunice returned to New York in mid-September, just about the time the judge in the Hines case declared a mistrial.

Eunice may not have been trying big cases for Tom Dewey, but her fame had spread well beyond New York. Reporters for mainstream publications wrote glowing stories about her, even though she was, syndicated columnist Dorothy Kilgallen would later write, "never on what you would call palsie-walsie-let's-go-out-and-have-another-beer terms with the working press." In the summer of 1938, the *Boston Daily Globe* published a long, adoring profile. *Life* magazine praised her as "one of New York District Attorney Dewey's smartest, most effective assistants." If reputation and advancement were what she sought, she was living her dream.

* * *

Her brother, Alphaeus, was pursuing different dreams. He and his wife, Margaret, attended all the right events and were featured admiringly in the columns. But their marriage had a secret side as well. Publicly they continued to hew to the traditional mores of the conservative black community from which both had sprung. Privately they were attending meetings of the Communist Party. In this they were hardly unique. By the mid-1930s, many Negro intellectuals found themselves attracted to the radical alternative. The Communists stood up for equality far more forcefully than either mainstream party. But the nascent civil rights groups kept a wary distance. Pressed, the NAACP even insisted that there were no Communists in its ranks and very few in all of Harlem.

The FBI would later conclude that Margaret went along not out of ideological conviction but to please her husband. And her husband's radicalization was now well advanced. As early as 1933, he had been spotted at a clandestine meeting in Washington, D.C., that was attended by a number of Negro intellectuals and James W. Ford, at that time the best-known black Communist, who the year before had run for Vice President of the United States on the Party's ticket. During the period when Eunice was rising in the district attorney's office, Alphaeus was at New York University, completing his Ph.D. dissertation on Tennyson's ideology. His adviser was Professor Edwin Berry Burgum, an avowed Marxist, who nudged him further left. From there, the step from belief to action proved entirely natural.

Around this time, the estimable Kelly Miller, the respected former dean of Howard University, penned a lengthy appreciation of his dear friend William Hunton, who had died some two decades earlier. The occasion for his essay was Addie's biography of her husband, published in 1938. The book, entitled *William Alphaeus Hunton: A Pioneer Prophet of Young Men*, is rich with long quotations from her husband's detailed, erudite, and often amusing letters from around the world. It has become a standard source for historians interested in the early work of the YMCA among young men of the darker nation. The book was met with enthusiasm, and not only by the Negro press. A white reviewer praised the volume for its comprehensive portrait of "a man of vision, striving to usher in a feeling at least of conciliation, good will and brotherhood between the white race and its dark-skinned brothers."

For Miller, the release of the biography provided an opportunity to express his concern about the intellectual course of the darker nation since William's death. Writing in the conservative *New York Age*, Miller praised William for his inspirational Christian character and his efforts with the young. Miller, long a critic of Howard University (his former home and now Alphaeus's) for inculcating what he saw as a dangerous radicalism, was concerned about what the young were now being taught. He might well have had Alphaeus in mind when he worried that the darker nation's "educated youth . . . are rushing to and fro, hither and yon in quest of rash social theories as a panacea for racial ills"—an oblique reference to Marxism. Miller added that what the radicals among the young needed was "the coolness and balm of the Hunton spirit." But even if his friend William's surviving son read Miller's essay, it probably had little influence. Alphaeus was not one to back down. Indeed, the passage of time would find him more not less committed to the Communist cause.

In the fall of 1938, Dewey ran for governor. He had been district attorney for less than a year, but his standing with the public was higher than ever. Somehow the embarrassment of the Hines mistrial had worked to his advantage. People believed the judge had let a guilty man walk free on a technicality. Events were unfolding just as Herbert H. Lehman, the incumbent, had feared. Lehman's concern that Dewey might one day challenge him had caused the governor to leave the young lawyer's name off the list of potential special prosecutors he had presented to Dodge back in 1935. Now his worry had come to pass.

Once again, Eunice campaigned enthusiastically for her mentor. Dewey painted himself as a moderate, promising to strike the proper balance in "a generation torn by strife between extremists and fanatics." Although the candidate himself was popular, he had difficulty making headway against a governor whose record of integrity and success was hard to criticize. Running hard, Dewey slowly gained ground, and by election eve the race was considered a dead heat. It was not enough. In the end, Dewey lost, by one and a half percentage points. But Eunice's star went right on shining. Toward the end of the year, a column in the *Amsterdam News* named her as one of the three "official political counsels of Harlem." The honor was meant as a paean to Eunice's growing influence in the Republican Party.

Hines's retrial began late in January 1939, and this time he would be convicted.* Once more, Eunice would have no involvement in the case she had helped create. But no matter. Things were different now. In the darker nation, her name remained firmly associated with the arrest and trial of Hines. In 1938, Million Dollar Productions had released *Gang Smashers*, a movie about a female police detective who goes undercover to help break up a Harlem protection racket. The film had an all-black cast and was dedicated to "colored men and women . . . who unflinchingly risk their lives in the interests of good government" and who had prevailed in "the daily battle against organized crime." The Negro press quickly concluded that the film was inspired by "the 'Hines trial' and the policy racket in Harlem and Eunice Carter on Thomas E. Dewey's staff."

Although Eunice remained dedicated to her duties, she still found time to tend to her increasingly public persona. She was much in demand as a speaker, and not only before colored audiences. February of 1939 found Eunice in Baltimore to address the Co-operative Women's Civic League. Part of what she had to say was civic boilerplate. She urged the members to use their votes, no matter which side they happened to be on. She might have been describing her own career: "Take an active part in politics, begin by asking for what is wanted and what is needed and end by demanding because of your strength."

But there was more. Eunice argued that the accident of birth does not make some more worthy than others: "None of us has the privi-

---

* After Hines's second trial, the numbers kings, Ison and Pompez, were right back in business. Pompez returned not only to policy banking but, more important for history, to his beloved New York Cubans. He would later become a scout for the New York Giants and is credited with discovering, among others, major league baseball stars Juan Marichal and Orlando Cepeda. Today Pompez is (no joke!) the only numbers runner in the Baseball Hall of Fame at Cooperstown.

Portrait photograph of Eunice, taken at her home at 409 Edgecombe Avenue in 1942. Her picture often appeared in the Negro press.
PHOTOGRAPHS AND PRINTS DIVISION, SCHOMBURG CENTER FOR RESEARCH IN BLACK CULTURE, NEW YORK PUBLIC LIBRARY

leges by divine right. The spinning of the wheel of fate gave us or our parents enough foresight to see opportunities and make use of them."

Maybe she was thinking of her own life; maybe she was thinking of her brother's. In either case, Eunice must surely have been telling herself that after a few false starts, she had seen her opportunities and made the most of them. She was trying cases, she was supervising a staff of lawyers, she was traveling to make speeches, she was in and out of politics. She never slept. She lived on coffee. "I don't know where she gets the energy," her husband marveled. "It's hard keeping up with her these days."

Now on the cusp of forty, my grandmother was an esteemed prosecutor in the district attorney's office, a Czarina of high standing in Harlem sassiety, and one of the best-known black women in America. I suspect that she was happy.

PART II

PASSION

Yes, there is black and white but between there is red,
the red of rivers of blood, of red hot iron, of glowing
coals and barbarous fires, and too, oh God, the red of
flaming passion!

—EUNICE ROBERTA HUNTON,
review of *Holiday* by Waldo Frank,
Opportunity magazine (1924)

CHAPTER 15

THE CELEBRITY

EUNICE'S PERSEVERANCE PAID OFF. AT SOME POINT IN 1938 OR 1939 she was promoted to succeed Sol Gelb as head of Special Sessions, where virtually all misdemeanors were tried. She did not succeed to Gelb's munificent five-figure salary, but she nevertheless received a significant increase to $6,500 a year—around $112,000 in 2017 dollars. Managing Special Sessions was a crucial job. It handled more cases than any other bureau in the district attorney's office. And, of course, heading a bureau was considered a stepping-stone to higher things.

Once news broke of Eunice's new post, the pioneering black attorney Sadie Alexander wrote to relate how impressed she was that Eunice was trying cases and, especially, supervising other lawyers: "I cannot say too much for the ability that you have shown as well as the diplomacy which you must have exercised to have obtained such a position." No one had ever seen anything like this. White men, well trained, graduates of the top schools, all taking orders from a Negro.

A Negro *woman*.

Evidently, Eunice handled her new job well. Dewey would later point to her work as a major reason that the conviction rate in Special Sessions rose from 47 percent under Dodge to over 60 percent under the new regime. The press described Eunice in her new job as "one of New York's busiest women."

A few weeks after her appointment, Eunice described for a reporter her typical day. She would usually rise at seven-thirty, she said, and fortify herself for the day with orange juice and black coffee. Leaving her apartment at 103 W. 141st Street, she would drive her own car to her office on Leonard Street. At half past nine she would meet with her assistants ("all of whom are white"), then head off to court, where she would remain until the one o'clock lunch break. (Another admiring profile noted that she "manages on very little food, unaccountably.") At two p.m. Eunice would typically return to the court. Three hours later, she would be back at her desk, usually until seven, although about three nights a week she would work until eleven.

Asked about hobbies, she listed bridge (where she regularly won prizes), reading books, and riding horses "to keep her figure under control." And she described as her "greatest thrill" annual visits from Lisle Jr., who "spends his time" in Barbados "because the climate is better suited to his health." She added that she made regular "flying visits" to her brother, Alphaeus, in Washington. The term referred to the brevity, not the manner, of her trips to Washington. She would always drive or take the train. It was notorious among family and friends that Eunice had a fear of flying.

Eunice did not mention to the interviewer another passion: she was a great sports fan. Even in law school she had taken time out to attend the big football games between the prominent colored universities, usually with her husband at her side. She went to baseball games. And like so many in the darker nation of the day, she loved boxing. She was seen ringside at big fights. She visited Joe Louis's training camp. Later, when the champ was inducted into the armed forces, she would attend Harlem's testimonial dinner in his honor. (Like Eunice, Louis was a well-known Republican, and would endorse Wendell Willkie's presidential run in 1940.) To be sure, in those days the well-to-do of the darker nation were often of two minds about boxing, cheering Louis while worrying whether association with a sport considered low-class would simply intensify stereotypes of Negroes as primitive and savage. But soon their reluctance yielded to the general enthusiasm, and the hero worship became general.

Eunice, too, was viewed in the darker nation as a hero. There is a story in the family that she hoped to write a book about her experiences. Certainly her account of the Luciano trial would have been a big seller. But she never got around to it, most likely because she was too busy. The other possibility is that a memoir requires introspection of the sort that she had always resisted. Eunice lived entirely in her role, and so remained stern and distant, essentially unreachable. Her grammar and diction were sufficiently perfect that both served as a reproach to those who spoke more casually. She was judgmental and often dismissive. She was impatient. But nobody denies her remarkable legal talent.

In her new position, Eunice was involved in one headline case after another. She twice prosecuted the infamous "Dr." Anna Swift, accused of operating a house of prostitution under cover of a medical massage facility. Swift worked out of a building located at 8 East Seventieth Street known as the "Danish Institute." She had as her clients many of the most prominent men of the city. Convicted of the same offense in 1936, she had spent three months in the workhouse. Upon her release, she went straight back to the same business.

Swift's second trial was in the summer of 1940. Eunice tried the case. She successfully adopted the technique that had brought down Luciano: the women who worked for Swift testified against her and, in return, had their charges reduced or dropped. Of course, to the modern reader, the strategy seems commonplace. But once upon a time it was new. Dewey, on Eunice's urging, had helped pioneer it. Before the Luciano case, the prostitutes themselves were prosecuted. Persuading them to turn against their bosses was at the time an innovation, and a controversial one. Legal ethicists and stalwarts of the bar were appalled, although the women's "low social status" likely muted many voices that would otherwise have been raised in criticism. In any event, once proved worthy, the tactic became a permanent addition to the armamentarium of the prosecutor's office. Street-level prostitutes brought down

Luciano; street-level prostitutes brought down Anna Swift. And although the news of the madam's conviction did not make headlines—the story appeared on the back page of the *New York Times*—Eunice must surely have been thrilled to find this sentence: "Mrs. Eunice H. Carter, assistant district attorney, led the prosecution."

Not long after came a small coda from the Luciano trial. Eunice had a letter from Frances Blackman of East Thirty-second Street, a madam whose house had been raided during the February 1, 1936, surprise arrests leading up to the Luciano trial, and who had turned state's evidence. According to the letter, which was addressed to "Mrs. Cotter," Blackman had later also testified for Eunice in the grand jury, giving evidence against someone named "Harlem Tom." Probably this was Tom Morro, also known as "Big Tom," against whom Eunice interviewed witnesses to build a case for compulsory prostitution in January of 1938.* (Whether Morro was ever brought to trial is not recorded in the files.) Now Blackman had been arrested again, once more for running a brothel. She reminded Eunice of the promise prosecutors always make to reluctant witnesses—"You said that if ever you could help me in any way that you would gladly do it"—and asked for a meeting before her trial. Eunice agreed to talk to her. What happened next does not appear on the record, but it is almost certain that Eunice told her that there was nothing to be done: turning state's evidence is not a license to commit further crimes.

Eunice was a meticulous courtroom advocate who meticulously displayed her attention to detail. In a prostitution case Eunice handled in January of 1938, she gave what could easily serve as a textbook example of how to lay a foundation in order to introduce evidence of a telephone call based on the witness's familiarity with the voice on the other end. The following month, in a trivial case involving a break-in, Eunice took considerable care in crafting questions that would enable a witness to make clear without ever saying so that there could not have been a legitimate reason for the defendants to be on the premises. (The care was necessary because the witness would not have been allowed simply to

---

* It is unlikely that this is Harlem Tom Evans, the gangster who had a bit part in D. W. Griffith's 1912 film *The Musketeers of Pig Alley*.

state an opinion.) Other examples of Eunice's careful work in minor cases abound.

But if many of the prosecutions she handled were routine, a few of them still wound up on the front page. The most prominent defendant she faced in a courtroom was Jules Brulatour, whose case arrived in 1939 not long after she began running Special Sessions. Brulatour was a titan of the film industry. He had made a fortune in cheap silents of the *Perils of Pauline* type and was now making another fortune in talkies. Out in Hollywood there were those who whispered that he had been one of Orson Welles's models, along with William Randolph Hearst, for Charles Foster Kane. Kane's boozy ex-wife is supposed to have been based on Brulatour's ex-wife Dorothy Gibson, whom he scandalously wed while still married to an earlier wife. In January he was found in his five-story townhouse at 1145 Park Avenue, bleeding from a gunshot wound. He was rushed to the hospital. His third wife, the actress Hope Hampton, was the press's favorite suspect. But Brulatour, once he regained consciousness, insisted that he had accidentally shot himself, even though the path of the bullet was downward into his neck.

The case was a big deal—and not just in New York. Newspapers around the country ran headlines. Foreigners, too, took an interest. "Brulatour Arrested in Shooting, Hope Hampton Called as Witness" headlined the Montreal *Gazette*. Brulatour and Hampton whirled through New York society. According to a *Life* magazine profile, a pair of front-row seats was reserved for the couple at every Broadway opening; the Brulatours "through sheer fortitude have become Broadway's No. 1 first-nighters." Just a few years before the shooting, the government of France had conferred upon him the Legion of Honor.

Given Brulatour's celebrity, the newspapers ebulliently covered every development in the case. At first the stories were ominous. Stains on the pistol, wrote the *Times*, had been "made by blood." The article went on to paint a maudlin picture: Brulatour incommunicado in the hospital, attended only by his wife and his physicians. But just days later, arriving for his arraignment in felony court, he was described by the *Times* as "jovial" and "enjoying the experience." In the corridor, the filmmaker took off his hat to show reporters where the bullet had nicked his ear and lodged in his neck. Asked about arriving on time,

Brulatour "smilingly" explained, "Punctuality is the politeness of kings—that is, it was when there were more of them than today." The prosecution admitted that it was unable to prove a felony, so the judge sent the case to Special Sessions. This meant that the matter now rested in Eunice's lap.

The following day, Brulatour staggered into the courthouse—"weak on the pins" by his own description, a condition he blamed on the weather—and entered a plea of guilty in Special Sessions to having violated the Sullivan Act, which required that New Yorkers have licenses for guns small enough to be concealed. Eunice, who handled the case herself, made no sentencing recommendation. But she did make clear that the district attorney's office was skeptical of the story that Brulatour had shot himself. For one thing, the gun he had produced and claimed to have used was the wrong caliber. "[T]here has been a shooting which has not been satisfactorily explained," Eunice told the court. Given the filmmaker's refusal to back off his story, however, there was little for the prosecution to do but plead the case out. Still, she had the satisfaction of presiding over the conviction of one of the wealthiest men in the city.

Eunice was known as a tough prosecutor, but she could also dispense mercy. Consider the case of Ruth Anderson, who brought sixteen cartons of cigarettes from New Jersey into New York, and was fined twenty-five dollars for possession of unstamped cigarettes in violation of a city ordinance. She then faced state charges for the same offense. Eunice agreed to hold the state's case over, pending Anderson's appeal of her conviction. The appellate court overturned the judgment, ruling that the tax stamp was not required where the cigarettes were for personal use. In light of the ruling, Eunice moved to throw out the state charges as well, even though it was not obvious that the state was bound. The court concurred. Similarly, when six men were convicted in Special Sessions of concealing their police records when they applied for jobs as private detectives, Eunice recommended that their sentences be suspended because that was the sentence handed down for others who had done the same but were tried in General Sessions.

A trickier case involved a man named Joseph Stillman who had served as a witness in a minor prostitution case in 1938. When Eunice spoke to him after the trial, she discovered that he had perjured himself. Evidently he had testified that he had visited the defendant only once for the purpose of paying her for sex. Actually he had been to the house two weeks earlier. He explained to Eunice that he would not admit under oath to the earlier visit because to do so might cause trouble for the friend who brought him there. In a memorandum to Paul Lockwood, Dewey's top assistant, she wrote that Stillman's misstatement was not material and therefore "is not such perjury as would lend itself to a charge and prosecution for perjury." She was not sweeping anything under the rug: materiality is legally relevant.

Eunice's work in Special Sessions also led her to a particular concern about the way the system treated juveniles. She would see the same young men come back again and again for the same petty offenses, receiving each time a sentence more severe than the last. Finally she decided that enough was enough, and in 1940 she was instrumental in developing (and shepherding through the legislature) New York's first-in-the-nation system under which nonviolent offenders between the ages of sixteen and eighteen would in most cases have their names kept secret and be spared prison terms, in the hope of furthering their rehabilitation. Dewey gave Eunice full credit.

And like any prosecutor, Eunice had her share of encounters in the realm of the bizarre. In December of 1939, she had a man named Andrew Solomon arrested in her office on Leonard Street. The arrest followed a strange courtroom event in which he pretended to be the defendant in a case to which he apparently had no connection. The judge called the defendant's name and Solomon stepped forward instead—not by accident but on purpose. He answered the judge's questions as though he were the one being arraigned. The proceeding might have continued for some while had a police officer not noticed that the wrong man was being arraigned.

What the actual defendant's lawyer was thinking is not recorded.

Yet with all of the time spent at the office, in the courthouse, or on the road, Eunice found time to maintain her standing at the summit of the Great Social Pyramid. She was still out and about in sassiety, as

Eunice would proudly tell interviewers that she drove herself to work every morning, from upper Harlem down to lower Manhattan. PHOTOGRAPHS AND PRINTS DIVISION, SCHOMBURG CENTER FOR RESEARCH IN BLACK CULTURE, NEW YORK PUBLIC LIBRARY

the columns were pleased to record. She made occasional trips under the auspices of the NAACP. More important, at some point in 1939, Eunice and her husband left 141st Street and moved to an apartment at 409 Edgecombe Avenue. This was the most prestigious address in Sugar Hill; and Sugar Hill, in turn, was the most prestigious Negro neighborhood in New York—some would have said in the entire country. The historian David Levering Lewis described Sugar Hill as "a citadel of stately apartment buildings and liveried doormen." At 409 Edgecombe, some lucky residents could look out their windows and watch baseball games at the Polo Grounds, home of the New York Giants. Among the Huntons' new neighbors were the Walter Whites, the Thurgood Marshalls, and the Roy Wilkinses. Eunice had less time to entertain, but her credentials as a Czarina remained solid. Her parties and receptions, if less frequent than in the past, were still praised by the social columns. She was still out on the town regularly. One week she would be at a dance during the New York convention of the National Bar Association. The following week would find her at opening night of the latest

Eunice in a posed photograph for a profile in the press, 1942. She did not cook at home very often.
PHOTOGRAPHS AND PRINTS DIVISION, SCHOMBURG CENTER FOR RESEARCH IN BLACK CULTURE, NEW YORK PUBLIC LIBRARY

Harlem cabaret show. Or attending a cocktail party to raise money for the *Crisis*, the NAACP's magazine. Or addressing a Republican club in Rockaway. Or speaking at an event organized by the National Council of Negro Women, where she had risen to become a key lieutenant of Mary McLeod Bethune's. If the Harlem glitterati descended upon a luxurious new nightclub for its grand opening, Eunice was sure to be among them. If the colored American Legion paraded on Memorial Day, you could be sure that Eunice would be an honored guest. If legendary civil rights lawyer Charles Hamilton Houston came to town, you could be sure that Eunice would co-host the reception.

The Negro press followed Eunice slavishly. So eager were editors to cover her doings that she could make the papers simply by sitting down to bridge. If she went on vacation, it got mentioned in the columns. Even her clothing was news. One gossip columnist remarked on how Eunice looked "tops wearing an expensive wolf coat" but "may shed it for lighter apparel if she decides to bask in the sunshine at Nassau before the winter ends." Another noted that Eunice wore suits during the day because "she passes very little of the daytime . . . filling social engagements."

And, always, there were more speaking engagements. She addressed colored Republicans throughout the region. She drew a packed house in Albany. At the annual convention of the National Council of Negro Women in Washington, D.C., she warned that if America did not end the scourge of Jim Crow, it would "be held up to scorn by the rest of the civilized world."

Not all of her audiences were black.

In February of 1939, Dewey was invited to make remarks at a huge Brooklyn gala in honor of John R. Crews, chairman of the county Republican Party. Some seven thousand guests would be present, many of them powers in the party. Given Dewey's plans to go after the GOP presidential nomination the next year, his attendance was de rigueur. But his trial schedule left him unable to go; he was in the midst of preparing the Hines summation. He sent Eunice to address the group in his place. This was an act of considerable faith in her abilities—and also in her star power. Her audience this time did not comprise colored Republicans. The GOP might have styled itself the party of Lincoln, but the room would be overwhelmingly or perhaps entirely white. And these were people Dewey had to impress, people who could affect his future. He sent her anyway.

Actually the risk was small. Eunice was by now one of the best-known Negro women in the country, and certainly one of the best-known Negroes in the Republican Party.

So prominent had she become that in the summer of 1939 her photograph was featured, along with pictures of Booker T. Washington and George Washington Carver, at a Stanford University exhibit on Negro "racial achievements." At the New York World's Fair she received a medal at a "Women of Today" event; afterward, she and the other honorees were given tea by Mrs. Vincent Astor. She joined Vivien Leigh and Laurence Olivier on a radio show. She was profiled in national magazines. For the next decade she would be a fixture in the Negro press, so much so that in the headlines there was never a need to explain to the readers who she was. Just "Mrs. Carter" or "Eunice Hunton Carter" would be enough.* Apart from Mary McLeod Bethune and a handful of entertainers, no other Negro woman received this homage.

---

* Although the press sometimes called her "Mrs. Lisle Carter," she was almost never "Eunice Carter." She insisted on including "Hunton," and the press went along. Some publications even hyphenated the name: "Hunton-Carter."

* * *

The portrait of Eunice painted by both the Negro and the mainstream press was mostly accurate. She was smart and talented, she was hard-working and well-spoken. She commanded respect, even among those unaccustomed to respecting, in any serious intellectual sense, either Negroes or women. Eunice could impress and even intimidate. She was widely admired for her brilliance and her success. She generated stories galore. But not all the stories are true. The most tantalizing fiction involved Stephanie St. Clair, the colorful Harlem numbers runner.

Several sources assert that St. Clair was living at 409 Edgecombe when Eunice and Lisle moved in, meaning that the prosecutor and the gangster were neighbors. The stylish St. Clair was one of the Black Queens who ran the policy racket in Harlem before the Mob moved in. She is also the one who sent the taunting note to Dutch Schultz when he was on his deathbed. Long a figure of popular fascination, St. Clair has appeared in countless novels and has been portrayed in the movies by the talented actresses Novella Nelson and Cicely Tyson. Alas, the well-worn story that she and Eunice lived in the same building seems not to be accurate. Certainly St. Clair resided at 409 Edgecombe from the late 1920s to the late 1930s. But in March of 1938 she was sentenced to two to ten years in prison for shooting her husband. By the time Eunice and Lisle moved in, St. Clair was behind bars.

A related and equally popular myth holds that Eunice, in her official capacity, investigated or even sought to prosecute St. Clair. After all, their careers overlapped. Eunice joined Dewey in 1935; St. Clair was active until she went to prison in 1938. Unfortunately, this account is supported neither by the records of the New York County District Attorney nor by contemporaneous news accounts. Most likely the tale began as a misunderstanding of the purpose of the January 1937 numbers raids Eunice coordinated in Harlem, which were aimed ultimately not at black policy bankers but at Tammany leader Jimmy Hines. Too bad: it would make a great vignette.

Yet stories about a connection between the two women persist, and small wonder. Both were smart and strong-willed, both were successful and glamorous, both were admired by passersby as they strolled the Harlem streets sporting jewelry and furs. They were on opposite sides of the law. Each would have made a formidable adversary for the other. A confrontation would have been great theater. But it never happened.

In September of 1939, as evidence that "there is no room for prejudice" in New York, Dewey cited his hiring record:

> I have more Jews working in the department than has ever been true before, and, for the first time, a Polish assistant is employed. There are more colored persons in outstanding positions than has been true of any other administration, as you have observed. In fact, a colored woman lawyer is the head of the largest bureau in this office.

The Chief was already preparing another run for higher office, and Eunice, whether or not she knew it, would be an important prop in the campaign.

Not that she would have minded.

CHAPTER 16

THE DECISION

During the run-up to Thomas Dewey's 1940 presidential campaign, the black press ran puff pieces. A story in the Baltimore *Afro-American* touted the candidate's supposed lack of racial prejudice. And considering the era, what he had done with appointments was indeed impressive. The story gave considerable space to Eunice's role in running the office's work in Special Sessions ("more cases than any other bureau") and Francis Rivers's role as head of homicide prosecutions ("he has no rivals in the nation"). When asked what he would do for the Negro as president, Dewey answered by citing the high salaries paid to the two black lawyers. The pair of them, declared a letter to the *New York Age*, were "making Negro history."

Eunice of course was a big Dewey backer. Her hard work on behalf of the man expected to receive the Republican nomination prompted the Negro papers to write stories about the friendly disagreement between Eunice and Mary McLeod Bethune, who was part of Roosevelt's "Black Cabinet" and campaigning nearly as hard for the New Deal as Eunice was against it. The Baltimore *Afro-American* was catty: "Mrs. Carter belongs to the new school with its emphasis on efficiency and expertness. She is naturally more active than Mrs. Bethune, being much younger." The story went on to call the two women "well matched," but Bethune, who could be thin-skinned, would surely have noted the slight.

Eunice by this time was implementing the new juvenile affairs program while still running Special Sessions. She balanced her duties with travel on behalf of the campaign. She went to Washington, where on Capitol Hill she represented the candidate in a meeting with what the press called "powers that be." She went to Bridgeport, Connecticut. At one point she somehow squeezed seven talks for Dewey into as many days. She went to Baltimore to interview potential speakers, evidently with an eye toward selecting surrogates to campaign on Dewey's behalf. While in the state, she stopped in Easton to address the Maryland Colored Republican League, delivering a talk entitled "Taking Stock of the Negro in America in 1940." Her message was characteristically clear and sharp:

> Seventy-five years after 1865 we still have in the United States lynching, disfranchisement, discrimination by public utilities and tax supported institutions of learning and an undetermined place in the American economic scheme.

She added a sharp swipe at the Democrats, for whom more and more Negroes, by this time, were casting ballots: "We cannot in good conscience support a party whose controlling factors and guiding spirit fail to recognize that all men are created equal."

A month later, back in Maryland, she pressed the same case before the Progressive Republican Club. It was the Democrats, Eunice said, who had killed the federal anti-lynching law that was the top priority of the civil rights leadership. She accused the Roosevelt administration of "hobnobbing with the exponents of the antilynching bill and promising them help and support." She admitted that she admired Eleanor Roosevelt, whom she considered "a great lady, perhaps one of the greatest." But she warned her audience not to allow their admiration of the First Lady to move them to vote for her husband:

> She is not to be confused with the President, himself, or with the present administration. Do not be misled into believing

that the actions and attitudes of a very great lady and great
American are indicative of the attitude of the Democratic
party.

Eunice's attack on Roosevelt was harsh but fair. For the third election
cycle in a row, the President was counting on the votes of segregationist
whites in the South, many of whom, on issues apart from race, were fairly
liberal and supported the New Deal. The White House, along with congressional Democrats, determined not to alienate this crucial bloc
with loose talk about equality—or about a federal lynch law. Dewey,
touting his record on race, hoped to secure enough colored votes to
make up the difference.

But first he had to secure the nomination. Apart from his work as
a prosecutor, Dewey had never held any public office. Nevertheless, by
the time the convention opened in Philadelphia on June 24, 1940, Dewey
had the most primary votes and pledged delegates. Still, the great majority of delegates were unpledged. There was work to be done. Eunice
was present, heading an operation to swing Negro delegates his way. A
reporter for the Democratic-leaning *Chicago Defender* mocked her as
the snob she surely was. Dewey headquarters, he wrote, "is manned in
part by the elite"—including "Eunice Carter, who never allows one to
forget who is who."

The hard work was all for naught. Having the most delegates is not
the same as having a majority of the delegates, and the machinations
of the convention proved beyond Dewey's control. He had aimed too
high too fast. He was widely seen as too young and lacking adequate
foreign policy experience. As the convention took vote after vote, unable
to coalesce around a candidate, Dewey's support began to crumble. On
the sixth ballot, the delegates agreed unanimously to nominate Wendell Willkie, a lawyer and corporate executive who had never held public
office either, and who, until a year ago, had been a Democrat. Eunice
was crushed. Her proud dream of accompanying her mentor to Washington had turned into a humiliating nightmare.

But Eunice, ever a creature of duty, soldiered on. Back in New York,
she joined a biracial group of prominent members of the Republican-
Fusion coalition who signed a letter criticizing Mayor La Guardia for

throwing his support to Roosevelt. The group backed Willkie instead. She went ahead even though she must have known there were risks. But at least she was in good company. Fellow signatories included La Guardia's former campaign manager and the legendary parks commissioner Robert Moses. Though La Guardia, the great reformer, by now had a tight grip on the city's political machine, Eunice stuck to her principles. She disliked the New Deal, and was not afraid to say so. Although she admired Eleanor Roosevelt, she distrusted Franklin, most particularly on issues of race. Willkie spoke out forcefully on civil rights, which the President rarely did. The GOP nominee promised to end segregation throughout the federal government: "discrimination in the civil service, army, navy, and all other branches of the government must cease." No major party candidate had ever said such a thing. The *Pittsburgh Courier* not only endorsed Willkie but decorated the facade of its building with a large portrait of the candidate surrounded by red, white, and blue bunting. Eunice campaigned hard for Willkie, and toured Harlem with his wife.* But come November, Willkie—the last "dark horse" candidate ever nominated by a major party—lost to Roosevelt in a landslide. Once again, Eunice's political hopes were dashed.

Whether your candidate wins or loses, one of the oft-overlooked joys of Election Day in the United States is that Thanksgiving Day follows so closely upon it. In 1940, Thanksgiving fell on Thursday, November 21. Fifteen-year-old Lisle Jr. came home from Cazenovia, New York, a small town near Syracuse, where he was attending preparatory school. In early August he had returned from Barbados for good. Eunice had wanted her son back, but once he arrived she did not know what to do with him. She sent him to prep school—so he always believed—not because he needed it but simply to get rid of him. He was wounded, but the pattern was familiar. When he was small, his mother had sent him to stay with her husband's family in New Jersey. When he was nine, she had sent him to Barbados for five years. And now, as a teenager, he was being exiled once again.

This final exile, unlike the others, did not involve more gentle and

---

* By a bizarre coincidence, Willkie, in his youth, once dated a woman named Eunice Carter.

loving surroundings than home. At Cazenovia, Lisle Jr. was respected by his teachers, and earned high marks. He was one of the very few black students on campus, however, and many of his classmates subjected him to pranks—some merely irritating, others actually dangerous. No doubt a part of this was simple hazing. He was the statistician and part-time coach for the baseball team, but when he was pressed into emergency service as a pinch-hitter, Lisle Jr. was warned not to swing at any pitches; he was told to hope for a base on balls instead. Playing defense, he was put in right field but told to let the center fielder make all the catches. Of course, being teased for not being much of an athlete is just boys being boys. When the other boys set fire to the door of your room, however, it becomes more difficult to tell yourself that race is in no way involved.

Lisle Jr. probably welcomed a respite, and at least he came home that Thanksgiving to pleasant surroundings. So spacious were the Carters' premises at 409 Edgecombe that Eunice could throw parties for sixty guests or more. The apartments at the north end of Sugar Hill were called "oatmeal flats," because by the time you shelled out the money to live there, all you could afford to eat was oatmeal. Eunice did not have that problem. The building was chock-full of lawyers and physicians, judges and business owners. Still, in 1940, Eunice's salary of "$5,000+"— the actual figure was $6,500, but the census takers went no higher—was matched by fewer than half a dozen of her fellow tenants. And this was without taking into account what Lisle Sr. earned from his dental practice, unreported to the census because it was income from self-employment. All by herself, Eunice out-earned Walter White, the head of the NAACP. She out-earned Thurgood Marshall, head of the just-created NAACP Legal Defense Fund. She out-earned the famous artist Aaron Douglas. She out-earned a tenant who was an assistant attorney general of the state of New York. Few of her neighbors, even those with multiple incomes, earned half what Eunice alone did.

These statistics bear mention because by all accounts she liked to spend her money. Eunice had a taste for the finer things in life. Fur coats. Expensive jewelry. Rare wines. Fancy vacations. When she traveled by ship, a thing she did often, she traveled first class. (She also insisted that Lisle Jr. travel to and from Barbados first class.) Each time she changed addresses, she moved to a more prestigious and more expensive building. Her home was sumptuously furnished. She spent money as swiftly as she and her husband earned it. She saved nothing.

This was the home to which Lisle Jr. returned from Cazenovia in November of 1940. There were seven for Thanksgiving dinner. In addition to Lisle Jr. and his parents, Judge and Mrs. Charles Toney, fellow 409 Edgecombe residents, were there. So was Addie. So was Alphaeus, but without his wife. Eunice's younger brother was on his own. For the second time in a decade, his marriage had come a cropper. Once more he was scandalizing the Czarinas. For a good two years during which he was living in Washington as a dutiful husband to Margaret, he had been having an open and unapologetic affair with a woman named Dorothy Williams, who lived in New York. He was repeating the same pattern. He had cheated publicly with Margaret while still married to Ethelyn, and was now cheating publicly with Dorothy while still married to Margaret. He was as rebellious in his personal life as in his politics.

It is difficult to imagine that Addie greeted her wayward son's womanizing antics with anything but icy disapproval. Eunice, for her part, must have been furious. Here she was, fighting to maintain, as best she could and at considerable personal cost, the traditions to which she and her brother had been raised; and here was her younger brother doing as he liked as usual, disdaining the marital virtue that Addie insisted was the only true salvation of the race.

There was a deeper reason for Eunice's fury at her brother: by this time she was fighting to hold her own marriage together. The union that had once seemed so shiny and bright was beginning to show its cracks. Lisle Sr. was tall and dashing, with a disconcertingly straight stare that was softened by his penchant for reciting poetry by the yard. He was popular around Harlem. His dental practice at 2307 Seventh Avenue welcomed children, who always felt gently treated, and if you happened to be short of funds, you could always pay him later. He was patient and reflective and was admired for his sense of humor. He ran several of Harlem's more prestigious men's clubs. And the whisper was that he had girlfriends galore. A cousin who worked briefly in his dental office recalled that he was seeing a young woman who lived around the corner. They made no secret of their relationship; Lisle Sr. would make plans to see the girlfriend quite openly on the telephone. The whole office knew; probably the whole neighborhood knew; which meant that all Harlem knew. All of Eunice's Harlem, anyway.

Eunice had been raised to different values. Both her father and her mother had stressed the integrity of the family as central to the progress of the race. Addie in particular, as the apostle of Negro womanhood, believed that the female of the species demonstrated her virtue by a lifelong committed wedlock. She had been pressing that argument in writing and in speeches for forty years now.

To be sure, Eunice might not have followed her mother's advice that the first duty of the Negro woman was the rearing of children, but she did manage—at what effort we can only guess—to put an outward face of amity on her difficult marriage. And if reverence for her mother proved not enough to keep Eunice on the straight path, she had also seen the vehemence with which the Czarinas had gone after Alphaeus when he'd married a stage girl. Eunice was now very much in the public eye and boiling with ambition; she could not afford to have her reputation soiled.

Nevertheless, she considered ending the marriage. One summer, when Lisle Jr. was visiting from Barbados, the mother who was usually too busy to know what to do with her son took him on a surprise vacation of several days to Saratoga Springs. Lisle Jr. enjoyed this time away—until the sunny afternoon when Eunice told him she was in love with another man.*

---

* According to Lisle Jr., this conversation took place when he was about eleven or twelve. He also said that he came home from Barbados only twice during his years there. Available records indicate that apart from his move back to the United States, which occurred in early August of 1940 and which he would hardly describe as a visit, Lisle Jr. did indeed come home only twice, both times sailing to Boston. The first visit, confirmed by immigration records, occurred in July of 1937, when he was eleven. The second, confirmed by news accounts, was in early August of 1939, when he was thirteen. (See "Chatter and Chimes," *New York Amsterdam News*, Aug. 12, 1939, p. 12.) Of course there may have been other trips the records of which do not survive. But if these were the only trips, and if we suppose that six decades later Lisle Jr. correctly remembered his age at the time of the visit to Saratoga, then Eunice's confession occurred during the summer of 1937, which would place it about a year after the Luciano trial ended.

On the other hand, the society columns in the Negro press regularly covered who was

And asked how he would feel if she left his father.

The question took her son by surprise. He was angry that she would even ask. Angry, and also wounded. He did not hesitate. He told his mother that he would mind very much. He wanted his parents to stay married. And stay Eunice did. Perhaps she believed that in this way she would make up for the pain that repeated exile had caused her son. Or perhaps Addie's lessons on marital fidelity would have prevailed in any case.

Some years later, Lisle Jr. discovered that the other man in Eunice's life was the bandleader Fletcher Henderson. Henderson, small and dapper, is considered one of the premier arrangers in jazz history. He studied chemistry in college but, after arriving in New York to pursue graduate work at Columbia, quickly turned to music instead. (His biographer tells us that his appalled parents viewed music as no more than an extracurricular activity.) Like Eunice, Henderson was married. Unlike Eunice, he was known to stray. How had they first met? Perhaps their paths crossed during the year Eunice spent teaching in Louisiana after receiving her degree from Smith in 1921. As it turns out, Henderson was in New Orleans in 1922. Or Eunice might have met him later, in her Harlem Renaissance days. However their relationship began, Addie would surely have put a stop to it, for a bandleader, in her estimation, would have been little more than a rung or two above a showgirl. So if their romance predated Eunice's marriage, her sacrifice might have been even larger. Not only did she stay with Lisle Sr. to avoid upsetting her son too greatly; she might well have married him in the first place while in love with another man. And history contains an intriguing nugget in support of this thesis: Henderson married his wife, Leora, exactly one month after Eunice married Lisle.

In any case, Eunice stayed. Caught between her son's fear and anger and her own worry about what her mother would think, Eunice chose

---

heading to Saratoga Springs, which was at this time a frequent destination for the well-to-do of the darker nation. Eunice is mentioned as vacationing there only in the summer of 1941. (See "Grand Season at Saratoga Spa Pleased Folk from Many Cities," *New York Amsterdam Star-News*, Sept. 6, 1941, p. 6.) It is possible, then, that Lisle Jr.'s memory indeed played him false, and that the conversation in which Eunice discussed leaving her husband took place not when he was visiting from Barbados but in the summer of 1941, when he had just completed his year at Cazenovia and, not quite sixteen years old, was about to enter Dartmouth College.

the course of duty. If maintaining fidelity to her vows included her own pain, she was nevertheless obeying the demands of the moral tradition in which she had been raised. Probably Eunice never mentioned Fletcher Henderson to her mother. If she had, Addie doubtless would have told her daughter that by staying with her husband, she was doing the right thing. Addie had spent nearly half a century campaigning for the proposition that what the Negro family most needed was a stable household, where moral guidance and example were provided by a dutiful wife. In Addie's world, the need of the individual for love and happiness was less important than the need of the community for stable families.

To be sure, Addie had encountered difficulty in living up to her own standards, and Alphaeus had rejected them entirely. But Eunice had never thought of herself as a rebel. Having a career of her own was defiance enough of the mores to which she had been raised. Divorces were not supposed to happen in the better families. She was also quite conscious that she had already pressed the limits of her mother's vision of what the Negro woman was supposed to do. So she stayed.

Perhaps as a penance, Eunice became earnest in pressing for better treatment for women, both in marriage and in the workplace. In a May 1937 speech to the Howard University Alumnae Club, she spoke happily of women's changing place in American economic life: "[W]e are molding a new system and a new order." Negro women in particular, she said, were moving into the job market, but there were pitfalls along the way. She described the treatment of female employees as "one of the most vicious things in our economic and social order." She had in mind particularly men who supervise women:

> There are men who exact from women a personal relation-
> ship of a rather intimate nature in order that the women may
> feel secure in their jobs. Boiling in oil is just a little too good
> for those kind of men.

She reminded her audience that much remained to be done to be sure that younger women would have a place. And, echoing her mother's emphasis on self-reliance, she warned that the task would be difficult because many young people "have not learned the habit of working." It was up to Negro women, she concluded, "to see that the path is being broken in the right direction."

At other times, however, she backed off on the harshness of her rhetoric. In a rambling March 1938 address to the Essex County League of Colored Women Voters on the role of women, Eunice seemed conflicted. Her advice reflected her own marital disarray: "Never argue with a man. I believe that I have quarreled with a man only six times in my life. Always it resulted in disaster." And in a bit of counsel that must have surprised her listeners, she warned women to be modest in pursuit of ambition: "Women's influence should be from behind the throne, not on it." She added, "The girl of today no longer waits at home for marriage but immediately goes to work and finds more opportunities than the colored man. The latter has lost the proverbial occupations." And a remark near the conclusion surely confused her audience:

> Women must never forget that men should dominate the race and that a race is only as strong as its men. We must continue to inspire them. Otherwise, there will be a decline of this and other races.

But then, at the end, Eunice reversed field: "I believe in the independence of women nevertheless."

Here was neither the smooth, confident intellectual of Eunice's days as a darling of the Harlem Renaissance, nor the sharp, brilliant advocacy she brought to the courtroom, nor even the cool Christian logic through which Addie had linked domesticity, racial pride, and the fight for justice. Eunice's remarks were more in the nature of an apologia. Perhaps the message was intended not for the colored women of Essex County but for her own husband. Perhaps she had decided that the discord in their marriage arose not simply from his affairs or hers but from a sinking sense that what the Barbadian traditionalist to whom she was married found so disturbing was the success of her career.

Later that year, Eunice took time off to head for Washington, where she sat with her mother and her brother at a memorial hosted by

Howard University in honor of her father, William. Both children spoke. While Alphaeus settled for banalities, expressing the hope that the YMCA's next half century would be as fine as the previous one, Eunice took the occasion to tell the group that "any success I have gained" was due to the spirit of her father and the guidance of her mother.

She made no mention of her husband.

Six decades later, Lisle Jr. would tell an interviewer that his parents were living separately, "probably by 1935, and certainly by 1940," the year he returned from Barbados. There is no reason to doubt his recollection. However, the Negro press, which at this time gave bold headlines to the smallest hint of marital strife in sassiety, makes no mention of the separation. Eunice and Lisle Sr. were recorded as living together in the 1940 census, compiled in April, and later that year they jointly hosted Thanksgiving dinner. Eunice had told an interviewer in February that the "system" that kept her going included "having dinner regularly with her husband." Probably the estrangement had ended by then. In any case, if they had indeed set up separate housekeeping at some point, Eunice and Lisle Sr. hid it well—not from their son, to be sure, but from the Czarinas up on top of the Great Pyramid.

On the other hand, they had developed the habit of taking separate vacations, and nobody would say that all was well with the marriage. And in 1939, unlike in other years, all the mentions of Eunice in the gossip columns omit any mention of Lisle Sr., as if she is doing the social whirl alone. So perhaps they were indeed living apart for a time. In the end, however, Eunice persevered. The traditional standards mattered to her. That they made less and less difference to a changing world—and no difference at all to her brother—would only have made a woman like Eunice more determined to live the values she preached. So Addie's daughter reached the same decision as millions of others whose spouses stray: she would stick it out and hope that things would improve. The work might sometimes be painful, but it was work in which she believed.

True, Eunice would have to do the work largely alone. She was not the sort of woman to have best friends. Here the coolly mannered distance she presented to the world militated against her. A neighbor at 409 Edgecombe remembered later: "Carter was a very serious woman who never engaged in banter or discussion. When she came to our apartment to have her hair done, she always brought a book and read in silence."

Eunice read in silence, she brooded in silence, and she suffered in silence. She had been raised by a father who never shared his worries with his wife, and a mother who never shared her worries with anyone. Both had been models of stoicism. And even had she considered behaving differently, her brother's relative flamboyance would have acted as a standing reproach. So she kept the world at a distance and wound up with no one to talk to.

Certainly Eunice had a social circle through which she whirled, acquaintances with whom she might play bridge or grab a few days' vacation at a resort. Then, too, she still sat high in the councils of the Czarinas who directed the course of sassiety. When she could, she continued making the rounds of the appropriate fund-raisers and galas. But she had no one with whom she could discuss the difficulties in her marriage. She was attractive but not approachable; impressive but not open; intimidating but not confiding.

To remain in the broken marriage, Eunice would be forced to reinvent herself, to build a world around more than the traditions to which she had been raised. The world she chose to build revolved around ambition and profession. If she could not be happy at home, she would at least be a star at the office. Eunice saw the path of her future: a few more years as a prosecutor, followed by an appropriate judgeship, and after that—who could say? Her rise seemed certain. She had no way to know that one of the major props on which she relied in her climb was about to vanish.

CHAPTER 17

THE FILE

IN 1942, TOM DEWEY LEFT THE DISTRICT ATTORNEY'S OFFICE AFTER just a single term in order to run for governor of New York. He won easily, succeeding the popular Lehman, who had gone to Washington to help with the war effort.

Eunice was a Dewey delegate at the state Republican convention at Saratoga. In the general election she campaigned for her mentor, and when jubilant members of the Square Deal Republican Club staged a victory dinner, Eunice was the featured speaker. Following his victory, Dewey took others to Albany with him, but Eunice remained in the district attorney's office. Perhaps this was by her own choice. She was now running the juvenile justice program that she herself had created, listed by Dewey as one of his proudest achievements. Nevertheless, with Dewey's departure, Eunice learned where she truly stood in the office's pecking order. Dewey proposed four potential successors, all white men. Eunice had no earthly reason to suppose that one of the names should have been hers. Even the most progressive politicians of the era would not have proposed a Negro for an elective citywide office, and a Negro woman, whatever her talents, would be even worse. This was not merely an era of segregation. This was an era when many a white family owned a Be-Bop the Jivin' Jigger toy and seasoned their food from what were referred to, literally, as nigger salt and pepper shakers. This was an era when a black man planning to drive from New York to Florida had to have a family to stay with in every town south of Pennsylvania, because few hotels took colored guests and a Negro sleeping in his car invited arrest. This was an era when the nation was fully mobilized for war but only 3 percent of all employees in the defense industries were black.

Still, the fact that Eunice could not even be considered must have rankled, reminding her forcefully that no matter how her talent, drive, and achievement were rewarded within the confines of the office, the nation in which she lived still drew lines she would not be allowed to cross. She had always believed that she was special—in particular, that she was special to Thomas Dewey. But the web of racial expectations that she had trained herself to ignore turned out to have snared her after all. Perhaps she was less special than she thought.

From Dewey's list, the Republican-Fusion machine selected Frank Hogan, with whom Eunice had worked on the Luciano case. Hogan was a Democrat, but not Tammany-connected. He enjoyed a reputation as a reformer. He was also three years Eunice's junior. Hogan, in turn, promised to retain all of Dewey's people. As it transpired, he kept sixty-eight out of the seventy-four lawyers in the office. One of them was Francis Rivers, a graduate of Yale College and Columbia Law School; he, Eunice, and the very young James M. Yergan were the only black lawyers on the staff. With enormous hoopla and a public statement of thanks, Hogan raised Rivers's salary from $7,500 to $10,000, a decision, he said, that was "based on merit alone." He retained Eunice as a deputy assistant (still not a full assistant) but moved her out of Special Sessions and placed her in charge of the Special Part for Adolescent Offenders, a second program for sixteen- to eighteen-year-olds that she had developed, but not a full bureau. Special Sessions went to Lawrence J. McKenna. Eunice's salary remained at $6,500. At this time of course women, married women in particular, routinely earned less than men in similar jobs, on the theory that men had families to support and women had husbands to support them. The theory was widely embraced. Equal pay for equal work was yet at the fringe of the women's movement. Still,

Eunice must have been stung. Francis Rivers was a figure of experience and gravitas, and he had been out of law school longer than Eunice. But she had been in the office longer. At the time Hogan took over, Rivers was spending part of his time as a trial lawyer in Special Sessions. Eunice had formerly run Special Sessions.

Hogan kept bringing in new faces. Within a few years, there were some two hundred attorneys, of whom seventy-five were assistant or deputy assistant district attorneys—that is, Eunice's rank or higher. "We have our pick of a lot of good men," Hogan would later tell a reporter. He made no mention of women. And, in particular, none of the new hires were black women. Eunice's new boss never promoted her, and she no longer prosecuted any cases of note. From the time of Hogan's ascension onward, although Eunice's name was still frequently in the newspapers, she was almost always featured in the account of some political campaign or on the society pages. Her public profile remained high. She was still a power in the Republican Party and a big name in the darker nation. As a lawyer, however, she was on the verge of becoming what all her life she had worked hard to avoid: a face in the crowd.

Eunice's career at the district attorney's office would likely have gone in a different direction had the Fusion machine chosen not Hogan but Paul Lockwood, whose name was also on Dewey's list. Eunice had worked closely with Lockwood on a number of matters, and the pair spent part of their precious free time in each other's company. (They even went to a Negro League ball game together.) Many Republican insiders also favored Lockwood. But Hogan was seen as giving the reformers a better chance to retain the office in the coming election. Lockwood might well have lost to a Tammany Democrat. Hogan was seen as—and probably was—a man of transparent rectitude. Under his leadership, the office as a whole flourished. Eunice, however, became an outsider.

There is no indication that her trial skills had atrophied. Something had changed. Race was not the problem: Francis Rivers was cruising upward through the ranks. So perhaps what was holding Eunice back was her gender or, more likely, gender and race together: people who

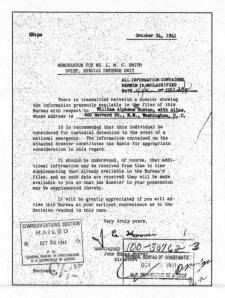

Alphaeus's FBI file ran to almost seven hundred pages, most of it focused on his activity as a clandestine member of the Communist Party. To her dying day, Eunice believed that her younger brother's radical activities destroyed her career. She was probably right.

PUBLIC RECORD OBTAINED FROM FEDERAL BUREAU OF INVESTIGATION

would readily accept a Negro man or a white woman would not necessarily be comfortable around a Negro woman. Hogan, with reason, stands as a heroic and admirable figure in the history of New York City, but he could have been heroic and yet not entirely beyond the reach of the prejudices of the era.

Eunice, however, never blamed Hogan. She offered a different possibility for her lack of advancement: that even at the apex of her fame, people in positions to advance her career were starting to worry about her brother.

Alphaeus Hunton first landed in the files of the Federal Bureau of Investigation early in 1941, after he was spotted in Washington, D.C., in the company of Florence Plotnick, a functionary of the Communist Party and an avowed Marxist. Plotnick had long been in the Bureau's sights. Her father was a Communist. Her mother was an anarchist. Plotnick herself had joined the Young Communist League at age twelve and "had been arrested more than two dozen times by the time she was 18." She was believed to run one of the Party's "underground" printing facilities, which in reality would likely have been little more than a basement room with a mimeograph machine for pamphlets. The file contains vague hints that she and Alphaeus might have had an intimate relationship, but had the agents had hard evidence that this was true, they presumably would have spelled it out. (At this time, Alphaeus was still married to his second wife, Margaret, but openly seeing third-wife-to-be Dorothy, so Florence would have been a third woman in his life.)

According to the earliest memorandum in Alphaeus's FBI file, he and Plotnick were plotting a pair of heinous acts. First, they were registering Negroes to vote. To the Bureau, this was bad enough. Second, they planned to print fifteen thousand forms on which Negroes could list their qualifications for employment, "so that 'pressure' can be brought upon the Federal government to require the hiring of these negroes." The agents were suitably shocked. Plotnick was named as Alphaeus's "constant adviser" as well as the individual who would make arrangements for printing—presumably via her "underground" press. In March, a watch was placed on his mail and arrangements were made for agents occasionally to follow him. By July, the file stated confidently that Alphaeus was a member of the Communist Party. According to a confidential informant, he worked out of the national office in New York and had not joined the branch in Washington, "to hide his party connection."

The Bureau would keep Alphaeus under intermittent surveillance for the rest of his life. By the time he died, his file would run to nearly seven hundred pages. His sister's name appears sparsely.* Two early reports mention that she works for Dewey. Not a scrap of paper suggests that she shared her brother's views or participated in his activities. But part of the danger of Hoover's files was that whether you had been exonerated was less important than whether your name appeared. There is no way to measure the effect of Alphaeus's avowed communism on his sister's career. Eunice always insisted that the effect had been enormous. It would fly in the face of our tortured history to suppose that the effect had been zero.

The influence of Alphaeus's commitment to the Party on his sister was more than just a matter of the damage it did to her career. They found themselves now on different sides of an issue of—literally—life and

---

* In response to my Freedom of Information Act request, the FBI stated that it holds no files on Eunice.

death. When World War II began in 1939, Alphaeus, as a member of the Communist Party, followed the Party line. At the outset of the war, Germany and the Soviet Union were allies. The Party therefore opposed Western entry into the war. So did Alphaeus. Negro leaders who supported the war effort were branded by the Party as "betrayers." Alphaeus agreed. When Hitler launched his invasion of the Soviet Union in June of 1941, the Party immediately switched sides. Now Western intervention was a matter of moral urgency. Alphaeus agreed.

Unlike her brother, Eunice never dithered. She unswervingly supported the war effort even when the government's official position was one of neutrality. In May of 1941, the newly created USO (known at the time as the United Service Organizations for National Defense) held a huge rally in Madison Square Garden in support of the forty-five thousand New Yorkers already drafted into the armed forces. Sitting among the sponsors, alongside Pan American Airways founder Juan Trippe and former Republican presidential candidate Alf Landon, was Eunice. Her presence was scarcely surprising. She was, at this time, one of the most prominent colored Republicans in the country, and in the face of popular isolationism, the Roosevelt administration wanted to showcase support for the coming conflict across lines of both party and race.

Once Japan attacked Pearl Harbor and the United States formally entered the war, Eunice worked even harder to rally support. In June of 1942 she appeared at a war bond rally together with such celebrities as Olivia de Havilland, Marian Anderson, and Supreme Court Justice Frank Murphy. That same year Eunice was a founding member of a multiracial organization called Democracy in Action that had as its stated purpose persuading "minorities" to support the war effort. Among the other notable members were Carl Van Doren, Noble Sissle, and Mrs. J. Borden Harriman, as well as Eunice's mentor Mary McLeod Bethune. At this time, there was serious question in the public mind about whether Negroes would or should fight for a nation that oppressed them. The historian John Hope Franklin summarized the difficulty: "Negroes schooled in the experiences of the 1920s and 1930s were unwilling to see the fight against Nazism carried on in the context of an American racist ideology." Alarmed by rising signs of colored indifference, the Roosevelt administration reached out to leaders of the race to put their concerns about domestic policy aside and endorse the war against Nazism as the lesser of two evils. Many prominent Negroes wrote articles taking precisely this line. The War Department also commissioned a series of propaganda films in the hope of turning black opinion around.

Democracy in Action was part of a larger complex of organizational and journalistic moves aimed at a Negro community thought to be indifferent. One Negro paper described the group's aims more broadly: "devoted to the primary purpose of working for a true democracy in this country." Another explained that Democracy in Action planned to "bring together a large number of minority peoples, including colored Americans and American Indians, anxious to contribute to the general war work, but often denied the opportunity." The organization explained that its founders offered their services to war relief groups but "received no encouragement," often "meeting with cruel rebuffs." At first, Democracy in Action was a big deal. The group's initial public meeting, in May of 1942, included the reading of a message of support from Eleanor Roosevelt. Famous artists raised funds. At a rally in Central Park in June, the featured speaker was the actress Tallulah Bankhead. In October 1942, the organization held a rally in Harlem, where residents were praised by the president of the city council for strictly following wartime blackout regulations—unlike, he said, the residents of Park Avenue. The idea was to get the darker nation thinking of itself as patriotic. Rallying minority support was an important goal of Roosevelt's policy.

Like most black leaders, Eunice cooperated enthusiastically. Her support for the war effort was public and unstinting. Lieutenant Colonel Harry Lofton, one of the few Negroes to command a combat regiment, visited Harlem early in 1943. Naturally sassiety gave him a glittering testimonial dinner. Naturally the organizers sat Eunice beside him on the dais. Later that year, at a conference sponsored by the National Council of Negro Women, Eunice led a panel discussion about discrimination in the armed forces. The panelists were Roy Wilkins of the NAACP and her brother, Alphaeus—one of the last times we know for sure that the two of them sat together.

Addie, too, supported the war, despite her long record as a peace activist. During the 1920s and 1930s, she had become the enemy of militarism generally but especially American militarism. World War II changed her mind. Perhaps Nazism stirred memories of her disillusionment and fear during her studies in Germany. Now she attended meetings with representatives of the Free French because "there is only one Paris." But that was not enough. Ailing and well on in years (she was probably seventy-six) but searching for a way to help, Addie enrolled in a first aid course. "[W]e don't know where we're going from here," she told a suitably astonished reporter, "and we must all be prepared for any emergency."

Although Eunice wholeheartedly supported the war effort, she remained a staunch Republican, and therefore a staunch critic of the Roosevelt administration. In September of 1942, she was part of a Constitution Day panel in New York that expressed strong support for the war but attacked Roosevelt's "Four Freedoms" speech. The panelists pointed out that the President's list of what America was fighting for omitted economic freedom. They also lambasted the "torrent" of new federal regulations—"this battle of the typewriters," one panelist called it—and expressed wariness at Roosevelt's hints of a larger United States presence in the world once the war was won. The conference was sponsored by the conservative Braman Fund Committee on Defense of the Constitution, some members of which had made headlines when they'd condemned the New Deal as "dictatorship." But speakers at Braman Fund events had been attacking Roosevelt and his political programs for almost a decade. That Eunice would join them provides a useful reminder: although she wore many different hats over the decades, she was no New Dealer. She did, however, make a friend of Eleanor Roosevelt during the war years, for she was always on the lookout for new connections.

There was the larger war that engulfed the world, and there was the smaller war that engulfed the family. At Christmas of 1942, Alphaeus came to New York to visit his sister at 409 Edgecombe. Addie, too, was present for the holidays. This may have been the last time Alphaeus and Eunice visited together; it was very likely the last time the three were together as a family. But the holiday must have been awkward. By this time, Alphaeus's politics had surged far to the left. He was already a member of the Communist Party. In his personal life, too, he continued to pile scandal upon scandal. He and Margaret were still married, but by the time of his Christmas visit he was openly and unapologetically seeing Dorothy. Worse, he and Dorothy were probably living together in Washington. Addie could not have approved. Four months after his visit, in a final slap at what would come to be called the politics of respectability—the social norms that so constrained his mother and his sister—Alphaeus married Dorothy. What must have shocked the Czarinas was not the fact that they were wed; no doubt sassiety was waiting for Alphaeus, in the old argot, to make an honest woman of her. No, the shocking part was *how* they wed.

Margaret received her decree of divorce on March 1, 1943—and all at once Dorothy, too, began to insist on the norms of respectability: "I refused to continue our relationship on the existing, unsatisfactory basis, and accused Alphaeus of lack of positiveness in his personal affairs, and trying to avoid the subject of our future." They apparently argued, but there followed an exchange of loving correspondence. Although Dorothy tries to explain away his reluctance as the natural response of a man who has made two bad marriages, at this point Alphaeus was pretty much out of excuses.

And so they wed. Without telling anyone except Dorothy's mother and one friend, they "slipped over to Virginia" on the blustery morning of Saturday, April 24, to be wed. Not in a church. By a justice of the peace. And not just any justice of the peace. By a showy, irreverent justice of the peace, who bragged in the press that he could marry a couple in fifty-five seconds. There was no religious ceremony, which was probably just as well, because few Christian pastors would have been willing to officiate: not on the Saturday between Good Friday and Easter Sunday. If the couple had planned the entire episode with the goal of shocking sassiety, they could hardly have done better. And if one combines Alphaeus's self-discipline with his utter disdain for the politics of respectability, it seems quite likely that the choice of Easter Saturday for the wedding was indeed intended as a slap.

And, probably, taken as one.

By this time, Alphaeus had rejected not only the traditionalism of his family but also the deep faith in God that had motivated his mother and father. Already in his childhood he had become at best an agnostic. To be sure, his sister Eunice's own religious life seems to have been broader than it was deep. She seems to have been the sort of Episcopalian who is more familiar with the Book of Common Prayer than with the Bible. But at least she carried on the forms of the faith that had shaped her. Alphaeus, on the other hand, was determined to be as open and public in renouncing his faith as he was in promoting his politics. He was an atheist and a Communist, and probably took pleasure in knowing that the Czarinas would despise him for both.

Quite possibly Eunice did not know for some while that her brother had wed for a third time. The couple did not allow Dorothy's family to announce the marriage until August. The family stories do not tell us why, but the truth is not difficult to guess. Addie was failing. Alphaeus might have longed to shake the foundations of the Great Social Pyramid, but he had no desire to make his mother's condition worse.

It made no difference. On Monday, June 21, two months after her son's wedding, Addie died.

Addie had been sick for some while, and before she was sick she was sickly. Her husband had suffered first from a form of malaria and finally from tuberculosis. Her own ailments were undisclosed. But what had been occasional hospitalizations had become more frequent. Recently she had started to turn down invitations even to local events that a few years before she would have attended. It does not appear that she was particularly close to either her daughter or her son. Alphaeus would visit her in Brooklyn when he came to the city, and Addie sometimes spent the holidays with Eunice. Yet to judge from the society pages, she and her children for the most part led rather separate lives. One has the sense that Eunice, having married and thereby freed herself from Addie's domineering ways, did all she could to preserve her independence. So she rarely went to Addie's house at 93 Bainbridge Avenue in Brooklyn, and Addie rarely visited Eunice at her several addresses in Manhattan. Mother and daughter also moved in different social circles,

Addie with her radical friends or with the ladies of Brooklyn, and Eunice among the mighty Czarinas. But Lisle Jr. spent many hours at Addie's house, reading from the large collection of books once owned by the grandfather he had never met, listening engrossed as his grandmother shared the family lore, and sitting reflectively at the famous table where John Brown did or did not plan his raid on Harpers Ferry.

The funeral was held at St. Augustine's in Brooklyn, the same Episcopal church where Eunice had been married and from which William Alphaeus Hunton Sr. had been buried. Her brother attended, but the arrangements were made by Eunice, and emphasized her side of the family. She was freezing him out. The officiant was the Reverend John Johnson of St. Martin's Episcopal Church in Manhattan, which Eunice and Lisle Sr. attended. Assisting was Addie's nephew, the Reverend Louis Berry from Montclair, New Jersey, whose brother, four decades earlier, had boarded with the Huntons in Atlanta. The active pallbearers included two judges, Hubert Delany and Myles Paige, both longtime friends of Eunice's. Another was a rising young novelist named Richard Wright, who was also an acquaintance. The other pallbearers, active and honorary, were mostly from Eunice's circle. Present to serve as one of the six honorary pallbearers was District Attorney Frank Hogan, Eunice's boss. Probably Hogan undertook this duty as a favor to Eunice; it is unlikely that he knew Addie. Of course, politics were likely involved. But given that Hogan had just recently acceded to the throne, it is not easy to tell who was trying to ingratiate with whom.

Addie, in death, continued to exert an influence on both her family and the larger community. Newspaper stories about Eunice went on at length about her mother. *Two Colored Women with the American Expeditionary Forces*, Addie's co-authored 1920 book chronicling the experiences of the black troops in World War I, was suddenly being praised by the federal government, which was recommending books portraying the role of Negro troops. There were Addie W. Hunton clubs. Years later, organizations she had founded were still honoring her.

Once Addie was buried, those "flying visits" between the siblings ceased. There was no more traveling back and forth—at least none recorded in the society pages, which watched the Hunton family's every move. So sudden was the estrangement that one wonders whether

Eunice blamed Alphaeus for their mother's death. Perhaps toward the end Addie learned of her son's sudden marriage. Perhaps Eunice only thought she had. Either way, one has difficulty resisting the conclusion that much of the later bad blood between the siblings had its origins in Eunice's belief that Alphaeus and his constant flouting of the norms for which the family stood had hastened their mother to her grave. Even an unfair sentiment is a sentiment.

True, 1943 proved a difficult year for Eunice in other ways too. In the fall, Governor Dewey decided to appoint a Negro as a judge of the City Court, nowadays known as the Civil Court. The *Times* described the post as "the highest-paid and the highest-ranking judicial job ever given to a member of the Negro race in the State and possibly in the nation." The salary was an eye-popping $17,500 a year—over $250,000 today. Eunice had been Dewey's loyal follower for almost a decade. She had paid her dues, both political and professional. She made no secret of her longing for a judgeship. But she did not get the appointment. Instead Dewey picked her rival, Francis Rivers. Eunice was stunned. If Thomas Dewey, the mentor she had supported unflinchingly, would not put her on the bench, it was unlikely that anybody else would.* Similarly, when Dewey decided to appoint a black woman as New York's secretary of labor—the first Negro ever in a governor's cabinet in the state—he chose not Eunice but veteran GOP politico Bertha J. Diggs. To be sure, Eunice made more money as a deputy assistant district attorney than she would have as a member of the cabinet. But a lucrative slot on the state Industrial Board (salary $8,500) also went to someone else. Positions in the state attorney general's office, too, were filled by other colored lawyers.

Even when she lobbied for others, Eunice was not able to get Dewey to choose her candidate. Earlier that same year, she was part of a group pressing the governor to name sports impresario Robert L. Douglas as the first-ever Negro to serve on the state's boxing commission. The *Age* described Douglas's selection as "certain." But the *Age* backed the wrong horse; and so did Eunice. Instead of Douglas, Dewey picked Cillian

---

* Back in 1940, Mayor La Guardia had also passed her over, promoting Eunice's friend Myles Paige, then a city magistrate, to be a judge in Special Sessions—the first Negro ever to serve there. Paige's promotion opened up a magistrate's spot, but Eunice was not offered that post, either.

Powell, publisher of the *Amsterdam News*, a larger paper than the *Age*, and one that had supported him consistently.

Eunice still had her moments. There she was in the *New York Times*, standing beside Mayor La Guardia as he opened the Citizens Emergency Conference on Interracial Unity, which sought to make racial justice a war aim and led directly to the establishment of what would later become the New York Human Rights Commission. (For its troubles, the conference was later labeled a Communist-front group by the House Committee on Un-American Activities.) There she was in August, seated in the front row at the annual East-West classic of the Negro baseball leagues, played, as usual, at Comiskey Park in Chicago. There she was, photographed in the paper as she partied with the likes of Carl Van Vechten and Langston Hughes. There she was, along with her husband, making the rounds of the late-season sassiety parties in Washington. There she was, immediately after, up in Baltimore, joining such luminaries as Thurgood Marshall in addressing the annual meeting of the National Bar Association. There she was, an honored guest at a reception at the Hotel Theresa for 150 members of the press. In other words, she was still doing the same things she had been doing for the past decade.

But running in circles is wasted motion. Eunice was keenly aware that in the big things—the career-building things, the ladder-climbing things—she was suddenly being left behind. The plums she had thought would be hers were being doled out as treats to others. Although she still had a seat at the banquet table, she was being crowded out. One wonders whether it could be entirely a coincidence that her Left-leaning brother, whose every move was watched by the FBI, had just that summer taken a leave of absence from his post at Howard to join the Council on African Affairs in Manhattan, a group that even the *Times*, then as now the voice of establishment liberalism, would shortly label a Communist-front organization.

Certainly Eunice thought she detected cause and effect. Although her career would in some ways continue to thrive, she would go to her grave believing that her brother's wild politics had stalled her rise in the district attorney's office and wrecked her lifelong dream of becoming a judge.

CHAPTER 18

THE CONNECTIONS

IN FEBRUARY OF 1944, A CONTROVERSY AROSE OVER FRANK CAPRA'S documentary film *The Negro Soldier.* The production was War Department propaganda, intended to persuade the darker nation to support the war effort. But once the film was screened for military officials, pressure mounted to cut it to a much shorter running time—twelve minutes rather than forty-three (originally ninety)—by removing scenes of Negro officers giving orders and white nurses caring for Negro soldiers, and by reducing to a minimum scenes of Negroes with guns. These scenes, the War Department feared, would be offensive to many whites and might even provoke race riots. At the very least, if the scenes remained, the film might hurt the war effort more than it helped. Capra, to his credit, resisted the cuts. But he was also careful to distance himself from the project in case it flopped. He might have helped produce the film, he said, but he had neither written nor directed it. The objectionable scenes were "news to me."

As the brouhaha intensified, civil rights groups got involved, prominent among them the NAACP and the National Council of Negro Women. For once, Eunice's politics were actually an aid to the organization. Jeanetta Welch Brown, executive secretary of the Council, wrote to Eunice on Mary McLeod Bethune's behalf, pleading with her to contact Wendell Willkie immediately and ask him to resist cutting the film. Willkie, the GOP's presidential candidate four years earlier, now chaired the board of Twentieth Century Fox, which, in turn, was part of the film consortium working with the Department of War. Perhaps the Pentagon would listen to him. As a leading Republican, Eunice knew Willkie well. During the 1940 election campaign, she had strongly supported the GOP ticket. She spoke on his behalf on a nationally syndicated radio program. She toured Harlem with Mrs. Willkie. So Eunice had a connection. And, indeed, soon after receiving the letter conveying Bethune's plea, Eunice wrote to Jeanetta Welch Brown from Chicago to say that she had been in touch with Willkie as requested— her letter does not say how—and that he had promised to raise the matter at a meeting of the company's board the very next day.

Negotiations continued. The dispute grew tense. Civil rights leaders also had concerns about the documentary. In particular, they disliked the suggestions that American whites and Negroes had long worked together in harmony and that colored troops were wildly cheered upon their return from World War I. They thought the film too unrealistic. They too wanted it changed. Eunice, who was still working for the district attorney, remained at the heart of the negotiations, nominally representing the National Council of Negro Women. There was a fresh problem, she reported to Bethune in mid-March. Even if they won the battle to run *The Negro Soldier* at its full length, they would face the tricky matter of persuading theater owners to exhibit the film. The fear in the industry was not that the documentary was incendiary but that it would not find an audience.

In the end, the middle ground prevailed. The film was finally released in its uncut form. The Associated Press praised the documentary for telling its story "with restraint and dignity." Alas, just as Eunice had predicted, *The Negro Soldier* performed poorly at the box office.

Nevertheless, she must have been pleased to be asked to help. Her brand of Republican traditionalism was going out of style in a darker nation growing rapidly Democratic. Yet the network of connections she had painstakingly built proved still useful to the race. Four years earlier, Wendell Willkie had been the GOP standard-bearer in the presidential race, a status that in theory made him titular head of the party.

Yet Jeanetta Welch Brown never evinced the smallest doubt that Eunice would be able to get him on the telephone. Neither did Eunice. There is no way to know whether Willkie's influence played a role in the film's ultimate release.* Nevertheless, the facts that Eunice knew how to reach him and that he took her call stand together as powerful testimony to her influence within the Republican Party.

But, of course, Mary McLeod Bethune was familiar with Eunice's talent for working both sides of the aisle, a talent that would be fully on display a bit later in the presidential campaign. When the new head-quarters of the National Council of Negro Women in Washington, D.C., was dedicated in October 1944, the guest speaker was Eleanor Roosevelt, who, after her remarks, ceremonially handed the keys not to Mrs. Bethune but to the chairman of the Council's board—Eunice. By then the hard-fought presidential campaign was in the home stretch, and the press did not miss the irony that Eunice was busily campaign-ing against Eleanor's husband: "Mrs. Carter is a Republican of national note. Mrs. Roosevelt is the wife of the Democratic President of the United States."

Actually, by this time tiny fissures were developing in Eunice's relation-ship with Mrs. Bethune, who had long been for her a sort of surrogate mother. It was at Bethune's home in Florida that Eunice had recuper-ated after her hysterectomy, and it was during their regular conversa-tions that she chose her life's course. Too, Bethune had invited Eunice (along with Addie) to the meeting at which the National Council of Negro Women was founded. Eunice had risen to chair the board, and she expected to succeed to the presidency if and when Bethune, near-ing seventy and in poor health, chose to step down. Meanwhile, the organization was habitually short of money—in 1937 the treasury held only $18.25—and Eunice often seemed to be the group's primary means of support. Out of her own pocket she made not only gifts but loans, few of which were repaid. Her constant pressure on Bethune to cut back on expenditures was the source of no small tension between them.

Despite their long history together, the two women moved in dif-

---

* A few months later Willkie had a heart attack and entered into a period of swift decline. He died in October.

Eunice, probably in the 1940s, with Mary McLeod Bethune (far right), Daisy Lampkin (second from left), and Ella Moten (left). Lampkin was a suffragist and fellow member of the National Council of Negro Women. Moten was a groundbreaking singer and actress, who in 1934 became the first African American woman to perform at the White House.

ferent worlds. It would never have occurred to Bethune to struggle up the slippery stones of the Great Social Pyramid. That was neither who she was nor what she wanted. And although Bethune's achievements made her in certain ways attractive to the Czarinas, she could never have sat among them. She came from the wrong class of people. She had been born poor. She was dark-skinned—another tragic Harlem prejudice. But she was a force with which the Czarinas had to reckon. She had been elected head of the National Association of Colored Women (co-founded by Addie) back when the group was thought to be a tool of the elite. She possessed a fine political touch. She could be a charmer. She had a considerable ego, to be sure, and what might be termed a non-indifference to praise. She could be prickly. But unlike Eunice, Bethune had little interest in surrounding herself with what used to be called the finer things in life. She was driven less by a desire to find a place on the Pyramid than by a powerful sense of mission.

These distinctions, to be sure, should not have affected the relationship between Eunice and her surrogate mother. The larger fissure was political—and, like so much in Eunice's life, it involved Alphaeus. In April 1944, Eunice had represented Mrs. Bethune and the National Council of Negro Women at a Pan-Africanist conference organized by her brother for the Council on African Affairs and held in New York City. By this time, Alphaeus had decided to remain at the CAA for the long term, even if it meant giving up his position at Howard University, which he ultimately would. Already he had become one of the organization's leading lights, with a rising profile (at least in radical circles) that excited jealousy from Max Yergan, the group's founder. Alphaeus and his third wife, Dorothy, found a place in Brooklyn, at 257 MacDonough Street. As it happened, Alphaeus was once more under FBI surveillance, and the information about his new address was duly recorded in his file. The agents did not mention that his new address was just around the corner from the townhouse at 93 Bainbridge Street, where his mother had lived out her final years. But the irony was unlikely to have been lost on Eunice.

So brother and sister were both in New York City full-time now, but their paths did not cross. Not socially. Eunice resided in Harlem and worked downtown at the municipal building on Leonard Street. Alphaeus resided in Brooklyn and worked on West Twenty-sixth Street. Neither their homes nor their offices were in close proximity. The siblings were distant now, and not only from each other. They had grown more remote from their relatives as well. When their Uncle Alexander—Addie's younger brother—died in Norfolk, neither attended the funeral.

The separation between Eunice and Alphaeus, however, could not be complete. Bethune served on the board of the Council on African Affairs, a choice that must surely have left her protégée rankled. To be fair, the CAA was at this time attracting significant support from a wide variety of the influential organizations of the darker nation. These included not only the NAACP and the National Urban League but even the venerable National Association of Colored Women. A few months later, in July of 1944, Bethune would sponsor the National Non-Partisan Political Conference in Chicago to demand the participation of the Negro leadership in structuring the postwar order. Delegates also agreed to call a future meeting of the "Darker Peoples of the World" to fight for the end of racism around the globe. But even as Bethune, Eunice's mentor and surrogate mother, inched further to the left, Eunice remained firmly within the establishment wing of the GOP, personified by her professional mentor, Thomas Dewey.

The CAA conference in April 1944 pulsed with radical energy. The black Communist leader Benjamin Davis Jr., whom the Hunton siblings had known when they were all children in Atlanta, was an enthusiastic participant. So were Francis Nkrumah (later to be known famously as Kwame Nkrumah) and Amy Ashwood Garvey, formerly wed to Marcus Garvey. This was a heady and unlikely mix for Eunice's conservative and traditionalist politics. Put aside her estrangement from her brother. Militating against even the smallest involvement in the event were her position in the district attorney's office and her ambitions, for she still longed for a judgeship. The career risk Eunice ran was not inconsiderable. That she attended anyway was likely a signal of her devotion not to Alphaeus or to Pan-Africanism but to Mary McLeod Bethune.

For the most part, Bethune returned Eunice's devotion. Whenever the National Council of Negro Women held an event, whether a conference or a panel, a fund-raising dinner or a White House tea, Eunice was always a featured speaker. This was no small thing. One cannot gainsay the importance of the Council during this era in the life of the darker nation. The Great Depression still lingered and had hit African America hardest. The movement for racial equality was sputtering, unable to breach either violent repression in the South or political intransigence in Washington. Yet here was this group of feisty colored women, stepping well beyond the usual bounds of club life to demand change at home and abroad. They somehow had entrée to the White House. Their national conferences drew thousands of delegates. African America was fascinated. The Negro press featured on the front pages the group's every meeting or statement. Bethune was a hero. And

*Eunice refusing to yield the floor at a meeting of black Republicans in Chicago in
1944. Through the group's influence, the GOP that year adopted the most progressive
civil rights platform plank of any major party up to that point in American history.*
PHOTO BY GORDON COSTER/THE LIFE PICTURE COLLECTION/GETTY IMAGES

Eunice, a front-page celebrity in her own right, was the hero's sidekick
and (everyone believed) her chosen successor.

Always shrewd about her professional opportunities, Eunice had a
clear eye on the road ahead. If by some chance things did not work out
with her legal career, Eunice had a backup plan.

Or so she thought.

When Eunice wrote to say that she had succeeded in getting in touch
with Willkie, she had just returned from Chicago. The reason for her
trip was a meeting of the Planning Committee for United Minorities, a
group of Negro Republicans pressing the party to take a tough line
against racial discrimination. GOP officials addressed the meeting.
One was Werner Schroeder, for years the shadowy hand behind Republican politics in Illinois. Eunice spoke too—the only woman to do so.
Other offices were contested, but she was elected first vice president

by acclamation. The meeting had a narrow and serious purpose. In November, the party would put up a fourth candidate against Franklin Roosevelt. The Planning Committee hoped to persuade the convention to adopt what amounted to a laundry list of strong positions on equality. What was left unspoken was their hope that the nominee would be Dewey, whom they knew to be on their side.

The Negro press followed, almost day by day, the committee's efforts to influence the GOP platform. When the convention arrived in July, the members got the candidate they wanted. This time, Dewey was better prepared. He secured the nomination with ease. The committee members got the platform plank on race that they wanted—a plank considered by far the strongest adopted up to that time by an American political party—and there again Eunice played the key role. Chicago Stadium, the site of the convention, was thick with Negro delegates and officials. Photo spreads, usually featuring Eunice, were splashed across the pages of the colored papers. She kept busy rallying support and trading horses. By reputation, she did both well. And yet there were reports of strife among Dewey's colored backers. The *Chicago Defender* named Eunice as part of a cabal trying to persuade Dewey not to name Francis Rivers, her longtime office rival, as head of his campaign among Negroes. The reasons were obscure. The fear cited in the article was that he would not do the job full-time, as he was currently on the bench and unlikely to step down. More likely, the infighting arose as a result of jockeying for power among influential Negro Republicans: Eunice felt squeezed out. In any case, the cabal failed, and Rivers remained central to Dewey's campaign.

Actually, the bickering over Rivers was a sideshow. Just before the start of the Chicago convention, Eunice was at the center of a more serious contretemps. Harrison Spangler, chairman of the Republican National Committee, wrote a letter to a subcommittee seeming to suggest that the bold GOP platform was a smokescreen, that Negro voters should not expect much after the election. The party then tried, in the hamhanded way of political organizations, to suppress Spangler's letter. Eunice fully supported the effort. "We don't want to make the letter public yet," she told a closed meeting on how to deal with the potential controversy. Her advice was to avoid the controversy by keeping the letter secret. To do otherwise, she said, would "hurt the GOP." In the way of such things, Spangler's letter wound up in the papers anyway. So did reports about the closed meeting, complete with quotations from Eunice: a small embarrassment, but for one who prided herself on a fine political instinct, an embarrassment nevertheless.

The convention also served as Lisle Jr.'s introduction to practical politics. At this time he was almost nineteen and a student at Dartmouth, where he waited tables to help pay his tuition. Eunice, who was present in Chicago not as a delegate but under the auspices of the Republican National Committee, brought her son along to show him "what a political convention is like." There might have been another reason, too. Perhaps she wanted them to spend some time together, just in case. With the war still on, Lisle Jr. was waiting to hear whether he would be called for military service. (He was, scant weeks later, but never served at the front.) Nevertheless, the convention would have been an important learning experience. Lisle Jr. would have been exposed, perhaps for the first time, to Eunice the hard-nosed political wheeler-dealer, stoic in public, forceful in private. Later on, when his own time came to enter public service, he would show a preference for quiet backroom bargaining. It is easy to imagine that he learned those skills at his mother's feet.

As the campaign neared, Dewey was brimming with confidence. He had told a reporter four years earlier that Roosevelt was "the easiest man in the world for me to beat." And Dewey had a strategy. He would court the Negro vote more explicitly and enthusiastically than had any presidential candidate of either party in the nation's history. No one had ever tried this approach: the risk of alienating white voters was too great. But for Dewey, the risk was worth taking. And so, once more, Eunice was in the thick of things, during both the primary season and the general election. She traveled the country, rallying Negroes on his behalf. On the campaign trail, Dewey repeatedly used her name to show his commitment to racial equality. Unsurprisingly, he pressed the point particularly with black audiences. In an interview with the *Chicago Defender*, he pointed out that his wife, a Texan, had "entertained at dinner Eunice Hunton Carter"—a social act, he said, that "would not

Eunice and her only child, Lisle Jr., probably around 1941, when he was in his teens. He had spent most of the previous six years in Barbados.

be acceptable to the south." In St. Louis, Dewey told a group of colored Republicans that in selecting Eunice and also Francis Rivers, he had simply "appointed people because they were good and merited it and not because of their race, color or creed." The GOP bought advertisements in Negro papers touting his black appointees, Eunice prominent among them. But the mainstream press also noticed. White journalists repeatedly warned the Democrats that they were in danger of losing black voters. The *Philadelphia Inquirer*, in explaining why, pointed to Eunice's appointment as the "first Negro woman in the country to actually function as a prosecuting attorney."

The Dewey campaign came along at the right moment for the darker nation—in particular, for the darker nation's journalists. Even as rank-and-file Negro voters were deserting the GOP in droves, black newspapers were fighting a humiliating battle to have their reporters permitted at the President's press conferences. They lost. Roosevelt's apologists blame the White House Correspondents' Association, which controlled credentials and was determined to stay lily-white. But the President or his press secretary could easily have forced a change. They chose not to. The outcome was belittling, a reminder of the true order of things: mainstream papers could get their people in, but the Negro press could not. And petty discriminations were not atypical of the Roosevelt administration. The President had rejected repeated advice to act decisively on race, including entreaties from his wife. Calls by his own supporters for desegregation of the armed forces he rejected as "destructive to morale" in the midst of war. Last time around—just weeks, in fact, before the 1940 election—the White House had issued a statement implying that Walter White of the NAACP agreed with the policy. This was a blatant lie. But preserving segregation in the military helped the Democrats secure, for yet another cycle, the Solid South. Over and over, Roosevelt proved himself willing to trade racial justice for Dixiecrat electoral votes.

One might reply that this made him no different from anyone else in the era, if not for the fact that during the 1944 campaign, Dewey courted the Negro vote so assiduously. He had carried Harlem, now a Democratic stronghold, in his 1942 gubernatorial campaign. Surely his appeal would be every bit as great on the national stage. True, colored voters were expected to go heavily for Roosevelt, but Dewey had hopes of luring some away—and *some* would be enough. "If only a small fraction of the Negroes shift away from the Democrats," wrote *Life* magazine, "this may be enough to give Republicans victory." And so Dewey did everything he could to signal voters of the darker nation that he was on their side. No candidate had ever attempted so radical a strategy. But Dewey plunged right in. He met publicly with the head of one civil rights organization after another. A West Virginia audience gave him a standing ovation when he accused Roosevelt of remaining "cynically silent" on racial equality while "relying for his main support upon a solid block of votes in States where millions of American citizens are denied their right to vote by the poll tax and by intimidation." When Dewey learned that the Dixiecrats were circulating throughout the South a photograph of himself with leaders of the darker nation, he added a caption—"Dewey Attends Negro Cocktail Party"—and ordered his staff to "flood Harlem with copies." (Governor Olin D. Johnston of South Carolina, who would be elected to the Senate in the fall, turned the trick around again, charging that Dewey had attended "a Negro drinking party.")

Dewey offered more than photo ops. He promised nearly every-thing the civil rights leadership wanted, the same list on which Frank-lin Roosevelt had never acted: A federal anti-lynching law. A Fair Employment Practices Committee with actual power to act against dis-crimination. An end to the poll tax. Negroes appointed to high offices. As governor, his supporters noted, he had proclaimed Negro History Week—in those days, no small thing. That fall, however, about as many Negro papers went for Roosevelt as for Dewey. (The white papers went overwhelmingly for Dewey.) Still, Dewey supporters could take heart from a survey by the National Negro Council purporting to show that he had the backing of some 72 percent of black voters in the North. The methodology was shaky, but the poll received extensive coverage.

As the campaign intensified, Eunice continued her tireless efforts on Dewey's behalf. Her name kept showing up beside his, even in the white press. "[W]hen he was special prosecutor," editorialized the pro-Dewey *New York Herald Tribune*, "one of his most trusted assistants was Mrs. Eunice Carter, a Negro woman." And although she supported her candidate and her party on the merits of their positions, she could hardly be unaware that should Dewey win the election, hundreds of federal posts would suddenly be within his gift. After all her labor, her reward would surely be considerable. And if by some chance he were to lose? Well, there was always 1948, and, in the meanwhile, judgeships and other plums were available in New York, too.

However enthusiastic Eunice's opinion of Dewey, her brother viewed the Republican nominee with undisguised contempt. In the summer of 1944, immediately after the convention, Alphaeus penned a scathing unsigned editorial in the journal *New Africa*, which he edited:

> What principally characterizes the foreign policy section of
> the Republican platform is a short-sighted, reactionary, and
> dangerous Americans-for-America spirit. . . .

The fury in Alphaeus's words might easily have been directed at Eunice. By this time, her brother's transition to a doctrinaire commu-nism was complete. He entirely lacked faith in the democratic system.

And, as we shall see, he may have been running little errands for intelligence officers on the staff of the Soviet consulate. Perhaps he was not even thinking of Eunice when he wrote about Dewey. But his words, however intended, implicitly accused his sister of wasting her life.

Lest he be misunderstood, on the eve of the election Alphaeus once more used the pages of *New Africa* to blast his sister's mentor: "On November 7 Americans will decide whether this country is to turn its back upon international cooperation and instead launch a new American imperialism." Nor was Alphaeus alone. Much of the traditional leadership of the race remained staunchly Republican, but the black Left had turned sharply Democratic. Mary McLeod Bethune was openly for Roosevelt. Addie's old friend Du Bois was passionate in his support. He argued that rather than choosing which party might be better on civil rights, the darker nation should vote against "the party of Big Business"—that is, the Republicans. (In today's terms, Du Bois was arguing that Negroes should ignore the social issues and vote their pocketbooks.) Eunice's friend Walter White, whom she had known since her Atlanta childhood, had, like most race leaders, backed Willkie in 1940. But he found Dewey "insufferable." Negro journalists, too, were among the skeptics. In an editorial, the *Chicago Defender* accused Negroes who supported the GOP of "shameful, myopic vision." The black appointments Dewey always bragged about, sniffed the paper in a news story, were mainly to jobs "large salaried but inconsequential." A columnist for the *Philadelphia Tribune* charged Eunice and other Negro Republican supporters with "playing the role of Quisling" because they allegedly remained silent while Dewey courted Southern whites.

The charges may have been absurd, but it is hard to see how Eunice could fail to take them personally.

The election was not even close. In the popular vote, Dewey lost by just under 4 million votes out of nearly 48 million cast—to be sure, a smaller margin of defeat than any of Roosevelt's three previous opponents, but still huge. The President's margin in the electoral college was as daunting as usual: 432–99.* The South had made noises about deserting the

---

* The 1944 election marked the fourth time in a row that Roosevelt crossed the 400-electoral-vote

President, but on Election Day Roosevelt swept the Jim Crow region for the fourth consecutive election: another white landslide. Even the strong racial equality plank that Eunice had fought so hard to get into the Republican platform was held against her candidate. When Dewey gave a speech to the effect that government power should not be used to set one race against another, the House majority leader, John W. McCormack of Massachusetts, shot back that the remarks were "reprehensible" because they injected race into the campaign. The subtext, intended for swing voters, was that race was a matter too troublesome and incendiary to discuss. (Again, today we would call this one of the "social issues.")

Democrats hammered Dewey on this point: by calling for racial equality, the GOP candidate was being divisive. At the same time, they accused him of cynicism for courting Northern Negroes and Southern whites at the same time. In a speech to a packed Harlem ballroom on election eve, Secretary of the Interior Harold Ickes accused Dewey of walking "hand in hand with the most vindictive enemies of the Negroes." True, the Democrats were doing exactly the same, but more effectively. The attacks worked. Roosevelt carried the Solid South and lost few Negro voters in the North. In the end, Dewey did not even carry New York, where he sat in the governor's mansion. Yet in defeat he seemed cheerfully undeterred. According to Arthur Vandenberg, Dewey had told him that he had actually hoped not to be nominated: "I was not going to be one of those unhappy men who yearned for the presidency and whose failure to get it scarred their lives." Dewey scarcely took a break, but plunged right back into his duties as governor.

For Eunice, the defeat was harder. Perhaps she had been infected by her mentor's optimism about his chances. Perhaps she had read the same tea leaves as everyone else and had known all along that the Chief had no chance. Either way, the result was the same: she had hitched her wagon to Dewey's star, only to see him fall from the sky. True, there was nothing odd in her decision to back her mentor. At that time, the most prominent Negroes were still overwhelmingly Republicans. The enormous support of the black masses for FDR was a new development, one

---

line. In the seventy-plus years since, the feat has been accomplished by only one Democratic presidential nominee—Lyndon Johnson in 1964.

that leaders of Eunice's generation had trouble fathoming and to which they were still adjusting.

The newspapers of the darker nation noticed the gap and mocked those who, like Eunice, were on the losing side. "Dr. Bethune Sole Survivor of Women's 'Old Guard' for FDR," proclaimed the *Atlanta Daily World* in a front-page headline, adding, "Most Other Oldtimers Were Aboard Gov. Dewey's Wagon." The article began, "The womens [sic] vote was one of the most important factors in the presidential election last week. Only one of the women identified with the older leadership among Negroes, however, was out working for Roosevelt, the victor. She was Mrs. Mary McLeod Bethune."

The next paragraph was less laudatory: "Practically every other woman whose name is nationally known, were Republicans." The piece went on to list the prominent members of the "old guard" who had backed Dewey—among them Mary Church Terrell, Nannie Burroughs, Crystal Bird Fauset, and, of course, Eunice Carter. The author then pointed to the rising generation, younger black clubwomen who were Democrats. Among them were Dorothy Height and Edith Sampson. Like Bethune, they had chosen the winning side.

Eunice had not. For one of the few times in her swift rise, she had miscalculated. And, at age forty-five, been labeled an "old-timer" to boot.

The darker nation had changed. Negro papers that had been staunchly Republican were suddenly running front-page stories about the doings of the local Democratic clubs. And Dewey, for all of his progressive racial politics, had scarcely dented Roosevelt's Negro support. The President had used his adroit political balance to keep peace with the South while bestowing just enough patronage on African America. Studies of the 1944 returns have suggested that had he carried the black vote in the North, Dewey would have won the election. But every election is decided by ifs.

In January of 1945, two months after the presidential election, Eunice resigned from the district attorney's office. Some part of her decision doubtless involved frustration at Hogan's diminution of her duties. And perhaps the work itself was beginning to weigh on her. In one case, a lawyer objected to his twelve-year-old client's being held in an adult jail while awaiting trial for a fatal stabbing. The judge kept the defendant where he was after Eunice investigated and reported that the boy "was being properly cared for." And, remarkably, in an office now spilling over with deputy assistant district attorneys by the score, unsolicited letters complaining about houses of prostitution were still being routed to her desk. No doubt Eunice would have preferred still to be running litigation in Special Sessions. But if wishes were horses, she would also have preferred to be riding off to Washington as part of a new Dewey administration. Those possibilities were gone.

Eunice still enjoyed professional standing and prestige, but her day-to-day life as a deputy assistant district attorney had become desultory. By the time she resigned, she was already living much of her professional life outside the office. She addressed conferences on racial equality organized by federal agencies. She sat on bar committees with the likes of Thurgood Marshall and sat down with industrialists to talk about how to enhance the role of women in the workplace now that the war was winding down and the men were coming home. On a résumé, all of this would be impressive. But it was not what Eunice had hoped to be doing. Her work no longer satisfied her itch to advance, and her prospects within the office were nil. Walking through the door had become a daily humiliation.

Still, she had her hopes. In March 1945, shortly after Eunice resigned, the New York legislature passed the Ives-Quinn bill, establishing the nation's first civil rights commission with actual power to investigate and punish discrimination on the basis of race, color, creed, or national origin. Each member of the commission would receive $10,000 annually, a princely sum for the era. The *Crisis* lauded the measure as "a signal victory in the fight for economic equality." After a brief hesitation, Dewey had invested considerable political capital in persuading skeptical Republican legislators to support the legislation. He had faced down business lobbyists who argued that Ives-Quinn would drive industry and jobs out of the state. Now the bill was law, and it was time for the governor to select the members. Eunice had publicly fought for the bill's passage. The *New York Times* named her as a likely appointee. But, once again, Dewey cast his eye elsewhere.

Was Eunice disappointed? No doubt. Although Hogan had failed to promote her, Dewey owed her. Yet here, as with the missed judgeship, she assigned the blame not to her mentor Dewey but to her Communist brother, whose politics were day by day bringing him further into the public eye. Dewey was known to be close to FBI Director J. Edgar Hoover. There is no telling what warnings might have passed between the two of them. Before Alphaeus left Howard for the Council on African Affairs, Hoover had lobbied behind the scenes, albeit unsuccessfully, to have him fired from what was, after all, a federally funded institution. Alphaeus's name also remained on the Bureau's Custodial Detention list, a special category reserved for individuals targeted for immediate arrest in the event of a national security emergency. Hoover probably would have said just enough to make Dewey realize that the second run for President he planned for 1948 would not be helped should he pick Eunice for a high post only to have her brother's case blow up in his face. Better not to take the risk. And so an appointment for Eunice was out.

Yet the loyalty that had guided so much of her life had not gone away. Just as she stuck with her husband after he cheated, she would stick with Dewey despite his betrayal. Possibly this was a matter as well of cool, calculating ambition. Eunice knew that Dewey planned to make another run at the White House. If he won in 1948, there was still time for her to cash in her chips. And if that turned out not to work, there was still the backup plan.

She hoped.

CHAPTER 19

THE DEFEAT

In the spring of 1945, with the war nearing its end, diplomats from around the world convened in San Francisco for the conference that would establish the United Nations. Eunice entrained for the West Coast along with Mary McLeod Bethune and Dorothy Ferebee, Bethune's personal physician. They would join representatives from forty-six countries to work out the final details for the proposed new international body.

Here a problem arose. The United States government understood the need for Negro representation at the conference, but refused to appoint any black delegates. Instead the State Department authorized the NAACP to choose three "consultants." The NAACP in turn selected Walter White, its secretary; W. E. B. Du Bois, its head of research; and Mary McLeod Bethune, who in addition to running the National Council of Negro Women served as one of several Association vice presidents. Informally, this meant that the only Negro groups represented by official observers at the creation of the United Nations were the NAACP and the National Council of Negro Women. The problem arose because much of the darker nation saw both organizations as essentially clubs for the elite, with little room for the voices or concerns of ordinary colored folk—that is, they saw the groups in much the same way that Harlemites had once seen Eunice. Consequently, the leaders of a large number of Negro organizations left out of the conference also converged on San Francisco. This group, comprising mainly religious and fraternal organizations, held a series of meetings at the Third Baptist Church to adopt resolutions criticizing the composition of the official delegation and demanding that the United Nations Charter include an explicit denunciation of colonialism. Du Bois addressed the group, seeking to reassure its members that the official consultants shared their concerns. Eunice, along with Bethune and Ferebee, attended at least one of these alternative sessions in early May. A surviving photograph shows the three of them outside the Third Baptist Church.

It is difficult to exaggerate the importance of the San Francisco Conference to the darker nation. From small Southern towns to big Northern cities, the air seemed to crackle with a palpable excitement. In the colored imagination, the United Nations would in some way smite the race bar at home and the oppression of Africa abroad. All across the country, black organizations large and small held meetings, drafted resolutions, signed petitions, and raised money to send their representatives to San Francisco. If all the darker nation went, surely the rest of the world could not ignore the honest plea for simple justice.

Much of what has been written about Eunice asserts that she was present in San Francisco as an official observer for the National Council of Negro Women. She was not. Neither was Bethune, who insisted that she was in San Francisco to represent "the colored women of America." Although some press accounts were confused even at the time, most correctly identified Bethune as a representative of the NAACP. Walter White made heavy weather of this point, facing down the formidable Mrs. Bethune and reminding her that she was there only as part of the NAACP delegation. Du Bois would later write to Arthur Spingarn that Bethune had been "rather a nuisance but a harmless one." Eunice had no official status at all.

At least White and the others thought she didn't. But they reckoned without the Hunton fortitude. Because Eunice, unofficial or not, attended most of the conference sessions, sometimes in Bethune's place. After Bethune left for home, Eunice stayed on in San Francisco. She continued to attend the United Nations conference, waltzing into meetings as if she belonged. Outside the formal sessions, she became co-sponsor of a caucus called the League of Races, an effort to unite "the darker races and smaller nations of the world." Representatives of various countries joined Eunice and other Negro leaders from the United States at a series of three banquets, each held at a fancy hotel. It does not appear that NAACP officials attended; most likely they were not invited.

In June, Eunice took time off from her labors to head down to Los Angeles for the annual Interracial Film and Radio Guild Unity Awards dinner, where on behalf of the group she presented an award to keynote speaker Orson Welles. (Other honorees at the event included Lena Horne and Bette Davis.) Afterward she returned to the San Francisco Conference.

Where there was no earthly reason to allow her back in.

Yet somehow Eunice managed to gain reentry to the conference, where she continued representing the National Council of Negro Women (which was not an official observer), taking the place of Mrs. Bethune (who had been chosen by the NAACP and was not permitted a substitute). Perhaps Eunice worked her way in by charm or cleverness or simply the good graces of the other delegates. Perhaps Eleanor Roosevelt or another of Eunice's influential friends pulled a string or two. But what more likely was at work was the Hunton fortitude: the same fortitude her father had displayed half a century ago when he talked the railway conductor out of sending him and his wife to sit in the colored train car.

As 1946 dawned, the signal achievement of Eunice's career was turned upside down. Governor Thomas E. Dewey, the man she had helped convict Lucky Luciano, commuted the mobster's thirty-to-fifty-year prison sentence, contingent on his agreement to allow himself to be deported. The commutation came after heavy pressure from federal officials, in return for assistance Luciano was said to have rendered during the war. From his prison cell, Luciano was reported to have contacted associates on behalf of the United States Office of Naval Intelligence to end labor strife on the docks. He was also said to have given the military information on leaders of the Sicilian Mafia who might be helpful when the Allies invaded the island. The press took these claims at face value. Even as he set Luciano free, Dewey admitted to skepticism about the basis for the release, pointing out that "the actual value of the information procured is not clear." His doubts were well-founded. Luciano's contribution to the war effort would later turn out to have been greatly exaggerated. The commutation would come back to haunt the governor in his reelection campaign. He would be forced to deny charges that he had been duped by organized crime figures who had built up Luciano's war record.

What Eunice thought of Dewey's decision is not recorded. Probably she was too busy to give the matter much thought. By this time, she had reopened her legal practice. She commuted every weekday to a dark, vaguely baroque building at 516 Fifth Avenue, on the corner of Forty-third Street, a rabbit warren housing everything from remailing services to the American Research Bureau to the City-Wide Citizens Committee on Harlem. U.S. Airlines, a freight carrier, had space there. So did the World Children's Foundation, which, despite its impressive-sounding name, was a one-woman shop dedicated to finding homes for "wild oats" babies—children of black American soldiers and British mothers. At the same address one could stop in at the American War Blinded Veterans, which would turn out to be a fraud.

Opening her own law office had been a bold move when Eunice had first done so, back in the 1930s. It was only slightly less bold now. There are no figures for 1946, but four years later, in 1950, there would be 31,707 male lawyers in New York State. There would be 1,275 female lawyers in New York State. There would be 19 Negro women lawyers in New York State. Put otherwise, black women constituted about six ten-thousandths (0.06 percent) of all the state's lawyers, a proportion so small that it is less a minority than a rounding error. But Eunice had faced worse odds the first time around and still managed to make her way. Besides, she was nothing if not bold. The trick now would be to play on her earlier celebrity and begin to collect clients.

She also expected to have a junior associate join her practice soon: her son. After finishing his studies at Dartmouth in 1944, Lisle Jr. had gone into the army. With the war over, he was granted early discharge in 1946. He worked for a while as a restaurant inspector for the city, then entered St. John's School of Law. Eunice had wanted Lisle Jr. to go somewhere else—perhaps Fordham, as she had, perhaps one of the

Ivies—but he'd refused to consider the idea. A family tale holds that Lisle Jr. preferred studying in Queens because he was courting a young lady. And perhaps Eunice was not, after all, unhappy with her son's choice to remain in the city. He had returned from the war safely when many others had not. Better still, he had chosen to live at home, meaning that his mother could see him often.

But home was no longer 409 Edgecombe Avenue. In the summer of 1946, Eunice and her husband had purchased an elegant townhouse at Number 10 Jumel Terrace; when Lisle Jr. moved back home following his military service, he occupied the basement apartment.

Jumel Terrace was a short, lovely cobbled lane running south to north between 160th and 162nd Streets, technically just north of Harlem, although many Negroes came to see it as the highest point in Sugar Hill. On the southeast side of the street was the mansion occupied in the early nineteenth century by Eliza Jumel, said to have been the wealthiest woman in the country. Across from the mansion stood a row of tall, fancy townhouses dating from the turn of the century. Number 10, constructed in 1899 in the Romanesque Revival style, had last been sold in 1917 to Gustav Scholer, a physician and alienist who served for some years as the city coroner, and whose testimony at several sensational murder trials early in the twentieth century had made him something of a celebrity.

Eunice and Lisle were fortunate to get the house. Racially restrictive covenants had begun to appear in Harlem shortly before World War I, part of the last-ditch effort to keep the neighborhood white. Harlem's racial complexion had changed sharply since the townhouses were built, but Jumel Terrace had remained a bastion of whiteness as the darker nation swarmed around it. The Carters were the first Negro family to buy on the street. Most of the other townhouses were encumbered with racial covenants, but—probably because it had not changed hands in nearly three decades—Number 10 was not.

The sale closed in July of 1946, at a price of $10,500. The seller was the German Society of the City of New York, which had received it by devise from Scholer's widow, Emma, earlier that year. Even accounting for inflation, the price was a steal—a mere $139,000 in 2017 dollars. The value of the house had fallen enormously over the preceding three decades. But the neighborhood was changing fast, and was about to start changing faster.

After purchasing the property, Lisle and Eunice immediately hired architect Frank B. Dorman (who happened to be white), and on December 3 filed plans for a $5,000 renovation. There is some reason to think that Emma Scholer had fallen on hard times after her husband's death—a friend had moved in, and evidently the two women shared expenses—and it is possible that the house was in disrepair. In any case, the work was swiftly completed, and the Carters occupied their new home early in 1947. The restored mansion had nearly four thousand square feet of floor space, not counting the basement. There was a walled garden in the rear, and finely turned wood inlays were every-where. The master suite and the other front rooms enjoyed a view out across Jumel Terrace to the famous manor house and its gently sloping grounds.

Eunice immediately set about entertaining. Her receptions drew raves. The Negro press referred to the house as a "manse." Events at 10 Jumel quickly became de rigueur for what the *Amsterdam News* called the "social register names" of the darker nation. The most sought-after invitation each year was to what the society pages gleefully labeled Eunice's annual "beeg, beeg Christmas party at her Jumel Terrace house in Upper Manhattan [on] Christmas Eve." Each winter's event, gushed the columnists, was expected to be "bigger and better . . . if that's possible."

Bit by bit Eunice and Lisle had moved up in the world, geographi-cally as well as socially. They had moved from apartment to apartment, each address more prestigious than the last. Finally they had reached 409 Edgecombe Avenue, the summit of sassiety. Now they were the first Negroes to occupy the peak of Sugar Hill, the highest point in Harlem. They had made it, literally, to the top.

And for Eunice, even that was not enough.

Eunice's ambition continued to burn. She remained heavily involved in GOP politics, even attending meetings of the Republican National Committee. But politics did not pay the bills. Worried that she would not earn enough from the practice of law, Eunice sought other sources of income. By 1946, she was attending meetings of the National Negro

Publishers Association. A year later, she partnered with journalist and businessman Ernest E. Johnson to form Carter-Johnson Associates, a public relations firm specializing in outreach to the darker nation. The Negro press predicted that the new firm would "be a whale of a success." Eunice did not abandon her legal practice; in fact, Carter-Johnson shared space with her law office. The firm swiftly picked up several substantial pieces of business, including a rumored $10,000 consulting fee from the National Council of Negro Women. The National Negro Newspaper Publishers Association agreed to pay the company for a "minimum program." A Carter-Johnson survey of minority news outlets was covered by *Billboard* magazine. The press suggested that Eunice, on some of her trips abroad, was hunting for business. Some bits and pieces came in. But in the end, bits and pieces were not enough. After a strong start, the firm would dissolve in October of 1948, just over a year after opening. The partners would keep working in public relations, but separately. Said Johnson: "It didn't work out, that's all. It's not like a marriage that you can't break up, you know."

Or like siblings. Sometimes that doesn't work out, either.

For a long time, the legal problems besetting other leading radicals of the era had passed Eunice's brother by. Now the circle was closing. So was the nation's mind. Across the country, states were creating their own versions of the House Committee on Un-American Activities. Portraits of leftists were coming down. Groups on the attorney general's list of subversive organizations could no longer rent most venues for their meetings or rallies. In 1949, eleven leaders of the Communist Party went on trial for the crime of being eleven leaders of the Communist Party. The Council on African Affairs, where for the past several years Alphaeus had served as executive director and leading light, was slowly drowning beneath the McCarthyist wave. The liberals on the board (including Mary McLeod Bethune) had fled, and the radicals who remained were fighting nasty and very public internecine battles. The Jefferson School of Social Science, the Communist-run educational center where Alphaeus offered evening classes, was being so closely monitored by federal investigators that the registrar had stopped recording the names of students, assigning them numbers instead. Alphaeus's friend and colleague W. E. B. Du Bois would soon be indicted on dubious but serious charges of failing to register as a foreign agent. Yet for all of this, Alphaeus himself somehow remained unmolested. (Except that he remained on Hoover's secret list of those to be detained in an emergency.)

By this time he and Eunice were barely in touch, and small wonder. She was Republican and traditionalist, whereas her brother had become a well-known activist and Communist. He was being noticed, moreover, not just by the nation's radical Left but by the radical Right as well. Writing in the *Chicago Tribune*, an official of the conservative Church League of America described him as "a Negro who has been associated with various 'fronts' and is one of the writers for the Communist Daily Worker." But Alphaeus had long ago ceased worrying about what people thought of him. In the Council's hard-left magazine *New Africa*, which he edited, Alphaeus argued that Truman's policy on aid to Europe was intended to stop Russia while opening up Africa to exploitation by American capitalists. The only just way to develop the world, he concluded, was under the aegis of the United Nations, with the involvement of "the major powers, including the Soviet Union." Truman saw the Marshall Plan as a bulwark against communism; Alphaeus saw the United Nations as a bulwark against America. When the NAACP nevertheless endorsed the Marshall Plan, Alphaeus turned his ire on its leaders—most of them close friends of his sister's.

The Federal Bureau of Investigation was not entirely sure what to make of him. Throughout the 1940s, files on Alphaeus were opened and closed repeatedly without any clear design. More than once, agents reminded each other that his sister worked for Dewey. Possibly this was a warning to tread with care. Several times the New York field office promised to follow his activities and make a report, but the organized surveillance was at best intermittent. Agents kept a brief watch on his mail, abandoned as unproductive, and a brief tap on his phone, which also seems to have led nowhere. (Alphaeus's file includes the transcript of only a single innocuous conversation about a meeting, in the course of which he largely limits his replies to "Yes" and "No"—probably because he guessed correctly that the Bureau was listening.)

Looking back from the Internet age, one has trouble appreciating the difficulties the FBI faced in developing information. Agents complained in their memoranda that they had learned from neighbors that "the subject" had remarried but they could not ascertain the name of his new wife. They needed informants in order to discover Alphaeus's home address and where he was employed. The agents interviewed the postman and the local credit bureau to no avail. To learn what Alphaeus was working on, they would buy copies of the *Daily Worker* and clip out his essays—or even retype them afresh, word for word. Their researches were extensive, but in the end they found only the innocuous. They managed to establish that Alphaeus was a Communist, but found no evidence that he was an important one. In 1947, the investigation was closed once more.

A year later, the Bureau's interest suddenly revived. According to an informant, in August 1947 (the very month when his sister announced with great hoopla the founding of Carter-Johnson Associates), Alphaeus was involved in a curious incident. Pavel Fedosimov, formerly the Soviet consul in Washington, asked him "to prepare a report concerning the treatment of the Negro both in the United States and Africa." Ten days later, Alphaeus was summoned to the Soviet consulate in New York to meet with several officials, among them Fedosimov and Jacob Lomakin, the consul general.* (Fedosimov was an agent of the NKVD, the Soviet intelligence organization, as very likely was Lomakin.) Lomakin told Alphaeus that the report was too long. They needed "a more brief and concise document." With the help of an aide at the Council on African Affairs, Alphaeus provided the shorter memorandum, which was used by the Soviet delegation at the United Nations to attack the United States and Britain for "imperialism and discrimination against Negroes."

One must take the story with a grain of salt. Even the FBI memorandum uses the word "allegedly." No American in the postwar years would lightly meet with Soviet diplomats, least of all at the consulate, which was under constant surveillance. But the tale is consistent with

---

* This is the same Lomakin who the following year would be expelled from the United States after leading the raid that kidnapped Oksana Kasenkina, a schoolteacher and would-be defector, from an upstate New York farm for Soviet dissidents. His team would drive her back to the city and refuse to allow anyone into the consulate to visit her. Kasenkina would finally, and dramatically, escape Soviet custody by leaping from a third-floor window of the consulate in an apparent suicide attempt.

Alphaeus's character. At the height of the Cold War, he would not have hesitated an instant either to attend the meeting or to provide the report, the contents of which appear to have been entirely consistent with what he said publicly and often. Moreover, if we concede that Alphaeus was indeed a dedicated Stalinist, on easy terms with the leaders of the CPUSA and perhaps even secretly one of them, he would have been the obvious person for the Soviets to ask for the report. The reader might object that the same information could be gleaned from the press, and there would be no need to involve Alphaeus. Any assistant could have produced the same work. But that is a non sequitur. An American would do the best job, an American Negro better still—and which American Negro should the NKVD have asked instead? The Soviets had no reason to hesitate to seek his help, and they might well have believed, given the depth of his knowledge and the force of his writing, that he would do the best job. And of course it's possible that Alphaeus, like many a true believer, was performing little tasks for the Soviets already.

Nevertheless, in the end there was not enough meat to satisfy the hunger of Hoover's men. After adding two memoranda about the meeting at the consulate, the Bureau closed Alphaeus's file yet again. He was still considered a small fry.

This status would soon change.

Eunice, at this time, was busily pursuing her backup plan. With the failure of Carter-Johnson Associates, she had become more and more the strong right hand on which her mentor Mary McLeod Bethune relied in running the National Council of Negro Women, and she was still expected to succeed to the throne one day. But tensions had begun to develop. By the mid-1940s Eunice had risen to become chairman of the executive committee and of the board. ("Chairman" is what the position was called.) She had also become a key financial backer, making frequent contributions and even advancing loans, because the coffers of the NCNW were often empty. Bethune, moreover, had a tendency to make lavish promises that the organization's finances could not support. She believed that God would provide, and so she would make commitments to staff or to outsiders without worrying about where the money might come from. Eunice, along with fellow attorney Edith

Sampson, led the faction of the board that kept pressing Bethune to scale back her vision. Bethune, in turn, came to resent the constant reminders that the cupboard was bare.

Early in 1947, these tensions came to a head when the NCNW laid off two employees—both of whom happened to be members of the United Office and Professional Workers of America. The UOPWA, chartered by the Congress of Industrial Organizations, was a racially integrated union of clerical workers, and it would come down hard in the anti-Communist era a few years later. The union had a reputation for radicalism. Members were accused of illegal secondary boycotts. In short, the UOPWA was not a group to be trifled with. And, predictably, it responded with fury to the layoffs. Stories in the colored press, almost certainly planted, accused the NCNW's leadership (that is, Bethune) of feathering its own nest—for example, with expensive overseas travel— while refusing to pay a fair wage.

Eunice took charge of the settlement negotiations. One has the sense that she took charge of most things, instinctively. She met with Joseph H. Levy, the union's international vice president, a hard-liner known for the contrarian position that nonprofits could best perform their charitable functions by paying high salaries. The result was an amicable letter signed by both parties, in which the union accepted that the employees had been laid off only because of the NCNW's "critical financial position" and the Council agreed that members of its staff were free to join the UOPWA if they chose. The press gave Eunice full credit for the successful resolution of the crisis. Bethune was hardly mentioned—an omission she likely noticed.

And resented.

The relationship between the two women remained cordial on the surface, but deep tensions were developing. In autumn of 1947, Mrs. Bethune was scheduled to travel to Paris to represent the NCNW at the triennial conference of the International Council of Women, after which she would travel through Europe on related business. Word came that she was too ill to make the trip. Eunice, as chairman of the executive committee, would go to France in Bethune's stead. Actually, the change represented a significant savings. The NCNW had planned to cover travel expenses for Bethune and Dorothy Ferebee. Eunice, however, was able to pay her own way—neither the first nor the last time she would go abroad on Council business at her own expense. Given that she reasonably expected to run the organization one day, such an investment was perfectly sensible. But Bethune would later hold the trip against her, perhaps because, according to the gossip columns, she was not ill at all: she was simply embarrassed to be caught spending so many of the NCNW's scarce dollars on overseas junkets. (We'll come back to this trip in a moment.) There had already been some tension between the women over Ferebee's role. Eunice had expressed concern that the NCNW, by leasing space to Ferebee for her medical practice, was endangering the group's tax-exempt status.

Eunice's trip to Europe in Bethune's place was a grand success. She impressed her new colleagues at the International Council of Women, so much so that the following year she would be Europe-bound once more, this time as a representative of the International Council itself at a United Nations conference of nongovernmental organizations in Geneva. After that she would continue on to a meeting of the Council of the World Union of Peace Organizations, of which she had somehow managed to get herself elected as treasurer. This was no small deal: in 1949, Sir John Boyd Orr, president of the World Union, would go on to win the Nobel Peace Prize.

It would be a mistake to suppose that all of this was accomplished because of the happenstance of Mary McLeod Bethune's falling ill in 1947. Rather, what we are seeing is Eunice's partially successful reinvention. Of course, some accident had to occur to provide the opportunity for her talent and determination to come to the fore. But the accident need not have involved Mrs. Bethune. Eunice's ambition had her always on the lookout for opportunity. Once she had determined to point her life toward the international arena, something would have turned up.

And even what we might think of as Eunice's day work slowly began to take on an international flavor. The press reported that Eunice was now practicing international law. And she somehow met Simone Sohier-Brunard, a Belgian who was the head of the Union des Femmes Coloniales (Union of Colonial Women). The union was not an organization of women from European colonies; it was an organization of European women interested in improving the status of women in the colonies. In 1947, Mme. Sohier-Brunard hired Carter-Johnson Associates to plan a guided tour of America so that she might learn about the lives of Negroes in the United States.

Around this time, Eunice gave an interview to the *New York Age*. The article described her as "quite a striking lady—very regal—and with the sort of personality that makes her a very delightful and charming person." This is a theme that runs through accounts of her life going back to the 1920s. The word "regal" appears not infrequently. Eunice was, to use the old terms, cultured and mannered. Her diction was always precise. Despite her occasional bouts of temper, no one ever accused Eunice of letting her hair down, even among friends. She was not so much tightly wound as carefully withheld. She did not so much look down on others as stand apart from them.

This attitude, although perhaps off-putting to her fellow Americans, likely was key to her ability to win influence abroad, particularly among Europeans, who warmed to this cool, well-dressed, articulate Negro who spoke excellent German and more than passable French as they had never warmed to Mrs. Bethune. One might even suppose (as the mercurial Bethune probably did) that Eunice, in dealing with the International Council of Women, had not so much represented her as replaced her.

In May 1948, before leaving for Europe for the follow-on conference of the International Council of Women in Geneva, Eunice threw a party for friends in her suite aboard the *Queen Mary*. She liked to live lavishly. By most accounts, the standard she demanded was often somewhat above even the comfortable income she and her husband earned. By 1948, of course, Eunice was no longer a prosecutor, and she was probably earning less in her combined private practice of law and public relations than she had in government service. Put otherwise, although she and her husband had a smaller income than when she had been a prosecutor, Eunice insisted on maintaining the same lifestyle as they had before—or perhaps an even more elaborate one.

And that taste included her living arrangements.

Which brings us back to that trip to Paris in the autumn of 1947, the one where Eunice replaced Mrs. Bethune, due to either illness or fear of scandal. Before Eunice left the country, her husband, Lisle, gave her a bon voyage party, reported in the columns to be "one of those 'like old times' affairs when the Carters used to have the gang often in the apartment they used to have at 409 Edgecombe Avenue." It was as though, with the move to Jumel Terrace, Eunice no longer entertained "the gang"; now it was formal parties and exclusive guest lists—a busy yet lonely existence.

Right around the time Eunice departed for Europe, her brother was suddenly news again—and not cast in a flattering light. The Council on African Affairs, which Alphaeus had left Howard to join, was falling to pieces. Max Yergan, the executive director, having tried and failed to fire Alphaeus, had been ousted by the board. But Yergan refused to leave, barricading himself in his office. Yergan told the press that Communists were trying to take over the Council. After finally vacating the premises, he filed a complaint with the police, charging that what the press called "members of a left-wing faction in the organization" had broken the locks on his door and stolen $900. One of those Yergan accused was Alphaeus Hunton. The decision on what to do fell to District Attorney Frank Hogan, who had eased Eunice out of prosecuting cases. After a brief investigation, Hogan announced that no charges would be brought. Each side in the contretemps then sued the other, leading to more bad press. Eunice was surely embarrassed, and the incident must have stoked her anger at her brother. Probably she was glad to be out of the country as the scandal unfolded.

CHAPTER 20

THE BREAKUP

IN THE AUTUMN OF 1948, DEMOCRATIC REPRESENTATIVE WIL-
liam L. Dawson, a black congressman from Chicago, arrived in New
York to organize the Truman campaign's get-out-the-vote effort among
Negroes. Eunice of course was on the other side, spearheading what
one columnist labeled "a 'Do for Dewey' group . . . which says Truman
forces shall not pass." This group "will create a heck of a lot of bogie in
the Big Town's barnyard before they let Dawson or any of his clan walk
off with any of the Empire State for Truman."

Once again, Eunice's mentor, Governor Dewey, was the nominee.
But this time, with Franklin Roosevelt dead and Harry Truman in the
White House, everyone knew that Dewey was going to win. The governor's optimism had never flagged. True, he had lost to Roosevelt in a
landslide, but everybody lost to Roosevelt in a landslide. A postmortem
analysis made clear that the size of the landslide was deceptive. Yes,
Roosevelt had carried thirty-six of the forty-eight states. Yes, the vote
in the electoral college was an overwhelming 432–99. As unhappy
Republican editorialists pointed out, however, a shift of just 300,000
votes in key states—less than 1 percent of the total votes cast—would
have meant a Dewey victory. In fact, Dewey came closer to Roosevelt in
the popular vote than had any other opponent. Party leaders therefore

talked themselves into giving Dewey another shot. With a tweak here and a dollar there—and against a lesser candidate—Dewey should be able to win it all.

Certainly Eunice would be hoping so. The new international twist to her activism had never quite flattened her ambition. The chimera of the judgeship still drew her; but so did the possibility of political office. Earlier that year, as the party sought a strong candidate to challenge Representative Adam Clayton Powell Jr., in the 1948 election, a gossip columnist for an out-of-town Negro paper had asserted that Eunice "might be persuaded if the right people asked her." But either the story was made up or the right people never asked. Certainly nothing came of the matter. Still, the fact that a newspaper would bruit such a tale suggests that journalists and their readers were still waiting to find out what Eunice Hunton Carter would do next.

For the moment, the answer was that she would hit the campaign trail with her mentor one last time.

Like Dewey, Truman had come to recognize the importance of the Negro vote. An adviser sent the President a memorandum arguing that the era of machine politics was over. What would matter henceforth, he noted presciently, was "the pressure groups." Among them were the Negro voters, who were "geographically concentrated in the pivotal, large and contested electoral states." But they disliked the Southern wing of the Democratic Party and could no longer be bought "with a Tammany turkey on Thanksgiving." Winning them over would require "real efforts," as opposed to "mere political gestures which are today thoroughly understood and strongly resented by sophisticated Negro leaders."

But would the strategy work? Maybe so. This time around, having learned from his rout in 1944, Dewey soft-pedaled the issue of racial justice. Once more, the Negro press mostly endorsed him, and the NAACP wondered why the candidate did not do more "to exploit his excellent record on civil rights." Actually, Dewey had not long before infuriated activists by his refusal to appoint a special prosecutor to investigate the February 1946 fatal shootings of two unarmed Negroes, one a veteran, and the wounding of a third, all by the same quick-trigger white Long Island policeman. So in a sense, even as Dewey decided not to make racial equality the centerpiece of his campaign, he had ground to make up with some of his black supporters. The Republican platform retained from four years earlier the promises to pass a federal anti-lynching law, end the poll tax, and desegregate the armed forces. Omitted, however, was the 1944 plank calling for the establishment of a permanent federal Fair Employment Practice Commission. (Roosevelt had created the agency by executive order, but without legislative backing it could be disbanded at any time.) The convention adopted a fair substitute, one of the strongest calls for civil rights ever seen in a major party platform:

> One of the basic principles of this Republic is the equality of all individuals in their right to life, liberty, and the pursuit of happiness. . . . This right of equal opportunity to work and to advance in life should never be limited in any individual because of race, religion, color, or country of origin. We favor the enactment and just enforcement of such Federal legislation as may be necessary to maintain this right at all times in every part of this Republic.

Moreover, just as in 1944, the GOP could point to actual Negro appointments as evidence of their candidate's lack of racial prejudice. Once more, Dewey supporters cited Eunice's rise during his term as district attorney to prove their candidate's bona fides. A columnist for the *Los Angeles Sentinel* not only posited her success under Dewey as a reason to vote Republican but also quoted an attack on Truman by the prominent black pastor Clayton D. Russell: "If he double-crossed the Jews on the Palestine question what will he do to the Negro on the civil rights issue?"

Truman's campaign had recognized from the start that Dewey would try to win the Negro vote by promising a civil rights agenda very much like the one the black leadership was seeking. Given the need to placate the Southerners, the Democrats could hardly promise the same. Instead, their strategy would be to remind the darker nation "that the really great improvement in the economic lot of the Negro of the North has come in the last sixteen years only because of the sympathy and policies of the Democratic administration." Here again, we might say that the Democrats and Truman wanted black voters to ignore the divisive social issues (civil rights) and vote their real interests (economic progress).

Once again Eunice campaigned for her mentor. Once again they made public appearances together. But she did not travel as widely as in 1944. Dewey's crowd of prominent Negro supporters and appointees was much larger now. As governor, he had named any number of colored officials. In short, he did not need Eunice quite as much as he had in 1940 and 1944. Add to that Dewey's decision to downplay the commitment to equality that had been the centerpiece of his campaign four years earlier, and there was simply less for Eunice to do.

As Election Day approached, nobody thought Truman had a chance. The bookmakers quoted odds as high as 15-to-1 for anyone so foolish as to bet on the President's victory. All the national polls were in Dewey's favor. In some his lead was in the double digits. On election night, the candidate and his closest friends and aides held victory parties across Manhattan. As everyone knows, the *Chicago Tribune* declared Dewey the winner in its morning editions. The *Tribune* was not alone. That same Wednesday morning, the *Washington Post* ran a long profile of "Thomas Edward Dewey, yesterday elected to become the thirty-third President of the United States." But of course Dewey had actually lost, in one of the great upsets in American political history. The crucial Negro vote had stuck with the Democrats—and, by sticking, determined the outcome.

A few weeks after the election, Eunice was hospitalized again. The Negro press assured readers that she suffered from nothing serious— just "a checkup"—and, more to the point, that "[t]he election had nothing to do with it even though Eunice is a top Republican." Probably Eunice had been ill for some while. She had done less campaigning this time around than she had in 1944, and after the election, rather than resume her whirlwind schedule, she had limited herself to a single outing: the Harvard-Yale game in Boston on November 20, which she had attended with friends. She was released from the hospital around mid-December, just in time to return to 10 Jumel Terrace to begin preparing for that "beeg, beeg" Christmas party, invitations to which were so hard to come by—which she promised this year would be "bigger and better" than ever.

In January of 1949, Harry Truman struck a small but important blow for equality. For the first time, every inaugural event was open to Negroes. In particular, he broke the long tradition that only whites were invited to the inaugural ball. The elite of the darker nation flocked to Washington for the week of festivities. Eunice joined the general migration. The society pages of the colored papers wrote about the colorful designer gowns that well-to-do Negro women wore to the ball, but Eunice chose basic black. The society pages of the mainstream papers pretended no Negroes were present.

Still, if we judge by the steadiness of Eunice's grip on the Pyramid, the year started out as a success. But in other ways, 1949 began to shape up as Eunice's annus horribilis. To begin with, things went bad with Mrs. Bethune. As recently as the year before, Eunice and Bethune were so closely associated in the public eye that when the post office received a letter from Liberia addressed only to "Mrs. Bethune, American Educator, New York City, U.S.A.," the envelope was promptly delivered to Eunice, in the expectation that she would send it on to the addressee. But now all at once the simmering tension in their relationship began to boil over. The flame was lit early in the year when the State Department invited the National Council of Negro Women to send a representative to join the international tour of the Town Hall Meeting of the Air. This was a junket—a prestigious junket—whose members would travel for months, circling the globe. At each stop, the group would make presentations about life in America. The idea was to win hearts and minds and so set back the Soviets in the Cold War.

It is difficult for us, looking back, to understand how important such an opportunity was. There would be publicity galore. And everybody wanted in. The American Legion had a spot. So did the American Bankers Association, the United States Conference of Mayors, the American Federation of Labor, the NAACP—pretty much every major interest group in America. Eunice believed that the spot reserved for the National Council of Negro Women was hers for the asking. Eunice was the one who, through her connections (probably Chester Williams at the State Department), had finagled the invitation for the NCNW to choose a member. She was by now the group's accredited observer at the United Nations, and, in her own right, a consultant to UNESCO. At her own expense, she had represented the Council in Greece and Finland and France. The Town Hall trip, too, she could finance without any cost to the group. She spoke German and French. She would seem to have been the obvious choice. On the other hand, one never knew. Bethune had become prickly on the subject of who represented the NCNW abroad. She was annoyed that for reasons of money and energy she could not go everywhere, and was openly wary of letting anyone other than herself become the public face of the group. Nevertheless, Eunice believed, with reason, that the outcome was a foregone conclusion.

To her surprise, however, Bethune made no selection at all. Instead, she presented the choice to the board, which, in Eunice's helpless presence, selected instead Edith Sampson, a fellow lawyer who had once been Eunice's friend and was nowadays her rival. Bethune suggested that she thought the honor of representing the group abroad should be spread around. But it was an insult to Eunice to be forced to chair a meeting at which her own candidacy was rejected. She evidently hit the ceiling—not during the meeting but shortly after. She and Bethune exchanged sharp words. Both went away angry. A few days later, Eunice fired off a handwritten note that was not quite an apology. She was sorry, she wrote, "not for what I said but for the manner in which I said it." She admitted that she should not have been disrespectful to an elder. On the other hand, Eunice still saw herself as the victim: "I do not think that I shall ever [recover]." In the face of so grudging an expression of regret, Bethune, unsurprisingly, did not yield an inch. She accused her protégée of saying "that I had stabbed you, I was impolite, I was a liar." A few days later, Eunice responded with a more straightforward but still cool apology.

And yet she was unable to put the dispute behind her. In early June she resigned as the NCNW's representative to the National Peace Conference. This was actually clever of her—and related to what happened next. In June of 1949, Eunice departed for yet another conference in

Europe. She wrote to Bethune from aboard ship. In her letter, Eunice accused her mentor of being the one who was refusing to let the matter rest. She had heard somewhere that Bethune had described the incident in ways unflattering to her onetime protégée. Her letter disputed Bethune's version of the facts. And she added words difficult to take back: "At [first] the whole affair was a bitter disappointment, now I realize that this is perhaps the better way. I go on to continue the work which I have begun in [quarters] where it is apparently appreciated." Eunice was signaling her anger but also her surrender. She was headed to another meeting of the International Council of Women, where she had already begun to rise. But that was not what she had been longing for. The backup plan she had long ago conceived—the plan to run the National Council of Negro Women—had obviously failed.

The failure was driven home in November, when the NCNW met in Washington to choose a successor to Mrs. Bethune, who at long last had announced her retirement. The press, still believing that Eunice was the protégée, touted her chances. Although some stories hinted at a dispute with Bethune, as late as October pundits were still proclaiming that the "brilliant" Eunice Carter's name was "right up there" in the mix of potential successors. There were even whispers that she was the favorite. But when the convention arrived, Eunice did not even toss her hat in the ring. She knew that without Bethune's support, she had no chance.

As it happened, the favorite going into the election was Eunice's rival, Edith Sampson. Rumors flew that the delegates from New York, who contributed heavily to the Council's finances, would revoke their support should Sampson be chosen. The press reported that one member of the board said she would "see Sampson in hell first." The stories did not give the board member's name, but the signs point to Eunice. By this time, she could not control her pain and fury. When the board convened on the eve of the vote, Eunice—hobbled by a broken leg from a fall she had suffered in Switzerland over the summer—had what might best be described as a meltdown. She could not let the controversy go. She insisted that the minutes reflect that the Town Hall position had arisen from her work and hers alone. This was nine months after the board had chosen Sampson, and Eunice was now fighting for recognition of exactly the proposition she had denied in the letter to Bethune from aboard ship. Small wonder that Eunice would soon find herself turned out of her position as chair.

Of course, in truth the fury that she directed at Bethune could just as easily have been aimed at Dewey, or Alphaeus, or even J. Edgar Hoover. All her life, Eunice was never not in control of herself, a trait that no doubt made her rage even more surprising. There are people whose anger is constantly on display. Eunice was not among them. People who knew her always talk about her cool distance, even when others would lose their tempers. But she had been cool about too much for too long. Her inability to put aside her anguish, together with her very public frenzy at the November board meeting, point to a woman on the edge. She had reason to be. A public career that had never moved in any direction but forward had over the past two years been swiftly and decisively derailed. Eunice had committed no error. She had been touched by no scandal, she had not lost her talent or her intellect, she had put no foot wrong. But life had blown up in her face nevertheless.

Still, she might have derived some small satisfaction from the result of the balloting to select Bethune's successor. When the votes were tallied, the delegates had rejected Sampson decisively. Instead, the lot fell upon Dorothy Ferebee, Bethune's friend and personal physician—the same Dorothy Ferebee who two years earlier had been scheduled to accompany Bethune to Paris for the start of what was to have been a monthlong tour of Europe—the trip that Eunice more or less snatched from under their noses. Members explained later that they were tired of having the organization run by members of the elite, which was most assuredly how both Eunice and Sampson saw themselves.

Bethune, still steaming, was unable to resist playing a small and humiliating but public game with her onetime protégée. Eunice still chaired the board of directors and the executive committee, and although she would soon be stripped of both titles, the plan was originally for her to give her usual International Night address to the assembled members from the podium. At the last minute, Bethune sent a curt note informing her of a change of plans. This year, for the first time, Eunice's talk would be from her seat in the audience; and it was limited to three minutes.

The backup plan had imploded. Eunice would not be running the National Council of Negro Women. With her uncontrollable fury at the board and at Mrs. Bethune, Eunice herself no doubt was a contributor. Nor did her sharp tongue help. According to the historian Christine Lutz, Eunice had made an intemperate joke after Bethune missed a meeting in 1948—a comment promptly reported to the leader by Edith Sampson. But there is another explanation for the collapse of Eunice's hopes. Both the National Council of Negro Women and Bethune herself had been under scrutiny from the FBI and various Communist-hunting congressional committees, and the group was working hard to showcase its strong and shining commitment to American ideals. By the late 1940s, Bethune was busy putting distance between herself and associates who might be viewed as too radical. Participating in the Town Hall Meeting of the Air was but one of the ways the NCNW was ostentatiously displaying its patriotism. Another was ensuring that the top ranks of the Council were free of the Communist taint. Bethune and Dewey traveled very different paths but seem to have reached the same destination: Alphaeus's increasingly wild political stances made backing his sister too risky. Bethune's abandonment of her protégée might well have been the judgeship all over again.

Eventually the two women settled their differences, after a fashion. Bethune retired, and the National Council of Negro Women passed into other hands. She and Eunice once again attended the same Council events, handed each other awards, and, in public, spoke highly of each other. But they never again exchanged the warm correspondence that had marked most of the 1940s; their relationship outside of official duties essentially ceased. Twice more over the years Eunice would be spoken of as a likely candidate for the presidency. But although for the rest of her life she served the NCNW in various positions, she never again threw her hat into the ring to lead the organization she had helped her mentor found. When Bethune died a few years later, many friends and colleagues had formal roles at her funeral. Eunice was not among them.

CHAPTER 21

THE REINVENTION

ONE HAS TO PICTURE EUNICE AT THE TURN OF THE DECADE: ABAN-doned by both her mentors, deprived of her mother, estranged from her brother, shipwrecked in politics, her public career dead in the water, her backup plan gone awry, stuck in a dreadful marriage, living upstairs from a son she barely knew. For better than a decade now, she had been the great Eunice Hunton Carter, the colored woman who brought down Lucky Luciano, honored by the white world and adored by the black. Her name had been constantly on the front pages of the Negro papers. Her life, although not wanting in its pains, had nevertheless been rewarding. Eunice had never been a woman who would stoop to win a popularity contest. She believed to the bottom of her soul in merit and hard work. By being better than anyone else at whatever she chose to do, she would continue to rise. She would be honored and admired. But in the middle of 1949, just as she turned fifty years old, her ascent had stalled. The plan was not working. Being the best at what she did was not enough. She had become, quite suddenly, just another face in the crowd. Worse, she had never had so much time to herself. At the district attorney's office, Eunice had barely had a free hour. Back then, brooding would have cost precious moments she could not spare. Since her resignation, however, her efforts to replicate that sense of being constantly busy had failed. Her law practice and her public relations firm had come to naught. Of course she still held the celebrated beeg, beeg parties at her fortress on Jumel Terrace, including a hugely successful November gala to celebrate her silver wedding anniversary, and people still fought over invitations. Nevertheless, with her career becalmed, Eunice was slipping in spite of herself into the role she had fled two decades ago: another Czarina, presiding over Harlem society because she had little else to do. Her life became in certain ways spooky. She collected model cars and shot glasses, and displayed them all over the house.

True, Eunice managed a handful of minor victories in the course of her dreadful year. In particular, she might have gained some small solace from *Ebony* magazine's big July 1949 write-up on the ten women leaders of the race. She was included, along with Mrs. Bethune, while her rival, Edith Sampson, was absent. Still, the satisfaction must have been bittersweet. Where others were listed with their profession (for example, "Elsie Austin—Lawyer" or "Gertrude B. Anderson—Businesswoman"), she was listed as "Eunice Hunton Carter—Republican." Some burdens we can never put down.

But quitting was not in her nature. Even if the career that had once seemed so easy had become a slog, Eunice was determined to push on. And at first it seemed as if her determination would be rewarded. The year 1950 began auspiciously. Eunice was the only Negro to testify before the Senate on the ratification of the Genocide Convention. The cause was dear to her heart. In 1948 she had framed the resolutions for both the Democratic and Republican National Conventions favoring the treaty. She lectured and wrote on the problem of genocide, and would soon appear on Eleanor Roosevelt's new television show to argue for ratification.

Yet her crusade was hardly uncontroversial. In the magical postwar world, opposition to Jim Crow was often cast, by some political alchemy, as sympathy for communism. Small wonder, then, that even the Genocide Convention would wind up cursed by the same spell. The Convention on the Prevention and Punishment of the Crime of Genocide (as it is formally known) had been adopted by the United Nations General Assembly in 1948. The Truman administration had been a prime mover in advocating for the treaty in the wake of the Holocaust. But the Senate was wary. Some of the worries will be familiar to modern ears: the touchy question, for one, of whether members of the American military should be subject to the jurisdiction of foreign powers. Other objections were peculiar to the era. In particular, Dixiecrats and their supporters were concerned lest the way their states treated their Negro populations should come within the treaty's prohibitions. Nobody wanted to go back home and tell his constituents that the United Nations now had a license to sit in judgment on the racial norms of the American South. Supporters had to find a way to thread this tricky needle.

Among the Genocide Convention's more passionate supporters was Eunice. She had spoken to audiences about genocide for years. Her testimony in support of the treaty came at a hearing before the Senate Foreign Relations Committee in January of 1950. All the major civil rights organizations were in support. As a formal matter, Eunice was on Capitol Hill representing the National Council of Negro Women. Ratification was also a major goal of Alphaeus's; he surely would not have been displeased by the fact that the document, for all of its virtues, was carefully drafted to let Iron Curtain governments off the hook: the prohibitions applied to crimes against populations based on race, religion, or ethnicity, but excluded crimes based on political views. Opponents argued that the Genocide Convention had been created to allow the rest of the world to chastise the West. American citizens, they warned, would be at the mercy of foreign governments. Alphaeus was a strong supporter of the convention. One might think therefore that he was pleased by his sister's testimony. But he was not. In particular, he could not have been happy with a proviso Eunice added toward the end of her testimony. In words intended for opponents of the treaty, she argued that the convention would not apply to the oppression of the darker nation:

> The situation of the Negro people in this country is in no way involved. The lynching of an individual or of several individuals has no relation to the extinction of masses of peoples because of race, religion, or political belief.

Alphaeus, with his straightforward, take-no-prisoners style of advocacy, never understood what his sister saw clearly: that in the arena of practical politics, there is little point to telling the truth and losing. Sometimes (so she might have said to him were they still on speaking terms) one must obfuscate a bit and get what one can. Better to try to stop genocide abroad and leave racism at home untouched than to wind up improving neither.

Alphaeus, by contrast, would shortly help draft a report from the Civil Rights Congress entitled *We Charge Genocide*, a book that argued, contra Eunice, that the treatment of the darker nation in the United States was precisely the sort of thing that the Convention had been crafted to prevent. He would have been utterly unimpressed by the suggestion that he was making ratification that much less likely. Politics was for Alphaeus very much an all-or-nothing proposition—an attitude that would cost him dearly.

In the end, the Senate committee's report recommending approval of the bill attached an "understanding" that the word "genocide" did not encompass "lynchings, race riots or any form of segregation." Finally a branch of the national legislature had chosen to address lynching— but only by way of assuring the lynchers that they were safe from international law. Yes, Eunice's words were prudent and political, perhaps even necessary if the bill was to pass. Someone had to say what she said. And the compromise the committee worked out was exactly the one Eunice had suggested.

But the treaty did not come to a vote in the full Senate. In fact, the United States did not adopt the Genocide Convention until the late 1980s. Eisenhower, Kennedy, and Johnson gave essentially no support. Nixon did press for ratification, but without success. In 1986, in a much-changed nation, Ronald Reagan managed to persuade the Senate to adopt the treaty, albeit with reservations. Yet Eunice was correct back in 1950. Rather than dragging its feet, America should have led the way.

Eunice's international success was largely driven, of course, by her still-burning ambition to make her mark in the world; but another factor was the determination that had fired her two decades earlier, the fear of winding up as a Harlem Czarina and nothing else. To be sure, she was at times required to play that role, and for the most part, she played it well. But on one occasion Eunice's efforts exploded in her face, leading to a very public embarrassment in the Negro press—an embarrassment that, although she might not have seen things quite this way, actually pointed to something admirable in her character.

The occasion was a March 1950 tea she hosted at 10 Jumel Terrace on behalf of the Friends of the NAACP, the fund-raising arm she had co-founded. The guest was Elizabeth Waring, the wife of a federal judge in South Carolina who had come down hard against segregation, becoming, in the process, an enemy in his home state and a hero within the darker nation. His wife, who turned out to be even more adamant an egalitarian than her husband, was a guest for whose presence any Czarina would readily do battle. For Eunice, landing her was an enormous coup. The printed invitations went out to the great ladies of Harlem. The mansion was expensively decorated for the event. The embarrassment came when the tea was snubbed at the last minute by the guest of honor.

Mrs. Waring refused to attend.

The reason may seem trivial, but behind it lies a lesson about Eunice herself. Walter White, head of the NAACP and at the time the most influential civil rights leader in the country, had recently left his wife, Gladys, and married Poppy Cannon, a white journalist from South Africa with whom he had long been involved. Eunice was close to Gladys, and invited her to the tea. Poppy was not on the list. Mrs. Waring, close to the new wife but not the old, sent a telegram on the day of the event saying she would not come. As I said: trivial. Except that it wasn't. The great Eunice Hunton Carter had committed a social faux pas. Papers as far away as Pittsburgh and Chicago gave her embarrassment front-page headlines.

And yet the sin for which Eunice was so publicly punished was no sin at all; she had acted, for once, out of affection and human feeling rather than calculating ambition. A true Harlem Czarina, ever mindful of her position on the Great Social Pyramid, would have seen the trouble looming, crossed her friend off the guest list, and promptly invited the new Mrs. White—the better to gleam and glitter in the columns. To have Mrs. Waring as a guest could only help one's position in sassiety. A true Czarina would be able to talk herself into sacrificing a wounded friend in exchange for the opportunity to climb a few levels.

All of which is to say that Eunice was not really suited to the life of jostling constantly for position on the Pyramid. Loyalty was once more her curse—and, being loyal, she was no more cut out for life as a Czarina than Addie, the great apostle of Negro motherhood, had been cut out to put the home before everything. In the postwar years, the path Addie had blazed and Eunice had followed was no longer so unusual: there now were black women aplenty who chose to pursue careers rather than spend their efforts scrambling upward in sassiety. But Eunice was unusual in having made that decision back in the 1920s. Whatever disappointment she might have felt about the later course of her own life, the choice she made so long ago could stand as an inspiration to a new generation of Negro women—and, whether she knew it or not, probably did.

The crisis blew over. Eunice did not lose her place in sassiety. The faux pas was soon behind her, and she continued to give her talks and host her events. In May she traveled to Philadelphia to speak at a colored YWCA about her recent visit to Germany. Later that year she was listed in the *Times* as one of the "patronesses" of a benefit luncheon at the Waldorf-Astoria for the American Women's Voluntary Services work in veterans hospitals. But none of this could possibly be enough to satisfy that driving ambition. She continued to cast about for a more public role, preferably one befitting her newly acquired taste for internationalism.

And found one.

Because 1950 was the year when the Truman administration decided to add a Negro woman to the American delegation at the United Nations. The post would only be as an alternate, but at this time even such a position carried enormous prestige. Everyone wanted the spot. This time the choice would not be up to Bethune; the State Department would decide. And Eunice already possessed all the relevant experience. She had participated in the San Francisco Conference, where the United Nations was founded. For the past four years she had been the National Council of Negro Women's accredited observer to the U.N. and served as a consultant to UNESCO. Surely this time the mantle would fall upon her shoulders.

But no. Once more she lost out to Edith Sampson. In retrospect, given Sampson's success at the Town Hall tour, it is hard to see how Truman could have chosen anyone else. That such doors as this would be flung open was simply another reason Eunice had coveted the Town Hall spot for herself. But she had not gotten that appointment, and she did not get this one. Sampson was the star. To compound the insult, Eunice's old and dear friend Walter White sang Sampson's praises. And Eunice must have writhed at the fawning press coverage in black and white papers alike. A columnist in the *Chicago Defender* was derisive, even cruel, as he twisted the knife:

> We understand that Philadelphia's Crystal Byrd [sic] Fauset, of doubtful Republican-Democrat political vintage, was one of the chief pawers for the spot, and there is talk that New York's Eunice Hunton Carter considered herself a made-to-order for the post.... But we say the appointment has been made, and the gals oughta throw in the towel and line up behind this first for the race. Strikes me the hell-raising could more profitably be used to open up some more spots for men and women of color.

Of course, it did not help matters that Eunice had come to prominence as a Republican, and had campaigned so vigorously for Truman's opponent. Nevertheless, the wound surely lingered.

In October, Governor Dewey threw her a sop, naming his old ally to a committee "to promote public observance of United Nations Day." Now it was her task to celebrate the very organization she was doing her best to forget. To be sure, the committee members included such luminaries as Francis Cardinal Spellman and David Sarnoff, head of RCA. Nevertheless, this final reward for her unstinting support of Dewey over the years was considerably less than Eunice had hoped for and expected. Uneasy thoughts of what might have been must have flitted through Eunice's head in November when, as usual, she delivered one of the principal addresses at the annual convention of the National Council of Negro Women, held that year in Washington, D.C. And 1950, which had begun so auspiciously, ended on a sour note when December rolled around and the *Pittsburgh Courier* published its annual list of the year's accomplishments by women of the race. Eunice, just yesterday the darling of the Negro press, did not even make the cut.

CHAPTER 22

THE SIBLINGS

BUT SOARING AMBITION WAS NOT ENOUGH TO KEEP EUNICE FREE of the weight of her brother's problems. As it happened, 1950 was also the year when a Soviet spy and defector named Louis F. Budenz fingered Alphaeus as a "concealed Communist"—meaning "one who does not hold himself out as a Communist and who would deny membership in the Party." The category was important in Cold War ideology. In his 1958 book *Masters of Deceit*, J. Edgar Hoover would claim that the United States harbored many concealed Communists, often "so deeply hidden that only top leaders know their identity." Concealed Communists were to hide from others, including lower-ranking comrades, the fact that they were members at all. The secrecy helped ensure that even fellow Party members could not betray them, and left the concealed Communist free to insinuate himself into circles that would otherwise be closed to one of openly radical views. But like Senator Joseph McCarthy, who often used the term "concealed Communists," Hoover never offered proof for his allegation that the number of such individuals was large. Although Budenz himself, who became a darling of Washington's Red hunters, provided a list of some four hundred concealed Communists, much if not most of the list was almost certainly fabricated. The principal function of the category of concealed

Communist, then, was not to root out genuine subversion but to further the influence of the Red hunters who wielded it.

Yet even if Hoover and others greatly exaggerated the numbers, no one disputes that a significant number of Party members kept their membership secret, in many cases because they were ordered to. That Alphaeus might have been among them is perfectly plausible. Concealed Communists were important to the movement, because the Party itself believed that the time would come when those who were open about their membership would be persecuted by the satraps of America's reactionary authorities. And in Alphaeus's case, Budenz specifically recalled meetings at which Alphaeus admitted his Communist Party membership. This was important because senior members of the Party sometimes performed tasks on behalf of the Soviet intelligence apparatus. Many knew exactly what they were doing; others had no idea. This work might be no more complex than a phone call and a code word and someone saying, "Pick up a package at ten o'clock tonight at such-and-such an address and leave it under the bench at the corner of so-and-so street." There is not a shred of evidence that Alphaeus was involved in anything of the sort, but one still might have expected Budenz's claims about Alphaeus to lead to a large investigation.

Instead, there was only a small one. The FBI seemed willing to let him go. His name remained on the Custodial Detention list, but his investigative file was closed once more. The government was after headlines, and there were more prominent Communists in abundance for the Justice Department to chase. In a spectacular trial the previous year, eleven leaders of the Communist Party had been convicted under the Smith Act of the crime of being leaders of the Communist Party, for this was an era much like our own, when punishing unpopular beliefs was very much in fashion. As it happened, that headline-grabbing trial, already completed, would soon lead to the reopening of Alphaeus's file.

And this time it would stay open.

None of this did much to help Eunice's career, and she remained keenly aware of the costs imposed upon her by her brother's Communist activity. Even much later, my grandmother never blamed the paranoia of the era for undercutting her ambition. She always blamed Alphaeus.

And, certainly, Alphaeus showed no signs of a willingness to mute his politics for her sake. Why, then (Eunice must have wondered), should she mute her ambitions for his? Neither was prepared to back down, forgive, or even reach out. Both siblings had inherited the stubbornness of both their parents.

And Eunice went further. She did her best to keep her son from any contact with his uncle. She warned Lisle Jr., pleaded with him, finally ordered him. One might dismiss her edict as simple pique. More likely, she had begun to worry that Lisle Jr., whose politics were far more liberal than her own, might find his future prospects damaged by too close an association with her brother the Communist. Eunice was looking ahead, for she was determined that her son would have a public career that would not be sidetracked like hers, but would be marked instead by a steady upward climb. So far the auguries were favorable. In 1950, her son and several friends founded a law firm called Carter, Smith, Watson & Wright, which either shared office space with Eunice at 516 Fifth Avenue or leased separate premises in the same building. Unlike his mother, Lisle Jr. had no trouble snagging clients. Soon Eunice would be bursting with pride when her son won a racial discrimination suit against the swanky Pierre Hotel on behalf of her friend Mollie Moon, the doyenne of Harlem society, whose rental of the roof garden had been revoked once management learned that she was not white. Lisle Jr. would be written up in all the Negro papers. In Eunice's terms, her son was on his way.

And just as she wanted to keep Lisle Jr. away from Alphaeus, Eunice herself had no intention of allowing her brother's troubles to slow her own whirl through society. If anything, she picked up the pace, as if only by keeping furiously active could she exorcize the demons that plagued her career: A reception for the Ladies of the Pullman Porters Auxiliary. A speech in Philadelphia during National YMCA Week. A committee to support Republican Edward Corsi's bid to become mayor of New York. (The bid was unsuccessful.) A reception for her rival, Edith Sampson. (Yes, Eunice tried to swallow that bitter pill.) The list of events rolled on and on. In June Eunice took charge of organizing a gala in honor of Ethel Waters and Todd Duncan at the Belmont Plaza to benefit the NAACP. In July Eunice and her husband found themselves in Wonder Lake, New Jersey, honoring Sylvanus Olympio, head of the representative assembly in what was then French Togoland. (Olympio, later the first president of independent Togo, would be assassinated in 1963.) In August at Jumel Terrace, the Carters hosted what the columns labeled a "brilliant gathering" for Frank Horne and Mercedes Rector Horne, at the time perhaps the most prominent couple in Washington sassiety.

By this time, Eunice had been named the official observer of the National Council of Negro Women at the United Nations, a consolation prize but one she came to value. She even made her peace with the new leadership. Dorothy Ferebee, the president who had defeated the favored Sampson after Eunice dropped out of the race, began to sing Eunice's praises. Eunice even resumed her representation of the NCNW abroad. She once more attended conferences in Europe on the group's behalf. Yes, the travel was still at Eunice's own expense. Still, she was on the verge of coming full circle. With her legal career behind her, Eunice was seeking a way to combine her new commitment to internationalism with the task of holding on to her place atop the Great Pyramid.

Keeping her balance would prove tricky.

In early December of 1950, Eunice's son married a young woman named Emily Ellis, from New Rochelle. The couple had met at a party in New York, and Lisle Jr. had wooed Emily from afar by sending her love poems he had written for her. Once when he had annoyed her by not writing for months, he won her back with a letter describing a glorious spring day in Manhattan and explaining that it made him think of how he missed her. The engagement was brief. The small wedding was held in the rectory of an Episcopal church in Mount Vernon.

The nuptials evidently brought Eunice little joy. She never approved of her son's choice of bride. In Eunice's view, Lisle Jr. could have had his pick of young women from the elite of the darker nation and then had the huge Harlem wedding that had once been de rigueur, but that she herself had been denied. Instead he chose a woman whose parents were shopkeepers. They stood nowhere on the Pyramid. That Emily was an honors graduate of Adelphi University impressed her mother-in-law

Eunice's son, Lisle Jr., with his fiancée, Emily Ellis, in Manhattan, around 1950. Eunice never approved of the marriage.
CARTER FAMILY PHOTOGRAPH

not at all. So unknown to sassiety was the bride's family that the *Amsterdam News*, in announcing the nuptials, misspelled the names of both of Emily's parents.

Not that Eunice was about to allow any of this to affect her own role in sassiety. That very December, wedding or no wedding, she was out and about as usual. Still, she could hardly pretend that her life was unchanged. After their three-night honeymoon, Lisle Jr. and Emily (known as Betty) moved into the ground-floor apartment at 10 Jumel Terrace. The press, charmed by Betty, immediately labeled her an "attractive Westchesterite." But her charms were lost on Eunice. The feeling was mutual: family legend has it that the young bride found her prominent mother-in-law overbearing and difficult.

Lisle Jr.'s marriage heightened Eunice's sense of having lost control of the forces that ruled her life. She tried her best to accept her son's choice, but could not entirely overcome the prejudices that had formed her. She was a thoroughgoing traditionalist, uneasy with the idea that the old order changeth, yielding place to the new; the things she had valued decades ago she valued still. She found her daughter-in-law insufficiently cultured. Betty had not been to Europe and had no plans to go. She had not read the great books in German or hobnobbed with Presidents of the United States. She had no ambition to obtain an advanced degree.

For her part, Betty tried to make her mother-in-law happy. She dutifully made the rounds of Harlem cocktail parties and receptions. But the Czarinas (Betty called them "old biddies") swiftly figured out that Eunice's new daughter-in-law had little interest in the scramble up the Great Social Pyramid—even though, on account of her marriage, she would start the journey fairly high up the trickily twisting slope. Nobody should have been surprised. Lisle Jr. had largely rejected the ways of Harlem sassiety. He had been inducted into the proper fraternity and joined a useful club or two, but he soon came to dismiss that entire world as silly and even oppressive. Just twenty-five years old, Lisle Jr. was showing signs of an independence that must have been, for his mother, a simultaneous source of puzzlement and pride.

Even as Eunice's domestic worries mounted, trouble loomed on another front. As 1950 slipped into 1951, her brother's legal fortunes were running swiftly downhill. Alphaeus was a trustee of the Bail Fund of the Civil Rights Congress, which had posted bond for the eleven Communist Party leaders convicted in 1949 of the crime of being Communist Party leaders. His fellow trustees included the novelist Dashiell Hammett and Frederick Vanderbilt Field, scion of two fabulously wealthy clans. The defendants were freed pending appeal, and the Supreme Court would soon decide their fate. If, as most observers expected, the Justices ruled against them, the Party leaders would be ordered to prison. Rumors began to circulate that at least some of the defendants might go underground rather than serve time. Running the Party from some backstreet walk-up apartment in a murky corner of a grimy city would be a lot easier than running it from a prison cell. But if the defendants fled, the trustees—Alphaeus included—would be in far deeper trouble. In the right circumstances, they might even face imprisonment. And in the Red-hunting hysteria of the age, the right circumstances happened a lot.

One might suppose that Alphaeus would turn to his sister. One might imagine that Eunice, former prosecutor and experienced trial lawyer, would be by her brother's side in his time of trouble. One would be in error.

Eunice continued to share her office at 516 Fifth Avenue with her son's law firm. Her career might have been in a decline, but she still had her courtroom skills and her contacts. Her son, too, was developing no mean reputation as a trial lawyer. Singly or together, they might have helped Alphaeus with his defense. But there is no evidence that he sought assistance from either. And we have no reason to suppose that assistance would have been forthcoming. Eunice certainly would have refused; and her firm command would likely have kept her son from helping.

At least in public, Eunice ignored her brother's troubles. She continued her nearly constant effort to reinvent herself. In March of 1951, she was replaced as the National Council of Negro Women's official observer at the United Nations. But the change barely slowed her down. Instead, it accelerated her move from the black club world into the white. In particular, the whirlwind of her international activity picked up speed. In April she traveled to Athens, Greece, to deliver one of the opening addresses at the triennial conference of the International Council of Women of the World. This was Eunice's second time attending the conference. (Remember that she had also been a delegate in 1948, in effect snatching away the slot reserved for Mary McLeod Bethune.) Now Eunice had been brought into the group's leadership, chairing its legal committee. And in June, even as Alphaeus's legal problems mushroomed and prison became a real possibility, Eunice was back home, being feted and giving talks about her trip.

Eunice does not seem to have made any mention of Alphaeus's case, whether in these or any other public appearances. In the fraught ideological moment, had she breathed a word in her brother's defense, the press would have roused itself to frothing fury. Eunice knew that. More to the point, she thought that Alphaeus was in the wrong. Better, she decided, simply to ignore the whole thing. By now her indifference to his fate was genuine. Alphaeus had cost her too much.

In June of 1951, the Supreme Court decided *Dennis v. United States*, upholding the convictions of the Party leaders. With their appeals exhausted, the eleven defendants were ordered to begin their sentences. Just as rumor had predicted, four chose to go underground instead. Their bail was forfeited. Alphaeus and his fellow trustees were commanded to appear before a federal judge, who would demand to know the names of those who had contributed to the fund. The theory was that those who put up the bail for the fugitives might know where they were hiding. If the trustees refused to answer, they would go to prison.

The case was headline news all across the country. Still Eunice did her best to ignore it. Back home from Athens, she was out and about in sassiety as usual. In June, she was the guest speaker at a luncheon sponsored by the National Association of Colored Graduate Nurses, an organization she had assisted mightily. Two weeks before her brother's contempt hearing, she was up in Harlem at the Royal Manor, on 157th Street, where the National Council of Negro Women had arranged an afternoon program in her honor. (Now that she was out of power, the Council honored her regularly.) Days later, she collected another award at an NCNW event in Washington. And she gave one talk after another about her experiences in Greece.

In July, Alphaeus and his fellow trustees appeared before Judge Sylvester Ryan in the federal courthouse in lower Manhattan. They were asked by prosecutors for the names of the contributors to the bail fund. They refused to answer, citing their rights under the Fifth Amendment. They were asked to produce the written records of the fund. Again they refused. Judge Ryan held them in contempt. Alphaeus was sentenced to six months behind bars. The others received similar sentences.

Alphaeus's third wife, Dorothy, was present in the courtroom to watch as her husband was arrested, handcuffed, and led off to the Federal House of Detention—more commonly known as the West Street Jail—to await transport to the federal penitentiary. Eunice was not in

Alphaeus being led off to prison with Dashiell Hammett after they were found guilty of contempt of court for refusing to divulge the names of contributors to a fund that supplied bail to leaders of the Communist Party. Frederick Vanderbilt Field, heir to two great American fortunes, went to prison with them.
BETTMANN/CONTRIBUTOR/ GETTY IMAGES

court that day; hardly anyone else Alphaeus knew was present, either. Dorothy Hunton writes that she was accompanied to the courthouse that July morning only by a single friend, who risked her job with the public schools to be there.

A month after her brother began his sentence, Eunice was a guest at the biggest sassiety event of the summer, the twenty-fifth wedding anniversary of her old friends the Aaron Douglases. Having allowed Alphaeus to wreck her career, she was not about to let the fact that he had now committed contempt of court to ruin anything else. Until the last year or two, her standing on the Great Social Pyramid had rarely been uppermost in Eunice's thoughts; now she was clutching the treacherous sides with both hands.

Alphaeus could fend for himself, just as he always had.

Yet try as she might, Eunice could not entirely avoid entanglement between her place in society and her brother's legal difficulties. The *Amsterdam News*, upon first reporting that Alphaeus was headed to prison, reminded its readers in the very first sentence that "Mrs. Eunice

Hunton Carter" was his sister. She might preside over sassiety from her grand townhouse at the highest point in Harlem, but the anti-Communist flames of the age threatened to singe even those who sat atop the Great Social Pyramid.

While at West Street, Alphaeus and his colleagues were summoned several times before the grand jury, to see whether they had changed their minds. They had not. They were in the grand jury room for no more than five minutes each. They were ordered to respond and refused. Back to their cells. And to their body cavity searches. And their waiting. Field was also brought down to Washington, where he declined to answer questions before the McCarran Committee. He would later write that these interrogations were "frequent interruptions to our peaceful life in jail." As it turned out, federal prosecutors and congressional committees were not the only adversaries the trustees faced. New York's Banking Department also opened an investigation, to determine whether the CRC bail fund had violated state law by accepting deposits without a state banking license. Once more Hunton and the other trustees were dragged from their cells for questioning. Once more they refused to answer. And here we see another small irony as the circle closes: several of the state laws under which the Civil Rights Congress was being investigated had been enacted following the collapse of the Clarke Brothers private bank, the event that had brought a young Negro prosecutor named Hubert Delany to prominence in 1929, thereby establishing for the young Eunice the racist dirty tricks to which the Tammany Democrats were willing to resort and solidifying her lifelong commitment to the world of Republican politics.

In September, Alphaeus and his fellow trustees were transferred from the West Street Jail to two federal penitentiaries. Their appeals were still pending, but it was time to serve their sentences. Eunice had not visited her brother when he was locked up in downtown Manhattan; certainly she would not make the trip to see him in Petersburg, Virginia, the racially segregated prison to which he had been assigned. Lisle Jr. wanted to go, but once more his mother forbade him; and once more he obeyed her edict.

Well-wishers at LaGuardia Airport celebrating Alphaeus's release from prison,
December 1951. Left to right: Alphaeus, his wife Dorothy, and his close friends
Paul Robeson and W. E. B. Du Bois. Eunice was not present to welcome him home.
HUNTON FAMILY PHOTO

Events had proved the wisdom of Eunice's decision to reinvent herself as an internationalist. Once Alphaeus went to prison—and given
what he went to prison *for*—Eunice knew that her own career as a public figure in the United States was over. No one with a Communist sib-
ling, and a prominent one at that, could realistically aspire to high
office. The long-standing hope for a judgeship was gone. So was her
dream that the advent of a Republican administration in Washington
would lead to a major executive appointment. As she would learn a few
years later, even jobs on Capitol Hill were foreclosed. Yes, Eunice had
her international work, and she was passionate about it. But she felt the
rest of her dreams, and even her public persona, slipping away.

November brought the annual meeting of the National Council of Negro Women in Washington, and Eunice was reelected to the executive committee of the board she had once commanded. Dorothy Ferebee was reelected as president, the job that just three years earlier everyone had known would someday belong to Eunice. The convention adopted resolutions calling for an end to segregation in transportation and public accommodations. The members further demanded that the President of the United States, by executive order, require integration of all publicly funded facilities in the District of Columbia, where they were gathered. There were several more resolutions, all entirely predictable, all reflecting the agenda of the civil rights organizations. The group adopted no resolution about the growing threat to the freedom of speech or the prosecution of dissent.

On November 24, two days after Thanksgiving, Eunice appeared on a Women's Day panel at Concord Baptist Church in Brooklyn. A decade earlier, she would have required no identification; her name alone would have been enough. Back then she was still the Negro woman who had brought down Lucky Luciano. But that phase of her life had vanished into the mists of faded memory. Now a passing mention of the event in the colored press called her "former N.Y. Assistant Corporation Counsel"—a job Eunice never held. Her proudest years had been written out of the history of the darker nation.

In December, Alphaeus was released from prison a month early: time off for good behavior. Dorothy flew down to Virginia to escort him back home. A surviving photograph shows Alphaeus and Dorothy at the airport in New York after his release. The smiling well-wishers include his good friends Paul Robeson and W. E. B. Du Bois. Eunice, unsurprisingly, is absent. She skipped her brother's release, just as she had skipped his contempt hearings and his appeals. She had never visited him in prison, and she was not about to welcome him home. The estrangement between the siblings was complete.

They never spoke again.

EPILOGUE

That, at least, is what my father always told me—that the mother he loved and the uncle he admired became such bitter enemies that they never spoke again. No friend or relative whom I have interviewed remembers matters differently.

And yet, as with so much else about the siblings' lives, the truth may be more complex than the stories. As I write these words, beside me on the table is a first edition of Alphaeus's 1957 book *Decision in Africa*, inscribed by him "For Eunice and Lisle with love." In Alphaeus's papers at the New York Public Library is a copy of the note that accompanied the book, sent right around the time he left the country for good. There is no response. Most likely he was reaching out to his sister, hoping to end the cold war between them that was much more on her side than his. But Eunice was still too bitter. My father recalled later how Eunice forbade him from seeing his uncle during the hearings that sent him to prison or during his incarceration. After Alphaeus's release, Lisle Jr. defied his mother's orders and visited him several times at his home in Queens. Alphaeus, said my father, was always warm toward him, with a scholarly turn of conversation that his nephew admired.

As for Eunice, her effort to reinvent herself as an internationalist was essentially a success. Her involvement in the International Council of Women deepened, and she regularly attended the group's triennial conferences. But she no longer represented the National Council of Negro Women. Now she traveled on behalf of the larger and more influential National Council of Women of the United States. For years Eunice would run the law committee of the International Council. She regularly addressed its meetings. She became a member of the Conference of International Organizations, a semiofficial umbrella for what we would today call nongovernmental organizations. In Geneva, a few years later, she would be elected president. She would become a formal consultant to UNESCO and travel the globe as a regular participant in meetings of the United Nations Commission on the Status of Women. At the invitation of the United States embassy in Bonn, she would lead a seminar on the role of the United Nations. She would become an influential member of the International Board of the YWCA. Three or four times a year, like clockwork, the columns would recount her departure for some conference in Europe or Asia.

She did not get everything she wanted. She was never a judge. And although her profile among nongovernmental organizations rose, her perch on the Great Social Pyramid proved difficult to maintain. Even 10 Jumel had become a dangerous place for her. After a period of reconciliation, her husband had resumed his wandering. Now and then, late at night, Eunice would call her son and beg him to come to the house, where in her separate bedroom she would unburden herself about how casually Lisle Sr. treated the marriage. Sometimes on such occasions she had been drinking. But the next morning, everything would be fine. And when a few years later her husband was diagnosed with cancer and had to sell his dental practice, Eunice would suspend her activities to care for him.

Eunice's marital difficulties were only a stutter on her upward climb. She soon resumed her full slate of international activities. My memories of her from the 1960s feature endless images of waving her off at the dock or welcoming her back, meeting her at the airport—yes, sometimes she flew, despite her fears—and looking forward to the stream of postcards she sent from around the world, which I, as a very young stamp collector, particularly valued. She would usually come visit at Christmas, a holiday I have long associated with the delicious

Lisle Sr. receiving an award from his fellow dental school graduates, 1961.
With him at the table are his daughter-in-law Emily and his wife Eunice.
(Lisle Jr., who was speaking at the event, was seated at the head table.)
CARTER FAMILY PHOTOGRAPH

aroma of the Virginia hams she would spend a day and a half preparing. If a part of me never stopped being intimidated by my Nana, another part always found her fascinating. There was always the sense that she had been places and done things. Working on this project has made me wish I had gotten to know her better when she was alive.

If Eunice had a life's philosophy, it was probably summed up in her remarks at the triennial conference of the International Council of Women, held in Greece in January of 1951. She was advertised to be speaking on the topic of "Women in the Technical Assistance Program." (This was a United Nations initiative to render expert advice to developing countries, adopted by the General Assembly in response to a call from President Truman.) And Eunice did discuss the advertised subject. But she also went beyond it, offering a sort of cri de coeur about the suffocating norms of gender.

"Each individual in this world," she told the thousands of delegates, "has his own peculiar character and his own particular talent." The purpose of a democratic society was to allow each individual to flourish—or, in Eunice's words, "to develop his talents and to grow in character and in personality according to his own personal ability and according to his own desires." A dictatorship, in any of its "many political forms," preferred "regimenting the individual, forcing him to work and even slave at tasks which he would never choose for himself." Women faced particular costs in the effort to flourish, because "they are encumbered in many instances by traditions which relegate them to a second class role." Freeing women would inure to the benefit of the whole: "A country or community which fails to allow its women to choose and develop their individual beings in an atmosphere of freedom thrusts away from itself a large part of the human resources which can give it strength and vitality." Allowing individuals to choose their own lives, she concluded, would provide "the surest defense against the tyrant— against the dictator from within, against the oppression of poverty and disease, against the guns of a marching army."

The modern reader will look at this passage and marvel at the idea that so successful and brilliant a woman would nevertheless resort constantly to "his" and "he." Of course this was another era, but even so, Eunice was wise enough to see the problem, and even discussed it in the same speech: "It is one of the inadequacies of the English language that it is frequently necessary, when referring to an abstract individual who may be either masculine or feminine, to use the masculine gender. Skill, talent, and ingenuity prevail in woman-kind as well as man-kind."

Speaking these words, Eunice might have been arguing with her own mother, or even with herself, using the occasion to battle her way through the tangled notions of duty that on the one hand she believed in fervently and on the other she knew had always held her back. Gender roles. Racial expectation. Playing the dutiful wife when her husband philandered and she herself was in love with another man; playing the dutiful mother when she had no idea what to do with a child. For regimentation, like dictatorship, comes in many forms; and "the dictator from within" had whispered to Eunice her entire life.

And although the whisper of tradition was always loud, I suspect that the voice she heard most clearly was always the voice of ambition. Her anger at her brother was a consequence of her determination to rise. It would be wrong to draw from Eunice's story the conclusion that she was unusually envious or thought only of herself. Rather, she was

Three generations of the family on the occasion of Lisle Jr.'s appointment to federal office, 1966. Left to right: Eunice, daughter-in-law Emily, son Lisle Jr., and grandson Stephen, the author.
AFRO AMERICAN NEWSPAPERS ARCHIVES AND RESEARCH CENTER

ambitious at a time and in fields where there were few possibilities for a colored woman to shine. And before we decide that she was too ambitious, we must ask ourselves whether if Eunice had been white and male and had the same résumé, she would not have gone further in her career. If our answer is even a tentative yes, then to criticize her for ambition amounts to little more than demanding that she stay in her place.

This book has belonged to Eunice. Her brother has stalked the story without ever being fully a part of it. But Alphaeus is in his way every bit as fascinating as his sister, and what happened to him is instructive.

After his release from prison, Alphaeus found himself unemployable. His degrees from Harvard and New York University, his expertise in Tennyson, his mastery of multiple languages all meant nothing. He was a Communist. He had been to prison. He was on all the wrong lists. Within a few years of his release, the Council on African Affairs would shut down and turn its assets over to the federal government. This was the only way to escape the Red-hunting pressure. He worked in a factory for a while, and did bits of poorly compensated writing. In 1958, he left the country. For good.

He headed first to Ghana, for a Pan-Africanist conference, where, to his surprise, he was treated as a celebrity. After Ghana, Alphaeus traveled the continent, renewing acquaintances with leaders he had met during the long anti-colonial struggle. One of them, Sékou Touré, offered both Alphaeus and Dorothy teaching positions in Guinea, which they accepted. Shortly thereafter, W. E. B. Du Bois asked Alphaeus to come to Ghana and assist in completing his beloved *Encyclopedia Africana* project—"assist" in this case meaning "take over." The great scholar, now in his nineties, was looking for an heir. When Du Bois died in 1963, Alphaeus did indeed take over. He and Dorothy lived happily in Ghana until their host, Kwame Nkrumah, was ousted in a 1966 coup. The Huntons fled to Zambia, under the protection of President Kenneth Kaunda, where Alphaeus found employment with Kaunda's foundation and, in the feverish words of an internal FBI memorandum "was in the process of making friends in high places." Although he often traveled to Europe and Asia, Zambia was his home for the rest of his life.

For Alphaeus, leaving America constituted his own escape attempt. For Eunice, traveling abroad was routine. It was what she did. The columns followed her to Geneva. To Athens. To Paris. To Rome. She had found her swagger again. She could hardly attend a meeting of any international organization without finding herself elected to the leadership. The golden touch she had somehow misplaced at home she had managed to locate abroad. By the time the Democrats swept back into power in Washington (and her son along with them, for Lisle Jr. would serve both Kennedy and Johnson), Eunice was involved in over a dozen international organizations, a couple of which she had co-founded, and held office in most of them.

By this time, the trickle of middle-class Negro families out of Harlem and into the suburbs had become a flood. Sassiety was not a patch on what it had been. For the rising generation, the challenge of scaling the Great Social Pyramid was losing its appeal. The mighty domestic organizations—the National Council of Negro Women, for instance—continued to wield influence but slowly ceased to dominate the life of the darker nation. An era was rushing toward its end. *Brown v. Board of Education* had been decided, and African America saw its future as bright. Battles of the sort that Eunice had fought daily to rise in her career would no longer be necessary. Or so the darker nation thought. Asked about whether whites would resist court-ordered integration, Eunice's friend Thurgood Marshall told the *New Yorker* that such a thing would be unimaginable—the end of America. And unimaginable it was. Colored people were all Negroes now and soon would all be black. Barriers were falling. Laws were being passed. True, those on the far left fringe of the community—Alphaeus, for instance—protested that the changes about which everyone was so excited were only cosmetic, that the racist idea was embedded so deeply that it would never be exterminated by fiat. But their voices were drowned by the cheers in the general rush to celebrate the progress of the race.

In 1963, after several years of illness, Lisle Sr. died. A few years later, Eunice would sell the house on Jumel Terrace and move to a lovely high-ceilinged apartment on Central Park West. Her international activism would begin to slow. By this time, she had been largely forgotten by a darker nation that had once cheered her. Alphaeus remained in self-imposed exile in Africa, from which he would never return. In addition to his work on the *Encyclopedia Africana*, he led protests at America's embassies, including one timed to coincide precisely with Martin Luther King's speech from the steps of the Lincoln Memorial. He continued to write articles arguing that communism, not capitalism, was the only path forward for the darker nation. He and Dorothy traveled to Russia and then to China, where he encountered a friend who told him that she had recently spoken to Eunice, who had confided in her that perhaps Alphaeus's way was right after all. Maybe Eunice really said that. Maybe she said something else that, by the time the friend told Alphaeus and Alphaeus told Dorothy and Dorothy put it in her book about her husband, had a different meaning.

The siblings never fully reconciled, but at least by the time Richard Nixon was elected President they were exchanging Christmas cards, and bits of correspondence as well. In the late 1960s, Eunice sent Alphaeus a special pull-out section on Africa from the *Times*. They would never be best friends or particularly close but, come to think of it, they never had been. They shared a memory of a time in the history of the darker nation that had been buried beneath the loud immediacy of the sixties. No one would have believed that scrambling up the

Pyramid had ever been so vital; or that leaving your wife could have been seen as an act of rebellion; or that the NAACP would repeatedly have sent a black woman by herself into the worst corners of Klan country; or that the death of a tireless and beloved YMCA worker would lead hundreds of colored college men across the country to spontaneously hold memorial services; or that a young man just out of slavery and safely in Canada would plunge back into the maelstrom, heading all the way down to Mississippi to purchase his brother's freedom. History is so easy to forget. By the time Eunice and Alphaeus died, ten days apart in 1970, both from cancer, nobody would have believed that a black woman was responsible for putting the most powerful Mafia leader in the nation's history behind bars.

But that happened too.

One can imagine a different America with a different history: a nation in which two siblings so brilliant and ambitious might have attained the heights to which talent and hard work entitled them. But the darker nation has always been an ocean wave, a wave that began in Africa and has for centuries beat ceaselessly against the artificial but nearly impregnable barriers that whiteness built. The greatest talent in the world could not breach the seawall. Not by itself. Nevertheless, the remorseless pounding has made a difference. Over the years, the seawall that is race hatred has aged. The battering from without has weakened the wall's foundations. Cracks have appeared. Leaks have sprung. If you listen with the ears of history and optimism, you can hear the inner supports starting to slip.

Today the situation of the darker nation is enormously better than it was in the days when Alphaeus and Eunice crashed against the wall of race. To insist, as some still do, that nothing has changed is an act of willful ignorance—and an insult to the generations who have beaten at the wall. But to say that the wall is weakening is not to say that it is no longer there. The barrier of whiteness has proved resilient. Those who shelter behind the wall are constantly shoring it up, often without realizing what they are doing. No matter. The wall is weakening. It did not fall in the lifetimes of Eunice and Alphaeus. It will not fall in ours. In the end, however, the logic of justice and the demands for freedom will overwhelm it.

AUTHOR'S NOTE

About a decade ago, I published a novel called *Palace Council*, in which I tried to wrap a mystery and a thriller around a tale of life within upper-crust Harlem in the 1950s and 1960s. Looking back, I have come to realize that the story I tried to tell was meant as an homage to my grandmother and her generation. But a work of fiction wasn't enough; in the end, the only way to honor Nana was by setting forth the truth of her remarkable story. Thus the present project.

I could not have completed this book alone. I am deeply grateful to the several students at Yale Law School who over the past several years have served as research assistants on various aspects of this project: Sam Adkisson, Bonnie Robinson, Aisha Saad, Adeel Mohammadi, Justin Smallwood, and, especially, the indefatigable and indispensable Lauren Hobby. I am grateful as well to archivists and librarians without number for assisting in the quest.

This book would never have happened without my parents, Lisle and Emily Carter, who for decades shared the stories that help drive the narrative. Among the many other individuals who graciously shared their memories of my grandmother or of the era (or their memories of the memories of others) are A'Lelia Bundles, Jane Livingston, John Minck, Mildred Persinger, Bernice Cosey Pulley, Beryl Rice, and Constance Wright. (I apologize if there are any I have omitted.) I wish to thank my older brother, Eric Carter, for tracking down the letter from Alphaeus to Eunice the year before they died. I am also grateful to the historian

Christine Lutz, whose dissertation on the Hunton family has proved a very fine resource. I have benefitted from the hard work of librarians and archivists without number. Among those who pointed me to particular sources I might otherwise have missed are John Q. Barrett, Carrie Johnson, Peter Kougasian, and Karen White. I have had the benefit of invaluable assistance and advice from my good friend Henry Louis Gates Jr., as well as a number of colleagues at Yale Law School, and I have had the privilege of discussing parts of this story in front of audiences at both Harvard University and the Key West Literary Seminar.

Lynn Nesbit, my literary agent, believed in the project from the beginning, and constantly encouraged me to continue when I had doubts. My editor, John Sterling, kept me from many a blind alley as he patiently and gracefully guided the book to its completion. Among the many good people at Holt who labored to bring this project to fruition, I must single out particularly Caroline Wray and Chris O'Connell, who between them kept countless balls in the air.

As always, I am grateful to my wife, Enola Aird, and my son, Andrew Carter, for their swift readings of the drafts, and for thoughtful criticism that enormously improved the story.

Finally, let me reiterate the dedication: this book would have been impossible without the work of my daughter, Leah Carter, who left lucrative employment in order to assist with the project. She was the one who traveled to distant archives, interviewed sources, collated thousands of pages of information, and helped structure the narrative. I quite literally could not have done this book without her tireless work.

I am grateful that for a brief moment of my life I had the great fortune to know Eunice herself. Given what I have learned in the course of this project, I only wish that I had known her better.

Foremost among God's gifts I count my family: Enola, Leah, and Andrew, our son-in-law Kyle Moore, and now our first grandchild, Addison Liam Carter-Moore, who arrived just as the story of his great-great-grandmother was going to press. Welcome, little one, and may your life be rich with wonder and joy.

Cheshire, Connecticut
July 2018

NOTES

Several of the sources I consulted are abbreviated here.

Bethune Papers Refers to Bethune's correspondence either from the papers of the National Council of Negro Women, accessed at the National Archives for Black Women's History, Landover, Maryland, or from the Bethune Foundation Collection, accessed at the Schomburg Center for Research in Black Culture, the New York Public Library.

Du Bois Papers Refers to W. E. B. Du Bois Papers (MS 312). Special Collections and University Archives, University of Massachusetts Amherst Libraries.

Hunton FBI file Refers to the seven hundred heavily redacted pages produced by the Federal Bureau of Investigation in response to my Freedom of Information Act request.

Moorland Papers Refers to the papers of Jesse Edward Moorland at the Manuscript Division of the Howard University Libraries and the Moorland Spingarn Research Center, Washington, D.C.

NYCDA archives Refers to Archives of New York County District Attorney's Office, New York City Municipal Archives.

Prologue

xiii **One woman fled** See "41 Raids Jail 77 in Dewey War to Smash Vice Racket," *New York Herald Tribune*, Feb. 3, 1936, pp. 1, 7.

xvi **"psychologically enduring"** Jonathan Scott Holloway, *Jim Crow Wisdom: Memory and Identity in Black America Since 1940* (Chapel Hill: University of North Carolina Press, 2013), pp. 28–29.

xvii **of the darker nation** I coined the term "darker nation" in my novel *The Emperor of Ocean Park* (2002), placing it in the mouth of one of my characters, never planning to use it again. But it has grown on me. Over the years I have come across similar but not identical usages in the essays of Alain Locke, the poetry of Langston Hughes, the speeches of Mary McLeod Bethune, and the original subtitle of the NAACP's magazine, the *Crisis*.

1. The Burning

3   **"pent-up hate and envy"** Addie Waites Hunton, *William Alphaeus Hunton: A Pioneer Prophet of Young Men* (New York: Association Press, 1938), p. 133.

4   *Plessy v. Ferguson* *Plessy v. Ferguson*, 163 U.S. 537 (1896).

4   **rival Democratic candidates** See, for example, "Issues Are Discussed by Howell at East-man: Primary Open to All Who Pledge Loyalty to the Democratic Party; Negroes Disfran-chised by Poll Tax Provision," *Atlanta Constitution*, Jan. 1906, p. 7. Historians typically lay a good deal of the blame for the racially charged atmosphere at the feet of Hoke Smith, who won the primary and the governorship. See, for example, John Dittmer, *Black Georgia in the Progressive Era 1900–1920* (Urbana: University of Illinois Press, 1977), pp. 100–101.

4   **The violence continued** There are several excellent histories of the riot. I particularly rec-ommend Rebecca Burns, *Rage in the Gate City: The Story of the 1906 Atlanta Race Riot*, rev. ed. (Athens: University of Georgia Press, 2009), and David Fort Godshalk, *Veiled Visions: The 1906 Atlanta Race Riot and the Reshaping of American Race Relations* (Chapel Hill: Univer-sity of North Carolina Press, 2005). There is also a short, useful account of what occurred in Allison Dorsey, *To Build Our Lives Together: Community Formation in Black Atlanta, 1875–1906* (Athens: University of Georgia Press, 2004), pp. 158–62. To truly understand the riot, one should also peruse the local papers, particularly the *Atlanta Constitution*, at the time the voice of elite white opinion in the city, and the *Atlanta Independent*, a controversial and widely read Negro-owned newspaper.

5   **A white neighbor** This story is related in a memoir by Mary Ovington, who heard it from Addie. See Mary White Ovington, *The Walls Came Tumbling Down* (1947; repr., New York: Arno Press, 1969), p. 59. The story is not dated in Ovington's book, but elsewhere she wrote that the dinner at which she heard the tale took place in the spring of 1906.

5   **most colored households** See Nicholas Johnson, *Negroes and the Gun* (Amherst, N.Y.: Pro-metheus Books, 2014). For a particular discussion of the Atlanta riot, see pp. 181–82. Else-where in the book, Johnson quotes Du Bois's well-known response to the riot: "I bought a Winchester double-barrelled shotgun and two dozen rounds of shells filled with buckshot. If a white mob had stepped on the campus where I lived I would without hesitation have sprayed their guts over the grass" (p. 151).

5   **"literally sold to"** Godshalk, *Veiled Visions*, p. 26.

6   **he was scheduled** On the importance of Japan to the YMCA, see Jon Thares Davidann, *A World of Crisis and Progress: The American YMCA in Japan, 1890–1930* (Bethlehem, Pa.: Lehigh University Press, 1998).

6   **Scant weeks after** J. W. E. Bowen, "The Atlanta Race Riot and Our Schools," *Christian Advo-cate*, Oct. 18, 1906, p. 16.

6   **"the dangerous period"** "Clarke [sic] and Gammon Safe—Washington," *New York Age*, Oct. 4, 1906, p. 2.

6   **The migration frightened** To be sure, most residents of the Fourth Ward stayed. But the city continued to burn with prejudice long after the riots ended. The future was not difficult to predict. Racial restrictions in Atlanta grew. What they had not accomplished by the vio-lence of the mob, Atlanta's whites tried to accomplish by the violence of law. They would eventually adopt ordinances restricting neighborhoods by race. The idea, which came to be call "redlining," was invented not by Southern racists but by Northern progressives. See Garrett Power, "Apartheid Baltimore Style: The Residential Ordinances of 1910–1913," *Maryland Law Review*, vol. 42, no. 4 (1983), p. 289. For a contemporaneous reaction, see "Baltimore Tries Drastic Plan of Race Segregation," *New York Times Magazine*, Dec. 25, 1910, p. 2.

6   **A few states** This effort is discussed in detail in Dewey H. Palmer, "Moving North: Migra-tion of Negroes During World War I," *Phylon*, vol. 28, no. 1 (1967), p. 52.

6   **"With the Huntons' departure"** Godshalk, *Veiled Visions*, p. 107.

7   **you could buy pieces** I had always thought that the story of the window displays of bits of Sam Hose's body was mere rumor, but apparently it was true. See Edwin T. Arnold, *"What*

Virtue There Is in Fire": Cultural Memory and the Lynching of Sam Hose (Athens: University of Georgia Press, 2009), pp. 118–19. That Hose was badly mutilated should hardly be surprising, given the way the local press egged on the mob. For a particular egregious example, see "Hose Is a Will o' the Wisp to His Determined Pursuers," *Atlanta Constitution*, April 16, 1899, p. 2. Although the newspapers characterized Hose as a "brute," he was short and skinny and weighed no more than 140 pounds. See W. Fitzhugh Brundage, *Lynching in the New South: Georgia and Virginia, 1880–1930* (Urbana: University of Illinois Press, 1993), pp. 83–84.

7 **the Huntons considered leaving** Addie Hunton, *Pioneer Prophet*, pp. 132–33.

7 **Two earlier children** How do we know that at least one of the first two children died of tuberculosis? Consider: Addie, in the biography of her husband she would later publish, describes his "quiet fortitude" at the moment "when we were taking our dying baby northward to Asheville" (Addie Hunton, *Pioneer Prophet*, p. 74). It is not clear which baby Addie meant. Both Bernice and the first William Alphaeus Jr. died when the family still lived in Norfolk, so Asheville would have been southward, not northward. It may be that the Huntons were elsewhere in the South—Alabama, for example, where she was teaching—when one of the children fell ill, in which case Asheville might indeed have been northward. The alternative is that the family did indeed rush southward, and either Addie's memory failed her or her pen slipped in recording the events more than forty years later.

The important point is not which direction they were traveling but that they were heading toward Asheville. In the late nineteenth century, Asheville, North Carolina, had become a destination for people seeking a cure for tuberculosis. The first tuberculosis sanitarium was built there, and by the 1900s, there were several. See Thomas M. Daniel, *Wade Hampton Frost, Pioneer Epidemiologist, 1880–1938: Up to the Mountain* (Rochester, N.Y.: University of Rochester Press, 2004), pp. 95–97. This was at a time when many physicians believed that sunlight and fresh air were the best way to battle the disease, and Asheville offered both. The Huntons were rushing their failing infant to Asheville in desperate hope.

At this time, the ravages of tuberculosis were significantly worse in African America than among whites. At the turn of the century, black sufferers were four times as likely as white sufferers to die. See Marion M. Torchia, "The Tuberculosis Movement and the Race Question, 1890–1950," *Bulletin of the History of Medicine*, vol. 49, no. 2 (Summer 1975), p. 152. Many Americans, including many doctors, considered the data a mark of the Negro's physical inferiority. Others, more egalitarian in outlook, suggested that "the poor and the ignorant" needed to be "impressed with the importance of having an abundance of fresh air and sunshine in the living-rooms." "Society Reports," *Medical Record*, vol. 53, no. 20 (May 14, 1898), p. 707 (remarks of Dr. Edward G. Janeway, president of the New York Academy of Medicine). That the poor and ignorant might not have living rooms to ventilate and open to the sun did not figure into the calculation. Although tuberculosis sanitariums were by this time being built everywhere, most segregated their patients by race. Many others, in the North as well as the South, did not admit Negroes at all. See Torchia, "The Tuberculosis Movement and the Race Question," pp. 155–58.

7 **So cautious were they** See William A. Hunton to Jesse Moorland, June 13, 1899, Moorland Papers.

7 **"Have lots to tell"** William A. Hunton to Jesse Moorland, April 25, 1899, Moorland Papers.

7 **"Sugar"** William A. Hunton to Jesse Moorland, July 24, 1899, Moorland Papers; William A. Hunton to Jesse Moorland, July 29, 1899, Moorland Papers; William A. Hunton to Jesse Moorland, Aug. 8, 1899, Moorland Papers.

7 **"Wife, Eunice Roberta"** William A. Hunton to Jesse Moorland, Aug. 22, 1899, Moorland Papers.

7 **"Eunice came and bound"** Addie Hunton, *Pioneer Prophet*, p. 133.

7 **"their handsome new home"** "What the Negro Is Doing," *Atlanta Constitution*, Nov. 5, 1899, p. 23. The *Constitution*, the dominant paper in town, featured a regular column entitled "What the Negro Is Doing: Matters of Interest Among the Colored People," and that is

where the story of the family's new home appeared. The column was penned by a prominent black physician named Henry Rutherford Butler—"H. R. Butler" to readers. Among Butler's many accomplishments was the first effort to write a history of a black medical association. See "Henry Rutherford Butler, M.D., 1862–1931," *Journal of the National Medical Association*, 51, no. 5 (Sept. 1959), p. 406.

7   **is usually described** See, for example, Hunton, *Pioneer Prophet*, p. 133: "We put much joyous enthusiasm into the building of our modest but precious home."

7   **"lived quite comfortably"** "Cal Coolidge Helped Her Get Her M.A. Degree," *Boston Daily Globe*, July 3, 1938, p. B18.

8   **"It's too nice"** Quoted in Walter White, *A Man Called White: The Autobiography of Walter White* (New York: Knopf, 1948; Athens: University of Georgia Press, 1995), p. 11.

8   **"served as a busy gathering place"** Burns, *Rage in the Gate City*, p. 34.

8   **"the most costly one"** See, for example, advertisement for the Gate City Drug Store, *Atlanta Independent*, Jan. 23, 1904, p. 2. On the opposite side of the page is an ad for the competitor, Carter's Drug Store, which includes a photograph of the pharmacist, perhaps to make sure potential customers know he is black.

8   **At 66 Peachtree Street** Dorsey, *To Build Our Lives Together*, p. 49.

8   **"[T]he colored people insisted"** Ibid., p. 92.

9   **other plans for Negro education** For example, a 1902 essay in the *Atlanta Constitution* advised: "Take the money that is now wasted on Latin and algebra, and use it in teaching them to cook, wash, sew, and do general housework." Mrs. T. W. Greene, "Trained Servants for the South and How to Get Them," *Atlanta Constitution*, Aug. 24, 1902, p. D2. The author saw only four possible futures for young colored women: they would teach; they would "become wives of prosperous colored men"; they would remain in "poverty, idleness, and shame, breeding a race of criminals to menace the citizen of the future"; or they would become "good servants." She argued that for most, the last was the only reasonable choice. Thus education should point all but a handful in that direction.

9   **commitment to excellence** The Houston Street School was admired throughout the Fourth Ward for the ways in which it inspired confidence and racial pride. When Eunice enrolled, the principal was the legendary William Baxter Matthews, who served in that position for more than two decades. At this time, the South's black-run schools were under ideological attack. Benjamin W. Hunt, a wealthy New Yorker banker who had moved to Georgia in the 1870s, complained that the schools were training "[y]oung negroes in the South . . . to regard the white race as enemies, not as friends." They were not being taught the proper attitude of respect for "superior" and other "civic duties." Instead, "the altruistic money of the white people is spent in teaching colored children anarchism" (Benjamin W. Hunt, letter to the editor, *New York Times*, Sept. 27, 1903, p. 14). The reason whites had to fund and control the black schools, wrote another Southerner in the *Outlook,* was to ensure that young Negroes were "educated under proper influences" (Clarence H. Poe, "Should Southern Whites Aid Negro Schools? A Southerner's View," *Outlook*, vol. 71, no. 17 [Aug. 23, 1902], p. 1010). Otherwise, the South risked "a vastly larger number educated beyond the control of the Southern white man and in an atmosphere calculated to produce constant friction between the races."

    Yet many whites admired the school. Justifiable pride in the institution, wrote the *Atlanta Constitution* in an 1897 article, "is felt not only among those who have children in the school, but by all the better negroes in the district" ("The Mitchell and Houston Street Schools: Houston Street School," *Atlanta Constitution*, March 10, 1897, p. 4). An article in the *Advance*, a Christian magazine, used the school's teachers, mostly graduates of Atlanta University, to illustrate the benefits of higher education for the "emancipated race" ("Shall the Emancipated Negro Be Liberally Educated?" *Advance*, vol. 45 [May 28, 1903], p. 658).

9   **just after her fifth birthday** Although the school is long gone, its reputation justifiably lingers. One particular object of pride is a widely told story of how Antoine Graves, the legendary

principal of the school, was fired by the city board of education in 1885 or 1886 after refusing to have his students join in the parade honoring Jefferson Davis as the train bearing the former Confederate president's remains passed through Atlanta. Even today the account appears in many a historical narrative. See, for example, Kenneth Robert Janken, *Walter White: Mr. NAACP* (Chapel Hill: University of North Carolina Press, 2003), p. 8; Howard N. Rabinowitz, "Half a Loaf: The Shift from White to Black Teachers in the Negro Schools of the Urban South, 1865–1890," in Rabinowitz, *Race, Ethnicity, and Urbanization: Selected Essays* (Columbia: University of Missouri Press, 1994), p. 111, n. 61; and C. T. Wright, "The Development of Public Schools for Blacks in Atlanta, 1872–1900," *Atlanta Historical Bulletin*, vol. xxi (Spring 1977), pp. 115–28.

Particularly given the era in which it occurred, the tale is both powerful and inspiring. Alas, it is also apocryphal. It could not have happened. In the first place, Graves's term as principal ended in 1886, and Davis did not die until three years later, in December 1889. Moreover, the train that carried Davis's remains through the South did not begin its journey until 1893, when his body was exhumed. (I am writing a separate article on the origins of this story.) Nevertheless, the pride with which the myth is repeated even today by those two or three generations removed tells a story of its own about the remarkable spirit with which parents of the Fourth Ward infused their children. Eunice, young as she was, could not help but be imbued with the same sense of confidence. Although she would study at Houston Street for only two years, the habits of thought that were reinforced there surely contributed to her lifelong belief that barriers existed to be overcome.

9   **the Christian warriors** An excellent account of William's work may be found in Nina Mjagkij, *Light in the Darkness: African Americans and the YMCA, 1852–1946* (Lexington: University Press of Kentucky, 1994), particularly chapter 4. Mjagkij's book is also a fine introduction to the contributions of William's colleague and protégé Jesse Moorland.

9   **"a very desirable center"** Addie Hunton, *Pioneer Prophet*, p. 132.

11   **At one point William complained** William A. Hunton to Jesse Moorland, Dec. 12, 1899, Moorland Papers.

11   **"Eunice caused the blots above"** William A. Hunton to Jesse Moorland, Aug. 4, 1900, Moorland Papers.

11   **"Eunice is as sweet as sugar"** William A. Hunton to Jesse Moorland, Oct. 12, 1900, Moorland Papers.

11   **"My stenographer"** William A. Hunton to Jesse Moorland, Jan. 18, 1901, Moorland Papers.

11   **"She [won't] believe"** William A. Hunton to Jesse Moorland, Feb. 4, 1901, Moorland Papers.

11   **There are more letters** See, for example, William A. Hunton to Jesse Moorland, Feb. 19, 1901, Moorland Papers, and William A. Hunton to Jesse Moorland, June 29, 1901, Moorland Papers.

11   **he would quote** See Christine Ann Lutz, "'The Dizzy Steep to Heaven': The Hunton Family and the Atlantic World, 1850–1970" (Ph.D. diss., Georgia State University, 2001), p. 163.

12   **The Huntons moved** Several sources assert that the Huntons moved to Brooklyn in April or May of 1907. But in January, Addie was already using a Brooklyn address in her correspondence. See Addie W. Hunton to W. E. B. Du Bois, Jan. 14, 1907, Du Bois Papers.

12   **principal cause of the labor strike** For an account of the corruption in the Sanitation Department that helped cause the strike, see Daniel Eli Burnstein, "Progressivism and Urban Crisis: The New York City Garbage Workers' Strike of 1907," *Journal of Urban History*, vol. 16, no. 4 (Aug. 1990), p. 386.

2. The Legacy

14   *Plessy v. Ferguson* Plessy v. Ferguson, 163 U.S. 537 (1896).

14   **William talked the conductor** Addie Hunton, *Pioneer Prophet*, p. 74.

15   **Christine Lutz speculates** See Lutz, "'Dizzy Steep to Heaven,'" p. 55, n. 2. As to the reasons for my skepticism, see the next note.

15   **owned by one Gustavus Horner** The last will and testament of Gustavus Brown Horner Sr., who died on January 2, 1815, provides that land be set aside for his slaves, including a woman named Betty, age thirty, and her son Stanton, age five. As Stanton Hunton is thought to have been born around 1809, this Stanton would have been the right age. If this is the Stanton we're looking for, then as a young boy he would have been a Horner slave, not a Hunton slave, with ownership at some point transferred to Thomas Hunton. But if Stanton's mother was not owned by a Hunton, it is unlikely that William Hunton was his father.

15   **Hunton & Williams** See "Eppa Hunton, Jr., to Enter a Co-Partnership: Father Comes Also," *Richmond Dispatch*, Oct. 8, 1901, p. 7. The firm was originally known as Munford, Hunton, Williams, and Anderson.

15   **was one of fourteen slaves** See "Will of General Thomas Hunton," recorded in probate March 1, 1832. Thomas died around 1829. The 1830 census lists Mathilda as head of the household and in possession of some nineteen slaves.

15   **"kindhearted"** The "kindhearted" language is from Dorothy Hunton, in her biography of her husband, Alphaeus (Eunice's brother). Dorothy Hunton, *Alphaeus Hunton: The Unsung Valiant* (Richmond Hill, N.Y.: D. K. Hunton, 1986), p. 1. Addie Hunton, Eunice and Alphaeus's mother, calls the owner "a most humane maiden lady of the Virginia aristocracy." Addie Hunton, *Pioneer Prophet*, p. 2. Mathilda was not a "maiden lady" as the term was traditionally used—she had been married. Dorothy Hunton calls the owner "Miss Nettie"; there is also a family tradition that her name was Elizabeth. This tradition is consistent with the theory that Stanton, when he was very young, was owned by Gustavus Horner.

When Gustavus died, his slaves were distributed among his children, one of whom was a daughter named Elizabeth, whose married name was Moore. She could well have been the "kindhearted" Elizabeth who supposedly taught the young Stanton to read and write. She would have inherited him when he was still a child, an important point, for not even the most progressively "humane" Southern lady would have spent enough time alone with an enslaved adult male to teach him to read. A few years later the estate was tied up in litigation, and it is possible that the heirs had to sell property (including human property) to make ends meet. A subsequent sale of Stanton to Thomas Hunton would then make the circle complete.

15   **regularly lobbied** A copy of one petition is available via the Race and Petitions Project at http://library.uncg.edu/slavery/petitions/details.aspx?pid=2654. Frequent proposals to restrict or eliminate manumission in Virginia were routinely voted down in the legislature. See John Henderson Russell, *The Free Negro in Virginia, 1619–1865* (Baltimore: Johns Hopkins Press, 1913), pp. 73–75.

15   **Either Gaines, too, was experiencing** In Virginia at this time, as elsewhere in the South, slaves were permitted to hire themselves out to others with the consent of their owners. The practice was not only common but constituted an important economic pillar of the edifice of slavery. This was particularly true in Virginia, as the gradual move away from tobacco-based farming altered planters' calculations about how many slaves they needed. See Sarah S. Hughes, "Slaves for Hire: The Allocation of Black Labor in Elizabeth City County, Virginia, 1782–1810," *William and Mary Quarterly*, vol. 35, no. 2 (April 1978), pp. 260–86. Generally, the owner and the slaves split the profits. For excellent discussions of this practice, see John J. Zaborney, *Slaves for Hire: Renting Enslaved Laborers in Antebellum Virginia* (Baton Rouge: Louisiana State University Press, 2012), and Jonathan D. Martin, *Divided Mastery: Slave Hiring in the American South* (Cambridge, Mass.: Harvard University Press, 2004).

16   **Stanton Hunton's deed** Gaines's signature appears on Stanton's deed of emancipation, a copy of which is in my possession. Christine Lutz, in her very fine history of the Hunton family, suggests that Gaines was not Stanton's owner but an agent for his actual owner. Lutz, "'Dizzy Steep to Heaven,'" p. 55, n. 3. This is unlikely. The law was clear. The owner had to sign or the manumission papers were invalid. The only exception was when the signer held the owner's power of attorney, but the power of attorney had to be recited on the face of the document. That was not done here.

16   **In 1840, about 10 percent** See Ira Berlin, *Slaves Without Masters: The Free Negro in the Antebellum South* (New York: Pantheon, 1974), p. 137.

16   **So Stanton, had he wished** A useful (and illustrated) account of the history of the free black population of Fauquier County may be found in Donna Tyler Hollie, Brett M. Tyler, and Karen Hughes White, *African Americans of Fauquier County* (Charleston, S.C.: Arcadia Publishing, 2009).

16   **"a loyal and dutiful person"** "Fauquier Emancipations," in *Afro-American Historical Quarterly* (of Fauquier County), fragment undated, unpaginated.

16   **he filed a formal petition** See the Race and Petitions Project, http://library.uncg.edu /slavery/petitions/details.aspx?pid=2654.

16   **The petition was joined** Among Staunton Hunton's several co-petitioners were Lucy Malvin and her three children, whose story is touchingly told in Eva Sheppard Wolf, *Almost Free: A Story About Family and Race in Antebellum Virginia* (Athens: University of Georgia Press, 2012).

16   **If he could not produce them** See the discussion in John Hope Franklin and Loren Schweninger, *Runaway Slaves: Rebels on the Plantation* (New York: Oxford University Press, 1999), pp. 145–47.

16   **found his way to Chatham** For vivid descriptions of the world the formerly enslaved made in and around Chatham, see the essays in Boulou Ebanda de B'béri, Nina Reid-Maroney, and Handel Kashope Wright, eds., *The Promised Land: History and Historiography of the Black Experience in Chatham-Kent's Settlement and Beyond* (Toronto: University of Toronto Press, 2014). See also John Kenneth Anthony Farrell, "The History of the Negro Community in Chatham, Ontario, 1787–1865" (Ph.D. thesis, University of Ottawa, 1955).

17   **in and around Natchez** For a chilling example, see Todd A. Herring, "Kidnapped and Sold in Natchez: The Ordeal of Aaron Cooper, a Free Black Man," *Journal of Mississippi History*, vol. 60, no. 1 (Winter 1998), p. 341. Numerous further instances are recounted in Jaime Elizabeth Boler, "City Under Siege: Resistance and Power in Natchez, Mississippi, 1719–1857" (Ph.D. diss., University of Southern Mississippi, 2005).

18   **"stern but devoted"** Addie Hunton, *Pioneer Prophet*, p. 6.

18   **she refused to use** Dorothy Hunton, *Unsung Valiant*, p. 3.

18   **Her mother was probably** Addie Hunton, *Pioneer Prophet*, p. 7.

18   **Addie was christened** Lutz says that Adelina was born near Beaufort, South Carolina, and I have no reason to doubt her impeccable research. See Lutz, "'Dizzy Steep to Heaven,'" p. 102. But Addie, who admittedly gave varying accounts of herself, said at one point that her mother was born in Virginia. Furthermore, the 1880 census gives Adelina as born in North Carolina.

19   **Her mother died** Lutz, "'Dizzy Steep to Heaven,'" p. 102. In 1894, Jessie Waits remarried. His second wife, Sarah, was sixteen years his junior. She apparently bore him a son, Bernard Waits, who was born in 1895, when Sarah would have been thirty-six years old.

19   **In the late 1890s** Many sources, including several obituaries of Addie, assert that this was the Spencerian College of Commerce or the Spencerian Business College, but there seems to be no record of a school with either name in the city at that time. Most likely Addie enrolled at a business college that taught the Spencerian method, which was a form of shorthand. There existed at this time in Philadelphia both the Frankford College of Commerce and the Philadelphia Business College and College of Commerce. If she attended one of those, she was probably training to be a professional secretary—that is, to earn her own living in the job rather than working for her husband for free. It is not clear whether Addie ever completed her degree.

19   **William canceled his travels** William A. Hunton to Jesse Moorland, Dec. 17, 1898, Moorland Papers, and telegram from William A. Hunton to Jesse Moorland, Dec. 21, 1898, Moorland Papers.

19   **"A Pure Motherhood"** Addie's address on this occasion has been anthologized often. For the original text, see *The United Negro: His Problems and His Progress: Containing the*

Addresses and Proceedings; The Negro Young People's Christian and Educational Congress, Held August 6–11, 1902 (Atlanta: D. E. Luther Publishing, 1902), p. 433.

20 **Certainly William shared** As evidence of William's uneasiness with the behavior of those less mannered than himself, consider the following excerpt from a letter to Addie, which appears in her book about her husband: "There was an awful crowd of colored people who got on in Atlanta going to Goldsboro, North Carolina, to work. They began drinking (women and men) as soon as we left Atlanta. Every seat was occupied—a drinking woman was in my seat. It was awful." Quoted in Addie Hunton, *Pioneer Prophet*, p. 70. Addie does not give the date of the letter, but the context suggests that it may have been written around 1910 or 1911.

21 **"one of the greatest women"** "Midnight's Musings," *Afro-American* (Baltimore), June 20, 1908, p. 5.

21 **Even the mainstream papers** See, for example, "Negro Women to Meet in Brooklyn To-Morrow," *Brooklyn Daily Eagle*, Aug. 23, 1908, p. 41.

21 **She penned a plaintive note** Addie W. Hunton to Jesse Moorland, April 2, 1907, Moorland Papers.

21 **What Addie did not** Addie W. Hunton to W. E. B. Du Bois, April 8, 1907, Moorland Papers.

21 **"I did not mean"** Addie W. Hunton to Jesse Moorland, April 8, 1907, Moorland Papers.

21 **she found full-time employment** Judith Weisenfeld, *African American Women and Christian Activism: New York's Black YWCA, 1905–1945* (Cambridge, Mass.: Harvard University Press, 1997), p. 54.

21 **She was hired as** See Nancy Marie Robertson, *Christian Sisterhood, Race Relations, and the YWCA, 1906–46* (Urbana: University of Illinois Press, 2007), p. 25. In many ways, Addie's tenure with the YWCA tracked her husband's with the YMCA. She was the group's first Negro secretary. She was the group's first paid Negro employee. She redefined her job as building new colored branches, not just evaluating the old ones. And she concentrated on the colleges, where she wound up chartering thirty-eight new colored branches. See Laverne Gyant, "Working Toward the Betterment of the Community: Elizabeth Ross Haynes," in *Black Lives: Essays in African American Biography*, ed. James L. Conyers (1999; repr., London: Routledge, 2015), pp. 95, 98–99.

21 **"embarked on a five-month tour"** Weisenfeld, *African American Women and Christian Activism*, pp. 54–55.

21 **she continued to be invited** See, for example, "Women's Work for the Race," *Afro-American* (Baltimore), Aug. 29, 1908, p. 1.

22 **Some of the letters** In his private correspondence with his friend Jesse Moorland, William evinced enormous love for his wife and family. But there are hints in the letters of a lack of respect for Addie—a feeling that, if indeed it existed, must surely have seeped from time to time into their relationship. Call it a desire for male companionship. The great traditionalist perhaps shared the traditional view that the troubles of men are not for women. Of his love for his wife his letters and actions leave no doubt. Nevertheless, we might characterize his attitude toward her as an affectionate condescension. (I am grateful to Leah Carter for this important insight.)

Consider this excerpt from a letter to Moorland sent from New Orleans in March of 1900:

> I should say I do know what it means to have one's stenographer put one's letter in better style than the dictator can think out. Dear angels! They call for the last drop of patience on our parts. But say, boss, you had better not talk so loud, as the enclosed note warns (William A. Hunton to Jesse Moorland, March 30, 1900, Moorland Papers).

To understand the point, consider that Addie, when not traveling, worked as William's secretary—not merely in a casual but in a formal sense. (Remember that she had attended secretarial school.) Many of William's letters are typewritten, but Addie was generally the typist. This is indicated by a May 1901 letter to Moorland full of typographical errors and misspellings not common to his correspondence. At the end of the letter William apologizes: "This is my writing, but you would probably guess that" (William A. Hunton to Jesse Moorland, May 23, 1901, Moorland Papers).

That Addie was William's secretary was the aspect of their complex relationship that probably lay behind the half-joking reference in a letter he sent to Moorland in December of 1900:

> I think I shall have to advertise for another stenographer. I dictated some sentences to my "present incumbent" [Addie] which she refused to write. How can I endure it! Hope you are having more fortunate experience. And, yet, it is equally as bad when a man's wife thinks so little about the letters he [illegible] that she sends them back to him. Of course we capitalists and oppressed husbands must speak softly, or there will be a strike (William A. Hunton to Jesse Moorland, Dec. 4, 1900, Moorland Papers).

The last line is meant to be humorous, but it is also importantly gendered. William could make gentle fun of his wife for being so strong-willed, confident that although she might run the household and even talk back to him, he was head of the family. Yet the theme of being somewhat hapless at home was one on which he hammered. In the fall of 1899, when the family had at last moved into their new house at 418 Houston Street, William wrote to Moorland that he would "be simply an eater [&] sleeper here, with nothing to do with affairs, except to provide the money to pay the bills." William A. Hunton to Jesse Moorland, Oct. 24, 1899, Moorland Papers. The historian Christine Lutz, in her study of the Hunton family, puts the matter this way: "She was a pupil in his eyes, never a peer" (Lutz, "'Dizzy Steep to Heaven,'" p. 110). Children are sensitive to such nuances. Eunice and Alphaeus could not have helped noticing the air of superiority, however slight, that their father assumed around their mother.

They would also have noticed his reserve. William was not the sort to unburden himself to his wife when things went poorly. Addie would later describe her husband's almost stoic calm in the face of any setback. But with Moorland he was more frank. For example, when Addie wanted to accompany her husband to a conference in Boston, it was to Moorland, not Addie, that he privately worried about whether the family budget would stand the strain (William A. Hunton to Jesse Moorland, June 1, 1901, Moorland Papers). Two months later, after complaining humorously about a long day spent shopping with his wife, William added this: "I miss you very much, for I have no one with whom to talk my troubles over" (William A. Hunton to Jesse Moorland, Aug. 22, 1901, Moorland Papers). See also William A. Hunton to Jesse Moorland, Nov. 25, 1899, Moorland Papers: "Don't get lost any more. I am lonesome without a word from you."

Addie admired her husband. She loved her husband. She was proud of her husband. But she may nevertheless have grown tired of being condescended to, or perhaps of knowing that William was not prepared to confide in her.

22 **Under a pretext** See Lutz, "'Dizzy Steep to Heaven,'" p. 163.

22 **Addie enrolled at Kaiser Wilhelm** The information on what Addie studied in Germany is from "Traveled with Negro; Held," *Sun* (Baltimore), June 8, 1910, p. 13.

22 **"shows a marked superiority"** "The Negro in America," *Times* (London), Jan. 26, 1909, p. 9.

22 **"at the various courts of Europe"** "Courts and Capitals of the Old World," *Washington Times*, July 16, 1903, p. 6.

23 **an appreciation of jazz** See Jed Rasula, "Jazz as Decal for the European Avant-Garde," in Heike Raphael-Hernandez, ed., *Blackening Europe: The African American Presence* (New York: Routledge, 2004), p. 1.

23 **"boyishly joyous"** Addie Hunton, *Pioneer Prophet*, p. 134.

23 **Other sources say** The historian Christine Lutz, in her study of the Hunton family, suggests that Addie later became persuaded "that Germans were a heartless body of people, ingenious, disinclined to democracy, but inclined toward conquest." Lutz, "'Dizzy Steep to

Heaven,'" p. 165. Although Lutz includes this proposition in her discussion of Addie's time in Europe with the children, her source material is the book Addie co-authored after spending time in Europe during World War I. The book makes no mention of Addie's views during her earlier visit. See Addie W. Hunton and Kathryn M. Johnson, *Two Colored Women with the American Expeditionary Forces* (Brooklyn: Brooklyn Eagle Press, 1920).

23 **The stated reason was** Addie's was case number 83846. The ship's passenger manifest listed her as born in Africa, a non-immigrant alien, and living in Canada. All three were incorrect.

23 **was applied with some frequency** See Martha Gardner, *The Qualities of a Citizen: Women, Immigration, and Citizenship, 1870–1965* (Princeton, N.J.: Princeton University Press, 2005), pp. 91–92. At this time LPC was the most common reason for would-be immigrants to be refused entry. By one estimate, over 60 percent of those turned away in the early twentieth century were categorized as likely public charges. See Erika Lee and Judy Yung, *Angel Island: Immigrant Gateway to America* (New York: Oxford University Press, 2010), pp. 157–58. Martha Gardner puts the figure at two-thirds; see Gardner, *The Qualities of a Citizen*, pp. 90–91. There were famous cases of error, and frequent promises to do better, but in the anti-immigrant hysteria of the age, the catchall category remained a formidable weapon.

Women traveling without husbands were particularly likely to be detained. If they sought to enter the country with their children, the fear of their likely indigence was even greater. See Gardner, *The Qualities of a Citizen*, pp. 91–92.

23 **an immigration officer's racial nightmare** According to immigration records, most of the others from the same ship who were detained along with Addie, however, were held because of a certificate from a physician, presumably on grounds of illness. Hardly any were designated "LPC." So we are likely on safe ground with the assumption that skin color played a role.

24 **"might be ostracized"** "German Woman Detained; Negro Family Taken to Ellis Island and at Same Time Released," *New-York Tribune*, June 7, 1910, p. 14.

24 **"did not know there was any"** "Traveled with Negro; Held," *Sun* (Baltimore), June 8, 1910, p. 13.

24 **"was not aware of the color line"** "Admit Rodenbeck Girl; Young Woman Said She Didn't Know of Our 'Color Line,'" *New York Times*, June 8, 1910, p. 3.

24 **She told the *Tribune*** "German Woman Detained; Negro Family Taken to Ellis Island and at Same Time Released," *New-York Tribune*, June 7, 1910, p. 14.

24 **Addie told the *New York Age*** "Tells of Detention Incident," *New York Age*, June 30, 1910, p. 1.

25 **He seemed to recover** Addie Hunton, *Pioneer Prophet*, p. 134.

25 **She joined the boards** See, for example, "Clio School of Natural Science: Gives Special Instruction in the Higher Branches of Learning," *Afro-American* (Baltimore), May 13, 1911, p. 2.

25 **The press of the darker nation** See, for example, "Midnight's Musings," *Afro-American* (Baltimore), June 20, 1908, p. 5.

26 **The tea was canceled** "No Negroes and No Tea," *Courier-Journal* (Louisville), Feb. 26, 1911, p. 8.

26 **"dancing for joy"** Hunton, *Pioneer Prophet*, p. 135.

26 **at 575 Greene Avenue** In 1917, W. E. B. Du Bois would purchase a home on the next block. See W. E. B. Du Bois to State Bank, June 17, 1917, Du Bois Papers.

26 **"cure cottages"** Saranac Lake was the home of the Adirondack Cottage Sanitarium, which specialized in the treatment of tuberculosis. The institution had been founded by Dr. Edward Livingston Trudeau, an apostle of what has been called the "rest cure." He believed in the importance of exposing tuberculosis patients to sunlight and fresh, clean air, and that the best place to find both was in the mountains. Once the sanitarium and its vision became popular, townspeople began refitting their houses to Trudeau's standards, so that you could rent one of these dwellings—known as "cure cottages"—without regard to whether you were being formally treated at the hospital Trudeau founded.

27 **depending on his health** The cure cottages were expensive, and renting one regularly further damaged the family's already shaky finances. See Lutz, "'Dizzy Steep to Heaven,'" pp. 183–86.

27   **one of the few women to attend** Only seven women attended the conference, but eleven were invited (out of thirty-two participants). David Levering Lewis, *W. E. B. Du Bois: The Fight for Equality and the American Century, 1919–1963* (New York: Henry Holt, 2000), p. 633, n. 318.

27   **whose widow was a dear friend** See, for example, the correspondence quoted in Hunton, *Pioneer Prophet*, p. 165.

27   **The organizers hoped** See Simon Topping, "'Supporting Our Friends and Defeating Our Enemies': Militancy and Nonpartisanship in the NAACP, 1936–1948," *Journal of African American History*, vol. 89, no. 1 (Winter 2004), pp. 17, 18. Whether the conference made an important difference is another matter. See the critique in William Jordan, "'The Damnable Dilemma': African-American Accommodation and Protest During World War I," *Journal of American History*, vol. 81, no. 4 (March 1995), pp. 1562, 1571ff.

27   **"It was all so beautiful"** Hunton, *Pioneer Prophet*, p. 161. A monody is a poem of lament at another's passing.

28   **going back on tour** See, for example, "Women's Federation," *New Journal and Guide* (Norfolk, Va.), Aug. 4, 1917, p. 1, describing Addie's visit to Hampton, Virginia, in July, and "Civic League's Annual Luncheon: Working of Women Along Social and Civic Lines Thoroughly Discussed," *Afro-American* (Baltimore), Feb. 24, 1917, describing her visit to Baltimore. The Baltimore lecture, on the topic of "the many ways in which colored women could work for urban uplift," came just three months after William's death.

3. The Student

29   **When he asked why** See "She Helped Jail Luciano," *Amsterdam News*, Aug. 15, 1942, p. 4.

30   **"would read all night"** Dorothy Hunton, *Unsung Valiant*, p. 12.

30   **he won a medal** "The Horizon," *Crisis*, vol. 15, no. 2 (Dec. 1917), pp. 83, 90.

30   **His favorite activity** Dorothy Hunton, *Unsung Valiant*, p. 12.

30   **"Colored high school students"** "The Horizon," *Crisis*, vol. 23, no. 1 (Nov. 1921), p. 34.

30   **working as a Red Cap** Dorothy Hunton, *Unsung Valiant*, p. 15.

30   **boarding with the Hairstons** To be precise, the 1920 census places Alphaeus and Addie at the Hairston home. It is possible, of course, that they stayed elsewhere before that. In her book about her husband, Dorothy writes that Alphaeus stayed with the Hairstons while his mother was in France, but, as we have seen, he was actually in Philadelphia. However, he may have returned to Brooklyn and the Hairstons by the summer of 1919, if we imagine him able to begin working as a porter at age fifteen. More likely, however, his work as a porter came in the summers of 1920 and 1921.

30   **Harry was a Pullman porter** The Red Caps were station porters, and should not be confused with the Pullman porters, by then already organized by A. Philip Randolph. Harry Hairston was one of the latter; Alphaeus was one of the former, transporting passengers' bags back and forth from curb to train and vice versa. The work of a Red Cap was backbreaking. The conditions were dreadful. The Red Caps were poorly paid, and tipping by the passengers whose bags they carried was "unreliable." In the aftermath of World War I—that is to say, just about the time Alphaeus began work—the Penn Station Red Caps tried to organize a union, the Brotherhood of Railway Station Attendants. The effort failed. Management imposed pay cuts. It was the Depression, and jobs were scarce. The labor did not require particular skill. The Red Caps understood that if they quit, they could easily be replaced. See Eric Arnesen, *Brotherhoods of Color: Black Railroad Workers and the Struggle for Equality* (Cambridge, Mass.: Harvard University Press, 2001), pp. 158–60. Alphaeus could not quit; he needed the money.

30   **"the hard work supplied"** Dorothy Hunton, *Unsung Valiant*, p. 15.

32   **Addie was away** Addie presumably wrote to her children, but no letters survive. She also continued her correspondence with Du Bois. See, for example, Addie W. Hunton to W. E. B. Du Bois, March 10, 1919, Du Bois Papers.

32 **"military equivalent of chain gangs"** Arthur E. Barbeau and Florette Henri, *The Unknown Soldiers: African-American Troops in World War I* (Philadelphia: Temple University Press, 1974; rev. ed., New York: Perseus/Da Capo Press, 1996), p. 90.

32 **"showing a determined woman"** Mark Robert Schneider, *"We Return Fighting": The Civil Rights Movement in the Jazz Age* (Boston: Northeastern University Press, 2002), p. 56.

32 **"a delegation of ladies"** "Mrs. Hunton Welcomed Home," *New York Age*, Aug. 30, 1919, p. 7.

32 *Two Colored Women* See Addie Hunton and Kathryn Johnson, *Two Colored Women with the American Expeditionary Forces*. The third Negro woman in the group, Helen Curtis, was involved in an important lawsuit after returning from the war. She and her husband contracted to buy a house on S Street, not far from the house formerly owned by the Huntons. The neighbors sued to enforce a racially restrictive covenant, which the Supreme Court upheld in *Corrigan v. Buckley*, 271 U.S. 323 (1926). It would be more than two decades before the court changed its collective mind.

33 **celebrating their heroism** One of the colored soldiers, Victor Daly, received the Croix de Guerre for his wartime exploits and would return home to write *Not Only War: A Story of Two Great Conflicts*, which is believed to be the only novel about the war by a black author. In Washington, D.C., a few years later, Daly would become one of Alphaeus's closest friends.

33 **returned a year and a half later** For a perhaps overenthusiastic argument on the way the experience of the war altered Addie's politics, see Susan Chandler, "Addie Hunton and the Construction of an African American Female Peace Perspective," *Affilia: Journal of Women and Social Work*, vol. 20, no. 3 (2005), p. 270.

33 **Before she could depart** The application itself makes interesting reading. Previously—so the application recites—she had traveled on a British passport obtained on December 15, 1908, and (according to Addie) now "expired—still in possession." Her application says that she will be out of the country for less than a year, and further says that she resided outside the United States from December 1908 through June 1910, living in Belgium, France, Germany, Switzerland, Italy, and Holland. England is also included, but with a question mark appended to it. ("ENGLAND?") She certifies that she will be going abroad temporarily, on "Y.M.C.A. WORK" (not Y.W.C.A. work, as several sources mistakenly assert) in France and England, departing in May of 1918. At the top of the application is a typewritten note to the effect that she carried a British passport because she was married to a British citizen but "is now back in America and reverts to her original citizenship," with a handwritten addendum: "husband dead." Her name is given as Addie Waits Hunton, which was actually the correct spelling.

34 **Addie's true age** Christine Lutz gives Addie's birth date as 1867. See Lutz, "'Dizzy Steep to Heaven,'" p. 101, n. 25. Lutz does not say where the information comes from, but her source was presumably the marriage license. The license is actually made out in Addie's correct maiden name: "Waits," not "Waites." How her name came to gain an "e" is not clear.

34 **the median household income** Several sources state erroneously that the median income in 1920 was about $3,400. This figure is drawn from an Internal Revenue Service study of the median income of *those who filed tax returns*—which at that time many fewer were required to do.

34 **remains a mystery** Apparently the family had some savings for the children's education, and Addie was determined not to use the money for other purposes. See Lutz, "Dizzy Steep to Heaven," pp. 185–86. Nevertheless, by the time Alphaeus was ready for college, the funds were gone. Perhaps Addie had spent them on Eunice; or perhaps the savings had never been that large, and the family, in dire financial straits, had been forced to tap the money after all.

35 **"northern secretary"** See "The Horizon," *Crisis*, vol. 14, no. 2 (June 1917), pp. 85, 91. Possibly this was the same school where Addie taught during the missing year in her biography.

35 **"nobly beautiful"** Ovington, *Walls Came Tumbling Down*, p. 59.

35 **"Eunice and Alpheus"** Mary White Ovington, *Black and White Sat Down Together: The Reminiscences of an NAACP Founder* (New York: Feminist Press, 1995), p. 38.

35 **In time, the friendship** No less stern a critic than W. E. B. Du Bois himself insisted that Ovington was without prejudice. "There is no shadow of the thing in your soul," he wrote to

Joel Spingarn in 1914—"the thing" being a tendency to hew unconsciously to the color line. "The same is true of Miss Ovington," Du Bois continued, "because she has lived the life of colored people intimately." W. E. B. Du Bois to Joel Spingarn, Oct. 28, 1914, in Herbert Aptheker, ed., *The Correspondence of W. E. B. Du Bois* (Amherst: University of Massachusetts Press, 1997), vol. 1, pp. 203, 206.

35   **"How I miss you"** Addie W. Hunton to Mary White Ovington, March 25, 1921, NAACP Papers.

36   **"friend and advisor"** See, for example, "She Helped Jail Luciano," *New York Amsterdam Star-News*, Aug. 15, 1942, p. 4. Eunice also had more formal interactions with Calvin Coolidge during her time at Smith. See "Two New York Women Win Honors at Smith," *Chicago Defender*, June 25, 1921, p. 5.

     Addie had her own relationship with Coolidge. In 1920, when Warren G. Harding ran for President with Coolidge as his running mate, Addie had campaigned for the victorious ticket. She also stumped for Coolidge in his successful quest for the presidency in 1924, and maintained a connection to Coolidge when he was in the White House. The connection was sufficiently close that Du Bois sent her a memorandum with the request that she bring it to the attention of the President. See W. E. B. Du Bois to Addie Hunton, Nov. 9, 1926, Du Bois Papers. (The memorandum itself has not survived, so we don't know its subject.)

36   **made the honor roll** See *Smith Alumnae Quarterly*, Nov. 1918, p. 41.

36   **The battle pitted** Kendra Van Cleave, "Fashioning the College Woman: Dress, Gender, and Sexuality at Smith College in the 1920s," *Journal of American Culture*, vol. 32, no. 1 (March 2009), p. 4.

36   **Some were so concerned** Margaret A. Lowe, "From Robust Appetites to Calorie Counting: The Emergence of Dieting Among Smith College Students in the 1920s," *Journal of Women's History*, vol. 7, no. 4 (Winter 1995), p. 37.

37   **she immediately became enmeshed** See Joyce Blackwell, *No Peace Without Freedom: Race and the Women's International League for Peace and Freedom 1915–1975* (Carbondale: Southern Illinois University Press, 2004), pp. 73–75.

37   **"While white men have been preserving"** "'Thousands Died for a Lie'—J. W. Johnson," *Brooklyn Daily Eagle*, Oct. 13, 1919, p. 5.

37   **she corresponded with Du Bois** See, for example, W. E. B. Du Bois to Addie W. Hunton, Sept. 24, 1920, Du Bois Papers.

37   **Nannie Helen Burroughs wrote to Addie** Nannie Helen Burroughs to Addie W. Hunton, Oct. 20, 1923, Du Bois Papers.

37   **led to frequent correspondence** See, for example, Ida Gibbs Hunt to Addie W. Hunton, Sept. 1927, Du Bois Papers; W. E. B. Du Bois to Addie W. Hunton, March 1927, Du Bois Papers; and W. E. B. Du Bois to Addie W. Hunton, Aug. 3, 1927, Du Bois Papers.

37   **American military intelligence** Lutz, "'Dizzy Steep to Heaven,'" pp. 213–14.

38   **She was only the second** See, for example, "Wins Two Degrees at Once," *Afro-American*, June 24, 1921, p. 2; "'Judge Men by Their Souls,' Pastor Asks," *Chicago Defender*, June 28, 1924, p. A1, reprinting an essay from the *Indianapolis Sunday Star* written by the Reverend Ernest Fremont Tittle; and "Education Among Negroes," *Herald of Gospel Liberty*, Nov. 1, 1928, p. 1044.

     Christine Lutz has described Eunice's master's thesis as "undistinguished and clearly hurried." Lutz, "'Dizzy Steep to Heaven,'" p. 272. The judgment is understandable but not entirely fair. By the standards of today's scholarship, the thesis is slender indeed, containing mainly exposition and conclusion, with very little interstitial argument. But this was very much the style of the times. Still, it is true that Eunice was never a scholar in the model of her brother, who was the sort to devour every available bit of writing on whatever subject took his fancy and to track every idea to its furthermost source.

38   **won prizes at the mostly white** Dorothy Hunton, *Unsung Valiant*, p. 15.

39   **"After the formal observance"** Addie Hunton, *Pioneer Prophet*, p. 152.

4. The Czarinas

41   **the college bulletin listed** See *Smith Alumnae Bulletin*, July 1922, p. 460.

41   **"Christmas isn't Christmas"** Eunice Hunton, "Who Gives Himself," *Opportunity: A Journal of Negro Life*, vol. 2, no. 24 (Dec. 1924), p. 374. This was the Christmas 1924 issue of *Opportunity*, and Eunice's story was published alongside others by Zora Neale Hurston and Paul Robeson.

42   **Eunice left immediately** In September the newspapers had her in St. Louis to visit her aunt, Mrs. W. C. Gordon. (This was apparently her father's older sister Victoria.) Eunice was expected to stay for ten days, then to head home, making stops along the way at Indianapolis and Chicago. "Missouri," *Chicago Defender*, Sept. 2, 1922, p. 16.

42   **her mother embarked** "Expect Mrs. Hunton Back," *Chicago Defender*, Nov. 18, 1922, p. 9.

42   **had found Addie in Indiana** Brief accounts of both trips may be found in Schneider, *"We Return Fighting,"* pp. 238–44.

42   **essentially ran the state** See "Indiana Swayed Entirely by Klan: 'Hooded Forces' Domination There Seems to Be Complete and Opposition Is Silent," *New York Times*, Nov. 7, 1923, p. 15.

42   **Ministers defended the Klan** See "Minister Lauds Work of Klan," *Indianapolis Star*, June 12, 1922, p. 9.

42   **"Hear Mrs. Hunton"** Untitled notice, *Southern Indicator* (Columbia, S.C.), Jan. 27, 1923, p. 2.

43   **He was acquitted** A particularly effective account of the crime and the trial may be found in Virginia Van der Deer Hamilton, *Hugo Black: The Alabama Years* (Tuscaloosa: University of Alabama Press, 1972), pp. 84–92. Counsel for the defense was Hugo Black, whom two decades later Franklin Roosevelt would appoint to the Supreme Court.

43   **"reign of terror"** Quoted in Schneider, *"We Return Fighting,"* p. 239.

43   **"I had no idea"** Quoted in ibid.

43   **three days in the hospital** Melinda Plastas, *A Band of Noble Women: Racial Politics in the Women's Peace Movement* (Syracuse, N.Y.: Syracuse University Press, 2011), p. 53.

43   **leading gymnastics classes** Thelma Berlack-Boozer, "Woman of the Week," *New York Amsterdam Star News*, May 24, 1941, p. 15.

43   **"for the purpose of blending"** "Society News," *New York Amsterdam News*, Sept. 19, 1923, p. 8.

44   **The Blacker the Berry** See Eunice Hunton Carter, review of *The Blacker the Berry*, by Wallace Thurman, *Opportunity: A Journal of Negro Life*, vol. 7, no. 5 (May 1929), p. 162.

44   **may have been the only colored reviewer** For example, Eunice's friend Walter White criticized the novel's artistic merit and declared that "if the impressionistic, modernist manner in which *Holiday* is written is great art, then there is something vital which is missing in his makeup" ("The New Books," *Crisis*, vol. 27, no. 4 [Feb. 1924], pp. 174–75). Jean Toomer, in an unpublished review, blamed the book's flaws on the fact that the author was of "white descent." Quoted in Barbara Foley, "An Epistolary Friendship," *American Book Review*, vol. 35, no. 1 (Nov.–Dec. 2013), a review of Kathleen Pfeiffer, ed., *Brother Mine: The Correspondence of Jean Toomer and Waldo Frank* (Urbana: University of Illinois Press, 2010).

Eunice's view was far more favorable. She praised *Holiday* as "sheer poetry . . . an epic too rich in beauty, hate, and tears to be held in the bonds of meter and form" ("Our Book Shelf," *Opportunity: A Journal of Negro Life*, vol. 2, no. 14 [Feb. 1924], p. 59).

44   **Famous white editors attended** An evocative description of the event may be found in Jervis Anderson, *This Was Harlem: A Cultural Portrait, 1900–1950* (New York: Farrar, Straus and Giroux, 1982), pp. 200–203.

44   **among the small group** Johnson was a genius at spotting talent, a man whose "impresario touch" (as David Levering Lewis calls it) helped shape the Harlem Renaissance. Small wonder that Eunice came under his influence. "Sooner or later," writes Lewis, "the Harlem of Charles Johnson enveloped almost every young artist or writer." David Levering Lewis,

When Harlem Was in Vogue (New York: Alfred A. Knopf, 1981; repr., New York: Penguin, 1997), p. 126.

44 **Sources differ** For the assumption that the group was created as a result of the dinner, see, for example, Chidi Ikonné, *From Du Bois to Van Vechten: The Early New Negro Literature, 1903–1926* (Westport, Conn.: Greenwood Press, 1981), p. 92. For the assumption that the group existed prior to the dinner, see Eleanore van Notten, *Wallace Thurman's Harlem Renaissance* (Amsterdam: Rodopi, 1994), p. 40, n. 70.

44 **the group's ten members as of 1924** There is actually some dispute about the full membership list. In August 1926, the *Amsterdam News* listed the members as follows: "Mrs. Regina Anderson-Andrews, Miss Gwendolyn Bennett, Miss Jessie Fauset, Mrs. Eunice Hunton-Carter, Langston Hughes, Countee Cullen, Charles S. Johnson, Harold Jackman, Eric Walrond."

45 **"I didn't vote on them!!!!"** Quoted in George Hutchinson, *In Search of Nella Larsen: A Biography of the Color Line* (Cambridge, Mass.: Harvard University Press, 2006), p. 537, n. 85.

46 **"Most of us"** Anita Reynolds, with Howard W. Miller, *American Cocktail: A "Colored Girl" in the World*, ed. George Hutchinson (Cambridge, Mass.: Harvard University Press, 2014), p. 98.

46 **"to the world that a Negro"** Edward G. Perry, "Royalty and Blue-Blooded Gentry Entertained by A'Lelia Walker at Lewaro and Town House," *New York Amsterdam News*, Aug. 26, 1931, p. 11.

46 **"most elaborate social function"** "Thousands Defy Rain to View Fashionable Bridal Party," *New York Age*, Dec. 1, 1923, p. 1.

46 **"9,000 Guests Invited"** "9,000 Guests Invited to a Colored Wedding," *New York Times*, Nov. 22, 1923, p. 19.

46 **"'Cullud 400' on Edge"** "'Cullud 400' on Edge as Miss Mae Walker Awaits Wedding Gong," *Pittsburgh Daily Post*, Nov. 24, 1923, p. 2.

46 **with enthusiasm** The new clinic, operating under the name North Harlem Dental Clinic, received state approval to begin serving patients in the summer of 1924 ("License Granted for Harlem Dental Clinic," *Chicago Defender*, Aug. 7, 1924, p. A7). Shortly thereafter it opened its doors at 102 W. 136th Street, in space donated by the Urban League. Services were available to all children in Harlem. For those able to pay, the fee was twenty-five cents for the first visit, ten cents for subsequent visits. For those unable to afford the fee, services were provided without charge (Thelma E. Berlack, "Chatter and Chimes," *Pittsburgh Courier*, Aug. 2, 1924, p. 12). Errold Collymore was the first chairman of the clinic, although Lisle Carter Jr., Eunice's husband-to-be, would soon succeed him ("Local Dentists Conduct Meeting," *New York Amsterdam News*, Feb. 28, 1928). See also "Over 1,000 Children Visited Dental Clinic Last Year," *New York Amsterdam News*, Jan. 19, 1927, p. 9. Eunice ran the women's auxiliary (Thelma E. Berlack, "Chatter and Chimes," *Pittsburgh Courier*, Oct. 25, 1924, p. 12). The clinic became so well known that Broadway shows and dance orchestras put on special benefits to support it. See "Theatrical Notes," *New York Times*, Jan. 16, 1925, p. 14; "J. A. Jackson's Page," *Billboard*, Jan. 31, 1925, p. 50; "'Round Li'l Ol' New York with 'Billboard' Jackson," *Afro-American* (Baltimore), May 24, 1924, p. 4; and "New York Society Notes," *Chicago Defender*, May 10, 1924, p. A4.

47 **Columbia Dental School** Lisle's military service record tells us that he spent his entire eight months in the military in the Students Army Training Corps. An added notation reads, "Dental & Oral Surgery NY to disch.," meaning, one presumes, that he was in school until discharge.

47 **His academic achievements were featured** "The Horizon," *Crisis*, vol. 22, no. 4 (Aug. 1921), pp. 176, 178.

48 **"queenly, sometimes portly"** Quoted in Anderson, *This Was Harlem*, p. 340.

48 **prejudice had mostly faded** For more on this prejudice, see Irma Watkins-Owens, *Blood Relations: Caribbean Immigrants and the Harlem Community, 1900–1930* (Bloomington: Indiana University Press, 1996).

48 **she loaned money to friends** See "Receipt for money borrowed," April 30, 1924, Du Bois Papers.

49 **had administered the last rites** Hunton, *Pioneer Prophet*, p. 161.

49 **Afterward he had conducted** Miller was also a story himself. He was a graduate of Howard and a major Christian intellectual. His 1905 book *Adventism Answered (the Sabbath Question)* remained influential for years. He was a radical anti-capitalist who wrote for the *Messenger*, A. Philip Randolph's Socialist-leaning magazine. He had been part of the Niagara Falls conference that began the process of establishing the NAACP. He corresponded regularly with Du Bois. In 1918, he had made headlines when he ran for Congress on the Socialist Party ticket. (He lost.)

49 **"very impressive ceremony"** "Dr. L. C. Carter Marries Popular School Teacher," *Chicago Defender*, Dec. 6, 1924, p. A4.

50 **Floyd was a considerable activist** In early 1921, for example, Floyd was part of a Jacksonville, Florida, delegation that visited Senator Warren G. Harding, the president-elect, and was "informed that men of color would receive appointments throughout the South." James Weldon Johnson, "Report of the Secretary for the Board Meeting of March 1921," reprinted in Sondra K. Wilson, ed., *In Search of Democracy: The NAACP Writings of James Weldon Johnson, Walter White, and Roy Wilkins, 1920–1977* (New York: Oxford University Press, 1999), pp. 23, 25. See also Megan Ming Francis, *Civil Rights and the Making of the Modern American State* (New York: Cambridge University Press, 2014), pp. 84–85.

50 **the only family member to attend** See "Captain Floyd Marries Mrs. Addie Hunton," *Buffalo American*, May 17, 1923, p. 1. See also "Mrs. A. W. Hunton Marries Captain Floyd of Florida," *New York Age*, May 19, 1923, p. 2. The articles correctly give Addie's maiden name as "Waits" rather than "Waites."

50 **finally ruled in Floyd's favor** The case was decided on May 13, 1926. The opinion of the Florida Supreme Court may be found at *Floyd v. Floyd*, 108 So. 896, 91 Fla. 110 (1926), and is cited to this day on the issue of alimony. Justice Terrell, the author of the opinion, wound up serving until 1964. His forty-one-year term on the state's highest bench remains the longest in state history.

The trial court originally awarded alimony. In January of 1925, the Florida Supreme Court had dismissed Floyd's initial appeal on the motion of his counsel. See *J. W. Floyd v. Addie Hunton Floyd*, 105 So. 157, 89 Fla. 537 (1925). Before dismissing his own appeal, a lawyer in the midst of negotiations would first secure the agreement of the other party that he would be free to refile the appeal should the negotiations break down. Negotiations did indeed break down after Addie reportedly demanded a lump-sum settlement of $10,000 (about $140,000 today).

51 **"Hunton-Floyd"** See, for example, "Notables Pay Final Tribute to Mrs. Talbert," *Pittsburgh Courier*, Oct. 27, 1923, p. 5, and "New Jersey," *New York Age*, July 28, 1923, p. 3.

It's difficult to say how much sassiety knew about Addie's second marriage. On the one hand, her new husband was the father-in-law of the prominent J. Rosamond Johnson. On the other hand, even those of her correspondents who were Addie's close friends seemed not ready to acknowledge that she was now Mrs. Floyd. See, for example, Nannie Helen Burroughs to Addie W. Hunton, Oct. 20, 1923, Du Bois Papers. But by August of 1923, when Addie attended the meeting of the International Council of Women of the Darker Races (ICWDR) at the Nannie Helen Burroughs Training School in Washington, D.C., and was elected first vice president, she was already going by Hunton-Floyd. See Ashley N. Robertson, "The Drums of Africa Still Beat in My Heart: The Internationalism of Mary McLeod Bethune and the National Council of Negro Women (1895–1960)," Ph.D. dissertation, Howard University (ProQuest Dissertations Publishing, 2013), p. 59. However, Addie's report to the NAACP on the meeting was apparently signed "Hunton." When she addressed a luncheon in St. Louis in September, the *Chicago Defender* similarly called her "Mrs. Addie Hunton Floyd." The following year, however, when she spoke in Springfield, Illinois, on the occasion of Abraham Lincoln's birthday, she was simply Mrs. Hunton. "Illinois State News," *Chicago Defender*, March 1, 1924, p. A5. Similarly, when in June she co-hosted a dance for the

World Student Federation Committee of New York and New Jersey, she was Mrs. Hunton ("Among the Harlem Society Leaders Who Sponsored Dance Wednesday Night," *Pittsburgh Courier*, June 28, 1924, p. 13). For a similar example, see "Mrs. Addie Hunton Spears at Mothers and Daughters Banquet," *Philadelphia Tribune*, May 17, 1924, p. 13.

In August of 1924, the *Crisis*, published by her own employer, would at last refer to her by her married name, Hunton-Floyd ("The Horizon," *Crisis*, vol. 28, no. 4 [Aug. 1924], p. 169). The *New York Age* continued to use Hunton-Floyd, at least occasionally, well into 1925. See *New York Age*, May 19, 1923, p. 2; *New York Age*, July 25, 1925, p. 3; and *New York Age*, Aug. 8, 1925, p. 4. But the hyphenation was never consistent in the black press, and did not last long. That same month, in an article about the controversy over efforts of the National Women's Party "to exclude colored people" from graveside services for the suffragist Inez Milholland, she was called of all things "Miss Addie W. Hunton"—an appellation she never used ("The National Woman's Party Snubs Race at the Grave of the Late Inez Milholland," *New Journal and Guide* [Norfolk, Va.], Aug. 30, 1924, p. 7). A November item in the *Chicago Defender* similarly stuck with "Mrs. Addie W. Hunton" ("Y.M.C.A. Briefs," *Chicago Defender*, Nov. 22, 1924, p. A10). She was Mrs. Hunton-Floyd again in an *Amsterdam News* story in July about her election as head of the Empire State Federation: "Mrs. H. Floyd Heads Empire State Federation," *New York Amsterdam News*, July 15, 1925, p. 7. Similarly, the *Chicago Defender* called her "Hunton-Floyd" in an April 1925 snippet on her recent illness. The item read, in its entirety: "Mrs. Addie Hunton-Floyd, noted Y.W.C.A. and welfare worker, of 452 Bedford Ave., who has been ill, is on the road to recovery." See "Brooklyn Notes," *Chicago Defender*, April 11, 1925, p. A2. (Note that "452" is a typographical error for "1452.") But the usage was not consistent, and in most of the many stories mentioning her she remained "Mrs. Hunton." See, for example, "Y.W.C.A News," *New York Amsterdam News*, Jan. 14, 1925, p. A14; "La Mode Ultra to Be Displayed at Big N.A.A.C.P. Spring Dance," *Pittsburgh Courier*, March 21, 1925, p. 14; "New York Club Women Organize," *Pittsburgh Courier*, June 27, 1925, p. 6; "Moton Again Heads Negro Bus. League," *Pittsburgh Courier*, Aug. 29, 1925, p. 3; and "Newark," *Pittsburgh Courier*, Oct. 17, 1925, p. 6.

51   **There seem to be no** For example, the historian Christine Lutz, noticing that in August 1924, the *Crisis* referred to Addie as "A. Hunton-Floyd," says that this was done "mistakenly." Lutz, "'Dizzy Steep to Heaven,'" p. 252. But Hunton-Floyd (or Hunton Floyd) was indeed Addie's name at the time.

51   **"Their protocol"** Quoted in Anderson, *This Was Harlem*, p. 340. Powell meant, of course, the Court of St. James's.

51   **cackled the *Pittsburgh Courier*** "Addie Hunton-Floyd Sued for Divorce, Gossips Say," *Pittsburgh Courier*, Oct. 25, 1924, p. 1.

51   **kept coming to Harlem** See, for example, Bessye Bearden, "New York Society," *Chicago Defender*, Nov. 1, 1930, p. 11.

52   **students from Howard** Alphaeus's belated realization that he would have to spend a second year led to an extraordinary chain of correspondence with George W. Robinson, the longtime legendary dean of Harvard's graduate school. See William Alphaeus Hunton [Jr.] to George W. Robinson, Feb. 18, 1925 (expressing surprise at being required to spend two years and seeking an exemption); George W. Robinson to William Alphaeus Hunton [Jr.], Feb. 20, 1925 (coldly refusing the request); William Alphaeus Hunton [Jr.] to George W. Robinson, March 3, 1925 (seeking help with financial aid to remain a second year); and George W. Robinson to William Alphaeus Hunton [Jr.], March 4, 1925 (offering no firm answer).

52   **He could hardly escape** Alphaeus was not the first Howard student to face this barrier, and the practice (we needn't call it a rule) had been in place for some time. A decade earlier, Lorenzo Dow Turner, another Howard graduate, had also been told by Robinson that he was being admitted to the master's degree program contingent upon his agreeing to spend a second year in residence. Turner, too, was warned that he must complete his course work "with distinction." See Margaret Wade-Lewis, *Lorenzo Dow Turner: Father of Gullah Studies* (Columbia: University of South Carolina Press, 2007), p. 26.

Yet one mustn't get the wrong idea. Harvard did not apply this requirement to all Negro applicants. A year after Alphaeus arrived, Sterling Brown, a Phi Beta Kappa graduate of Williams, applied for the same program and was promptly accepted for a one-year master's degree. The two men became close friends, and even shared an office for a time when both wound up teaching at Howard. See Keith Gilyard, *John Oliver Killens: A Life of Black Literary Activism* (Athens: University of Georgia Press, 2010), p. 38. Brown, who went on to become an award-winning poet, would later teach, among others, Kwame Nkrumah and Toni Morrison.

53 **Alphaeus petitioned** See William Alphaeus Hunton to George W. Robinson, March 3, 1925, and George W. Robinson to William Alphaeus Hunton, March 4, 1925, both at Harvard University Archives.

53 **"inevitable counter-offensive"** John Livingston Lowes, *Convention and Revolt in Poetry* (Boston: Houghton Mifflin, 1919), p. 220.

53 **who credited the great scholar** That Alphaeus might have been radicalized in part through his contact with Professor Lowes is not far-fetched. The Communist writer, critic, and theorist Granville Hicks reported exactly that experience. See Elmer Borklund, *Contemporary Literary Critics* (London: Palgrave Macmillan, 1977), pp. 259–60.

5. The Escape

54 **listed as "Dentist"** Lisle, although he earned an excellent living, also had a penchant for get-rich-quick schemes. Two years later, along with his brother Cecil and his friend Dennis Edwards, a realtor who also was a fellow Barbadian, he would form the C. E. E. Corporation. The plan was to borrow money and loan it at above-market rates to Negroes seeking to buy Harlem homes who could not get financing. The profit would come in the spread. The company does not seem to have succeeded.

55 **cute stories** "Side Lights on Society," *New York Amsterdam News*, June 2, 1926, p. 10.

55 **traveling to Haiti** Du Bois's wife, Nina, was among those seeing Addie off at the dock as she left. See Nina Du Bois to W. E. B. Du Bois, Feb. 16, 1925, Du Bois Papers. In the letter, Nina says that Addie "was asked to go by some womans [sic] club." For an account of the WILPF trip to Haiti, see Plastas, *A Band of Noble Women*, pp. 114–20. On the question of how much of the controversial final report Addie drafted, see Plastas, pp. 54–55. See also Brandon R. Byrd, "'To Start Something to Help These People': African American Women and the Occupation of Haiti, 1915–1934," *Journal of Haitian Studies*, vol. 21, no. 2 (Fall 2015), p. 154, and Lutz, "'Dizzy Steep to Heaven,'" pp. 244–45.

55 **"peace school"** Lutz, "'Dizzy Steep to Heaven,'" p. 252.

55 **In an address to** "Society," *Pittsburgh Courier*, Jan. 21, 1928, p. 7. The address was delivered at the Founders' Day luncheon in Pittsburgh.

55 **Eunice served for a time** See, for example, Anna M. Dingle, Eunice Hunton Carter, Lottie M. Cooper, and Eva T. Parks to W. E. B. Du Bois, March 8, 1927, Du Bois Papers. On the activities of the Circle during the period of Eunice's involvement, see Plastas, *A Band of Noble Women*, pp. 53–53, and Lewis, *W. E. B. Du Bois, 1919–1963*, pp. 208–9.

55 **she helped Addie organize** See Lutz, "'Dizzy Steep to Heaven,'" pp. 231–32.

56 **a Great Social Pyramid** As far as I am aware, the first to call Harlem sassiety a "social pyramid" was Alain Locke in his 1924 review of Jessie Fauset's first novel, *There Is Confusion*. See Cheryl A. Wall, *Women of the Harlem Renaissance* (Bloomington: Indiana University Press, 1995), p. 68.

56 **joining a committee** See Shannon King, *Whose Harlem Is This, Anyway? Community Politics and Grassroots Activism During the New Negro Era* (New York: New York University Press, 2015), p. 91.

56 **"society matrons"** "North Leads South in Producing Harlem Society Matrons," *Pittsburgh Courier*, June 18, 1927, p. 3.

57 **"always had intended to do"** Elizabeth Galbreath, "Typovision," *Chicago Defender*, Feb. 24, 1940, p. 16.

57   **did not actually admit another** See Philip S. Anderson, "Striving for a Just Society," *ABA Journal*, Feb. 1999, p. 66.

57   **increased by 69 percent** Lewis, *When Harlem Was in Vogue*, p. 240.

57   **"most of whose students"** Robert J. Kaczorowski, *Fordham University School of Law: A History* (New York: Fordham University Press, 2012), p. 99.

57   **immigrant urban populations** See John M. Breen and Lee J. Strang, "The Golden Age That Never Was: Catholic Law School from 1930–1960 and the Question of Identity," *Journal of Catholic Social Thought*, vol. 7, no. 2 (2010), pp. 489, 502–5.

57   **opened its doors to women** Kaczorowski, *Fordham University School of Law*, pp. 37–38.

58   **The first Negro students** Ibid., p. 45. Contrary to what is frequently repeated in history books, Eunice was not the first black woman to be graduated from Fordham Law School. That distinction belongs to Ruth Whaley, whose degree was awarded cum laude in 1924. One later writer reports that Whaley graduated "at the top of the class of 1924." See Constantine N. Katsoris, "In the Service of Others: From Rose Hill to Lincoln Center," *Fordham Law Review*, vol. 82 (2014), pp. 1533, 1550. This should not be taken to mean literally that she was first in her class. Kastoris's source, Kaczorowski's book, merely reports that she graduated cum laude. Kaczorowski, *Fordham University School of Law*, p. 46.

Whaley's graduation was touched by controversy when she claimed that a prize to which she had been entitled on the basis of examination scores was awarded to a white student instead. See "Women Law Student at Fordham University Charges Discrimination," *Pittsburgh Courier*, June 14, 1924, p. 1, and "Negro Graduate Says Fordham Is Unfair to Her," *New York Herald, New-York Tribune*, June 8, 1924, p. 1. Ignatius Wilkinson, the dean of the law school, denied any racial discrimination, and the book company that sponsored the prize said that Whaley had misunderstood the rules. "Fordham Law Dean Denies School Was Unfair to Negro," *New York Herald Tribune*, June 10, 1924, p. 12. Her cause was unsupported by her classmates. See, for example, George M. Feigen, "No Prejudice at Fordham" (letter to the editor), *New York Herald Tribune*, June 18, 1924, p. 12.

The faculty, weirdly, decided to withhold Whaley's degree until she withdrew her charges. "Univ. Law Student Who Charged Bias, Will Not Graduate: Mrs. Whaley's Degree Will Be Withheld, Faculty Announces," *Pittsburgh Courier*, June 21, 1924, p. 1. But the decision was apparently short-lived. Kenneth W. Mack, *Representing the Race: The Creation of the Civil Rights Lawyer* (Cambridge, Mass.: Harvard University Press, 2012), p. 135. Oddly, the dispute is not mentioned in Robert Kaczorowski's history of Fordham Law School.

Eunice could hardly have been unaware of the Whaley controversy, which was the talk of the colored middle class. Whaley herself would later suggest that any discrimination she suffered was because of sex rather than race. Mack, *Representing the Race*, p. 135.

58   **enrolled some 535** Kaczorowski, *Fordham University School of Law*, p. 97.

58   **Only seven women graduated** Ibid., p. 43.

58   **A year behind were** For details of these and other notables who overlapped with Eunice, see Constantine N. Katsoris, "A Tribute to the Fordham Judiciary: A Century of Service," *Fordham Law Review*, vol. 75 (2007), pp. 2303, 2316–18.

58   **"excessive absences"** Kaczorowski, *Fordham University School of Law*, p. 100.

58   **"Students were required"** William R. Meagher, "A Long Association with Fordham," *Fordham Law Review*, vol. 49 (1980), p. xl.

59   **fully one-third** See Katsoris, "In the Service of Others," p. 1533. Katsoris's account of these matters is based on contemporaneous sources, principally the reports of the dean and the minutes of faculty meetings.

59   **more full-time professors** Katsoris, "In the Service of Others," pp. 1564–65.

59   **first women's lavatory** Kaczorowski, *Fordham University School of Law*, p. 100.

59   **"By sending forth students"** Quoted in "Discerns Evil in Education: Dean Wilkinson of Fordham Law School Assails Materialism," *New York Times*, May 14, 1928, p. 19.

59 *Gunning v. Royal* See William A. Keener, I. Maurice Wormser, and John T. Loughran, *A Selection of Cases on the Law of Contracts*, 2nd ed., Part 1 (New York: Baker, Voorhis & Co., 1914), pp. 358 (*Gunning v. Royal*) and 734 (*Boone v. Eyre*).

59 *Boone v. Eyre* Boone v. Eyre, 1 H. Black 273, note (a) (1777).

60 **She would tell interviewers** See Elizabeth Galbreath, "Typovision," *Chicago Defender*, Feb. 24, 1940, p. 16.

60 **working for the Bamberger Fund** See Margaret Blake, "Eunice Hunton Carter 1921, Attorney," *Smith Alumnae Quarterly*, Nov. 1935, p. 26.

60 **running the Harlem branch** "Hoover Women Give Bridge-Whist Party," *New York Amsterdam News*, Oct. 31, 1928, p. 4.

60 **"[E]verything that we have had"** "Negro Voters Urged to Back Republicans," *Democrat and Chronicle* (Rochester, N.Y.), Oct. 24, 1928, p. 18.

61 **state's banking industry** See the discussion in Daniel Roland Fusfield, *The Economic Thought of Franklin D. Roosevelt and the Origins of the New Deal* (New York: Columbia University Press, 1956), pp. 183–86.

61 **The president of Columbia** "Butler Endorses Delany," *New York Times*, Oct. 27, 1929, p. 3.

61 **"Don't vote for me"** See Wil Haygood, *King of the Cats: The Life and Times of Adam Clayton Powell, Jr.* (New York: Houghton Mifflin, 1993), p. 39.

62 **"the interest of the Negro"** "La Guardia Contends Tammany Proves Enemy of Negro by Fighting Delany," *New York Amsterdam News*, Oct. 30, 1929, p. 3.

62 **Eunice campaigned hard for La Guardia** See "Cong. La Guardia Denounces Prejudiced Federal Judge," *New York Age*, Aug. 3, 1929, p. 3; "LaGuardia Talks to Bethel Lyceum: Congressman Slams Racial Bigotry as 600 Acclaim Him at Testimonial Meet," *New York Amsterdam News*, July 31, 1929, p. 2.

62 **"You've got to stop depending"** "Fish Urges Harlem to Support Delany," *New York Amsterdam News*, Oct. 23, 1929, p. 2. See also "Fish Stumps for Delany: Strongly Urges Election of Negro to Congress," *New York Times*, Oct. 30, 1929, p. 26.

62 **to create the Women's Political Council** "Women Organize to Help Registration," *New York Amsterdam News*, Oct. 9, 1929, p. 2.

62 **called him "Hobart"** See "Designate H. T. Delany," *New York Times*, Aug. 7, 1929, p. 4.

62 **Some voters were bewildered** Charles Pearce, "New York's Spiritualists, Mediums and Fakers Mulct Gullible Suckers of Thousands Yearly," *Afro-American* (Baltimore), July 4, 1931, p. 10.

62 **"victory celebration"** "Banquet for Delany," *Afro-American* (Baltimore), Nov. 2, 1929, p. 5.

62 **"Do You Want a Negro Congressman?"** "Delany Confident of Election Day Victory: Tammany Frantic in Effort to Beat Republican Rival," *New York Amsterdam News*, Oct. 30, 1929, p. 1.

62 **promised an investigation** "Sees Fraud in Fight on Negro Candidate," *New York Times*, Nov. 4, 1929, p. 3.

62 **Like all of Harlem's** See Gilbert Osofsky, *Harlem: The Making of a Ghetto* (Chicago: Ivan R. Dee, 1996), pp. 176–77.

62 **made an impassioned plea** "Harlem Must Elect Delany to Prove Interest in Self, LaGuardia Avers," *New York Amsterdam News*, Sept. 11, 1929, p. 3.

63 **constituted only about 30 percent** The 30 percent figure comes from the 1930 census, conducted a few months after the election. By 1940, the Nineteenth District would be 95 percent black and only 5 percent white.

63 **incumbent, Joseph Gavagan, won** "Delany Loses by 12,000," *New York Amsterdam News*, Nov. 6, 1929, p. 1. The actual plurality was 13,436. For precise totals, see "Final Results of the Election on Tuesday," *New York Times*, Nov. 7, 1929, p. 20. Delany was defeated, in David Levering Lewis's fine phrase, by the "ethnic algebra of the Twenty-first Congressional District." Lewis, *When Harlem Was in Vogue*, p. 216.

63 **"sending out spurious literature"** "Delany Alleges Fraud in N.Y. Election," *Afro-American* (Baltimore), Nov. 16, 1929, p. 4.

63 **Harlemites complained** "Negroes Make Charges: Many Unable to Vote, They Say, as Gavagan Defeats Delany," *New York Times*, Nov. 6, 1929, p. 6.

64 **she had become a supervisor** See "Supervisor," *Chicago Defender*, April 9, 1932, p. 7.

64 **sassiety wives asked** See "Launch New $100,000 Drive," *Pittsburgh Courier*, Jan. 24, 1931, p. 4.

64 **"a more respectful hearing"** "Cooperate to Aid Unemployed," *New York Age*, Nov. 14, 1931, p. 4.

64 **tea with Mrs. John D. Rockefeller** Bessye Bearden, "Tid-Bits of New York Society," *Chicago Defender*, May 24, 1930, p. 11.

65 **"Howard Professor Weds Stage Girl"** "Howard Professor Weds Stage Girl," *Afro-American* (Baltimore), Jan. 7, 1928, p. 5.

65 **how the colored press put it** "Prof. Hunton, Mate Split," *New York Amsterdam News*, Sept. 16, 1931, p. 1. The show in question was *Rang Tang*, an all-black revue, and appears to be the only show in which Ethelyn ever appeared. However vague the meaning of the phrase "run off," one should note that the show closed on October 22, 1927, and the couple was not wed until two months later.

65 **"disapproved" of the match** See "Prof. Hunton, Mate Split," *New York Amsterdam News*, Sept. 16, 1931, p. 1. The society columns billed Ethelyn as an actress, which was how she preferred to describe herself. She had appeared in the Broadway musical *Rang Tang*, a sort of sequel to *Shuffle Along*, the hugely popular all-black revue that produced countless imitators and, among well-to-do whites, a demand for Negro instructors to teach them the latest dance steps. According to gossip columns, Ethelyn "deserted" the cast to marry Alphaeus.

Nevertheless, a showgirl was a showgirl, and *Rang Tang* was a big deal. After opening in July of 1927, it ran for 119 performances, at the time a record for a Negro show. The plot was absurdly far-fetched, in the manner of the vaudeville stage of the era. Two Negro men on the run from creditors in their small Southern town steal a plane and fly off to Africa, hoping somehow to strike it rich. The plane begins to fall apart and they are forced to land near Madagascar. (Yes, the writers seem to have their geography confused. Madagascar is off the east, not the west, coast of Africa. And as Madagascar is an island, the escapees could land only on it, not near it.) A series of comic adventures ensue, at the end of which the two stars discover a diamond mine. They return to the United States, not to the South but to Harlem, where, thanks to their newfound wealth, they join the highest ranks of society. At this time the Negro musical was beginning to move downtown, both on and off Broadway. Producers were on the lookout for valuable properties. The Negro shows always included a lot of dancing. Enthusiastic white audiences would go home and mimic the latest steps. *Rang Tang* seems to have created a couple of brief dance crazes in downtown clubs, but, unlike other hit musicals of the day, the show produced no popular songs.

Given the success of *Rang Tang* the coverage was lavish, and the newspapers naturally mentioned by name several members of the cast. Ethelyn Boyd was not among them. She obtained not the smallest notice. Small wonder. According to ovrtur.com, Ethelyn was a member of the chorus—a "lady of the ensemble"—and not a featured player. The website lists no other Broadway credits under her name.

65 **even seen out and about** See, for example, "D.C. Society," *Afro-American* (Baltimore), Oct. 26, 1929, p. 2; "Personals," *Afro-American* (Baltimore), Feb. 1, 1930, p. 2 ("Personals" was a society column, not a space for advertising); and "Washington, D.C.," *Chicago Defender*, May 3, 1930, p. A16.

65 **Eunice visited the couple** "Visits," *Chicago Defender*, Dec. 6, 1930, p. 6. The brief piece described Eunice as a "charming matron." Her brother's name was spelled "Alphius."

65 **Alphaeus served as a groomsman** "Miss Du Bois Weds Countee Cullen," *New York Amsterdam News*, April 11, 1928, pp. 1, 6.

65 **"Harlem social event of the decade"** Lewis, *W.E.B. Du Bois, 1919–1963*, p. 221.

66 **crowd estimated at three thousand** "1,200 Invited; 3,000 Attended DuBois Wedding," *Afro-American* (Baltimore), April 14, 1928, p. 1. A number of sources incorrectly place the wedding at the Mother AME Zion church.

66 **extra patrolmen** See "Miss Du Bois Weds Countee Cullen: Wedding Guests sans Invitations Arrive Very Early," *New York Amsterdam News*, April 11, 1928, p. 1.

66 **"separating the sheep from the goats"** Charles Molesworth, *And Bid Him Sing: A Biography of Countée Cullen* (Chicago: University of Chicago Press, 2012), p. 135.

66 **Neither Eunice nor Addie** Only a partial guest list has survived in Du Bois's papers. I have been able to confirm via press reports that Addie was present at the wedding. See the partial guest list in "1,200 Invited; 3,000 Attended DuBois Wedding," *Afro-American* (Baltimore), April 14, 1928, p. 1.

66 **spotted at the beach** See "Washington Society," *Pittsburgh Courier*, Aug. 22, 1931, p. 8. One paper reported that Alphaeus and Margaret were both in Atlantic City, but as widely separated items in the same gossip column, as though their visits were independent of each other. Alphaeus was simply described as traveling with his friends, Mr. and Mrs. Victor Daly. See "D.C. Society," *Afro-American* (Baltimore), Aug. 22, 1931, p. 2.

67 **In the ensuing battle** For a stirring and well-documented account of the war between Schultz's forces and the Black Kings and Black Queens, see Shane White, Stephen Garton, Stephen Robertson, and Graham White, *Playing the Numbers: Gambling in Harlem Between the Wars* (Cambridge, Mass.: Harvard University Press, 2010), chapter 7.

67 **The press covered what it described** See, for example, "Negro Bankers and Collectors Said to Be Hanging On to the Numbers Business by a Thread," *New York Age*, Aug. 20, 1932, p. 1, and "Declare Strike Against Schultz Numbers' Banks; Expect Bloody Gang War," *New York Age*, March 4, 1933, p. 1.

67 **Joe Ison, who managed** Albert Fried, *The Rise and Fall of the Jewish Gangster in America* (New York: Holt, Rinehart, and Winston, 1980; repr., New York: Columbia University Press, 1993), p. 184.

67 **Schultz was the clear winner** See "Negroes No Longer Control Harlem Numbers Business as Kings Work for Bronx Beer Racketeer," *New York Age*, Aug. 15, 1932, p. 1.

67 **Martin L. Harris** See "Blacks, Whites War to Control Harlem Digits," *Afro-American* (Baltimore), March 25, 1933, p. 3. See also "First Degree Murder Indictment Returned Against Four Alleged Slayers of Numbers Banker, M. L. Harris, Who Opposed Schultz," *New York Age*, July 22, 1933, p. 1.

67 **it remains unclear** White, Garton, Robertson, and White, *Playing the Numbers*, p. 188.

67 **St. Clair openly appealed** "Nip Plot to Kill Mme. St. Claire: Harlem Policy Queen on 'Spot Asks Police Help," *Chicago Defender*, Sept. 24, 1932, p. 1.

67 **she promised publicly to kill Schultz** "Promises to Crimp Dutch Schultz," *New York Amsterdam News*, Sept. 21, 1932, p. 2.

68 **Some of the major** This intriguing point is made by Watkins-Owens, *Blood Relations*, pp. 138–39.

68 **Others who survived** See Rufus Schatzberg and Robert J. Kelly, *African American Organized Crime: A Social History* (New Brunswick, N.J.: Rutgers University Press, 1997), pp. 79–80.

68 **"It is ironical"** Quoted in Watkins-Owens, *Blood Relations*, p. 29. The quotation is from the *Amsterdam News*, Aug. 27, 1938, but the editorial page (in this case, p. 4) is illegible in the online sources.

6. The Candidate

69 **The guest list confirmed** "New York Society," *Chicago Defender*, Nov. 5, 1932, p. 11. By an interesting coincidence, Eunice graduated the same year Fordham awarded its first-ever doctorate to a Negro. See "Willis N. Huggins First Negro to Get Doctor's Degree at Fordham Uni.," *New York Age*, Aug. 20, 1932, p. 1.

69 **She brought a party of guests** "New Jersey State Personal Notes," *New York Age*, Nov. 19, 1932, p. 8.

69 **She served actively on the board** "Harlem Experimental Theatre Begins Season," *New York Age*, Oct. 15, 1932, p. 6. See also "Three Years with the Harlem Experimental Theatre—Its Purpose," *New York Age*, April 11, 1931, p. 6. Eunice was apparently involved from the found-

ing of the group in 1927. Her involvement probably came through her friend Regina Andrews, whose brainchild the group largely was. Previous efforts to establish a legitimate theater troupe in Harlem had consistently failed. See Errol G. Hill and James V. Hatch, *A History of African American Theatre* (Cambridge: Cambridge University Press, 2003), pp. 225–28.

69   **"a rousing mass meeting"** "New Jersey State Personal Notes," *New York Age*, Nov. 5, 1932, p. 8.

69   **Eunice had been a regular** See, for example, Bessye Bearden, "New York Society," *Chicago Defender*, Nov. 1, 1930, p. 11; Gerry [Gerri Major], "New York: The Social Whirl," *Afro-American* (Baltimore), March 28, 1931, p. 7; "Charlotte Hawkins Brown Is Guest of Honor at Tea Given in Brooklyn," *New York Age*, March 16, 1929, p. 7; "Harrison Addressed Group at Tea Sunday," *New York Amsterdam News*, Oct. 29, 1930, p. 10; "Clubs Sponsor Bridge Tournament for the Katy Ferguson Home," *New York Age*, Feb. 13, 1932, p. 2; and Bessye Bearden, "Tid-Bits of New York Society," *Chicago Defender*, Feb. 1, 1930, p. 11. Eunice often hosted events at her apartment on 141st Street. See, for example, Bessye Bearden, "New York Society," *Chicago Defender*, March 14, 1931, p. 11.

70   **"Getting the degree seemed to"** Ira Wolfert, "Cal Coolidge Helped Her Get Her M.A. Degree," *Boston Daily Globe*, July 3, 1938, p. B18.

70   **declared to have passed** See "Two New York Women Pass Bar Examinations," *Chicago Defender*, May 20, 1933, p. 6. Only 645 of the 1,786 who sat for the examination passed. "Bar Test Passed by 645 Students; Of Total Who Entered for March Examination 1,141 Were Unsuccessful," *New York Times*, May 11, 1933, p. 36. The other black woman who passed with Eunice was Lucille Edwards, later Lucille Edwards Chance, whose obituary years later would call her, incorrectly, "the second black woman admitted to the New York bar." See "Lucille Chance, Leader in Harlem and Lawyer," *New York Times*, April 8, 1987, p. 30.

70   **she hung out her shingle** Some sources give the address as 2143 Seventh Avenue. The 2145 address is taken from the Martindale-Hubbell legal directory for 1935.

70   **She took the view that** Margaret Blake, "Eunice Hunton Carter 1921, Attorney," *Smith Alumnae Quarterly*, Nov. 1935, p. 26.

70   **Alphaeus came to stay** Bessye Bearden, "New York Society," *Chicago Defender*, May 20, 1933, p. 17.

71   **Her operation made the papers** See "Eunice Carter in Sanitarium," *Pittsburgh Courier*, Dec. 9, 1933, p. 9. One of the surgeons was Dr. Peter Marshall Murray, who would later become the first Negro elected to the House of Delegates of the American Medical Association.

71   **"At press time"** "Society," *New York Amsterdam News*, Dec. 6, 1933, p. 4.

71   **"The eighty-five socialites"** "Chooses Roerich Museum for Tea for Philomathian Club," *New York Amsterdam News*, Feb. 28, 1934, p. 4.

72   **They had co-founded** Lutz, "'Dizzy Steep to Heaven,'" p. 246.

72   **They had even protested together** Plastas, *A Band of Noble Women*, p. 163. Unfortunately, Plastas does not provide a citation for this story, so I am unable to offer more detail.

72   **"Mrs. Carter has been ill"** Bessye Bearden, "New York Society," *Chicago Defender*, March 10, 1934, p. 9.

72   **"Mrs. Eunice Hunton Carter"** Neil Occomy, "Harlem by Night," *Afro-American* (Baltimore), March 17, 1934, p. 14.

72   **she was one of the best-known** In a survey of black college students in the 1930s, some 89.3 percent correctly identified Bethune as black, one of the highest figures in the study. The study is discussed in Ralph J. Bunche, *A Brief and Tentative Analysis of Negro Leadership* (1940; repr., New York: New York University Press, 2005), pp. 207–9 (Appendix II).

72   **She had also become** See the account in Ashley N. Robertson, *Mary McLeod Bethune in Florida: Bringing Social Justice to the Sunshine State* (Charleston, S.C.: History Press, 2015).

73   **she and her son returned** "Society," *New York Amsterdam News*, May 19, 1934, p. 4.

73   **offices high and low** See, for example, "7 Negroes Seek Seats in Congress from Mich.," *New York Age*, Aug. 13, 1932, p. 1.

74 **Eunice had stood up** "Hilles Repudiates Support by Bigots; Stresses Dry Issue," *New York Times*, Sept. 25, 1928, pp. 1, 2. This was Eunice's first appearance in the *Times*, which referred to her as "a negro campaign worker."

74 **unsuccessful run for governor** See "Negro Committee Pledges Aid to Tuttle," *New York Age*, Nov. 1, 1930, p. 1. On the same day the story ran, Eunice was among the signatories of a full-page ad for Tuttle in the same paper. See "Harlem Is on Trial" (advertisement), *New York Age*, Nov. 1, 1930, p. 5.

75 **an astonishing 50 percent** Nancy J. Weiss, *Farewell to the Party of Lincoln: Black Politics in the Age of FDR* (Princeton, N.J.: Princeton University Press, 1983), pp. 45–46.

75 **Half of the city's Negroes** Cheryl Greenberg, *"Or Does It Explode?": Black Harlem in the Great Depression* (New York: Oxford University Press, 1991), p. 174.

75 **three thousand holiday baskets** Anderson, *This Was Harlem*, p. 243.

75 **Harlem's once-dominant black Republican** Greenberg, *"Or Does It Explode?,"* p. 97.

75 **every candidate caught in a scandal** "Order Issued for Stephens," *New York Amsterdam News*, Aug. 25, 1934, p. 1.

75 **His time in Albany** Later in his career, Stephens did more. In particular, he proposed a ban on certain forms of racial discrimination; the bill passed. Baseball buffs may also be interested to know that it was Stephens who introduced in the assembly a resolution expressing the state's "deep regret" after the Yankees sold Babe Ruth to the Boston Braves in 1935. The resolution never came to a vote.

75 **the Negro press was rife** "Stephens, Steele Face 'Ax' at Polls," *New York Amsterdam News*, Oct. 20, 1934, p. 2.

75 **Eunice established a campaign headquarters** One contemporaneous account places Eunice's headquarters in the Lafayette Building, home of the Lafayette Theatre. See "The Feminist Viewpoint: Give Eunice Carter a Chance," *New York Amsterdam News*, Oct. 13, 1934, p. 9.

75 **Originally closed to Negroes** A frequent performer at Connie's was Fletcher Henderson, who would come to play a major role in Eunice's life; see chapter 16.

75 **"colored vaudeville"** See Vere E. Johns, "In the Name of Art," *New York Age*, Dec. 31, 1932, p. 6.

76 **paid tribute to the Mob** Of course the rest of the city paid tribute, too. Even heavyweight champion Jack Dempsey found it easier to pay the Mob than to resist. See William Donati, *Lucky Luciano* (Jefferson, N.C.: McFarland & Co., 2010), p. 92.

76 **which all Harlem knew** Several years later, District Attorney Thomas E. Dewey would mention this address in his opening statement in the corruption trial of Tammany leader Jimmy Hines. Quoted in "Dewey Says Hines Influenced Police," *New York Times*, Aug. 18, 1938, p. 1, which includes a reprint of his entire opening statement. See also *Matter of Davis*, 252 App. Div. 591 (N.Y. App. 1937).

76 **By one estimate** See "White Racketeers Take Over Harlem 'Numbers': Madden Operating Wide Open Shops," *New York Amsterdam News*, Aug. 10, 1932, p. 1.

76 **Certainly nobody was prepared** There was a short-lived and unsuccessful boycott of the numbers, aimed at allowing the black bankers who had previously been independent and now worked for the Mob to keep a larger share of the take.

76 **"smoking the pipe of peace"** "Harlem Primary Designations," *New York Age*, Sept. 1, 1934, p. 6.

76 **So Eunice was unopposed** "Primary Thursday to Be Bitter Here," *New York Times*, Sept. 9, 1934, pp. 1, 2.

76 **soon considered the favorite** "Without a Penny or Picture, Stephens Is Re-Elected—Again," *New York Amsterdam News*, Nov. 10, 1934, p. 5. Eunice's campaign manager was apparently Melvin Ware, a prominent black Republican. See Ted Yates, "New York After Dark," *Chicago Defender*, Dec. 29, 1934, p. 10. Ware later went into the advertising business. See Archie Seale, "Man About Harlem," *New York Age*, Aug. 8, 1936, p. 8.

77 **"has defeated every attempt"** Editorial, "Making Your Vote Count," *New York Amsterdam News*, Oct. 27, 1934, p. 8.

77 "exceptionally well qualified" "Eunice Hunton Carter Nominee in 19th A.D.," *New York Age*, Aug. 4, 1934, p. 1.

77 "with certainty" Julie A. Gallagher, *Black Women and Politics in New York City* (Urbana: University of Illinois Press, 2012), p. 60.

77 "First, her platform is practical" Ebenezer Ray, "Dottings of a Paragrapher," *New York Age*, Nov. 3, 1934.

77 "college-bred and unruffled" "Six Run for Office in New York's Election Nov. 6," *Afro-American* (Baltimore), Nov. 3, 1934, p. 10.

77 "an old, well-known family" "Runs Good Race," *Crisis*, vol. 41, no. 12 (Dec. 1934), p. 366.

78 "For myself I make no plea" Quoted in "Eunice Carter Has Busy Time," *New York Amsterdam News*, Nov. 3, 1934, p. 7.

79 "the dais of any number" "Eunice Carter Has Busy Time: Assembly Candidate Is Qualified for Job," *New York Amsterdam News*, Nov. 3, 1934, p. 7.

79 were dominated by women See Greenberg, *"Or Does It Explode?,"* pp. 105–8.

79 Middle-class black women Gallagher, *Black Women and Politics in New York City*, p. 60.

79 A Eunice Carter Club "Eunice Carter Club Launched by Women," *New York Amsterdam News*, Sept. 22, 1934, p. 14. See also "Women's Non-Partisan League Backs Candidacy of Eunice H. Carter," *New York Age*, Sept. 22, 1934, p. 2.

79 "A woman would have" "Eunice Carter Has Busy Time," *New York Amsterdam News*, Nov. 3, 1934, p. 7.

79 "much in demand" "Woman Assembly Candidate Gives Platform: Seeks Legislative Job in New York City," *Chicago Defender*, Oct. 20, 1934, p. 4.

79 "a convincing speaker" "Four Candidates for N.Y. Assembly Close Campaigns," *Afro-American* (Baltimore), Nov. 10, 1934, p. 12.

79 to draw enormous crowds See, for example, "Eunice Carter Has Busy Time:," *New York Amsterdam News*, Nov. 3, 1934, p. 7. The five thousand figure is from the story. The sanctuary apparently holds only one thousand.

79 She promised to ease "Woman Assembly Candidate Gives Platform: Seeks Legislative Job in New York City," *Chicago Defender*, Oct. 20, 1934, p. 4.

80 "Attention, Hairdressers and Operators!" Advertisement, *New York Amsterdam News*, Oct. 13, 1934, p. 15. Her appearance was sponsored by the National Beauty Culturists' League, the organization for black hairdressers.

80 But the cosmetologists See Tiffany M. Gill, *Beauty Shop Politics: African American Women's Activism in the Beauty Industry* (Urbana: University of Illinois Press, 2010), pp. 62–64.

80 "enhanced her chances" "Eunice Carter Wins Freedom for Couple," *New York Amsterdam News*, Nov. 3, 1934, p. 3.

81 "the voters turned deaf ears" "Stephens and Andrews Win: Harlem Goes Heavily Democratic in All Sections," *New York Amsterdam News*, Nov. 10, 1934, p. 1.

81 "greatest surprise" "Andrew [sic] Stephens Wins; Mrs. Carter, Steele Lose in New York," *Afro-American* (Baltimore), Nov. 10, 1934, p. 1.

81 "virtually invulnerable" For details of this race, and of its two colorful contenders, see Weiss, *Farewell to the Party of Lincoln*, pp. 80–89.

81 Two years later For an account of this race, see Jacqueline A. McLeod, *Daughter of the Empire State: The Life of Judge Jane Bolin* (Urbana: University of Illinois Press, 2011), pp. 34–36.

82 "I know she will love" Maurice Dancer, "Harlem Night by Night," *Pittsburgh Courier*, Nov. 17, 1934, p. A8.

82 "[l]ovely Eunice Carter's campaign" Maurice Dancer, "Harlem Night by Night," *Pittsburgh Courier*, Nov. 10, 1934, p. 18.

82 The old one had been See "'Tree of Hope,' Famous Harlem Landmark, Gone," *New York Age*, Aug. 25, 1934, p. 5. The story made news far from New York City. See, for example, "Axe Dooms Wishing Tree of Harlem's Stars," *Ithaca Journal*, Aug. 21, 1934, p. 1.

82 **who touched the tree in the hope** Anderson, *This Was Harlem*, p. 242. The Tree of Hope also appears as an important prop and metaphor in Dorothy West's short story "Amateur Night in Harlem."

82 **There is an extant photograph** See the photograph appended to "Harlem Gets Back Its Tree of Hope," *Chicago Defender*, Oct. 18, 1941, p. 6.

82 **She does not look** This is not to say that Dancer's version could not have happened before the photograph was taken. For one thing, there was indeed a dais on which only some of the large crowd was seated. See "Mayor, Moses and Hundreds Witness Tree Dedication," *New York Age*, Nov. 10, 1934, p. 1.

83 **The columnist ranked the Carters second** Roi Ottley, "This Hectic Harlem," *New York Amsterdam News*, Dec. 29, 1934, p. 9.

83 **the case was front-page news** "Maurice Dancer Held on Alimony Charge," *Chicago Defender*, Jan. 29, 1935, p. 1.

83 **never actually married** See Stephen Bourne, *Ethel Waters: Stormy Weather* (Lanham, Md.: Scarecrow Press, 2007), p. 10.

83 **He had been in trouble before** "Maurice Dancer, Benefit Promoter, Faces Graft Quiz," *Chicago Defender*, Aug. 4, 1934, p. 1, and "Maurice Dancer Held on Charges of Embezzling Benefit Funds of N.A.A.C.P. National Defense Fund," *New York Age*, Aug. 4, 1934, p. 1. Ironically, the *Age* announced Dancer's arrest and Eunice's nomination for the state assembly on the same date and on the same page. See "Eunice Hunton Carter Nominee in 19th A.D.," *New York Age*, Aug. 4, 1934, p. 1.

83 **The previous spring** "Maurice Dancer in Town to 'Put Over' Mammoth Defense Fund Benefit, June 17," *Pittsburgh Courier*, June 2, 1934, p. 1.

84 **"It is safe to say"** "New York Society Parade Latest at Huge Benefit," *Pittsburgh Courier*, June 2, 1934, p. 8.

84 **The Negro papers warned** See, for example, "Dancer and the NAACP" (editorial), *Afro-American* (Baltimore), Sept. 15, 1934, p. 4.

84 **The charges were ultimately dropped** "Judge Scores O'Ryan and Frees Maurice Dancer," *New York Amsterdam News*, Aug. 4, 1934, p. 1.

84 **"foul play"** "Maurice Dancer Is Vindicated, Tells Own Story," *Pittsburgh Courier*, Aug. 11, 1934, p. 1.

84 **something "big"** "Maurice Dancer Released in Benefit Probe; New Angle in Case Looms," *Chicago Defender*, Aug. 11, 1934, p. 2.

84 **His estranged second wife** The estrangement must have been recent. Just a few months before, Maurice and Myrtle Dancer were on the town together. See "A Chicagoan in Harlem," *Afro-American* (Baltimore), June 2, 1934, p. 9.

84 **And she had nursed** "'Sweet and Unaffected,' Says Nurse of Marva," *Pittsburgh Courier*, June 20, 1936, p. 9.

85 **"at her palatial home"** Bessye Bearden, "New York Society," *Chicago Defender*, Dec. 7, 1935, p. 17. Given the address, the "palatial home" would have been an apartment, not a townhouse. Eunice had also been a guest at Myrtle's birthday party two years earlier. See "Harlem Matron Feted at Gay Birthday Party," *Pittsburgh Courier*, Dec. 9, 1933, p. 9.

85 **She pressed the intriguing legal argument** "Maurice Dancer Jailed Failed to Pay Alimony," *Chicago Defender*, Feb. 2, 1935, p. 1.

85 **the magistrate rejected Eunice's plea** "Detroit Cops Take Dancer," *New York Amsterdam News*, Jan. 26, 1935, p. 1.

85 **despite Eunice's efforts** "Dancer in Jail; Ducked Alimony Since Year 1925," *Afro-American* (Baltimore), Feb. 2, 1935, p. 6.

85 **"volunteer assistant"** The sources differ on exactly when Eunice first took on these responsibilities. In an interview a few years later, she would imply that she began volunteering in the Women's Courts in 1935. Thomas Dewey, in his memoir, says she worked there for several years before 1935. And, as we shall see, some of the information Eunice is said to have gleaned from the Women's Courts could only have been obtained before March of 1934.

86　**Municipal reformers had argued** An excellent discussion of the history is Val Marie Johnson, *"Defining 'Social Evil': Moral Citizenship and Governance in New York City, 1890–1920,"* Ph.D. diss., New York University, 2002, chapter 5.

86　**The Women's Courts handled** See Lawrence Baum, *Specializing the Courts* (Chicago: University of Chicago Press, 2011), pp. 112–13.

86　**Eunice took up her position** See "Finds Gain in Vice Here," *New York Times*, June 6, 1932, p. 5. Before World War I, arrests and prosecutions had been in decline, leading reformers to argue that credit should go to the establishment of the Women's Courts. See, for example, Frederick H. Whitin, "The Women's Night Court in New York City," *Annals of the American Academy of Political and Social Science*, vol. 52 (March 1914), p. 181.

86　**probation or a fine** See "Probation to Be Extended to Higher Criminal Courts," *New York Times*, Feb. 8, 1925, p. 15.

86　**one judge threatened to resign** "Brooklyn Justices Confer on Inquiry," *New York Times*, Feb. 12, 1931, p. 2.

86　**Other judges were accused** See "Seabury Asks Court to Oust Silbermann," *New York Times*, June 12, 1931, pp. 1, 14. Magistrate Jesse Silbermann, alleged to have taken bribes, spent about one-fourth of his time sitting in the Women's Courts.

86　**had a tawdry reputation** In New York, the Women's Courts became the center of one controversy after another. In 1914, for example, suffragists had demonstrated outside the courthouse, complaining that female lawyers could argue before the judges but not vote in the elections where the judges were chosen. See "Plan 'Reproach' Meetings; Suffragettes Will Make Demonstrations Before Women's Courts," *New York Times*, July 10, 1914, p. 10.

7. The Commission

88　**The police made a constant** This account is drawn from an amalgam of sources. These include the *Complete Report of Mayor LaGuardia's Commission on the Harlem Riot of March 19, 1935* (New York: Arno Press, 1969).

88　**The *Times* nevertheless** See "Store Wrecked in Harlem and Boy Who Caused the Riot," photo caption, *New York Times*, March 21, 1935, p. 16.

89　**Popular fury was rising** For a useful account of the boycott campaign, see William Muraskin, "The Harlem Boycott of 1934: Black Nationalism and the Rise of Labor-Union Consciousness," *Labor History*, vol. 13, no. 3 (1972), p. 361. See also Winston McDowell, "Race and Ethnicity During the Harlem Jobs Campaign, 1932–1935," *Journal of Negro History*, vol. 69, no. 3–4 (Summer–Autumn 1984), p. 134, and Greenberg, "*Or Does It Explode?*," pp. 114–36. Tragically, the boycott was at times touched by anti-Jewish sentiment. Among the leaders of the boycott was the rabble-rousing anti-Semite Sufi Abdul Hamid, known widely as "the Black Hitler" or "the Harlem Hitler." (Hamid was briefly married to Stephanie St. Clair, the queen of the Harlem numbers racket, who tangled with the mobster Dutch Schultz. Hamid divorced St. Clair after she shot him.)

89　**"awaiting its immediate cause"** Lewis, *When Harlem Was in Vogue*, p. 306.

89　**Some Harlem merchants** "Harlem's Stores Ask Soldier Guard," *New York Times*, March 21, 1935, p. 16.

89　**The request was denied** See "12 Indicted in Riot; Troop Plea Denied," *New York Times*, March 22, 1935, p. 1.

89　**"These people feel"** Malcolm Aage Jackson, letter to the editor, *New York Times*, March 23, 1935, p. 14.

89　**The same Communists** See Mark Naison, *Communists in Harlem During the Depression* (Urbana: University of Illinois Press, 1983), pp. 140–41.

90　**The six Negro members** The rising black sociologist E. Franklin Frazier was appointed as director of research, a role that helped bring him to prominence. Several histories of the period, misunderstanding Frazier's duties, refer to him as a member of the commission, which he was not.

90　**She went yachting** See "Social Notes," *New York Amsterdam News*, June 8, 1935, p. 6.

90   to watch Joe Louis train "Johnny Dundee, Claude Hopkins Visit Louis Camp," *Afro-American* (Baltimore), June 5, 1935, p. 20.

90   She gave public addresses See "Confab Opens, Priest Speaks," *New York Amsterdam News*, June 8, 1935, p. 20 (speaking on the status of Negroes), and "3 Groups Get Delta Prizes," *New York Amsterdam News*, June 1, 1935, p. 7 (judging the competition).

90   She bought tickets "New York Society Parade Latest at Huge Benefit," *Pittsburgh Courier*, June 2, 1934, p. 8.

90   Edith Sampson, a Negro lawyer See Bessye Bearden, "New York Society," *Chicago Defender*, July 6, 1935, p. 6.

90   She hosted Idalee Thornton McGill "Mrs. McGill to Be Guest of Brownings," *Pittsburgh Courier*, June 15, 1935, p. A11. For the spectacular divorce, see "McGill's Wife Is Given Divorce," *Pittsburgh Courier*, April 22, 1933, p. 13.

91   "made the motion . . . that brought" Sue Bailey Thurman, ed., *The Historical Cookbook of the American Negro* (Washington, D.C.: National Council of Negro Women, 1958), p. 130.

91   Her early and enthusiastic endorsement See, for example, "New Council Has Its Place, Says Addie Hunton," *Pittsburgh Courier*, Jan. 4, 1936, p. 9. Addie called the group the "National Council of Colored Women"—"colored" having long been her preferred term.

91   because she felt badly treated See Plastas, *A Band of Notable Women*, p. 53. In its generous statement announcing her resignation, the NAACP board called her "one of the best equipped and most distinguished women in the country," and added that the organization "regretted exceedingly" that she "found it necessary to give up her position with the organization." See "Resignations," in *Fifteenth Annual Report of the National Association for the Advancement of Colored People for the Year 1924* (New York: NAACP, 1925), p. 60; and Lutz, "'Dizzy Steep to Heaven, pp. 261–63.

    Addie would later resign from the WILPF as well, this time on the ground that the group was not "ready for an interracial program." Quoted in Lutz, "'Dizzy Steep to Heaven,'" pp. 247–48. But, in truth, Addie had developed serious qualms about racism in the women's movement, after she and another Negro were invited to speak at a memorial for the lawyer, pacifist, and suffragette Inez Milholland, only to be told that they would not be permitted to deliver their remarks. See "The National Woman's Party Snubs Race at the Grave of the Late Inez Milholland," *New Journal and Guide* (Norfolk, Va.), Aug. 30, 1924, p. 7. The ostensible reason was that the National Women's Party, under whose auspices the ceremony was held, was trying to win elections in the South. The group subsequently apologized. See "Inez Milholland Memorial," in *Fifteenth Annual Report of the National Association for the Advancement of Colored People for the Year 1924* (New York: NAACP, 1925), p. 16. (Milholland, to whom Addie had been close, died in 1916, four days before William Hunton.)

    It also bears mention that Addie had recently embarrassed the NAACP. In 1922, in her role as a surrogate for the organization, she had helped defeat a New Jersey congressional candidate who opposed federal anti-lynching legislation. Up to that point, Addie was simply doing her job. Unfortunately, she then went on the attack against Senator Joseph S. Frelinghuysen Sr., also of New Jersey, for missing a key vote. The trouble was that the Jersey City branch of the NAACP was busily cultivating him. See Schneider, *"We Return Fighting,"* pp. 186–87. The organization was forced to mail out an apology, but Frelinghuysen still lost.

    Racism also finally drove Addie from the YWCA. See Lutz, "'Dizzy Steep to Heaven,'" p. 248. That break, however, did not seem to leave ill will, because her daughter later joined the board.

91   "a famous hostess" Thurman, *The Historical Cookbook of the American Negro*, p. 130. In a small snippet on her mother, Eunice also praised Addie for "her role as author and lecturer and her leadership participation in the fields of education, religion, and civic affairs" (p. 130).

93   "were merely symbols" Quoted in "Harlem Riot Laid to Economic Ills," *New York Times*, March 26, 1935, p. 5.

93   Some critics worried See "Riot Probe Commission of LaGuardia Criticized," *Afro-American* (Baltimore), March 30, 1935, p. 2.

93 **Others insisted that the members** See "Mayor's Committee Under Fire: Varied Groups Hit Body Appointed to Probe Harlem Riot," *New York Amsterdam News*, March 30, 1935, p. 1.

93 **Harlem ministers pointed out** See "Harlem Rioters Face Anarchy Indictments," *New York Herald Tribune*, March 26, 1935, p. 17.

93 **The Consolidated Tenants' League** Quoted in "Mayor's Committee Under Fire: Varied Groups Hit Body Appointed to Probe Harlem Riot," *New York Amsterdam News*, March 30, 1935, p. 1. See also Lindsey Lupo, *Flak-Catchers: One Hundred Years of Riot Commission Politics in America* (Lanham, Md.: Lexington Books, 2011), pp. 73–74.

93 **"smokescreen"** See "Inquiry on Harlem Scored as Sham," *New York Times*, May 29, 1935, p. 6.

93 **"high-toned"** Quoted in "The Man in the Street: Average Harlemite Thinks Conditions Precipitated Riots," *New York Amsterdam News*, March 30, 1935, p. 9.

93 **The commission, in its wisdom** See "Harlem Riot Laid to Economic Ills," *New York Times*, March 26, 1935, p. 5.

94 **"Red plot"** See "Police End Harlem Riot: Mayor Starts Inquiry; Dodge Sees a Red Plot; District Still Is Tense," *New York Times*, March 21, 1935, p. 1. See also "Harlem Riot Guilt to Be Sifted Today: New Indictments Expected as Dodge Hunts Red Element in Area's Unrest," *New York Times*, March 25, 1935, p. 34.

94 **He announced a "city-wide"** "12 Indicted in Riot; Troop Plea Denied," *New York Times*, March 22, 1935, p. 1.

94 **if bad blood existed** See, for example, "Harlem Police Defended," *New York Times*, May 18, 1935, p. 9.

94 **The Hearst newspapers** Naison, *Communists in Harlem During the Depression*, p. 142.

94 **James H. Hubert** See "Unemployment and Reds Held Causes of Riots," *New York Herald Tribune*, March 21, 1935, p. 2.

94 **"the only persons who"** Eugene Gordon, "Semi-Starvation Justified Harlem Riot, Says Gordon," *Afro-American* (Baltimore), April 6, 1935, p. 16.

94 **None of those quoted** See "The Man in the Street: Average Harlemite Thinks Conditions Precipitated Riots; Very Few Put Blame on Communists for Recent Outbreak," *New York Amsterdam News*, March 30, 1935, p. 9. See also Naison, *Communists in Harlem During the Depression*, pp. 142–44.

95 **The judge found** See "Blamed for Riot, Harlem Girl Fined," *New York Times*, March 24, 1935, p. 19.

95 **the Harlem audience loudly jeered** "Police Are Hissed at Harlem Hearing," *New York Times*, May 5, 1935, p. 35.

95 **"I'll shoot you"** See "Scuffle Disrupts Hearing in Harlem," *New York Times*, June 15, 1935, p. 16.

95 **Many city officials** See the foreword to Mayor's Commission on Conditions in Harlem, "*The Negro in Harlem: A Report on Social and Economic Conditions Responsible for the Outbreak of March 19, 1935*" (unpublished typescript, 1935), unpaginated.

95 **The only reason Frazier's check** Lindsey Lupo, *Flak-Catchers: One Hundred Years of Riot Commission Politics in America* (Lanham, Md.: Lexington Books, 2011), pp. 72–73.

95 **The Communist Party, by contrast** Naison, *Communists in Harlem During the Depression*, pp. 143–50.

96 **spoke at a testimonial dinner** See "Socialites Pay Tribute by Way of a Banquet," *Chicago Defender*, June 15, 1935, p. 9.

96 **disagreement erupted** "Election Issue Disrupts Fete," *New York Amsterdam News*, June 8, 1935, p. 1.

96 **"I heartily agree with you"** Quoted in Lupo, *Flak-Catchers*, p. 76.

96 **"the most progressive leaders"** Ben Davis Jr., *James W. Ford: What He Is and What He Stands For* (New York: National Campaign Committee of the Communist Party, 1936), p. 28. (The paging of this pamphlet is idiosyncratic.) Davis, who along with Ford was one of the two leading black Communists of the day, grew up in Atlanta, where he was apparently a playmate of Alphaeus's. Davis's arch-conservative father, a friend of the Huntons, published

the *Atlanta Independent*, which claimed to be the most widely read Negro paper during the first decade of the twentieth century.

97   **"flimsy evidence"** Quoted in "Harlem Report Assailed," *New York Times*, Aug. 19, 1935, p. 4.

8. The Prosecutor

100   **predicting his downfall** Of the Negro press, this was particularly true. See, for example, "Declare Strike Against Schultz 'Numbers' Banks; Expect Bloody Gang War," *New York Age*, March 4, 1933, p. 1; "'Dutch' Schultz 'on Spot' as Mme. St. Clair, Numbers Queen, Says That She's Out to Get Him," *Philadelphia Tribune*, Dec. 27, 1934, p. 1.

101   **his handpicked police commissioner** See Mary M. Stolberg, *Fighting Organized Crime: Politics, Justice, and the Legacy of Thomas E. Dewey* (Boston: Northeastern University Press, 1995), pp. 48–50.

101   **kept promising** See "War on Rackets Outlined by Dodge; Prosecutor Calls on Public to Give Evidence Under Promise of Protection," *New York Times*, Jan. 22, 1934, p. 2; "Dodge Promises a Drive on Crime; Says He Will Win Confidence of Critics by Aggressive War Against Rackets," *New York Times*, Dec. 5, 1933, p. 4.

101   **out of the room** Donati, *Lucky Luciano*, p. 103. See also "Jurors Probing N.Y. Vice Oust Their Attorney," *Washington Post*, May 22, 1935, p. 5.

101   **The foreman** Stolberg suggests that the entire grand jury met with Lehman. Stolberg, *Fighting Organized Crime*, p. 61. This is possible but seems unlikely, as the jury comprised the usual twenty-three members. Most sources agree that only the foreman, Lee Thompson Smith, met with Lehman. See, for example, Richard Norton Smith, *Thomas E. Dewey and His Times* (New York: Simon & Schuster, 1982), pp. 148–49.

101   **"useless"** That, at least, is the word he uses in *Liberty* magazine's version of the events. See Fred Allhoff, "Tracking New York's Crime Barons: Part I," *Liberty*, Oct. 31, 1936, p. 6. The editors concede that some of the quotations are "reconstructed." Allhoff would later author *Lightning in the Night*, a popular alternative-history novel about a Nazi invasion of the United States. The book would be published in 1940, well before several better-known volumes on the same theme.

102   **Rumor had it** Donati, *Lucky Luciano*, p. 103.

102   **nothing of the kind** See "Racket Grand Jury Balks over Corbin, but Dodge Is Firm," *New York Times*, June 5, 1935, p. 1.

102   **editorialists were poking fun** See, for example, "Runaway Jury," *Boston Daily Globe*, June 26, 1935, p. 16.

102   **Governor Lehman stepped in** "Dodge Will Obey Governor's Order on Racket Inquiry: Notifies Executive He Will Pick Special Prosecutor from Those Suggested," *New York Times*, June 26, 1935, p. 1.

102   **wanted nothing to do with Dodge** Donati, *Lucky Luciano*, p. 103.

104   **"Three thousand lawyers"** Smith, *Thomas E. Dewey and His Times*, p. 154. Press reports on the number of applicants varied. The lowest estimate came from the *Herald Tribune*, which reported that "more than a thousand letters containing credentials and biographies of aspirants" had been received. "Dewey Studies Pleas of 1,000 for Staff Jobs," *New York Herald Tribune*, July 7, 1935, p. 3.

104   **brutal, even terrifying** Stolberg, *Fighting Organized Crime*, p. 89.

104   **"tracked back to the cradle"** Herbert Corey, "Formula for Beating the Rackets," *Nation's Business*, vol. 25, no. 8 (Aug. 1937), pp. 31, 112.

104   **presented her theory to Dewey** See, for example, Ellen Poulsen, *The Case Against Lucky Luciano* (Little Neck, N.Y.: Clinton Cook Publishing, 2007), pp. 54–55, and Stolberg, *Fighting Organized Crime*, pp. 121–22. The story also appears in any number of encyclopedia entries and museum exhibits.

105   **If her application received special attention** See, for example, "Negro Lawyer, Investigators Will Get Dewey Probe Posts: Negro Lawyer Will Be Placed on Dewey Staff for Racket Inquiry," *New York Amsterdam News*, Aug. 3, 1935, p. 1.

105   **"Republicans feel that in appointing"** "Harlem Democrats Throw 'Harmony' out of the Window," *New Journal and Guide* (Norfolk, Va.), Aug. 24, 1935, p. A4.

105 **the news accounts had her** See, for example, "Eunice Carter to Aid Harlem Racket Inquiry," *New York Herald Tribune*, Aug. 6, 1935, p. 3.

105 **The *New York Times* put the story** "Dewey Gives Post to Harlem Lawyer," *New York Times*, Aug. 6, 1935, p. 3. The *Times* being the *Times*, the story referred to Schultz as "Arthur (Dutch Schultz) Flegenheimer."

105 **The *Herald Tribune* conjectured** "Eunice Carter to Aid Harlem Racket Inquiry: Dewey Appoints Negro Woman Lawyer to Help Drive on Numbers Game," *New York Herald Tribune*, Aug. 6, 1935, p. 3.

105 **Out-of-town papers** See, for example, "Dewey Opens War on Policy Racket: Names Negro Woman Lawyer as Aide in Fight on Harlem Crime," *Sun* (Baltimore), Aug. 6, 1935, p. 12.

106 **And the Negro press** See, for example, "Eunice Carter on Important Staff," *Pittsburgh Courier*, Aug. 10, 1935, p. 1; "Eunice Carter on N.Y. Racket Probe Staff: Negro Woman Lawyer Will Aid Prosecution of Crime, Rackets," *Philadelphia Tribune*, Aug. 8, 1935, p. 3; and "Woman Named N.Y. Vice Probe Assistant: Is First Person of Color Given This Position," *New Journal and Guide* (Norfolk, Va.), Aug. 10, 1935, p. 1.

106 **"Orchids to Mrs. Carter!"** Lillian Johnson, "The Feminine Viewpoint," *New Journal and Guide* (Norfolk, Va.), Aug. 17, 1935, p. A7.

106 **"She'll Fight Policy Racket"** "She'll Fight Policy Racket," *Afro-American* (Baltimore), Aug. 10, 1935, p. 6.

106 **"culled from 3,000"** "Eunice Carter on N.Y. Racket Probe Staff," *Philadelphia Tribune*, Aug. 8, 1935, p. 3.

106 **Only her local paper** "Mrs. Carter Seen as Only Negro Appointee: Whites to Fill Other Positions in Dewey Probe of Rackets," *New York Amsterdam News*, Aug. 10, 1935, p. 1.

106 **"Mrs. Carter was a girl"** Hickman Powell, *Ninety Times Guilty* (New York: Harcourt, Brace, 1939), p. 89.

106 **"her command of Harlem poolhalls"** Smith, *Thomas E. Dewey and His Times*, p. 181.

106 **Dewey was signaling an intent** See, for example, "Dewey Gives Post to Harlem Lawyer; Naming of Mrs. Carter, Negro, as Aide Viewed as Move to Break Policy Racket," *New York Times*, Aug. 6, 1935, p. 3.

106 **"I hired Mrs. Carter the first day"** "Dewey Has 3 in His Office," *Afro-American* (Baltimore), Sep. 2, 1939, p. 2. One sees in the story the seeds of Eunice's rivalry with Frank Rivers, who was hired after she was and held the same rank but was earning $7,500 to her $6,000. Moreover, for all the praise that Dewey lavished on Eunice (including a mention of her doctor of laws degree from Smith), it was Rivers whom he described as "among the two or three ablest colored lawyers at the New York bar."

107 **In July she helped organize** See Bessye Bearden, "New York Society," *Chicago Defender*, July 20, 1935, p. 8.

107 **She addressed the national conference** "Women's Business, Professional Club Conference Starts Friday," *New York Age*, July 13, 1935, p. 5.

107 **She again had as a houseguest** Bessye Bearden, "New York Society," *Chicago Defender*, July 6, 1935, p. 6.

107 **Eunice took a few days** See "Montrose, N.Y.," *New York Amsterdam News*, Aug. 10, 1935, p. 18.

108 **"Motor cars whizzed"** Eunice Hunton, "The Corner," in *Opportunity: A Journal of Negro Life*, vol. 3, no. 28 (April 1925), p. 114.

109 **The implication is** Jervis Anderson puts the point this way: "In the twenties, most visitors—unless they were reporters sent up by the major metropolitan dailies—did not see the less attractive sides of life in Harlem." Anderson, *This Was Harlem*, p. 139.

9. The Premise

110 **"ablest group of lawyers"** Thomas E. Dewey, *Twenty Against the Underworld* (New York: Doubleday, 1974), p. 160.

110 **"a labyrinth of solid doors"** "Dewey Method of Crime Hunting: Privacy and Soundproof Walls Assure Testimony Without Leaks," *New York Herald Tribune*, Jan. 16, 1938, p. A2.

110   **the city denied him nothing** See "Estimate Board Gets $115,000 Dewey Budget," *New York Herald Tribune*, July 17, 1935, p. 1.

110   **"familiar with underworld characters"** Dewey, *Twenty Against the Underworld*, p. 156.

111   **The suite was guarded** The *Times* labeled this measure an "extraordinary precaution." "Police Post Guard at Dewey Offices," *New York Times*, Aug. 2, 1935, p. 3.

111   **"far down at the end of the corridor"** Powell, *Ninety Times Guilty*, p. 90.

111   **the office's first prosecution** See Donati, *Lucky Luciano*, p. 110.

111   **the gangster was not welcome** See, for example, "Schultz No. 1 Dewey Target; Mayor Closes City to Him," *New York Herald Tribune*, Aug. 3, 1935, p. 1.

112   **"Let them think"** Smith, *Thomas E. Dewey and His Times*, p. 172. Smith had the story from Herwitz, in an interview. Unfortunately, there is no follow-up in Smith's fine volume, so we do not know what came of the pretense.

113   **"There is today scarcely a business"** The speech is given in full in Dewey, *Twenty Against the Underworld*, pp. 13–20. Most sources agree that he spoke for about half an hour.

113   **New Yorkers in droves** See, for example, "Victims Give Dewey Facts on Rackets," *New York Herald Tribune*, Aug. 1, 1935, p. 1.

113   **Many wrote letters** See, for example, Jerry W. Koprivsek Jr. to "Dewey Investigating Committee," Aug. 7, 1935, NYCDA archives.

114   **As early as September** See, for example, "Six Witnesses Heard by the Racket Jury," *New York Times*, Sept. 18, 1935, p. 17, and "5 Heard in Rackets Inquiry," *New York Times*, Sept. 14, 1935, p. 7.

114   **eighteen-year-old Salvatore Marrone** Marrone and a friend were arrested for assault in late August after a seventeen-year-old girl jumped from their car in Central Park. See "Girl Leaps Out, 2 Autoists Held by Park Patrol," *New York Herald Tribune*, Aug. 27, 1935, p. 8. Eunice interviewed one of the complaining witnesses and both of the alleged perpetrators, and also researched the legal basis for charging the defendants, all on the same day. See Eunice Carter, *Statement of Helen Genta*, Aug. 28, 1935 (memorandum in NYCDA archives); Eunice Carter, *Statement of Salvatore Marrone and Fred Guli*, Aug. 28, 1935 (memorandum in NYCDA archives); Eunice Carter, *Memorandum of Law in re: Abduction*, Aug. 28, 1935 (NYCDA archives).

115   **were thoroughly corrupt** During the early 1930s, Samuel Seabury, a retired judge, was counsel to a legislative committee looking into municipal corruption. In the public eye, his name and the investigative work became inseparable. Soon the press wrote only of the Seabury Commission, even though that was not the committee's formal name.

116   **Romano accused** Statement of John Romano, taken by Eunice H. Carter and Victor J. Herwitz, New York, New York, Aug. 26, 1935, NYCDA archives.

116   **Eunice wrote a detailed memorandum** Letter, William Bernard to Thomas E. Dewey, Aug. 1, 1935 (with handwritten notation on top reading "prostitution," meaning that it is for Eunice's attention), NYCDA archives; Eunice H. Carter to William Bernard, Aug. 22, 1935, NYCDA archives; and Eunice H. Carter, memorandum, Complainant: William Bernard, Aug. 30, 1935, NYCDA archives.

116   **filed one memorandum after another** See, for example, Eunice H. Carter, "Statement of Samuel Horowitz," Oct. 7, 1935, NYCDA archives; Eunice H. Carter, memorandum, "Statement of Max Kraintz," Aug. 29, 1935, NYCDA archives, and attached transcript; and Eunice H. Carter, memorandum (untitled), Oct. 1, 1935, NYCDA archives.

116   **they immediately fired off memoranda** See, for example, memorandum from M. L. Robbins to Eunice H. Carter and Wayne Merrick, Feb. 13, 1936, NYCDA archives (Merrick, a former FBI agent, was Dewey's chief investigator), and memorandum of Paul E. Lockwood, "Re: Telephone Complaint Martin Balagur," Sept. 16, 1935 (typed notation in top margin: "FOR MRS. CARTER'S FILES"), NYCDA archives.

116   **She gathered reports from** Donati, *Lucky Luciano*, p. 108. See memorandum, Manuel L. Robbins to Eunice H. Carter, Dec. 21, 1935, NYCDA archives.

117   **Eunice pointed out that Kleinman** Eunice H. Carter, memorandum, "In Re: Complaint of Frances Kleinman Alias Frances Guiterer," Sept. 7, 1935, NYCDA archives.

117   **She wrote about a Harlem landlady** Eunice H. Carter, memorandum (untitled), Oct. 1, 1935, NYCDA archives.

117   **Eunice remembered an oddity** Dewey, in his memoir, would remember clearly what Eunice had learned in the Women's Courts but would state that her work there had been "some years before." Dewey, *Twenty Against the Underworld*, p. 187.

118   **Karp's clients always went free** Later investigation showed that a small subset—those actually caught naked with a client—did not go free. Karp was not a magician. Girls caught in the act simply failed to show up for trial. Warrants were issued for their arrests but never executed. Some of the girls left town, but most showed up again and resumed the same work, albeit under different names.

118   **The question was whether** Many historians give joint credit for the prostitution theory to Eunice and Murray Gurfein, one of Dewey's senior assistants. Here, for example, is William Donati, the author of an excellent Luciano biography: "Following reports that the Magistrate Court was corrupt, Eunice Carter and Murray Gurfein began a probe." Donati, *Lucky Luciano*, p. 110. But the paper record does not bear this out. Richard Norton Smith, Dewey's most comprehensive biographer, offers a slightly different slant, and probably the correct one. Eunice came up with the idea, and she and Gurfein presented it jointly to the boss. Smith, *Thomas E. Dewey and His Times*, p. 181.

10. The Raiders

119   **The police investigated** See "Schultz Dies of Wounds Without Naming Slayers," *New York Times*, Oct. 25, 1935, pp. 1, 16.

119   **She collected white elephants** "Wished Schultz Luck; Woman Explains Cryptic Message She Sent to Gangster," *New York Times*, Oct. 27, 1935, p. 33.

119   **"a total of 820 days"** Quoted in White, Garton, Robertson, and White, *Playing the Numbers*, p. 186.

120   **"If Dutch is eliminated"** Quoted in Smith, *Thomas E. Dewey and His Times*, p. 171.

121   **The committee's supporters** See Mara Keire, "The Committee of Fourteen and Saloon Reform in New York City, 1905–1920," *Business and Economic History*, vol. 26, no. 2 (Winter 1997), pp. 573, 574.

121   **the group closed its offices** For an excellent history of the Committee of Fourteen, including the often-valid bases for criticizing its methods, see Jennifer Fronc, *New York Undercover: Private Surveillance in the Progressive Era* (Chicago: University of Chicago Press, 2009), particularly chapters 3 and 4.

122   **As Baldwin himself described** See William H. Baldwin to George E. Worthington, Sept. 20, 1935, NYCDA archives.

122   **Baldwin, acting as though** It appears that in 1935 the trustees of the records were George E. Worthington, William H. Baldwin, and James Stewart Cushman. See George E. Worthington to William B. Herlands, Oct. 3 [5?], 1935, NYCDA archives. In an interesting irony, Cushman, the founder of the real estate firm that still bears his name, was married to Vera Scott Cushman, long a leading light and fund-raiser for the YWCA, who would have been acquainted with Addie.

122   **Merrick told Herlands** See memorandum from Wayne Merrick to William B. Herlands, Oct. 16, 1935, NYCDA archives.

122   **"practically the only assistant"** Ibid.; the handwritten note from Herlands to Eunice appears in the top margin.

122   **As if she could not have** Dewey's biographer includes an interesting sentence: "By October, Dewey himself was caught up in the hunt, dog-earing a Rockefeller Foundation study on prostitution." Smith, *Thomas E. Dewey and His Times*, p. 182. Other sources also mention a Rockefeller Foundation study. See, for example, Stolberg, *Fighting Organized Crime*, p. 123. But the "study" was not performed by the Rockefeller Foundation, and Dewey was not the one who dog-eared it. True, there were several studies of prostitution produced by the Bureau of Social Hygiene under grants from the foundation, but the most recent dated from

World War I. Since that time the BSH had moved into sex research more generally. The document to which the various sources refer is the Committee of Fourteen report, which indeed received significant support from John D. Rockefeller Jr. "By October," Dewey himself does not appear even to have consulted the report. The person who dog-eared it, working all alone, was Eunice. (Stolberg is one of the few who gets this part right.)

122 **rather prim exchange of correspondence** See Eunice H. Carter to K. D. Metcalf, Oct. 21, 1935, NYCDA archives, and K. D. Metcalf to "Miss" Eunice H. Carter, Oct. 22, 1935, NYCDA archives.

123 **"She has interviewed"** All quotes in this section are from Fred Allhoff, "Tracking New York's Crime Barons: Part II," *Liberty*, Nov. 7, 1936, p. 18.

125 **"I trusted their judgment"** Dewey, *Twenty Against the Underworld*, p. 187. Closer to the events in question, Dewey took significantly more credit. In a 1937 affidavit, he would describe the effort to attack the Mob through an investigation of prostitution as his own idea: "A few weeks after my office was organized, we began to receive confidential information that prostitution in New York had in the past three years become almost wholly controlled by a single syndicate of gunmen and narcotics peddlers." Affidavit of Thomas E. Dewey, Record on Appeal, pp. 355–56. Note Dewey's use of "we," obscuring the fact that he himself had not thought any of the "confidential information" particularly important. He went on to describe some of the information in more detail and then added the following entirely true yet somewhat misleading statement: "I asked Mrs. Eunice H. Carter, a Deputy Assistant District Attorney in my office, to undertake a completely confidential investigation of these reports, in addition to other duties which she already had."

Dewey fails to mention that he initially opposed taking this route because it would make him look like a morality crusader; that all his top assistants were busily pursuing what Dewey considered more fruitful avenues of inquiry; and that the prostitution angle had been dumped in Eunice's lap precisely because it was not considered particularly important.

126 **she all but vanished** In early December, Eunice did purchase a private loge for an Ethel Waters concert at the Renaissance Casino to benefit the Edgecombe Sanitarium. See "Boxes and Loges for Edgecombe Sanitarium Benefit About Sold Out," *New York Age*, Dec. 14, 1935, p. 5. It is not clear, however, whether she attended.

126 **"It would seem that I can never"** Eunice H. Carter to Thomas E. Dewey, Jan. 1, 1936, NYCDA archives.

126 **Then, on January 13** See Donati, *Lucky Luciano*, p. 122.

127 **The extra manpower** See, for example, memorandum, Eunice H. Carter to Murray Gurfein, Jan. 17, 1936, NYCDA archives.

127 **At first he had gone about** Donati, *Lucky Luciano*, p. 108.

127 **frequently in the papers** See, for example, "Portrait of a Racketeer (Streamlined)," *New York Times Magazine*, Nov. 10, 1935, p. 6, and "Luciano Fled on Newark Tip," *New York Herald Tribune*, Nov. 3, 1935, p. 36A.

127 **"the head of the mob"** Quoted in Donati, *Lucky Luciano*, p. 119.

129 **"a besieged castle"** "Assailant of Watchman Sought in Mazes of Woolworth Building," *Washington Post*, Jan. 27, 1936, p. 1.

129 **Police speculated** "'Phantom' Thief Eludes 200 Police All Day in Woolworth Building," *New York Times*, Jan. 27, 1936, p. 1.

129 **Apart from Eunice** Stolberg, *Fighting Organized Crime*, p. 124.

129 **He suggested that perhaps** Powell, *Ninety Times Guilty*, p. 97.

129 **On the other hand** See, for example, "Painters Are Raided in Rackets Inquiry," *New York Times*, Jan. 16, 1936, p. 9; "Truckmen's Data Seized by Dewey," *New York Times*, Dec. 5, 1935, p. 1; and "Six More Seized in War on Usurers," *New York Times*, Dec. 6, 1935, p. 8.

130 **Eunice and Murray** Affidavit of Harold M. Cole, Record on Appeal, p. 513.

130 **The instruction sheets were detailed** David J. McAuliffe, untitled memorandum of instructions, [1936], NYCDA archives.

130 **A decade later, Eunice would tell** "Negro Woman Sent 'Lucky' Luciano Away," *New York Amsterdam News*, March 1, 1947, p. 1. A few days after the raids, however, she took time off to deliver a lecture in Poughkeepsie to celebrate Negro History Week. "Negro History Week to Be Observed Here," *Poughkeepsie Eagle-News*, Feb. 7, 1936, p. 18.

130 **The Woolworth Building's freight elevator** Smith, *Thomas E. Dewey and His Times*, p. 186.

130 **"Treat them decently"** This is another reconstruction from *Liberty* magazine. Fred Allhoff, "Tracking New York's Crime Barons: Part III," *Liberty*, Nov. 14, 1936, p. 32.

130 **the team had set aside** Donati, *Lucky Luciano*, p. 125.

130 **"By midnight a hundred suspects"** Smith, *Thomas E. Dewey and His Times*, p. 186. The press reported that the actual number was slightly higher. See "110 Arrested in 41 Secret Raids by Dewey in Drive on Chain of 200 Disorderly Houses," *New York Times*, Feb. 2, 1936, p. 1. Dewey himself put the number at "eighty or ninety prisoners." Affidavit of Thomas E. Dewey, Record on Appeal, p. 357.

130 **"were crawling with them"** Quoted in Stolberg, *Fighting Organized Crime*, p. 125.

130 **A detained madam** See Mildred Harris, "What It Feels Like to Testify Against a Big-Shot Gangster," Exhibit "B" Attached to Affidavit of Edward J. Doherty, Record on Appeal, p. 632.

130 **"The customary angels"** Smith, *Thomas E. Dewey and His Times*, p. 186.

131 **"Vice Raids Smash '$12,000,000' Ring"** "Vice Raids Smash '$12,000,000' Ring; Leaders in Jail," *New York Times*, Feb. 3, 1936, p. 1.

131 **"New York Vice Raiders"** "New York Vice Raiders Break City-Wide Gang," *Chicago Daily Tribune*, Feb. 3, 1936, p. 5.

131 **It is commonly reported** See, for example, C. Joseph Greaves, "How Prosecutors Brought Down Lucky Luciano," *ABA Journal*, online version, Nov. 1, 2015: http://www.abajournal .com/magazine/article/how_prosecutors_brought_down_lucky_luciano.

131 **He chose not to** Dewey, *Twenty Against the Underworld*, p. 193.

131 **Pressed to explain** See "Valentine Seeks Way to Curb Vice," *New York Times*, Feb. 5, 1936, p. 5.

11. The Preparation

132 **Gurfein drafted a memorandum** Murray I. Gurfein, "Memorandum to All Assistants," Feb. 16, 1936, NYCDA archives.

132 **"schooled in perjury"** Quoted in Donati, *Lucky Luciano*, p. 131.

132 **They were housewives** Dewey, *Twenty Against the Underworld*, p. 193.

132 **she had been on the trail** On Kaplan's role as a procurer, see Donati, *Lucky Luciano*, p. 112.

132 **Prodded by Eunice** Eunice Carter, Digest of Statement of Sadie Kaplan, April 17, 1936, NYCDA archives.

133 **Mildred Harris (also known as** See Mildred Harris, "What It Feels Like to Testify Against a Big-Shot Gangster," Exhibit "B" Attached to Affidavit of Edward J. Doherty, Record on Appeal, p. 632.

133 **a mobster she knew** The patrolman who was guarding Mildred Harris testified in court to having witnessed the conversation but conceded on cross-examination that he was not aware that the man had made any threats. See Trial Transcript, pp. 16554–65.

134 **Dewey himself was still not persuaded** Stolberg, *Fighting Organized Crime*, pp. 126–28.

134 **Betillo usually gave the orders** See, for example, C.D.B. [Charles Breitel], Memorandum on Al Weiner, April 27, 1936, NYCDA archives. Betillo had little trouble taking over booking and bonding operations from the independents. He was greatly feared within the New York underworld because of rumors that he had served as a killer for Al Capone. Dewey tried and failed to get this evidence before the jury. See Trial Transcript, pp. 15893–904. In his memoirs, Dewey called Betillo "a smart and ruthless murderer and gunman." Dewey, *Twenty Against the Underworld*, p. 190. Certainly Luciano and Betillo were close. In his opening statement to the jury, Luciano's counsel denied that his client knew any of the co-defendants other than Betillo, with whom he conceded that his client was acquainted. Donati, *Lucky Luciano*, p. 150.

135 **The means included taking over** See, for example, Eunice H. Carter, Statement of Abe Henig, March 19, 1936, NYCDA archives; Eunice H. Carter, Statement of Hugo Madison, March 19 and March 23, 1936, NYCDA archives; and Eunice H. Carter, Statement of William Ricco, March 21 and March 23, 1936, NYCDA archives.

135 **under the assumed name** Donati, *Lucky Luciano*, p. 94.

135 **Eunice learned in an interview** See Digest of Statement of George B. Grant, taken by Eunice Carter, April 2, 1936, NYCDA archives.

135 **Luciano was at last in custody** For more detail on the comedy in Hot Springs, see Donati, *Lucky Luciano*, pp. 140–43. For news coverage, see, for example, "Law Agencies in West Fight over Luciano," *New York Herald Tribune*, April 4, 1936, p. 1, and "Extradition Stay Is Won by Luciano," *New York Times*, April 8, 1936, p. 24.

135 **ridiculed by the papers** "Luciano Due Today; Faces $350,000 Bail," *New York Herald Tribune*, April 18, 1936, p. 1.

135 **According to the press** "Luciano Held in $350,000 on 4 Vice Counts," *New York Herald Tribune*, April 19, 1936, p. 1.

135 **"such a messy charge"** "Lucania Is Jailed in $350,000 Bail," *New York Times*, April 19, 1936, p. 1. The *Times* referred to Luciano inconsistently, mostly using "Lucania" but often using the more traditional "Luciano."

136 **"Prosecutor Dewey"** Meyer Berger, "The 'Great Luciano' Is at Last in Toils," *New York Times*, April 26, 1936, p. E10.

136 **he had been Dewey's** See Smith, *Thomas E. Dewey and His Times*, p. 114.

136 **"take general charge"** Affidavit of Barent Ten Eyck, Record on Appeal, pp. 1400–1401.

136 **Neither was Gurfein** Ibid., pp. 467–68. Ten Eyck said later that for two weeks after the raids—that is, until the middle of February—"I had no idea that Luciano was connected with organized vice in New York City, and so far as I knew at the time, no one else in Mr. Dewey's office had any such idea." The claim is implausible—certainly Eunice and Murray Gurfein had the idea, whether or not they could yet prove it—but Ten Eyck phrased his comment this way for a reason. He was responding to allegations that witnesses had been coached to name Luciano. There could not have been coaching, he was saying, if nobody knew what to coach for.

136 **"way into the early hours"** "Negro Woman Sent 'Lucky' Luciano Away," *New York Amsterdam News*, March 1, 1947, p. 1.

137 **an undated five-page memorandum** Memorandum on Preparation for Trial of Evidence to Serve as Foundation for Introduction in Evidence of Charts of Prostitution Arrests and Case Dispositions, undated, in NYCDA archives.

137 **Who wrote the memorandum** There is some internal evidence suggesting that the memorandum was written by Murray Gurfein, or perhaps by Eunice herself. Certainly aspects of it are consistent with the assignment she was given. But the memorandum could also have been written by someone else, and thus could be summarizing the results of assignments from several assistants.

   In any case, the copy in the files appears to have been sent to someone else. The section of the memorandum dealing with Max Rachlin, the Mob lawyer, is marked "Dubious" in the margin, in a hand not Eunice's. Why is Rachlin's culpability dubious? Because all the memorandum really says about the evidence is that there is proof that Rachlin "handled all arising from bonded houses" except for a few handled by other lawyers when he was not available and that there is proof that Rachlin was paid for his services by Jesse Jacobs, the Mob's illegal bondsman. But being paid by a shady character to represent other shady characters is not a crime, and prosecutors hate to indict other lawyers. Although Rachlin was named in the course of the trial as a co-conspirator, he did not himself face any charges.

137 **was assigned only one** Memorandum, no header, April 27, 1936, NYCDA archives.

137 **She prepared an excellent memorandum** "Anthony Curcio" (undated memorandum), NYCDA archives.

138 **there are certain sad stories** Particularly poignant was the story of Polly Sorrell, related in Donati, *Lucky Luciano*, p. 110.

138 **One later writer suggests** See Poulsen, *The Case Against Lucky Luciano*, p. 54. Poulsen does not cite a source for this assertion.

138 **"Tommy Bull had obtained permission"** Supplement #1 to Vice Statements, p. 2, unpaginated, undated, NYCDA archives. Also quoted in Donati, *Lucky Luciano*, p. 132.

138 **"Jimmy Fredericks had obtained permission"** Supplement #1 to Vice Statements, p. 1, unpaginated, undated, NYCDA archives.

139 **had been beaten by police** For details of the beating, see Donati, *Lucky Luciano*, p. 96.

139 **"Do you understand"** Transcript, Part Eleven, April 6, 1936, 4:00 p.m., Before Justice Philip J. McCook, n.p., People's Exhibit 34, *People v. Luciano*, Record on Appeal, New York Supreme Court, Appellate Division, First Department, vol. 8422 (undated; likely 1936), between pp. 6202 and 6203.

140 **his bail was raised** See "Trial of Lucania Will Start May 11," *New York Times*, April 25, 1936, p. 3. The $50,000 bail would be nearly $900,000 today.

12. The Trial

141 **"[P]rotecting rights is one thing"** "Lawyers for Criminals," *New York World-Telegram*, May 29, 1936. This editorial led to an unsuccessful defamation lawsuit against the newspaper by Harry Kopp, the lawyer who represented Davie Betillo at the trial.

142 **Dewey excluded** Stolberg, *Fighting Organized Crime*, pp. 132–33.

143 **Pete Balitzer testified** There is a good argument to be made that this testimony was inadmissible hearsay.

144 **But the conspiracy was charged** See *People v. Luciano*, 277 N.Y. 348 (1938). Admittedly the court had to reach back to a case from 1894 to demonstrate that the indictment need not charge conspiracy so long as it charged the underlying acts.

144 **"my boss"** New York's highest court, in affirming Luciano's conviction, cited this testimony as one of several pieces of evidence directly connecting Luciano to the prostitution scheme. See *People v. Luciano*, 14 N.E.2d 433, 277 N. Y. 348, 356 (1938).

146 **went along to observe** This scene is in the transcript, but is nicely dramatized in Donati, *Lucky Luciano*, pp. 158–59.

146 **"She did a thoroughgoing job"** "Lucania Is Named Again as Vice Chief: Woman Narcotic Addict Says He Planned City-Wide Chain of Disorderly Houses," *New York Times*, May 23, 1936, p. 16. In its coverage of the trial, the *Times* pedantically insisted on referring to Luciano as "Lucania," using his birth name, until quite late in the proceedings.

146 **"Luciano Named Vice Ring Head"** "Luciano Named Vice Ring Head by Drug Addict: Florence Brown Testifies, Fortified by Brandy, That He Directed Syndicate," *New York Herald Tribune*, May 23, 1936, p. 2A.

147 **one can be convicted** Here's an example: **A** and **B** agree to rob a bank. **A** draws up the plan. **B** carries out the robbery itself with the help of **C**, whom **A** has never met. As a matter of law, **A** and **C** are co-conspirators.

147 **Dewey forced Luciano** "Luciano Is Forced to Admit Crimes," *New York Times*, June 4, 1936, p. 1.

147 **"stuttering"** "Luciano Lied Often Under Oath, Dewey Makes Him Say on Stand," *New York Herald Tribune*, June 4, 1936, p. 1A.

147 **"slightly intoxicated"** Trial transcript, pp. 16525–27. Although Heidt's testimony was quite brief and not particularly compelling, it continues to find a place in commentary about the case. See, for example, Stolberg, *Fighting Organized Crime*, pp. 145–46. (Stolberg calls him "Heidy.")

148 **"You were instructed to take"** Trial transcript, pp. 16538–39.

148 **"was a real wise guy"** Quoted in Dewey, *Twenty Against the Underworld*, p. 225.

149 **"definitely unworthy of belief"** Trial transcript, pp. 17450–51.

149 **"primarily upon the sworn words"** "Luciano Jury Gets Vice Case Against Nine," *New York Herald Tribune*, June 7, 1936, p. 1A.

149 **The chamber was empty** Dewey, *Twenty Against the Underworld*, p. 262.

149   **At a press conference** See "Lucania Convicted with 8 in Vice Ring on 62 Counts Each," *New York Times*, June 8, 1936, p. 1, and "Luciano and 8 Guilty on All 62 Counts in Vice Racket," *New York Herald Tribune*, June 8, 1936, p. 1.

150   **He also checked** See "Luciano Sentenced to 30 to 50 Years," *New York Herald Tribune*, June 19, 1936, p. 1.

150   **he offered his congratulations** See "Tops in Law, Heads World Organization," *New York Age*, Nov. 5, 1955, p. 1.

150   **Tony Luciano would be named** Smith, *Thomas E. Dewey and His Times*, p. 225.

150   **the police commissioner relieved** "Valentine Hails Dewey Victory as Racket Blow," *Brooklyn Daily Eagle*, June 8, 1936, p. 6.

150   **told Justice McCook under oath** Donati, *Lucky Luciano*, p. 195.

150   **Mildred Harris would testify** Ibid., p. 218.

150   **Heidt had banked over $83,000** "Heidt Banked $22,288 in '32 on $3,200 Pay," *New York Herald Tribune*, June 21, 1936, p. 1A.

150   **Heidt was fired** "Heidt Dropped by Police for Aid to Luciano," *New York Herald Tribune*, Sept. 1, 1936, p. 9.

151   **the evidence was insufficient** See *Matter of Heidt v. Valentine*, 252 App. Div. 626 (1937).

151   **Heidt's reinstatement** See "Defender of Luciano Is Policeman Again," *New York Times*, Feb. 2, 1938, p. 12.

151   **would retire for good** "Patrolman Heidt Files Retirement Application: Luciano Defense Witness Seeks $1,500 a Year Pension," *New York Herald Tribune*, April 25, 1940, p. 14.

151   **linked to Mob bookmaker** "Never Saw Erickson, Heidt Says; Heidt Calls Erickson Link 'Mistake,'" *Newsday*, May 23, 1950, p. 1.

151   **run by the gangster Meyer Lansky** Donati, *Lucky Luciano*, p. 238.

151   **"a killer, a gunman"** Ibid., p. 6.

151   **Joseph Bonanno insists** Joseph Bonanno, *Man of Honor: The Autobiography of Joseph Bonanno* (New York: Simon and Schuster, 1983), pp. 164–65.

151   **"Tom Dewey tried"** Jack Higgins, *Luciano's Luck* (New York: Stein and Day, 1981), p. 51.

151   **"one thing that doesn't seem to fit"** Ibid., p. 49.

151   **"many of them alcoholics and drug addicts"** Polly Adler, *A House Is Not a Home* (New York: Rinehart, 1953), p. 294.

153   **"the meaty parts of the meal"** "1921 and Its Fifteenth Reunion," *Smith Alumnae Quarterly*, Aug. 1936, pp. 386, 387. See also Adler, *A House Is Not a Home*, p. 390.

153   **In an early June battle** See "Negroes Threaten Racial Party Split; Several Groups Prepare for Floor Fight as Credentials Committee Bars Them," *New York Times*, June 10, 1936, p. 15, and "Republicans Seat 'Lily-White' Group," *New York Times*, June 4, 1936, p. 2.

153   **forced to sit behind chicken wire** Weiss, *Farewell to the Party of Lincoln*, pp. 7–8, 185.

13. The Visitor

154   **"[E]verybody is capable"** Smith, *Thomas E. Dewey and His Times*, p. 159.

154   **Dewey himself** Donati, *Lucky Luciano*, p. 111.

155   **Lisle Jr. traveled in first class** That Lisle had a relative with him was reported in the press. See Bessye Bearden, "New York Society" (regular column), *Chicago Defender*, March 2, 1935, p. 7. Extrapolating from the first-class passenger list, the relative was most probably "Miss Cecile Carter." See Passenger List, First Class, S.S. *Fort St. George*, sailing from New York, N.Y., February 14, 1935, Arriving at Port of St. Croix, V.I., February 19, 1935 (listing "Miss Cecile Carter" and "Master Lisle Carter").

156   **"Mrs. Carter is also a mother"** "Four Candidates for N.Y. Assembly Close Campaigns," *Afro-American* (Baltimore), Nov. 10, 1934, p. 12.

157   **"a short visit"** "Mrs. Eunice Carter Passed Through," *Virgin Islands Daily News*, July 7, 1936, p. 1. The story stated, erroneously, that she was "the only Negro woman attorney" in New York State.

157　the same newspaper published "In the News Columns," *Virgin Islands Daily News*, Aug. 8, 1936, p. 1.

157　"Aty. Eunice Hunton Carter" "Society," *New York Amsterdam News*, Aug. 8, 1936, p. 6. The *News*, whose owners had always been big backers of Eunice's, had by this time changed hands. After a December 1935 strike by employees represented by what was then known as the American Newspaper Guild, the company declared bankruptcy and was sold for $5,000 plus the assumption of $30,000 in debt. See "Feeling Bitter at 'Amsterdam News' Auction: Two Medicos Take Over Harlem Newspaper," *Chicago Defender*, Jan. 18, 1936, p. 4. See also "Negro Weekly Bankrupt," *New York Times*, Dec. 21, 1935, p. 18.

158　some historians even today In a nice irony, the *Liberty* articles would later form part of the basis for Luciano's appeal. Macfadden, the conglomerate that published the magazine, paid for the participation of two of the women who had testified against the Mob boss. Dewey helped them get their deal. Bad optics, as we might say today—but, as it turned out, not sufficient ground for a new trial.

159　the Pompez-Ison bank's share "70 Seized in Raids by Dewey to Break Huge Policy Ring," *New York Times*, Jan. 15, 1937, p. 1. The policy raids raised hopes, which never quite came to fruition, that somehow control of the Harlem numbers game would fall once more into black hands. See White, Garton, Robertson, and White, *Playing the Numbers*, pp. 240ff.

159　the raids were national news See, for example, "Police Move to Smash Policy Racket in N.Y.," *Sun* (Baltimore), Jan. 15, 1937, p. 14, and "Big Policy Ring Smashed in N.Y. Gambling Raids," *Chicago Daily Tribune*, Jan. 15, 1937, p. 13.

159　The headquarters for the raids Smith, *Thomas E. Dewey and His Times*, p. 215.

160　Dewey had assembled a raid force See "70 Rounded Up in Police Raids Led by Dewey," *New York Herald Tribune*, Jan. 15, 1937, p. 20. It is striking that the *Times* put the story on the front page but the *Herald Tribune* buried it.

160　she'd spent months preparing She did take one evening off early in January to deliver a lecture to the Harlem Economic Forum. Her topic, unsurprisingly, was the rackets. See "Harlem Economic Forum Plans Fine Lecture Series," *Pittsburgh Courier*, Nov. 14, 1936, p. 21. A few months earlier, but well into planning the raids, she had also taken time out to give a talk to the annual meeting of the National Bar Association. She warned her fellow Negro lawyers to make the same efforts that the white bar had recently undertaken to get rid of members who facilitated organized crime—or, as she put it, "purge themselves of lawyers with easy consciences." By this she meant those "who prostitute themselves to habitual criminals" and thereby "betray their positions of honor as officers of the court." Quoted in "Mrs. Carter Asks Lawyers for Social View of Law," *Pittsburgh Courier*, Aug. 15, 1936, p. 2.

160　she was named in See "70 Seized in Raids by Dewey to Break Huge Policy Ring," *New York Times*, Jan. 15, 1937, p. 1. Eunice and Grimes worked under the direction of top Dewey aide Jack Rosenblum. Richard Norton Smith, in his biography of Dewey, gives all the credit to Rosenblum. Smith, *Thomas E. Dewey and His Times*, p. 215.

160　"Eunice Carter's Sleuthing" "Eunice Carter's Sleuthing Lands Two Racketeers," *Pittsburgh Courier*, Jan. 23, 1937, p. 4.

160　Some eager journalists See, for example, "Gang Buster's Aide Forgets Crime at Dance," *Afro-American* (Baltimore), June 4, 1938, p. 9.

160　"numbers folk had suspected" "How Did Dewey Get His Facts on the Policy Racket in Harlem?," *Chicago Defender*, April 15, 1939, p. 13.

160　Harlem remained the most lucrative See the discussion in White, Garton, Robertson, and White, *Playing the Numbers*, pp. 238–49.

161　Pompez lived at See Adrian Burgos Jr., *Cuban Star: How One Negro-League Owner Changed the Face of Baseball* (New York: Hill and Wang, 2011), pp. 99–100.

161　Eunice had been a guest "N.Y. and Brooklyn Get Franchises in National Association of Negro Baseball Clubs at Meeting Here," *New York Age*, Jan. 19, 1935, p. 5.

161 **A Negro journalist** See LaShawn Harris, "Playing the Numbers: Madame Stephanie St. Clair and African American Policy Culture in Harlem," *Black Women, Gender, and Families*, vol. 2, no. 2 (Fall 2008), pp. 53, 62.

161 **Pompez was known** At this time, at least four Negro League teams were owned by numbers runners. See White, Garton, Robertson, and White, *Playing the Numbers*, p. 217.

161 **"made a virtually impregnable fortress"** "Harlem Doesn't Fear Effects of Recent Rading [sic]," *Atlanta Daily World*, Feb. 1, 1937, p. 2.

161 **The Negro papers reported** See "Harlem Not Hurt by Dewey's Raids," *New York Amsterdam News*, Jan. 23, 1937, p. 1.

161 **Dewey chose her** Dewey, *Twenty Against the Underworld*, p. 323.

162 **"When are Negroes"** "Let Us Grow Up," *New York Amsterdam News*, Jan. 30, 1937, p. 12.

162 **"Dewey rats"** See Donati, *Lucky Luciano*, p. 217.

162 **"Fear screams"** Quoted in Dewey, *Twenty Against the Underworld*, p. 225.

162 **"reek with perjury"** "Dewey Charges Perjury in 3 Luciano Pleas," *New York Herald Tribune*, April 21, 1937, p. 4.

163 **The papers loved it** See, for example, "'Lucky' Luciano Case Witnesses Said in City: Dewey Turns to Hartford in Effort to Locate Two Women," *Hartford Courant*, April 22, 1937, p. 1. For coverage outside Connecticut, see, for example, "Retrial Plea for Luciano Called Fraud," *Rochester Democrat and Chronicle*, April 21, 1937, p. 6.

163 **loved that story too** See "Luciano Case Women in Enfield for Time," *Hartford Courant*, April 24, 1937, p. 12.

163 **"utterly destroyed"** *People v. Luciano*, 164 Misc. 167 (N.Y. Supr. Ct. 1937), *affirmed*, 277 N.Y. 348 (1938).

163 **The press also loved** See, for example, "Luciano Plea Denied," *New York Times*, May 8, 1937, p. 10.

163 **"we would get plenty"** Donati, *Lucky Luciano*, p. 219.

163 **payments to the women stopped** See Dewey, *Twenty Against the Underworld*, p. 269.

163 **his conviction was affirmed** *People v. Luciano*, 277 N.Y. 348 (1938). The only relevant difference was that one dissenting judge on the Appellate Division thought the sentences too harsh and the recanting affidavits too swiftly dismissed, whereas nobody on the Court of Appeals agreed. The lone dissenter on the Court of Appeals wrote that "there were material and prejudicial errors committed during the trial which cannot be overlooked" but did not say what they were. See *People v. Luciano*, 277 N.Y. 348, 363 (J. Rippey, dissenting). Justice Harlan W. Rippey, a newcomer to the court, was himself an interesting story. He had actually resigned a federal judgeship in order to pursue the state court post.

14. The Politico

164 **Before announcing his campaign** See Smith, *Thomas E. Dewey*, pp. 238–41.

164 **She campaigned energetically** See, for example, "Women Battle for Dewey in Boro Campaign," *New York Amsterdam News*, Oct. 29, 1938, p. 14, and "Channing Tobias Endorses Candidacy of LaGuardia," *New York Age*, Oct. 9, 1937, p. 1.

165 **At that point** See "Judge Paige, Miss Carter on Upgrade," *Chicago Defender*, Nov. 13, 1937, p. 6.

165 **Negro press predicted big things** Ibid. The "Miss Carter" in the headline is a reportorial or editorial not a typographical error. Eunice is referred to as "Miss" throughout the story. The article also refers to her, mysteriously, as "a most capable secretary."

165 **That the city suddenly** See, for example, "Appointed to District Attorney's Staff," *Pittsburgh Courier*, Jan. 8, 1938, p. 7. See also "The Cover," *Crisis*, vol. 45, no. 2 (Feb. 1938), p. 38.

165 **"special work in special sessions"** See "Dewey Takes Oath; First Independent in Post in 20 Years," *New York Times*, Jan. 1, 1938, p. 1; "Dewey Gives Jobs to Eunice Carter and Francis Rivers," *Pittsburgh Courier*, Jan. 8, 1938, p. 4; "Dewey Takes Office; Selects 16 More Aids [sic]," *New York Herald Tribune*, Jan. 1, 1938, p. 1; and "Dewey Names 16 Assistants," *Brooklyn Daily Eagle*, Dec. 31, 1937, p. 1.

165 **Another potential hire** Smith, *Thomas E. Dewey and His Times*, p. 244.

165   **"one of the highest paid"** J. Clay Smith, *Emancipation: The Making of the Black Lawyer, 1844–1944* (Philadelphia: University of Pennsylvania Press, 1993), p. 406.

165   **proved excellent** For a good example, see the transcript of *People of the State of New York v. Terry*, which Eunice tried on January 3, 1938—that is, immediately upon being assigned to the Women's Courts. Docket No. 3878, NYCDA archives.

165   **gleefully pointed out** See "White Woman Named Eunice Carter Aide," *Philadelphia Tribune*, Feb. 3, 1938, p. 4. See also "Another Woman Aide Is Appointed by Dewey," *New York Times*, Jan. 21, 1938, p. 2. Florence Kelley was also, like Eunice, a graduate of Smith College. "We See by the Papers," *Smith Alumnae Quarterly*, Feb. 1938, p. 150. Kelley's father was general counsel of the Chrysler Corporation and a partner in a New York law firm. Her grandmother founded the Consumers League of New York.

    Note that Kelly did not work exclusively for Eunice, but also helped out in the Indictment Bureau.

165   **determined to take down** See "Dewey Says Ison Will Help State in Racket Trials," *New York Herald Tribune*, Oct. 8, 1937, p. 11A.

165   **Dewey set out to prove** See "'The Trial of Jimmy Hines': A New York Melodrama," *Life*, vol. 5, no. 9 (Aug. 29, 1938), p. 9.

166   **Samuel Battle, the city's first** Arthur Browne, *One Righteous Man: Samuel Battle and the Shattering of the Color Line in New York* (Boston: Beacon Press, 2015), pp. 176–79. On Browne's friendship with Eunice, see pp. 207–8.

166   **name was magic** See Donati, *Lucky Luciano*, p. 230.

166   **With the Dutchman gone** Stolberg, *Fighting Organized Crime*, pp. 232–33.

166   **Harlem noticed** See, for example, L. F. Coles, "The Hines Case" (letter to the editor), *New York Amsterdam News*, March 18, 1939, p. 10.

167   **The press drew analogies** One peculiar story identified Eunice as among Dewey's assistants at the Luciano trial but then, when listing those who had worked both cases, omitted her name. See "Ghosts of Lucania Trial Keep Drifting into Record of Policy Racket Case," *Brooklyn Daily Eagle*, Aug. 27, 1938, p. 3.

167   **published verbatim transcripts** See, for example, "Witness, Under Defense Counsel's Lash, Admits Being a Gangster," *New York Times*, Aug. 25, 1938, pp. 11–12.

167   **henceforth they were racketeers** See White, Garton, Robertson, and White, *Playing the Numbers*, p. 250ff.

167   **Pompez was finally brought back** See "'Numbers' Banker Seized in Mexico: Pompez Will Reveal Facts About Policy," *Chicago Defender*, Nov. 6, 1937, p. 2.

167   **Ison made the same deal** "2 Who Helped Dewey Convict Hines Go Free," *New York Herald Tribune*, May 17, 1939, p. 40. The Negro press found the story worthy of front-page treatment. See "Pompez and Ison Freed in Numbers Case," *Chicago Defender*, June 10, 1939, p. 1.

167   **Bold headlines told readers** "$125 Weekly to 'Hines' Club': So Informed by Schultz' Aids, Ison Says," *Boston Daily Globe*, Jan. 29, 1939, p. A15.

167   **He had failed to realize** See Stolberg, *Fighting Organized Crime*, pp. 231–33.

167   **The decision was front-page news** See, for example, "Hines 'Bug' Case Ends in Mistrial: Prosecutor Dewey Is Accused of a 'Very Serious and Prejudicial Error,'" *Atlanta Constitution*, Sept. 13, 1938, p. 1; "Hines Decision Grieves Dewey," *Boston Daily Globe*, Sept. 13, 1938, p. 1; "Judge Throws Out Boss Hines Racket Case," *Chicago Daily Tribune*, Sept. 13, 1938, p. 1; "Hines Wins Mistrial in Racket Case," *Washington Post*, Sept. 13, 1938, p. 1; and "Hines Mistrial Declared; Pecora Says Dewey Made 'Fatally Prejudicial' Error," *New York Herald Tribune*, Sept. 13, 1938, p. 1.

167   **that the question was proper** Dewey, *Twenty Against the Underworld*, pp. 389–90.

168   **thought he was mistaken** See Stolberg, *Fighting Organized Crime*, pp. 242–43.

168   **Eunice went off to Pittsburgh** "Talk o' Town" (regular column), *Pittsburgh Courier*, April 30, 1938, p. 9.

169   **the event was widely reported** Contrary to some reports, Eunice was not the first black woman to receive an honorary degree from an American college or university. Mary McLeod

Bethune was honored by Rollins College in 1935, and although the available lists of black degree recipients are by no means complete, I suspect that there may have been others even earlier.

169 **The *Times* was sufficiently impressed** See "Four Women Get Honors at Smith; Mrs. Eunice H. Carter, Aide on Dewey's Staff, Is Made a Doctor of Laws," *New York Times*, June 21, 1938, p. 15. Her fellow recipients that year included Nellie Neilson, a medievalist; Jane Downes Kelly Sabine, a surgeon; and Mira H. Wilson, the principal of the Northfield School for Girls.

169 **She drove up to Northampton** "What's Going on Around the Town," *Pittsburgh Courier*, June 25, 1938, p. 9.

169 **the commencement address** Kittredge, one should note, was part of the Committee of Ten, the group that back in the 1890s had largely set the stage for the modernization of the secondary school curriculum to better prepare students for the rigors of college. See Richard Hofstadter, *Anti-Intellectualism in American Life* (New York: Vintage, 1963), p. 330. I mention this bit of history only to point out that both Eunice and Alphaeus, in their educations in the public schools of Brooklyn, benefitted indirectly from his work.

169 **"brilliant abilities"** *Smith Alumnae Quarterly*, Aug. 1938, p. 369.

169 **"an example of what"** "In the Magazine" [regular column], *Pittsburgh Courier*, July 9, 1938, p. 14.

169 **"its greatest gift upon"** "The Editor Says," *Opportunity: Journal of Negro Life*, vol. 16, no. 9 (Sept. 1938), p. 261.

169 **Eunice was addressing** "Judge Watson to Be Principal Speaker at Nat'l Bar Meeting," *New Journal and Guide* (Norfolk, Va.), July 23, 1938, p. 3. On the way to Durham, she might have stopped to visit relatives in Charlottesville. See "Charlottesville, Virginia," *New Journal and Guide* (Norfolk, Va.), July 30, 1938, p. 14.

169 **a four-week motoring trip** See "Chatter and Chimes," *New York Amsterdam News*, Aug. 20, 1938, p. 8, and "Motor Trip Soon to End," *New York Amsterdam News*, Sept. 3, 1938, p. 8.

169 **"never on what you would call"** Dorothy Kilgallen, "The Voice of Broadway," *News-Herald* (Franklin, Pa.), July 3, 1944, p. 4. See also *Wilkes-Barre Record*, July 3, 1944, p. 12.

169 **a long, adoring profile** "Cal Coolidge Helped Her Get Her M.A. Degree," *Boston Daily Globe*, July 3, 1938, p. B18.

169 **"smartest, most effective assistants"** "Negroes: The U.S. Also Has a Minority Problem," *Life*, Oct. 3, 1938, pp. 49, 58.

170 **He and his wife, Margaret** See, for example, "Stage * Screen * Nite Spots," *New York Amsterdam News*, April 18, 1936, p. 8; "Celebrate the Blues: Socialites Take All Space in Theatre," *New York Amsterdam News*, Nov. 26, 1938, p. 8. See also Mabel Alston, "Overheard in the Capital," *Afro-American* (Baltimore), April 13, 1940, p. 17.

170 **many Negro intellectuals** A leading analysis on the pull exerted on Negro intellectuals by the hard Left of the 1930s is Naison, *Communists in Harlem During the Depression*. Another fine source, although dated, is Wilson Record, *The Negro and the Communist Party* (Chapel Hill: University of North Carolina Press, 1951), particularly chapters 3 and 4. For particular attention to the often-overlooked role of Negro women on the radical Left of the 1930s, see LaShawn Harris, "Running with the Reds: African American Women and the Communist Party During the Great Depression," *Journal of African American History*, vol. 94, no. 1 (Winter 2009), p. 21.

170 **spotted at a clandestine meeting** Louis Lautier, "Capital Spotlight," *Afro-American* (Baltimore), June 3, 1933, p. A1. The previous year Ford had been involved with the effort to make a film in the Soviet Union about conditions for Negroes in the United States. A number of black intellectuals were flown to Moscow. But things ended in disaster. The Americans were badly treated by the Russians, and the resources to make a serious film never materialized. For a good discussion, see Mark Solomon, *The Cry Was Unity: Communists and African Americans, 1917–1936* (Jackson: University of Mississippi Press, 1998), pp. 173–77. See also Naison, *Communists in Harlem*, pp. 72–74. The story bears mention because among the

NOTES TO PAGES 170–177 | 325

intellectuals who traveled to Russia was Eunice's and Lisle's friend Henry Lee Moon, whose wife Mollie would later become perhaps first among Harlem's Czarinas. Henry Moon was for a long time attracted to the radical alternative. He was on familiar terms with many leading Communists, including Ford and Benjamin W. Davis, who would later become the best-known black party member. Davis and Alphaeus were also quite close. Alphaeus and Moon must surely have been friends. It would be interesting to learn whether that friendship endured once Eunice and Alphaeus became estranged in the 1940s.

170 **"a man of vision"** H.L.S., "New Books Passed in Review," *Brooklyn Daily Eagle*, Aug. 2, 1938, p. 7.

171 **what he saw as a dangerous radicalism** Miller had at one time been a leading member of the United Front. See Mark Solomon, *The Cry Was Unity*, pp. 29–30. In time he had become disillusioned, and even attacked Howard University for supposed sympathy to the Communist cause; p. 250. See also Record, *The Negro and the Communist Party*, p. 43. In fact, Miller turned against radical solutions generally, and, as Negro intellectuals lurched left, became at least an iconoclast and perhaps even an outcast. A useful account of this transformation is Bernard Eisenberg, "Kelly Miller: The Negro Leader as a Marginal Man," *Journal of Negro History*, vol. 45, no. 3 (July 1960), p. 182. See also Naison, *Communists in Harlem During the Depression*, pp. 179, 182–83. So perhaps Miller, once among the most influential of the colored intelligentsia, was writing in part out of bitterness at his own growing isolation. Miller's own son, moreover, became radicalized, and even lived for a time in the Soviet Union. Solomon, *The Cry Was Unity*, p. 173. So perhaps Miller had in mind Kelly Miller Jr. as well as Alphaeus when he wrote so caustically about the younger generation in his appreciation of William Hunton.

171 **"the coolness and balm"** Kelly Miller, "Kelly Miller Writes About," *New York Age*, Nov. 5, 1938, p. 6. The problem, Miller argued, was this: "In the Antebellum era the Negro was vouchsafed religion without education; in these latter days the up to date college bred youth are absorbing education without religion." For an earlier Miller foray into this battle, see Kelly Miller, "Should Black Turn Red?," *Opportunity*, vol. 11, no. 11 (Nov. 1933), p. 328.

171 **Eunice campaigned enthusiastically** See, for example, "Women Battle for Dewey in Boro Campaign," *New York Amsterdam News*, Oct. 29, 1938, p. 14.

171 **"a generation torn by strife"** Quoted in Michael Bowen, *The Roots of Modern Conservatism: Dewey, Taft, and the Battle for the Soul of the Republican Party* (Chapel Hill: University of North Carolina Press, 2011), p. 21.

171 **he had difficulty making headway** See Smith, *Thomas E. Dewey and His Times*, pp. 266–69.

172 **"official political counsels"** Archie Seale, "Around Harlem," *New York Amsterdam News*, Dec. 17, 1938, p. 21. Probably the writer meant "unofficial"—the subject was who had the clout to persuade the mayor to stop the coming World's Fair from becoming a showcase for "jimcrowism"—but, in any case, Eunice had made a very short list of influential New York Negroes.

172 **"the 'Hines trial'"** Earl J. Morris, "Grandtown Day and Night," *Pittsburgh Courier*, Oct. 22, 1938, p. 20.

172 **"Take an active part"** Quoted in "Says Fair Chance Will Cut Crimes," *Afro-American* (Baltimore), Feb. 25, 1939, p. 24.

173 **"hard keeping up with her"** "Not That It's My Business, but . . . ," *New York Amsterdam News*, May 25, 1940, p. 13.

15. The Celebrity

177 **she was promoted** In November, Dewey referred to Eunice as "acting" head of Special Sessions. See "Dewey to Help Elect Harlem Congressman," *New York Amsterdam News*, Nov. 5, 1938, p. 1. The date of Eunice's permanent appointment is not on file, and there seem to be no relevant stories in the press.

177 **Managing Special Sessions** Although Eunice ran Special Sessions, she does not appear to have been promoted from deputy assistant district attorney to assistant district attorney.

The annual reports of the office continue to list her as a deputy assistant until the end of her tenure. On the other hand, both in court appearances and depositions she is usually listed as assistant district attorney from about 1938 onward. But in correspondence she mostly uses "deputy assistant."

177   **"I cannot say"** Correspondence quoted in Kenneth W. Mack, *Representing the Race: The Creation of the Civil Rights Lawyer* (Cambridge, Mass.: Harvard University Press, 2012), p. 140.

177   **conviction rate in Special Sessions** See "Dewey's Staff Sets Record in Convictions," *New York Herald Tribune*, May 31, 1939, p. 1. These figures include the work of Special Sessions under Sol Gelb as well as under Eunice.

178   **"one of New York's busiest women"** "Mrs. Eunice H. Carter Busy Speaking for Thos. Dewey," *New York Age*, April 27, 1940, p. 2.

178   **Eunice described for a reporter** See "I Earn $5,500 Per Year: Admits Eunice Hunton Carter, Who Studied Law After Becoming a Housewife," *Afro-American* (Baltimore), March 5, 1938, p. 9.

178   **"manages on very little food"** Elizabeth Galbreath, "Typovision," *Chicago Defender*, Feb. 24, 1940, p. 16.

178   **she regularly won prizes** See, for example, "Society Snapshots," *New York Age*, May 21, 1937, p. 4.

178   **"because the climate is better"** The columns by this time made no secret of the fact that Lisle Jr. "lives with his grandmother" in Barbados. See, for example, "Chatter and Chimes," *New York Amsterdam News*, Aug. 12, 1939, p. 12.

178   **had a fear of flying** So great was Eunice's fear of dying in a plane crash that for years after, the press would routinely report on her monthlong trips to do a week or two of work—the remaining time taken up by travel. See, for example, Betty Granger, "Conversation Piece . . . About Smart People," *New York Age*, April 9, 1949, p. 4.

178   **Even in law school** See, for example, Gerry [Gerri Major], "New York: The Social Whirl," *Afro-American* (Baltimore), March 14, 1931, p. 7, and Gerry, "New York: The Social Whirl," *Afro-American*, Nov. 8, 1930, p. 7.

178   **She was seen ringside** See, for example, "Stars of Stage See Slaughter of Black Uhlan," *Pittsburgh Courier*, June 25, 1938, p. 4, and "Talk o' Town," *Pittsburgh Courier*, Dec. 25, 1937, p. 8.

178   **She visited Joe Louis's** "Johnny Dundee, Claude Hopkins Visit Louis Camp," *Afro-American* (Baltimore), June 5, 1935, p. 20. Eunice's husband accompanied her on the visit. See Lewis E. Dial, "The Sport Dial," *New York Age*, June 15, 1935, p. 8. She would make another visit in 1941. See "Louis at Peak Form for Nova Go," *Pittsburgh Courier*, Sept. 27, 1941, p. 17.

178   **she would attend Harlem's testimonial** "Reveille Club Joined by Over 400 in Paying Tribute to Joe Louis at Testimonial Dinner, Thursday," *New York Age*, May 30, 1942, p. 4.

178   **Like Eunice, Louis was** See Dominic J. Capeci Jr. and Martha Wilkerson, "Multifarious Hero: Joe Louis, American Society, and Race Relations During World Crisis, 1933–1945," in *From Jack Johnson to LeBron James: Sports, Media, and the Color Line*, ed. Chris Lamb (Lincoln: University of Nebraska Press, 2016), pp. 86, 91–92.

178   **the well-to-do of the darker nation** See Stephen Tuck, "'You Can Sing and Punch . . . but You Can't Be a Soldier or a Man': African American Struggles for a New Place in Popular Culture," in *Fog of War: The Second World War and the Civil Rights Movement*, ed. Kevin M. Kruse and Stephen Tuck (New York: Oxford University Press, 2012), pp. 103, 116–18.

179   **one headline case after another** A gossip column in January of 1938 asserts that Eunice and the black lawyer Sarah Pelham Speaks had recently been on opposite sides of a case and Speaks had prevailed. See Al Monroe, "On the Avenue," *Chicago Defender*, Jan. 29, 1938, p. 10. This would mean that Speaks was defending someone Eunice was prosecuting. I have been unable to find any such case (which is not to say that it does not exist).

179   **She twice prosecuted** See "'Dr.' Swift Goes on Trial," *New York Times*, Aug. 15, 1940, p. 18.

179   **"Danish Institute"** See "Anna Swift and 9 Seized in Massage Parlor Raid: Captured in 'Danish Institute' as in 1936 Arrest," *New York Herald Tribune*, July 3, 1940, p. 16.

179 **three months in the workhouse** Swift's first conviction led to what was at the time a landmark decision about the admissibility of testimony by accomplices. See *People v. Swift*, 161 Misc. 851 (N.Y. Misc. 1936).

179 **She successfully adopted** See "Hearing in Swift Case; Five Women Freed on Vagrancy Charge, Then Held as Witnesses," *New York Times*, July 6, 1940, p. 26, and "5 Women, Jailed in Raid, Are Freed, Then Detained: Cleared of Vagrancy, They Will Be Witnesses Against Anna Swift," *New York Herald Tribune*, July 6, 1940, p. 9.

179 **a controversial one** For a discussion of how innovative the technique was and what the criticisms were, see Lawrence Fleischer, "Thomas E. Dewey and Earl Warren: The Rise of the Twentieth Century Urban Prosecutor," *California Western Law Review*, vol. 28, no. 1 (1991), pp. 1, 18–20.

179 **"low social status"** Stolberg, *Fighting Organized Crime*, pp. 130–31.

180 **"Mrs. Eunice H. Carter, assistant district attorney"** "'Dr.' Swift Convicted in Institute Raid; She Is Liable to Three Years and Fine as Second Offender," *New York Times*, Aug. 22, 1940, p. 40. The colored press gave the story more prominent play. See, for example, "Mrs. Eunice H. Carter Obtains Conviction of 'Dr.' Anna Swift," *New York Age*, Aug. 31, 1940, p. 3.

180 **Probably this was Tom Morro** See, for example, Statement of Aldine Avery (deposition taken by Eunice H. Carter), Jan. 7, 1938, NYCDA archives; Statement of Peggy Kelly (deposition taken by Eunice H. Carter), Jan. 7, 1938, NYCDA archives; and Statement of Frank Diaz (deposition taken by Eunice H. Carter), Jan. 7, 1938, NYCDA archives. According to the transcripts, these statements were all taken on the same evening, between ninety-thirty and midnight. This telescoping of the interviews suggests that a raid was involved, but I have found no further information about it.

Actually, the late-night interviews help illustrate how busy Eunice was. Scant days earlier she had been trying the case of Ruth Terry, discussed below.

180 **"You said that if ever"** Frances Blackman to "Mrs. Cotter" [Eunice H. Carter], Jan. 29, 1941, NYCDA archives.

180 **Eunice agreed** Eunice H. Carter to Frances Blackman, Feb. 6, 1941, NYCDA archives. Blackman's initial letter states that the trial was scheduled for February 4. Unless there was a postponement, or unless Blackman actually meant not trial but arraignment, Eunice's response came too late, and might even have been planned that way.

180 **a textbook example** See *People of the State of New York v. Ruth Terry*, Docket Nos. 3876 and 3878, Jan. 3, 1938, transcript, NYCDA archives.

180 **Eunice took considerable care** See *People of the State of New York v. Logoda*, Feb. 17, 1938, transcript, Record on Appeal, examination of Dr. Rosen.

181 **Other examples of** See, for example, *People of the State of New York v. Jacobsen*, April 29, 1938, Record on Appeal.

181 **Newspapers around the country** See, for example, "Brulatour Leaves Hospital on Arm of Actress Wife," *St. Petersburg Times*, Jan. 31, 1939, p. 8; "Brulatour Leaves Hospital," *Milwaukee Journal*, Jan. 30, 1939, p. 14; "Prosecutor Shows Curiosity over Shooting of Brulatour," *Pittsburgh Post-Gazette*, Jan. 26, 1939, p. 2; "Hope Hampton's Husband Held on Gun Charge," *Chicago Tribune*, Jan. 26, 1939, p. 11; and "Jules Brulatour Is Fined $500," *Arizona Republic*, Feb. 11, 1939, p. 1.

181 **"Brulatour Arrested"** "Brulatour Arrested in Shooting, Hope Hampton Called as Witness," *Gazette* (Montreal), Jan. 25, 1939, p. 5.

181 **"through sheer fortitude"** Tom Prideaux, "Apple of His Eye," *Life*, April 8, 1946, pp. 107, 110.

181 **the Legion of Honor** "Brulatour Is Decorated: France Confers Order of Legion of Honor on Film Man," *New York Times*, July 27, 1930, p. 8.

181 **"made by blood"** "Brulatour Pistol Tested," *New York Times*, Jan. 29, 1939, p. 26.

182 **"Punctuality is the politeness"** "Brulatour in Court: Seems to Enjoy It," *New York Times*, Feb. 1, 1939, p. 2.

182 **"weak on the pins"** "Brulatour Pleads Guilty: Sentencing on Pistol Charge Fixed for Next Friday," *New York Times*, Feb. 3, 1939, p. 18.

182   "[T]here has been a shooting" "Brulatour Fined in Shooting Case," *New York Times*, Feb. 11, 1939, p. 12. Eunice was not the original prosecutor on the case. Before the matter was sent to Special Sessions, it was in the hands of a young deputy assistant named Herman McCarthy, who had been hired by Dewey right out of law school. McCarthy had made his name prosecuting Fritz Kuhn, head of the German American Bund. Later he would assist in the prosecution of Jimmy Hines, the Tammany leader who had long been in Dewey's sights.

182   Eunice agreed to hold "Woman City Fined Faces State Cigarette Charge," *New York Herald Tribune*, Dec. 22, 1939, p. 17.

182   The appellate court overturned "Buyers May Bring in Jersey Cigarettes If They Are for Personal Use, Court Holds," *New York Times*, April 3, 1940, p. 1.

182   The court concurred See "Cigarette Suit Quashed," *New York Times*, June 13, 1940, p. 25.

182   when six men were convicted "Suspend Strike Breaker Terms," *New York Herald Tribune*, Dec. 2, 1939, p. 28.

183   "is not such perjury" Memorandum, Eunice H. Carter to Paul E. Lockwood, Feb. 26, 1938, NYCDA archives.

183   was instrumental in developing See "Dewey Eases Lot of Wayward Boys," *New York Times*, Nov. 15, 1940, p. 14.

183   Dewey gave Eunice full credit See "New Bureau to Aid Youths Freed by Courts; Dewey Views It as a Preventive of Crime," *New York Times*, April 29, 1941, p. 21.

183   a man named Andrew Solomon Andrew Solomon does not appear to have been any relation to Albert J. Solomon, one of the witnesses Eunice prepared for the Luciano trial. See Eunice H. Carter, Statement of Albert J. Solomon, March 24, 1936, NYCDA archives.

183   a strange courtroom event "Wrong Man Pleads Innocent," *New York Herald Tribune*, Dec. 22, 1939, p. 15A.

183   She was still out and about See, for example, Alan McMillan, "Hi Hattin' in Harlem," *Chicago Defender*, Nov. 27, 1937, p. 11.

184   She made occasional trips See, for example, "Branch News," *Crisis*, May 1940, pp. 150, 151.

184   This was the most prestigious address For a discussion of the distinctions among Harlem neighborhoods, see Anderson, *This Was Harlem*, pp. 339–43, and passim.

184   "a citadel of stately apartment buildings" Lewis, *When Harlem Was in Vogue*, p. 217.

184   Her parties and receptions See, for example, "Carter's Cocktail Hour Brilliant," *New York Amsterdam News*, July 8, 1939, p. 12 (with photograph).

184   she would be at a dance "Society Snapshots," *New York Age*, Aug. 26, 1939, p. 4.

184   the latest Harlem cabaret Floyd G. Snelson, "Harlem: Negro Capital of the Nation," *New York Age*, March 18, 1939, p. 7.

185   to raise money for the *Crisis* See "Society Snapshots," *New York Age*, Feb. 19, 1938, p. 4.

185   addressing a Republican club R. L. Reid, "Far Rockaway & Arverne," *New York Age*, Nov. 9, 1940, p. 8.

185   Or speaking at an event See, for example, "The Women Have Their Day at Fair; 18 to Be Honored," *Pittsburgh Courier*, July 27, 1940, p. 10.

185   If the Harlem glitterati descended Floyd G. Snelson, "Harlem: Negro Capital of the Nation," *New York Age*, March 18, 1939, p. 7.

185   If the colored American Legion paraded "Memorial Day Parade Features Marching of Crack Negro Units," *New York Age*, June 10, 1939, p. 3.

185   Charles Hamilton Houston came to town "Society Snapshots," *New York Age*, Aug. 26, 1939, p. 4.

185   So eager were editors See, for example, "Talk o' Town," *Pittsburgh Courier*, April 30, 1938, p. 9.

185   If she went on vacation See, for example, "Out of Billy Rowe's Harlem Notebook," *Pittsburgh Courier*, April 15, 1939, p. 11.

185   "may shed it for lighter apparel" Floyd G. Snelson, "Harlem: Negro Capital of the Nation," *New York Age*, Feb. 15, 1941, p. 5.

185 **"she passes very little"** Elizabeth Galbreath, "Typovision," *Chicago Defender*, Feb. 24, 1940, p. 16. Galbreath added that Eunice favored "cooler sports attire in the summer" and liked to dress for dinner.

185 **addressed colored Republicans** See, for example, "Far Rockaway & Arverne," *New York Age*, Nov. 9, 1940, p. 8, and "State Organizations of Women G.O.P.s Meet in White Plains," *New York Age*, Oct. 29, 1939, p. 10.

185 **drew a packed house** "Albany, N.Y.," *New York Age*, Nov. 19, 1938, p. 11.

186 **"be held up to scorn"** Rebecca Stiles Taylor, "Activities of Women's National Organizations," *Chicago Defender*, Nov. 29, 1941, p. 18.

186 **Not all of her audiences** See, for example, Alice Cogan, "Club Women," *Brooklyn Daily Eagle*, Oct. 11, 1940, p. 11.

186 **He sent Eunice** "7,000 Acclaim Leader Crews at 6th A. D. Ball," *Brooklyn Daily Eagle*, Feb. 25, 1939, p. 3.

186 **So prominent had she become** "Loan Exhibit Shows Negro Achievements," *Stanford Daily*, Aug. 3, 1939, p. 2.

186 **she received a medal** The event made the mainstream as well as the Negro press. See "13 Noted Negro Women Get Medallions at Fair," *New York Herald Tribune*, June 26, 1939, p. 9, and "'Women of Today' Honored with Medals at the Fair," *New York Amsterdam News*, July 1, 1939, p. 7. Along with Mrs. Astor, the tea was co-hosted by . . . Addie Hunton.

186 **She joined Vivien Leigh** See "Mrs. Carter on Air Program with V. Leigh," *Afro-American* (Baltimore), June 1, 1940, p. 13. The story amusingly calls Olivier "Lawrence Oliver."

187 **Several sources assert** See also, for example, LaShawn Harris, *Sex Workers, Psychics, and Numbers Runners: Black Women in New York City's Underground Economy* (Champaign: University of Illinois Press, 2016), p. 70. For example, Eunice and St. Clair are both residents of the building in the stage play *409 Edgecombe Avenue: The House on Sugar Hill*, by Katherine Butler Jones.

188 **"I have more Jews working"** "Dewey Has 3 in His Office," *Afro-American* (Baltimore), Sept. 2, 1939, p. 2. The same story affirms that Francis Rivers is already earning more than Eunice, $7,500 to $6,000. This is also one of several places where Dewey tells the story of how he came to hire her.

16. The Decision

189 **The story gave considerable space** "What 72 Aides Think of Dewey," *Afro-American* (Baltimore), Oct. 7, 1939, p. 5.

189 **Dewey answered by citing** "GOP Candidate Pledges Square Deal to Negro," *Philadelphia Tribune*, April 4, 1940, p. 4.

189 **"making Negro history"** "Pseudo Political Leaders" (letter to the editor), *New York Age*, Sept. 2, 1939, p. 5.

189 **"Mrs. Carter belongs to the new school"** "Presidential Fight to Bring Prominent Women into Arena," *Afro-American* (Baltimore), May 18, 1940, p. 16.

190 **"powers that be"** Al White, "A Little Bit of Everything from the Nation's Capital," *Philadelphia Tribune*, June 13, 1940, p. 19.

190 **She went to Bridgeport** See "Bridgeport, Conn.," *Pittsburgh Courier*, May 11, 1940, p. 19.

190 **At one point she somehow** See "Mrs. Eunice H. Carter Busy Speaking for Thos. Dewey," *New York Age*, April 27, 1940, p. 2.

190 **"Seventy-five years after"** Quoted in "Lynching Evil in U.S. Scored by Dewey Aide: Urges Support of Men Who Realize All Are Created Equal," *Philadelphia Tribune*, March 28, 1940, p. 5.

190 **It was the Democrats** Actually, the Democrats did worse than simply kill the anti-lynching bill. They obfuscated the meaning of "lynching" itself. See Christopher Waldrep, "War of Words: The Controversy over the Definition of Lynching, 1899–1940," *Journal of Southern History*, vol. 66, no. 1 (Feb. 2000), p. 75.

190 **"She is not to be confused"** Quoted in "Says Antilynch Legislation Was Killed by Demos," *Afro-American* (Baltimore), April 27, 1940, p. 8. See also "Mrs. Eunice H. Carter Busy Speaking for Thos. Dewey," *New York Age*, April 27, 1940, p. 2.

191 **the great majority of delegates** See "Republicans Choose All but 8 Delegates," *New York Times*, May 30, 1940, p. 24.

191 **Eunice was present** See "9 Aides in Dewey's Convention Offices," *Afro-American* (Baltimore), June 22, 1940, p. 6. Rivers was also a delegate. There were evidently some 85 black delegates and alternates, and, according to the story, Eunice was personally acquainted with nearly all of them.

191 **"manned in part by the elite"** "At the G.O.P. Convention," *Chicago Defender*, July 6, 1940, p. 8.

191 **On the sixth ballot** A stirring account of the behind-the-scene machinations at the convention is Charles Peters, *Five Days in Philadelphia: The Amazing "We Want Willkie" Convention of 1940 and How It Freed FDR to Save the Western World* (New York: PublicAffairs, 2005). For a particular account of Dewey's miscalculations, see Smith, *Thomas E. Dewey and His Times*, pp. 307–14.

191 **joined a biracial group** See "23 Fusion Leaders to Back Willkie," *New York Times*, Oct. 14, 1940, p. 10, and "23 City Fusionists Bolt Mayor to Back Willkie," *Brooklyn Daily Eagle*, Oct. 19, 1940, p. 3.

192 **"discrimination in the civil service"** Quoted in Harvard Sitkoff, *Toward Freedom Land: The Long Struggle for Racial Equality in America* (Lexington: University Press of Kentucky, 2010), p. 133.

193 **Eunice could throw parties for** See, for example, "Carter's Cocktail Hour Brilliant," *New York Amsterdam News*, July 8, 1939, p. 12.

194 **In addition to Lisle Jr.** "Chatter and Chimes," *New York Amsterdam News*, Nov. 30, 1940, p. 14.

194 **For a good two years** "Affair" is the right word. According to Dorothy, she and Alphaeus began seeing each other in 1939, after a simple encounter on the street in Manhattan. They had been acquainted for some years, because he had previously courted her sister. That night they had dinner at Eunice's apartment (Dorothy does not say whether Eunice was present), and for much of the ensuing summer they were in each other's company, their time "filled with simple pleasures and delights of awakening love" (Dorothy Hunton, *Unsung Valiant*, p. 32). When they could not be together, they corresponded.

But what about his wife, Margaret? Whatever Alphaeus may have told Dorothy about the state of his marriage, he and Margaret spent the Christmas holiday of 1939 together in New York, splitting their time between Addie's home in Brooklyn and Eunice's apartment at 409 Edgecombe. (See Floyd G. Snelson, "Harlem, Negro Capitol of the Nation," *New York Age*, Jan. 13, 1940, p. 4.) That was after the August in which Alphaeus and Dorothy presumably fell in love. Moreover, the 1940 census lists Alphaeus and Margaret as husband and wife, living together in an apartment at 2719 Georgia Avenue in Washington.

If indeed Alphaeus and Margaret were still together in 1939 and 1940, then Alphaeus was traveling to New York to see Dorothy behind his wife's back. This would have been in keeping with his approach to relations with women, as he had earlier started seeing Margaret while still married to Ethelyn.

194 **He ran several of Harlem's** See, for example, "Karma Club Host to Friends at Gingham Party in Club Rooms," *New York Age*, June 29, 1940, p. 6, and "Survey of the Month," *Opportunity*, Dec. 1928, pp. 383, 384.

196 **Unlike Eunice** See "Henderson Injured," *Pittsburgh Courier*, Sept. 1, 1928, p. 12.

196 **Henderson was in New Orleans** For evidence that Henderson was in New Orleans that year, see Jeffrey Magee, *The Uncrowned King of Swing: Fletcher Henderson and Big Band Jazz* (New York: Oxford University Press, 2005), p. 25.

197 **"[W]e are molding"** Quoted in "Solution of Economic Ills Race's Salvation, Is Claim: Mrs. Eunice Carter, Dewey Aide in New York Crime Probe, Speaks to Howard University Alumnae Club," *New Journal and Guide* (Norfolk, Va.), May 15, 1937, p. A1.

198 **"Never argue with a man"** Eunice Hunton Carter, "How to Get Along with Men," *Afro-American* (Baltimore), March 19, 1938, p. 9. For a report on a similar talk, see "Eunice Carter Talks to Girls," *New York Amsterdam News*, April 8, 1939, p. 7.

199 **Eunice took the occasion** "Mrs. Addie Hunton Honored at Memorial to Y Founder," *Afro-American* (Baltimore), Nov. 12, 1938, p. 5. According to the story, William's sister, Mrs. Mary Hunton Gordon, sent "a message of congratulation and regret of her absence."

199 **"probably by 1935"** Lutz, "'Dizzy Steep to Heaven,'" p. 285, n. 37.

199 **"having dinner regularly"** Elizabeth Galbreath, "Typovision," *Chicago Defender*, Feb. 24, 1940, p. 16.

200 **"Carter was a very serious"** Katherine Butler Jones, *Deeper Roots: An American Odyssey* (n.p., 2012), p. 172.

17. The File

201 **Eunice was a Dewey delegate** "Harlem G.O.P. Set for State Convention: Delegates to Leave on Sunday for Saratoga After Thursday Rally," *New York Amsterdam Star-News*, Aug. 22, 1942, p. 1. See also "20 Negro Delegates and 15 Alternates to Attend GOP Convention from New York City," *New York Age*, Aug. 22, 1942, p. 5. At the previous state Republican convention, Eunice had formally seconded the nomination of the party's nominee for attorney general. See "Choice of McDermott for Attorney General Unites Boro G.O.P.," *Brooklyn Daily Eagle*, Sept. 30, 1938, p. 5.

   Eunice was also a founding member of the Crispus Attucks League, the semiofficial organization of black New York Republicans, which held its initial meeting in the fall of 1942. See "Harold C. Burton Is Head of New GOP State Organization," *New York Age*, Oct. 10, 1942, p. 5.

201 **Eunice was the featured speaker** "Square Deal Club's Victory Dinner Was a Gala Success," *New York Age*, Feb. 27, 1943, p. 4. The Square Deal Republican Club was a Negro version of the mainly white political clubs of the day. At its height it had several thousand members and, among the political clubs of Harlem, tended to attract the well-off and the traditionalists.

201 **listed by Dewey** Smith, *Thomas E. Dewey and His Times*, p. 341.

202 **This was an era when** For a recent account listing on this largely forgotten chapter of history, see David Gilson, "These Racist Collectibles Will Make Your Skin Crawl," *Mother Jones*, March–April 2016.

202 **James M. Yergan** James M. Yergan was the nephew of Max Yergan, a cofounder of the Council on African Affairs, who would soon become a colleague of Alphaeus's—until things turned sour.

202 **He retained Eunice** This was not a demotion. In 1940, Dewey had assigned Eunice as head of what was then called Social Adjustments. See *Annual Report of the Chief Clerk to the District Attorney for the County of New York 1940*, pp. ii and 102. It does not appear that this was established as a formal bureau within General Sessions until 1942. Even then, the list of her duties is inconsistent. Some news accounts say that she was assigned to "Adolescent Offenders Research," but the 1942 report from Hogan's office lists no such position. It does include the "Special Part for Adolescent Offenders"—the full name of what had been Social Adjustments—but no assistant or deputy assistant is listed as being in charge. Eunice appears only once in the report, in the very long list of deputy assistant district attorneys. See *Annual Report of the Chief Clerk to the District Attorney for the County of New York 1942*, typescript.

202 **Eunice's salary remained** "Rivers, N.Y. District Attorney Is Re-Appointed at $10,000 per Year," *Chicago Defender*, Jan. 17, 1942, p. 7.

203 **"We have our pick"** See "Father Hogan's Place," *New Yorker*, Aug. 16, 1947, p. 36. The article gives Hogan all the credit for persuading the prostitutes to testify against Luciano. The reporter obviously spent a great deal of time in the office, and he talked to several senior staffers. He discusses at length the work of Special Sessions. Yet the piece does not mention Eunice at all. True, she had left the office two years previously. But much of the article was about Luciano and other Mob figures in whose prosecution she had taken a hand.

203 **From the time of Hogan's ascension** See, for example, Al Monroe, "Swinging the News," *Chicago Defender*, Aug. 7, 1943, p. 9.

203 **Lockwood might well have lost** Smith, *Thomas E. Dewey and His Times*, p. 340.

204 **Alphaeus Hunton first landed** See Federal Bureau of Investigation, Form. No. 1, "Alpheus [sic] Hunton," Internal Security-C, File No. 100–1767, July 3, 1941.

204 **"had been arrested"** "Florence McDonald, 73, Berkeley Radical," *New York Times*, July 1, 1989. The singer Country Joe McDonald, formerly of Country Joe and the Fish, is her son.

204 **She was believed to run** Twelve years later, in a 1953 congressional hearing on "Communist Underground Printing Facilities," a witness would describe Plotnick as formerly having been "city organizer of the party" in Washington, D.C. *Communist Underground Printing Facilities and Illegal Propaganda: Hearings Before the Subcommittee to Investigate the Administration of the Internal Security Act and Other Internal Security Laws, Committee on the Judiciary, United States Senate*, 83rd Cong., First Session (1953), p. 61.

205 **According to the earliest memorandum** See Federal Bureau of Investigation, Form No. 1, "Alpheus [sic] Hunton," Internal Security-C, File No. 100–1767, July 3, 1941, pp. 1–2.

205 **a watch was placed on his mail** [Special Agent in Charge] S. K. McKee to the Director [J. Edgar Hoover], March 25, 1941 (from FBI file).

205 **"to hide his party connection"** Memorandum, "William Alphaus [sic] Hunton," July 3, 1941, File No. 100–647, FBI file.

206 **"betrayers"** See Record, *The Negro and the Communist Party*, pp. 185–88.

206 **Sitting among the sponsors** See "Trainees' Parents to Rally Tuesday," *New York Times*, May 18, 1941, p. 36.

206 **She was, at this time** The National Council of Negro Women, where Eunice as always was deeply involved, was an early supporter of the war, although there might have been more than one motive. In June 1942, Mrs. Bethune sent a letter inviting Eleanor Roosevelt to a forthcoming conference on national defense. Oddly, the letter does not pledge the NCNW's support for President Roosevelt's sharp increase in military spending. Instead, Bethune wants to figure out how "we"—presumably meaning the darker nation but possibly meaning the Council itself—"may get on the ground floor of some of the programs that are now being put into action." Mary McLeod Bethune to Eleanor Roosevelt, June 3, 1941, Bethune Papers. But the NCNW did correspond with Fiorello La Guardia, who by now was in Washington as head of the Office of Civilian Defense, on how it could help. See, for example, Fiorello H. La Guardia to Florence K. Norman, June 25, 1941.

206 **she appeared at a war bond rally** "Joe Louis, Marian Anderson and Others Appear on War Bond Rally," *New York Amsterdam Star-News*, June 20, 1942, p. 4.

206 **Eunice was a founding member** "New Group Seeks Aid of Minorities," *New York Times*, June 2, 1942, p. 14. See also "Group Here Seeking Negro Help in War," *New York Times*, March 5, 1942, p. 16.

206 **Among other notable members** Bethune's involvement in Democracy in Action made perfect sense. She had already realized that the war would provide a catalyst for domestic civil rights activism. Defeating Hitlerism abroad should logically be followed by abolishing the color bar within the nation's borders. See Mark Ledwidge, *Race and US Foreign Policy: The African-American Foreign Affairs Network* (London: Routledge, 2012), pp. 95–96 and passim. Bethune was an early supporter of what became known as the "Double V" campaign—*V* for victory abroad, *V* for victory at home. Eunice, her protégée, also joined this battle enthusiastically.

206 **"Negroes schooled in the experiences"** John Hope Franklin, "The Two Worlds of Race: A Historical View," in Franklin, *Race and History: Selected Essays 1938–1988* (Baton Rouge: Louisiana State University Press, 1989), pp. 132, 146.

207 **Many prominent Negroes wrote articles** See, for example, Walter White, quoted in Gunnar Myrdal, *An American Dilemma: The Negro Problem and Modern Democracy* (New York: Harper & Row, 1944), vol. 2, p. 850, and "Our Pledge of Allegiance," *Chicago Defender*, Sept. 26, 1942, quoted in Lester M. Jones, "The Editorial Policy of Negro Newspapers of 1917–18 as Compared with That of 1941–42," *Journal of Negro History*, vol. 29, no. 1 (Jan. 1944).

207 **The War Department also commissioned** See Clayton R. Koppes and Gregory D. Black, "Blacks, Loyalty, and Motion-Picture Propaganda in World War II," *Journal of American History*, vol. 73, no. 2 (Sept. 1986), p. 383.

207 **"devoted to the primary purpose"** "Form New Group to Aid United Nations' Effort: Interracial Body Holds Meeting in New York City," *Atlanta Daily World*, March 12, 1942, p. 1.

207 **"bring together a large number"** "Ambulance Affiliate Names Its Leaders," *Afro-American* (Baltimore), March 28, 1942, p. 20. Because the group's first action was to raise money for the Ambulance Corps, the paper formed the mistaken impression that the two organizations were related.

207 **"received no encouragement"** "All Races Are Accepted in New War Relief Unit: Group's Credo Pledges Stand for Democracy," *Atlanta Daily World*, April 27, 1942, p. 1.

207 **At a rally in Central Park** "New Group Seeks Aid of Minorities: 'Democracy in Action' Opens Campaign for Solid Backing of the War Effort," *New York Times*, June 2, 1942, p. 15.

207 **residents were praised** "Blackout Conduct in Harlem Praised," *New York Times*, Oct. 11, 1942, p. 59.

207 **The idea was** Negro newspapers began the routine use of "Democracy in Action" in headlines above stories showing how the war was benefitting the darker nation. See, for example, "Ship Is Democracy in Action," *New Journal and Guide* (Norfolk), Aug. 26, 1944, p. 8 (about a warship with a Negro skipper), and "Democracy in Action on the Home Front," *Cleveland Call and Post*, Feb. 6, 1943, p. 12B (about a newly integrated workplace). Even the sudden integration of the Girl Scouts of America in the fall of 1942 was credited by the *Amsterdam News* to the "'democracy in action' spirit." The *News*, whose pages seemed always to support whatever causes Eunice supported, used the phrase again when it published a photograph of a downtown coffee shop whose white owner had hung in the window a poster featuring a Negro aviator. See "An Example of Democracy-in-Action," *New York Amsterdam News*, May 26, 1945, p. 7A.

But others used the term less admiringly, as when the *Pittsburgh Courier* played on the group's name in a mocking headline. See "Army Calls White Boys—Leaves Negroes Behind; Some Democracy: Democracy in Action: Race Airmen Cannot Fly These Ships—U. S. Navy Policy; Democracy in Action:—Colored Pilots Will Fly These Ships—U. S. Army Policy," *Pittsburgh Courier*, Feb. 21, 1942, p. 1.

207 **Rallying minority support** A good discussion of the complexity of the problem may be found in Neil A. Wynn, *The African American Experience During World War II* (Lanham, Md.: Rowman & Littlefield, 2010). By some time in 1943, Democracy in Action had evidently ceased to do business, probably because the major wartime charity it supported, the civilian-led British and American Ambulance Corps, had been wound down and replaced by military rescue workers.

207 **Eunice cooperated enthusiastically** For a useful critique of the strategy of the black leadership during the war, see Lee Finkle, "The Conservative Aims of Militant Rhetoric: Black Protest During World War II," *Journal of American History*, vol. 60, no. 3 (Dec. 1973), p. 692.

207 **Naturally the organizers** See "Harry Lofton Is Feted Here," *New York Amsterdam Star-News*, Jan. 2, 1943, p. 16. Eunice can be seen sitting beside the guest of honor in the accompanying photograph.

207 **Eunice led a panel discussion** See "Interracial Forum Highlights Meeting," *Pittsburgh Courier*, Oct. 23, 1943, p. 11.

208 **"we must all be prepared"** "Laud World War Book on Negro's Position," *Brooklyn Daily Eagle*, June 28, 1942, p. 19.

208 **part of a Constitution Day panel** See "Bridges Opposes U.S. as 'Policeman'; Senator Says Theory That We Must Supervise World After War Is Dangerous," *New York Times*, Sept. 17, 1942, p. 9, and "Braman Committee in All-Day Conference on Winning the War," *New York Age*, Sept. 19, 1942, p. 2.

208 **They also lambasted** "Four Freedoms Criticized at Forum on War: Country's Economic Trend Also Decried by Speakers at Town Hall Conference," *New York Herald Tribune*, Sept.

17, 1942, p. 8. Eunice gave an address at the meeting, but I have not been able to find the text of her remarks.

208 **"dictatorship"** See, for example, "Dictatorship Seen in New Deal Rule," *New York Times*, July 19, 1939, p. 4; "New Deal a Servant of Pressure Groups, Professor Declares," *Chicago Daily Tribune*, July 19, 1939, p. 5; and "F.R. New Deal 'Dictatorship' Condemned by Professors," *Oakland Tribune*, July 18, 1939, p. 3.

208 **But speakers at Braman Fund events** See, for example, "Mills Leads Constitution Day Attacks on Roosevelt Policies," *New York Herald Tribune*, Sept. 18, 1934, p. 1.

208 **At Christmas of 1942** "Dr. Hunton and Mother Visiting Eunice Carter," *New York Amsterdam News*, Jan. 2, 1943, p. 9. Due presumably to a typographical error, the article refers to Eunice and her husband as "Dr. and Mrs. Leslie O. Carter."

209 **"I refused to continue"** Dorothy Hunton, *Unsung Valiant*, p. 35.

209 **"slipped over to Virginia"** Ibid. The marriage license gives 1112 W Street, N.E., as the address of each party. It is not clear whether Dorothy and Alphaeus were already cohabiting or simply filled in the address as a statement of intention.

209 **showy, irreverent justice of the peace** "Alexandria Wants Marriage Business," *Cecil County Star* (Elkton, Md.), Dec. 8, 1938, p. 8. Friedlander died the year after Dorothy and Alphaeus were married.

210 **started to turn down invitations** See, for example, "Annual Community Luncheon Held by Business, Professional Women," *New York Age*, Nov. 1, 1941, p. 4. But see "W. C. Handy Among Distinguished Guests at Sunday Afternoon Concert of Monarch Band," *New York Age*, March 7, 1942, p. 7.

211 **the six honorary pallbearers** "Addie Waites Hunton, YMCA Fame, Dies: National Civic Worker, a Native of Norfolk," *New Journal and Guide* (Norfolk, Va.), July 10, 1943, p. A18.

211 **was suddenly being praised** See "Laud World War Book on Negro's Position," *Brooklyn Daily Eagle*, June 28, 1942, p. 19. See also "Sailor Uttered Famous War Cry," *Pittsburgh Courier*, Feb. 14, 1942, p. 2. The book was one of eight recommended by the Works Progress Administration on the role of the Negro soldier.

211 **Addie W. Hunton clubs** See, for example, "Beacon, N.Y.," *New York Age*, March 22, 1941, p. 9; "Glen Cove, L.I.N.Y.," *New York Age*, Nov. 20, 1937, p. 11.

211 **were still honoring her** See, for example, Mary E. Finger, "By Way of Mention," *New York Age*, Feb. 19, 1944, p. 4.

212 **"the highest-paid and highest-ranking"** "Negro Prosecutor Made City Justice," *New York Times*, Sept. 14, 1943, p. 1.

212 **she was part of a group** "Rival Groups Back Candidates for Boxing Commission Post," *New York Amsterdam Star-News*, Jan. 9, 1943, p. 12, and "Drive to Have Bob Douglas Named to Boxing Post in N.Y. Continues," *Pittsburgh Courier*, Jan. 16, 1943, p. 17.

212 **The *Age* described Douglas's selection** "Douglas Appointment to Boxing Commission Viewed as Certain," *New York Age*, Jan. 9, 1943, p. 11. See also "Back Bob Douglas for Boxing Commission," *Chicago Defender*, Jan. 16, 1943, p. 17.

213 **standing beside Mayor La Guardia** See Martha Biondi, *To Stand and Fight: The Struggle for Civil Rights in Postwar New York City* (Cambridge, Mass.: Harvard University Press, 2003), pp. 11–12. For Eunice's participation, see the photograph accompanying "End to Prejudice Urged by Mayor," *New York Times*, Sept. 26, 1943, p. 13.

213 **at the annual East-West classic** Al Monroe, "Swinging the News," *Chicago Defender*, Aug. 7, 1943, p. 9. The crowds for the annual contest were large. The 1944 game, with temperatures near one hundred degrees, drew some forty-six thousand fans. See Neil Lanctot, *Negro League Baseball: The Rise and Ruin of a Black Institution* (Philadelphia: University of Pennsylvania Press, 2004), p. vii.

213 **partied with the likes of** "Nora Holt, Famed Hostess, Gives Season's Most Elaborate House Party," *New York Amsterdam Star-News*, Nov. 13, 1943, p. 8A. According to the press, Eunice was also one of three black women invited to a conference sponsored by the *New York Times*. See "Talk o' Town," *Pittsburgh Courier*, April 24, 1943, p. 9. The *Courier* article does

not say what the conference was about, and I have been unable to find any other references to it.

213 **the late-season sassiety parties** Louis Lautier, "Capitol Spotlight," *Afro-American* (Baltimore), Dec. 4, 1943, p. 4.

213 **such luminaries as Thurgood Marshall** "What They Said and Did at Lawyers Meet in Baltimore," *Afro-American* (Baltimore), Dec. 4, 1943, p. 15.

213 **a reception at the Hotel Theresa** "By Way of Mention," *New York Age*, April 4, 1942, p. 4.

213 **to join the Council** According to Alphaeus's FBI file, Florence Plotnick may have played a role in persuading him to move to New York. See Federal Bureau of Investigation, File No. 101-1500 William Alpheus [sic] Hunton, Oct. 26, 1943 (Hunton FBI file). The file also indicates that Alphaeus had left his wife, Margaret, and was living with a woman named Dorothy Strange. Dorothy Strange was a prominent black Communist in the Washington area, and well known to the Bureau. At this time Alphaeus was involved with Dorothy Williams. Alphaeus might well have been seeing both women, but an equally plausible hypothesis is that the agent compiling the information received a report that the subject was living with a black woman named Dorothy and jumped to an erroneous conclusion.

Amusingly, the same memorandum refers to "Alphaeus" as Alphaeus Hunton's "alias."

18. The Connections

214 **But once the film** For background both on Pentagon objections and on the subsequent pressure by Negro leaders to have the film distributed at its full length, see Thomas Cripps and David Culbert, "*The Negro Soldier* (1944): Film Propaganda in Black and White," *American Quarterly*, vol. 31, no. 5 (Winter 1979), p. 616.

214 **"news to me"** Quoted in Joseph McBride, *Frank Capra: The Catastrophe of Success*, rev. ed. (Oxford: University of Mississippi Press, 2011), p. 492.

214 **pleading with her to contact** Jeanetta Welch Brown to Eunice H. Carter, Feb. 15, 1944, Bethune Papers.

215 **During the 1940 election campaign** See, for example, "Harlem Women of All Parties Reveal They Will Support Willkie," *New York Age*, Nov. 2, 1940, p. 3.

215 **nationally syndicated radio program** See "Republicans Plan Next Week's Program," *Emporia Gazette*, Oct. 26, 1940, p. 5.

215 **toured Harlem with Mrs. Willkie** "Mrs. Wilkie [sic] Tours Harlem," *New York Amsterdam News*, Oct. 12, 1940, p. 17.

215 **Eunice wrote to Jeanetta Welch Brown** Eunice H. Carter to Jeanetta Welch Brown, Feb. 23, 1944, Bethune Papers. In the same letter, Eunice apologizes for not yet fulfilling her pledge but explains that obligations surrounding her mother's death, plus a trip she had made to Chicago, had "wiped out all of the surplus." She promised to get to the pledge as soon as she could. Brown's letter acknowledging Eunice's assistance was oddly cold. See Jeanetta Welch Brown to Eunice H. Carter, Feb. 29, 1944.

We do not know what role, if any, Willkie played in keeping the film at its original length. A few months later, he had a heart attack and went into a swift decline. He died in October.

215 **they disliked the suggestions** See Andrew J. Huebner, *The Warrior Image: Soldiers in American Culture from the Second World War to the Vietnam Era* (Chapel Hill: University of North Carolina Press, 2008), pp. 45–47.

215 **They too wanted it changed** Capra resisted efforts by Carlton Moss, the Negro screenwriter, to add "angry fervor" to the story. Frank Capra, *The Name Above the Title: An Autobiography* (1971; repr., Boston: Da Capo, 1997), p. 358.

215 **they would face the tricky matter** Eunice H. Carter to Mary McLeod Bethune, March 14, 1944, Bethune Papers.

215 **"with restraint and dignity"** "Negro Soldier's Part in War Is Theme of Frank Capra Picture," *Indianapolis Star*, Feb. 15, 1944, p. 11.

216 **"Mrs. Carter is a Republican"** "First Lady to Dedicate Women's Council Bldg.," *Chicago Defender*, Oct. 7, 1944, p. 6.

216 **treasury held only $18.25** Elaine M. Smith, "Mary McLeod Bethune and the National Council of Negro Women: Pursuing a True and Unfettered Democracy," Historic Resource Study for the Mary McLeod Bethune Council House, Alabama State University, 2003, p. 43. (The manuscript is in the archives of the Mary McLeod Bethune Council House, Washington, D.C.)

217 **from the wrong class of people** See the perceptive discussion in Joyce A. Hanson, *Mary McLeod Bethune and Black Women's Political Activism* (Columbia: University of Missouri Press, 2003), pp. 99–111.

218 **neither attended the funeral** See "Rites Held for Alexander Waites, Popular Citizen," *New Journal and Guide* (Norfolk Va.), March 22, 1947, p. B3. The article took pains to distinguish surviving family members who attended the services from surviving family members generally.

218 **CAA was at this time** See, for example, Gerald Horne, *Black and Red: W. E. B. Du Bois and the Afro-American Response to the Cold War, 1944–1963* (Albany: State University of New York Press, 1986), pp. 76–77.

219 **"Darker Peoples of the World"** See Brenda Gayle Plummer, *Rising Wind: Black Americans and U.S. Foreign Affairs, 1935–1960* (Chapel Hill: University of North Carolina Press, 1996), p. 125. Bethune would use this phrase for the rest of her life. For example, in 1954, addressing a conference in Switzerland, she would say, "When you see me, you see a representative of 16 million black people in America, and I think of the darker peoples of the world who have been hungering, thirsting, to join hands with mankind everywhere." Mary McLeod Bethune, "Address to a World Assembly for Moral Re-Armament," reprinted in *Mary McLeod Bethune: Building a Better World—Essays and Selected Documents,* ed. Audrey Thomas McCluskey and Elaine M. Smith (Bloomington: Indiana University Press, 1999), p. 56.

219 **That she attended anyway** The historian Christine Lutz suggests that Eunice's attendance might have been evidence of her own Pan-Africanism. Christine Lutz, "Another Post-War Settlement: Eunice Hunton Carter and Mary McLeod Bethune," *Selected Annual Proceeding of the Florida Conference of Historians,* vol. 16 (March 2009), p. 62. But although Addie certainly wound up moving in that direction, there is little in Eunice's career and nothing in her extant correspondence to suggest that she followed her mother and brother along this particular path.

219 **was always a featured speaker** In the fall of 1945, in what would become a regular event, Eunice was a featured speaker on International Night at the annual convention of the National Council of Negro Women. See Rebecca Stiles Taylor, "Federated Clubs," *Chicago Defender,* Nov. 17, 1945, p. 19.

220 **The reason for her trip** See "Political Pot Boils in Chicago and Washington," *Pittsburgh Courier,* Feb. 19, 1944, p. 1. The group met for two days at the ballroom of Chicago's Pershing Hotel. The sessions were open to the public. The committee's slogan was decidedly militant: "Let those who would be free strike the first blow." See *Conference: United Planning Committee for United Minorities* [undated flyer for 1944 meeting]. The slogan is borrowed from a similar line popular among radical trade unionists of the nineteenth century, which would become popular among revolutionaries in the 1950s and 1960s. See also "GOP Leaders Will Meet to Lay Post-War Plans," *Pittsburgh Courier,* Jan. 29, 1944, p. 5.

221 **strong positions on equality** At this point, Eunice proved the consistency of her conservatism. She did not trust big government, and apparently, she was no more comfortable with the existence of self-perpetuating committee structures within organizations. Now that the Planning Committee was through with its work, she moved that it agree to abolish itself once it had made its report to the convention. The motion was defeated.

221 **The Negro press followed** See, for example, Channing H. Tobias, "The Two Conventions" (letter to the editor), *New York Age,* July 29, 1944, pp. 6 and 8, and Hazel Reed, "Women's Whirl," *New Journal and Guide* (Norfolk, Va.), March 11, 1944, p. 5.

221 **Photo spreads** See, for example, "GOP Convention Attracts Colorful Figures," *Pittsburgh Courier,* July 8, 1944, p. 4. For nonphotographic coverage of her role, see, for example, "G.O.P.'s Meet in Chicago: Convention Highlites," *Philadelphia Tribune,* July 1, 1944, p. 1.

221 **part of a cabal** See "Factions Vie for Dewey Nod," *Chicago Defender*, July 18, 1944, p. 18.

221 **Eunice felt squeezed out** Some journalists also saw the contretemps as Eunice's bid for power. See, for example, "Factions Maneuver to Head Dewey Campaign," *Atlanta Daily World*, July 8, 1944, p. 1.

221 **the cabal failed** Some sources credit Rivers rather than Eunice with drafting the civil rights plank. See Joshua D. Farrington, *Black Republicans and the Transformation of the GOP* (Philadelphia: University of Pennsylvania Press, 2016), pp. 27–28.

221 **"We don't want to make"** Quoted in "Revolt Threat Rocks GOP; Spangler Note on Bilbo Brings Angry Outcry; Attempt to Suppress Letter from GOP Head Fails," *Chicago Defender*, July 1, 1944, p. 1.

222 **brought her son** "Highlights of GOP Confab," *New York Amsterdam News*, July 1, 1944, p. 2A.

222 **"the easiest man in the world"** Smith, *Thomas E. Dewey and His Times*, p. 397.

222 **He would court the Negro vote** Negroes were not the only ethnic constituency the Republicans targeted in 1944. The party also sought the votes of "American nationals from Poland, Finland, Latvia, Lithuania, Estonia, etc.," on the theory that the Roosevelt administration planned, in effect, to abandon their beloved countries of origin to the Soviet sphere of influence. But the GOP effort was inconsistent and ultimately unsuccessful. See the discussion in John Lewis Gaddis, *The United States and the Origins of the Cold War, 1941–1947* (New York: Columbia University Press, 1972), pp. 146–49.

222 **in the thick of things** To be sure, Eunice could not work full-time on Dewey's campaign. She had her other responsibilities. In addition to her work in the office, in May she traveled to Omaha to lecture on ways to keep young people from getting into trouble. See "Juvenile Delinquency Blame Placed on Parents, Friends," *Nebraska State Journal*, May 20, 1944, p. 5.

222 **rallying Negroes** See, for example, "Rally for Dewey Is Held by Negroes," *Philadelphia Inquirer*, Nov. 2, 1944, p. 6; "Republican Leaders Back Warner at Borough Confab," *New York Amsterdam News*, July 29, 1944, p. 4B; and "Rally to Hear Roosevelt Talk," *Pittsburgh Post-Gazette*, Nov. 1, 1944, p. 4.

222 **particularly with black audiences** See, for example, "Dewey Begins Drive to Woo Negro Vote," *Pittsburgh Courier*, Aug. 12, 1944, p. 1; "Cite Dewey's Record for Naming Qualified Negroes to High Jobs," *New Journal and Guide* (Norfolk, Va.), Oct. 7, 1944, p. A16; and "Dewey Outlines His Theory on Equality," *New York Amsterdam News*, Aug. 12, 1944, p. 1A.

222 **"entertained at dinner"** Quoted in "Dewey Lashes FDR on Poll Tax," *Chicago Defender*, Aug. 5, 1944, p. 1. It is notable that neither Dewey nor the editors saw any need to tell readers who Eunice was. The working assumption must have been that their audience would know.

223 **"appointed people because they were good"** "Dewey Points to His Record: St. Louis Republicans Told Color Is Ignored," *Afro-American* (Baltimore), Aug. 12, 1944, p. 1. See also "Cite Dewey's Record for Naming Qualified Negroes to High Jobs," *New Journal and Guide* (Norfolk, Va.), Oct. 7, 1944, p. 4.

223 **advertisements in Negro papers** See, for example, GOP advertisement, *Indianapolis Recorder*, Sept. 23, 1944, 2nd section, p. 8; GOP advertisement, *New York Amsterdam News*, Oct. 28, 1944, p. 11; and GOP advertisement, *New Journal and Guide* (Norfolk, Va.), Oct. 28, 1944, p. B11.

223 **White journalists repeatedly warned** Farrington, *Black Republicans*, pp. 29–30. See also Arthur Krock, "Dewey Tactics in Race Confusing to His Backers," *New York Times*, Sept. 24, 1944, p. E3.

223 **"first Negro woman"** "Gov. Dewey Can Lure Willkie's Supporters," *Philadelphia Inquirer*, Feb. 19, 1944, p. 5.

223 **They lost** See Weiss, *Farewell to the Party of Lincoln*, pp. 157–58.

224 **"destructive to morale"** Quoted in ibid., p. 277.

224 **This was a blatant lie** See "White House Blesses Jim Crow," *Crisis*, Nov. 1940, p. 350.

224 **"If only a small fraction"** "How Will Negroes Vote? They May Hold the Balance of Power," *Life*, vol. 17, no. 16 (Oct. 16, 1944), p. 89. See also "Negro Republican Vote May Set 20-Year Mark," *Philadelphia Inquirer*, July 2, 1944, p. 2B.

224 **He met publicly** See, for example, "GOP Platform Bids for Negro Vote," *Chicago Defender*, July 8, 1944, p. 1.

224 **A West Virginia audience** Quoted in "Dewey's Stand on Race Issue," *Pittsburgh Courier*, Oct. 14, 1944, p. 1. The *Courier*, a big Dewey backer, not only put the speech on the front page but gave it a huge banner headline. The speech was apparently given the previous Saturday (October 7), just hours before Eunice's friend Wendell Willkie died.

224 **When Dewey learned** Smith, *Thomas E. Dewey and His Times*, p. 408.

224 **"a Negro drinking party"** "South Carolina Governor Hits Dewey on Negroes: Charges He Attended 'A Negro Drinking Party' in N.Y.," *New York Herald Tribune*, July 7, 1944, p. 9.

225 **As governor, his supporters noted** "Dewey Proclaims Negro Week," *New York Times*, Feb. 6, 1943, p. 11. This was not merely an election-eve sop to a valued constituency. After losing to Roosevelt, Dewey made the same proclamation in 1945. See "Negro History Hailed," *New York Times*, Feb. 11, 1945, p. 34.

225 **about as many Negro papers** See David M. Jordan, *FDR, Dewey, and the Election of 1944* (Bloomington: Indiana University Press, 2011), pp. 268–99.

225 **a survey by the National Negro Council** "Poll Shows Negroes for Dewey," *New York Times*, July 9, 1944, p. 29. To be sure, many prominent Negroes insisted from early on that colored voters would favor Roosevelt. See, for example, "Prediction on Negro Vote: Two NAACP Leaders Say Roosevelt Is Favored over Dewey," *New York Times*, May 4, 1944, p. 36.

225 **"[W]hen he was special prosecutor"** Editorial, "They're in South Carolina!," *New York Herald Tribune*, July 7, 1944, p. 12.

225 **"What principally characterizes"** "Editorial," *New Africa*, vol. 3, no. 7 (July–Aug. 1944), p. 3 (unpaginated).

226 **"On November 7 Americans will decide"** "Editorial," *New Africa*, vol. 3, no. 9 (Oct. 1944), p. 3 (unpaginated).

226 **"the party of Big Business"** "Be Intelligently Selfish at Polls, Urges DuBois," *Chicago Defender*, Sept. 30, 1944, p. 3. Du Bois's steadfast advocacy for the Democrats apparently caused the Republican editors of the *Amsterdam News* to censor his columns. See Horne, *Black and Red*, pp. 83–84.

226 **"insufferable"** Quoted in Jordan, *FDR, Dewey, and the Election of 1944*, p. 19.

226 **"shameful, myopic vision"** "Where Negroes Belong: Liberalism or Reaction?," *Chicago Defender*, Oct. 7, 1944, p. 12.

226 **"large salaried but inconsequential"** "Dewey's Campaign Promises Just Hollow Talk, Record Analysis Shows," *Chicago Defender*, Oct. 21, 1944, p. 16. Two months after the election, the newspaper lauded Negro voters for seeing through "the Dewey deceit and duplicity." The paper asked pointedly whether Dewey had appointed any Negroes to office after Election Day. "It's Still Time for a Change," *Chicago Defender*, Jan. 20, 1945, p. 10.

The spat within the black press over whether to support Roosevelt or Dewey fascinated the white press. See, for example, "'Courier' Calls on Negroes to Support Dewey," *New York Herald Tribune*, Sept. 29, 1944, p. 13.

226 **"playing the role of Quisling"** Arthur Huff Fauset, "I Write as I See," *Philadelphia Tribune*, April 15, 1944, p. 4.

226 **The South had made noises** For a discussion of the Southern threats to vote Republican and the turnabout by Election Day, see William E. Leuchtenberg, *The White House Looks South: Franklin D. Roosevelt, Harry S. Truman, Lyndon B. Johnson* (Baton Rouge: Louisiana State University Press, 2005), pp. 134–40.

227 **"hand in hand"** "Ickes Calls Dewey Enemy of Negroes," *New York Times*, Nov. 2, 1944, p. 12.

227 **"I was not going to be"** Quoted in Smith, *Thomas E. Dewey and His Times*, p. 440.

227 **Perhaps she had read the same tea leaves** As one historian has put it, "In the face of a popular incumbent fighting a popular war, there was little about the current administration to criticize." Bowen, *The Roots of Modern Conservatism*, p. 23.

228 **"The womens [sic] vote"** Harry McAlpin, "Dr. Bethune Sole Survivor of Women's 'Old Guard' for FDR: Most Other Oldtimers Were Aboard Gov. Dewey's Wagon," *Atlanta Daily World*, Nov. 18, 1944, p. 1.

228 **Like Bethune, they had chosen** Mrs. Bethune's decision to back Roosevelt had itself been newsworthy. See, for example, "Mrs. Bethune to Campaign for Roosevelt," *New Journal and Guide* (Norfolk, Va.), Oct. 14, 1944, p. A17. Although Bethune described herself as nonpartisan and had been a member of what was known colloquially as Roosevelt's "Black Cabinet," she was generally considered a Republican. In the 1920s, she had campaigned for Republican candidates.

228 **suddenly running front-page stories** See, for example, "Carver Democratic Club Presents Prizes to Contest Winners," *New York Age*, March 8, 1947, p. 1.

228 **The President had used** A useful account of Roosevelt's balancing act is Durahn Taylor, "From Hyde Park to Harlem: The Emergence of Franklin Delano Roosevelt's Black Constituency in New York City," *Afro-Americans in New York Life and History*, vol. 37, no. 1 (Jan. 2013), p. 7.

228 **Studies of the 1944 returns** See Gary A. Donaldson, *Truman Defeats Dewey* (Lexington: University Press of Kentucky, 1999), pp. 98–99.

228 **Eunice resigned** "Eunice Hunton Carter Resigns D.A.'s Staff," *New York Amsterdam News*, Jan. 6, 1945, p. A1.

229 **"was being properly cared for"** "Valentine Denies Curbs by Mayor," *New York Times*, Nov. 29, 1941, pp. 1, 34.

229 **unsolicited letters** See, for example, Eunice H. Carter to Hon. William E. Ringel [city magistrate], March 21, 1941, NYCDA archives; this was a reply to William E. Ringel to "Miss" Eunice H. Carter, March 10, 1941, NYCDA archives. But this had been going on for some time, even while Dewey was still in power and Eunice was running Special Sessions. See, for example, Jeanette G. Brill [city magistrate] to Thomas F. [sic] Dewey, Aug. 10, 1939 (stamped "REFERRED TO" with "Mrs. Carter" added by hand), NYCDA archives; Eunice H. Carter to Raymundo Costosa, Sept. 15, 1936, NYCDA archives; and memorandum, Mrs. [Eunice H.] Carter to Murray Gurfein, "Re Interview with Mr. Milton Georgiades," Jan. 17, 1936, NYCDA archives. See also Paul E. Lockwood to Hon. Jeanette G. Brill, Aug. 12, 1939 (mentioning that the matter has been referred to Eunice, whom Lockwood describes as "Assistant District Attorney").

229 **She addressed conferences on** See, for example, "Brilliant Leaders Who Spoke Against Discrimination, Urged Loyalty," *Pittsburgh Courier*, Oct. 25, 1941, p. 9.

229 **She sat on bar committees** For Eunice's service on the bar committees, see, for example, "National Bar Association Fights Bias at Convention: Lawyers Meeting in Chi Frame Resolutions to End Discrimination," *Afro-American* (Baltimore), Dec. 9, 1944, p. 3. On the meeting with industrialists, see Mary McLeod Bethune to Eunice H. Carter, Dec. 30, 1944 (Bethune Papers). See also Eunice H. Carter to Mary McLeod Bethune, Dec. 17, 1944 (Bethune Papers). As this exchange of letters reflects, Eunice had become a major financial backer of the NCNW. For an account of the group's woeful finances in this era, see Diane Kiesel, *She Can Bring Us Home: Dr. Dorothy Boulding Ferebee, Civil Rights Pioneer* (Lincoln: University of Nebraska Press/Potomac Books, 2015), pp. 155–58.

229 **"a signal victory"** Julia E. Baxter, "New York State Bars Economic Jim Crow," *Crisis*, vol. 52, no. 4 (April 1945), p. 98.

229 **After a brief hesitation** Smith, *Thomas E. Dewey and His Times*, pp. 444–48.

229 **He had faced down** See "Bias Bill Assailed by State Chamber," *New York Times*, Feb. 12, 1945, p. 32.

229 **Eunice had publicly fought** See "Among Those Present at London Conference," *New York Amsterdam News*, Feb. 24, 1945, p. 5A. Note that the headline is apparently an error, intended for a different story.

229 **The *New York Times* named** "Dewey Will Sign Ives Bill Monday and Then Seek 5 for Commission," *New York Times*, March 7, 1945, p. 38. In some stories Eunice was the only person

mentioned as a potential appointee. See, for example, "Dewey Makes NY FEPC Bill Law," *Afro-American* (Baltimore), March 17, 1945, p. 1.

230 **Dewey was known** The idea that Dewey and Hoover conspired together refuses to die. See, for example, William C. Sullivan and Bill Brown, "Life with a Tyrant: J. Edgar Hoover Ruled the FBI as His Personal Kingdom; Presidents and Private Citizens Alike Were Not Spared His Scheming," *Washington Post Magazine*, Sept. 23, 1979, p. 14. Perhaps unsurprisingly, recent events have put the unproven allegations back in the headlines. See Jeff Kisseloff, "This Is Not the First Time the FBI Has Interfered with a Presidential Election," *Nation*, Oct. 31, 2016.

230 **Hoover had lobbied** See J. Edgar Hoover, Memorandum for Mr. Matthew F. McGuire, Aug. 30, 1941 (Hunton FBI file); J. Edgar Hoover to Paul V. McNutt, March [24?; date is slightly smudged], 1942 (Hunton FBI file).

19. The Defeat

232 **All across the country** A nice summary of the energetic preparations may be found in chapter 4 of Plummer, *Rising Wind*.

232 **"the colored women of America"** "Unofficial Observers Plead for Equality," *Pittsburgh Courier*, May 5, 1945, p. 1.

232 **Although some press accounts** See, for example, "Sidelights on Historic Frisco Conference: Interesting Personalities Incidents Revealed at United Nations Parley in San Francisco," *New Journal and Guide* (Norfolk, Va.), May 5, 1945, p. C10.

232 **Walter White made heavy weather** White would later call press accounts of his battle with Bethune "mythical." Quoted in Horne, *Black and Red*, p. 37.

232 **"rather a nuisance"** Quoted in Lewis, *W. E. B. Du Bois, 1919–1963*, p. 510.

232 **After Bethune left** Eunice and Bethune both spoke at a church in Oakland just before Bethune left. "Mrs. Bethune Is Speaker at Los Angeles Council Meeting," *Pittsburgh Courier*, May 19, 1945, p. 5.

233 **Outside the formal sessions** "League of Races Dinners Bind Darker Races at San Francisco," *New Journal and Guide* (Norfolk, Va.), May 19, 1945, p. B14.

233 **Orson Welles** "Film and Radio Stars Meet to Give Inter-Race Awards," *New York Amsterdam News*, June 2, 1945, p. 7A.

233 **at face value** See, for example, "Dewey Frees Luciano for Deportation to Italy as Reward for Aid in War," *New York Herald Tribune*, Jan. 4, 1946, p. 1A.

234 **"the actual value"** "Dewey Commutes Luciano Sentence," *New York Times*, Jan. 4, 1946, p. 25. Note that the *Herald Tribune* put the story on its front page.

234 **greatly exaggerated** A brief but useful summary of the evidence is Monte S. Finkelstein, *Separatism, the Allies, and the Mafia: The Struggle for Sicilian Independence, 1943–1948* (Bethlehem, Pa.: Lehigh University Press, 1998), pp. 23–26. For a more forceful rejection of the argument that Luciano's help was important to the war effort, see Tim Newark, *Mafia Allies: The True Story of America's Secret Alliance with the Mob in World War II* (Minneapolis: Zenith Press, 2007).

234 **516 Fifth Avenue** The Martindale-Hubbell legal directory continued to record Eunice's business address at the district attorney's office on Leonard Street until 1949, when the Fifth Avenue address appeared for the first time. This is mere indolence. As city directories and other sources confirm, she opened the Fifth Avenue office almost immediately after leaving government employ.

234 **turn out to be a fraud** See "Court Dissolves Blind Veterans Group as Fraud," *New York Herald Tribune*, March 1, 1951, p. 21.

234 **There would be 19 Negro women** These figures are drawn from Appendix C, Chart C1, in J. Clay Smith, ed., *Rebels in Law: Voices in History of Black Women Lawyers* (Ann Arbor: University of Michigan Press, 1998), p. 284.

235 **something of a celebrity** Scholer had played a controversial role in the murder trial of Hans Schmidt, the only Catholic priest ever executed in the United States. Scholer first testified

that Schmidt had been insane when he murdered Anna Aumüller, but days later, under pressure, he told the court he was not sure.

235 **with racial covenants** On May 3, 1948, two years after Eunice and Lisle purchased their Jumel Terrace home, the Supreme Court would hand down its decision *Shelley v. Kraemer*, 334 U.S. 1 (1948), holding unconstitutional the enforcement of racially restrictive covenants in real estate sales. The case was argued by the Carters' friend Thurgood Marshall, a neighbor during their time at 409 Edgecombe. Less than two weeks after the decision, an upscale Manhattan agent named Samuel Hurwitz announced that because of the "removal of restrictions against Negroes and other minority groups," he was now "able to make many offers in sections which formerly excluded the groups involved." Among the neighborhoods he mentioned expressly was Jumel Terrace, in upper Manhattan. See "Ghetto Ruling Results in Expanded Offerings," *New York Amsterdam News*, May 15, 1948, p. 16. Hurwitz's sudden announcement that he was prepared to sell homes on Jumel Terrace to Negroes probably would have come as a thunderclap, had not Eunice and Lisle already purchased there. (As far as I have been able to determine, the second house on Jumel Terrace to be sold to nonwhites was No. 16, purchased by Alphaeus's close friend Paul Robeson and his wife in about 1950 or 1951.)

235 **The sale closed** "Real Estate Transfers," *New York Herald Tribune*, July 29, 1946, p. 26.

235 **the price was a steal** Although the 1917 sales price is lost to history, newspapers of the day report, implausibly, that Scholer borrowed $50,000 (about $1 million in 2017 dollars) to finance the purchase. According to census records, the 1910 assessment of 10 Jumel Terrace was $10,000. I suspect that the figure of $50,000 is a transcription error in the published records. More likely Scholer borrowed $5,000, which would be $104,000 in 2017 dollars.

236 **After purchasing the property** "Building Plans Filed," *New York Times*, Dec. 3, 1946, p. 56.

236 **the Carters occupied their new home** Bill Chase, "All Ears," *New York Amsterdam News*, Feb. 22, 1947, p. 8.

236 **"manse"** Lucille Cromer, "Conversation Piece About Smart People," *New York Age*, Jan. 20, 1951, p. 8.

236 **"social register names"** See, for example, "They Were Merry—of Very Good Cheer," *New York Amsterdam News*, Jan. 1, 1949, p. 8. Eunice's husband, Lisle, also quickly took advantage of the capacious house, hosting gatherings of both fraternity and professional colleagues. See, for example, "Chapter of Omega Returns Officers," *New York Age*, Nov. 20, 1948, p. 13.

236 **"beeg, beeg Christmas party"** "Along Celebrity Row," *Chicago Defender*, Jan. 1, 1949, p. 9. See also Thelma Berlack Boozer, "Choice Chatter," *New York Age*, Jan. 8, 1949, p. 9.

236 **"bigger and better"** Thelma Berlack Boozer, "Choice Chatter," *New York Age*, Dec. 25, 1948, p. 13. (I omitted the single quotes around "bigger and better.")

236 **she was attending** See "Numerous Social Functions Given for Members of NNPA at 4-Day Session," *New York Age*, June 29, 1946, p. 4.

237 **she partnered with** "Eunice H. Carter and Ernest E. Johnson Announce Formation of Publicity Firm," *New York Age*, Aug. 2, 1948, p. 3.

237 **The Negro press predicted** Toki Schalk Johnson, "Toki Types," *Pittsburgh Courier*, Sept. 6, 1947, p. 8.

237 **including a rumored** Gerri Major, "Around 'n' About," *New York Amsterdam News*, Feb. 5, 1949, p. 12. Although Eunice still chaired the executive committee, a nonprofit organization is allowed to contract for services from its own board members, subject to restrictions to prevent "sweetheart" deals.

237 **"It didn't work out"** Quoted in Lillian Scott, "Along Celebrity Row," *Chicago Defender*, Oct. 16, 1948, p. 9.

237 **The liberals on the board** In addition to the anti-Communist pressure, the Council on African Affairs suffered from poor relationships with other groups and "its own inability to function as a mass organization." Plummer, *Rising Wind*, p. 158.

238 **"a Negro who has been"** George W. Robnett, "School for Revolutionists" (letter to the editor), *Chicago Tribune*, June 24, 1945, p. 16.

238 **Alphaeus argued that Truman's policy** [Alphaeus Hunton], "International Finance Looks to Undeveloped African Resources: Anglo-Saxon Scheme of Super-Exploitation Expected to Save Bankrupt Europe," *New Africa*, vol. 6, no. 11 (Dec. 1947), p. 1.

238 **Alphaeus turned his ire** See Carol Anderson, *Eyes Off the Prize: The United Nations and the African American Struggle for Human Rights, 1944–1955* (New York: Cambridge University press, 2003), pp. 125–26. One can understand the ferocity of Alphaeus's opposition to the Marshall Plan as an outgrowth of his Communist commitment. For example, in an unsigned front-page editorial in *New Africa*, he argued that Truman's policy on aid to Europe was intended to stop Russia while opening up Africa to exploitation by American capitalists. "[I]t is hardly likely," wrote Alphaeus, "that Britain, France and Belgium can oppose America's access to the wealth of their respective African empires." The only way to develop Africa, he concluded, was under United Nations aegis, with the involvement of "the major powers, including the Soviet Union." Editorial, "International Finance Looks to Undeveloped African Resources: Anglo-Saxon Scheme of Super-Exploitation Expected to Save Bankrupt Europe," *New Africa*, vol. 6, no. 11 (Dec. 1947).

For more on Alphaeus's criticism of the Marshall Plan and its supporters, see Mark Solomon, "Black Critics of Colonialism and the Cold War," in Michael L. Krenn, ed., *The African American Voice in U.S. Foreign Policy Since World War II* (New York: Garland, 1999), pp. 53, 72–75. For Alphaeus's own more detailed views on capitalist exploitation of Africa, see Alphaeus Hunton, *Decision in Africa: Sources of Current Conflict* (New York: International Publishers, 1957), particularly Part II. See also W. A. [William Alphaeus] Hunton, "Colonial Control Discussed" (letter to the editor), *New York Times*, March 28, 1945, p. 22.

238 **that his sister worked for Dewey** To be sure, Hoover and Dewey were hardly enemies. In 1948, Hoover openly supported Dewey's presidential campaign. Some believe that there was a quid pro quo. Ronald Kessler, in his book on the FBI, insists that there was an explicit understanding that if Dewey won, Hoover would be attorney general, and perhaps a Supreme Court Justice. Ronald Kessler, *The Bureau: The Secret History of the FBI* (New York: St. Martin's Press, 2002), p. 103. Longtime Hoover aide William C. Sullivan is more cautious, suggesting only that Hoover "believed" an appointment would be forthcoming. See Sullivan and Brown, "Life with a Tyrant," *Washington Post*, Sept. 23, 1979.

238 **a brief tap on his phone** President Franklin Roosevelt, through a secret order in 1940, had empowered the Justice Department to tap the telephone lines "of persons suspected of subversive activities against the Government of the United States." See "Confidential Memorandum," Franklin D. Roosevelt to the Attorney General, May 21, 1940. Roosevelt probably intended that the attorney general review all FBI wiretap requests. But Robert Jackson, then serving in the office, was reportedly so upset by the memorandum that at first he tried to delegate the authority entirely to the director of the FBI and asked not even to be advised of whose phones were being listened to. See Curt Gentry, *J. Edgar Hoover: The Man and the Secrets* (New York: W. W. Norton, 1991), pp. 232–33.

238 **Alphaeus's file includes the transcript** See Edward Scheidt to Director, FBI [J. Edgar Hoover], Feb. 17, 1948, attaching the transcript (Hunton FBI file). The caller was Max Weiss, a senior member of the Communist Party of the United States. How cautious was Alphaeus? His entire side of the conversation was as follows: "Hello.... Yes.... Yeah.... Uh huh.... OK.... Yes.... Uh huh.... OK.... Yeah.... Bye." The Bureau also interviewed Alphaeus. He denied being a member of any subversive organization. For a transcript, see Statement of William Alphaeus Hunton, Feb. 25, 1942 (Hunton FBI file).

239 **the investigation was closed** See Memorandum, SAC [Special Agent in Charge], New York to Director, FBI [J. Edgar Hoover], April 28, 1947 (Hunton FBI file).

239 **According to an informant** See Memorandum, William Alphaeus Hunton, File No. 100-52572, Feb. 23, 1949, pp. 5–6 (Hunton FBI file).

241 **would come down hard** See, for example, United States House of Representatives, Committee on Un-American Activities, *Investigation of Communist Activities in the Los Angeles Area*, Hearings, Part 5, pp. 887ff. (testimony of Anne Kinney, Dec. 22, 1952). Certainly the

UOPWA worked with the Communist Party, and this cooperation was part of what led to the union's downfall. See Lisa Phillips, *A Renegade Union: Interracial Organizing and Labor Radicalism* (Urbana: University of Illinois Press, 2013), pp. 133–39. See also Judith Stepan-Norris and Maurice Zeitlin, *Left Out: Reds and America's Industrial Unions* (Cambridge: Cambridge University Press, 2003), p. 13, n. 28.

241 **The union had a reputation** For example, by the time of the dispute with the National Council of Negro Women in 1947, when campaigning against the atomic bomb was seen as a radical aim, the UOPWA was firmly in the anti-nuclear camp. See, for example, Marjorie Carmichael to Albert Einstein, April 8, 1947, Special Collections and Archives Research Center, Oregon State University, http://scarc.library.oregonstate.edu/omeka/exhibits/show/ecas/item/26621.

241 **Members were accused** See, for example, *Gomez v. United Office and Professional Workers of America*, 73 F. Supp. 679 (DDC 1947).

241 **Stories in the colored press** See, for example, Toki Schalk Johnson, "Toki Types," *Pittsburgh Courier*, March 15, 1947, p. 8.

241 **known for the contrarian position** See Joseph H. Levy, "How Can Peaceful Labor Relations Be Assured in Social Agencies?," *Jewish Social Service Quarterly*, vol. 24, no. 1 (Sept. 1947), p. 25. The *Quarterly* was edited by Herbert Aptheker, a friend of Alphaeus's.

241 **The press gave Eunice full credit** See, for example, "Union Settles Difficulties Between National Council Heads, Employees," *Pittsburgh Courier*, April 12, 1947, p. 8.

241 **remained cordial on the surface** See, for example, Mary McLeod Bethune to Eunice H. Carter, April 23, 1948 ("I enjoyed your week end here very much. I always enjoy you. Lots of love"). See also Mary McLeod Bethune to Eunice H. Carter, June 30, 1948. Still, they continued to have disagreements. Not all of them were about money. For example, Eunice apparently cared—and Bethune did not—about ensuring an adequate white turnout at the group's public events. See, for example, Eunice H. Carter to Mary McLeod Bethune, Feb. 17, 1948, Bethune Papers.

241 **Eunice, as chairman** See "International Council of Women Holds Conclave in Philadelphia," *Pittsburgh Courier*, Sept. 27, 1947, p. 10. Although the matter is not entirely clear, it appears that the meeting in Philadelphia was preliminary to the follow-up meeting in Europe. Some sources refer to the Paris meeting as the "International Assembly of Women." That group, however, seems to have met in Paris in 1946, not 1947.

241 **to cover travel expenses** Ferebee's biographer Diane Kiesel offers the intriguing suggestion that Bethune backed out of the trip because of the potential for bad publicity after being criticized in the press for spending so much money when the NCNW was essentially broke. See Kiesel, *She Can Bring Us Home*, p. 157. The claim that Bethune was not healthy to go was, in this theory, just a smoke screen. Perhaps this is exactly what happened. The trouble is that the only mention in the press seems to be the one that Kiesel cites, a brief note by a *Chicago Defender* columnist. The criticism—that Bethune and Ferebee are off to Europe when the Council is "flat on its fanny in morale and finances"—appears well down in the column. See Charley Cherokee, "National Grapevine," *Chicago Defender*, Aug. 9, 1947, p. 13. I am skeptical that the mercurial Bethune would have changed her plans because of this single comment when her regular press coverage was as fawning as ever.

242 **Eunice had expressed concern** Eunice Hunton Carter to Mary McLeod Bethune, Feb. 3, 1948, Bethune Papers.

243 **Mme. Sohier-Brunard hired** See "Eunice H. Carter Among Delegates to Paris Talks," *Chicago Defender*, Sept. 13, 1947, p. 8.

243 **"quite a striking lady"** "Women of Merit," *New York Age*, March 22, 1947, p. 5.

243 **her suite aboard the *Queen Mary*** See "Randolph, Reynolds Eye Powell's Berth," *New Journal and Guide* (Norfolk, Va.), May 22, 1948, p. 3. See also Eunice H. Carter to Edith Sampson, April 20, 1948, Bethune Papers, in which Eunice invites her rival to visit her in New York before her departure.

244 **"one of those 'like old times' affairs"** Bill Chase, "All Ears," *New York Amsterdam News*, Sept. 20, 1947, p. 8.

244 **One of those Yergan accused** See "Battles Left Wing for Group's Offices," *New York Times*, May 29, 1948, p. 6. As Yergan's biographer notes, by this time the executive director's efforts to purge "left-wing elements" from the Council on African Affairs had caused "an outright schism between pro- and anti-Yergan factions" on the board. David Henry Anthony III, *Max Yergan: Race Man, Internationalist, Cold Warrior* (New York: New York University Press, 2006), p. 230. The dispute was largely between Yergan on one side and, on the other, Alphaeus and his good friend Paul Robeson. For a brief, clear account of the battle, see Hollis R. Lynch, *Black American Radicals and the Liberation of Africa: The Council on African Affairs, 1937–1955* (Ithaca, N.Y.: Cornell University Africana Studies and Research Center, 1978), pp. 35–37. For the internal debate, see W. Alphaeus Hunton to W. E. B. Du Bois, "Memorandum from W. A. Hunton on Current Work of the Council," Feb. 20, 1948; Paul Robeson to Max Yergan, April 7, 1948; and Du Bois to Hunton, March 26, 1948.

The ousting of Yergan further damaged the already weakened Council. Many liberal and moderate members resigned from the board, believing that the group was indeed now dominated by Communists. See Plummer, *Rising Wind*, pp. 191–92. Eunice's mentor Mary McLeod Bethune hung on longer than most, but she finally quit as well.

244 **After a brief investigation** "No Cause for Action: Hogan Takes Stand After Study of Dr. Yergan's Complaint," *New York Times*, June 2, 1948, p. 17.

20. The Breakup

245 **what one columnist labeled** James Hicks, "The Big Town: 'Do for Dewey' Vs. 'Do for Truman,'" *New Journal and Guide* (Norfolk, Va.), Aug. 14, 1948, p. 11.

246 **"might be persuaded"** James L. Hicks, "In the Big Town," *New Journal and Guide* (Norfolk, Va.), May 8, 1948, p. 5.

246 **Still, the fact that** As measured by Eunice's ambition, matters went from bad to worse. In July of 1948, the State Department named another black woman, Dr. Merze Tate, to serve as one of three American representatives to the United States Social and Cultural Organization. "Dr. Merze Tate Selected by State Dept. to Represent U.S. on U.N. Committee," *New York Age*, July 17, 1948, p. 4. Tate was considerably overqualified—she had been the first black woman to study at Oxford, held a degree from Harvard, and had published two books on arms control—but for Eunice the blow must still have been bitter. She was falling further behind.

246 **What would matter henceforth** Quoted in Donaldson, *Truman Defeats Dewey*, pp. 25–26. As Donaldson points out, this famous memorandum, long attributed to Clark Clifford, was actually written by former Roosevelt aide James Rowe (pp. 24–25).

246 **Dewey soft-pedaled the issue** See Smith, *Thomas E. Dewey and His Times*, pp. 523–24. See also Donaldson, *Truman Defeats Dewey*, pp. 187–91.

246 **"to exploit his excellent record"** Quoted in Farrington, *Black Republicans*, p. 36.

246 **infuriated activists by his refusal** For a discussion, see Biondi, *To Stand and Fight*, pp. 62–66.

247 **"One of the basic principles"** Republican Party Platform of 1948, June 21, 1948, available at the American Presidency Project, http://www.presidency.ucsb.edu/ws/index.php?pid =25836.

247 **Dewey supporters cited Eunice's rise** See "Tells of Dewey's Record Which Aided Negroes Here," *New York Amsterdam News*, Oct. 16, 1948, p. 1. The theme was a familiar one for the *News*. See, for example, "Gov. Dewey's Record Wins Votes," *New York Amsterdam News*, Oct. 9, 1948, pp. 1, 25.

247 **"If he double-crossed the Jews"** Quoted in Leon H. Washington Jr., "Wash's Wash," *Los Angeles Sentinel*, Oct. 28, 1948, p. 9.

247 **Instead, their strategy would be** Donaldson, *Truman Defeats Dewey*, p. 99.

248 **held victory parties across Manhattan** Smith, *Thomas E. Dewey and His Times*, pp. 40–44.

248 **"Thomas Edward Dewey"** "People in the News: 'Persistence' Is the Dominating Trait That Carried Dewey to the Presidency," *Washington Post*, Nov. 3, 1948, p. 2.

248 **determined the outcome** For a defense of the proposition that the Negro vote made the difference in 1948, see Simon Topping, "'Never Argue with the Gallup Poll': Thomas Dewey, Civil Rights and the Election of 1948," *Journal of American Studies*, vol. 38, no. 2 (Aug. 2004), p. 179.

248 **The Negro press assured readers** James L. Hicks, "The Big Town," *Atlanta Daily World*, Dec. 15, 1948, p. 2.

249 **"bigger and better"** Quoted in Thelma Berlack Boozer, "Choice Chatter," *New York Age*, Dec. 25, 1948, p. 13.

249 **For the first time** See Walter S. White, "Abolition of Racial Segregation at Truman's Inaugural Praised," reprinted in *In Search of Democracy: The NAACP Writings of James Weldon Johnson, Walter White, and Roy Wilkins, 1920–1977*, ed. Sondra Kathryn Wilson (New York: Oxford University Press, 1999), pp. 268, 269–70. See also Lem Graves Jr., "Truman Wasn't Kidding!," *Pittsburgh Courier*, Dec. 18, 1948, p. 1.

249 **the colorful designer gowns** See Toki Schalk Johnson, "Diamonds, Mink, Handsome Gowns Featured by Nation's Outstanding Men and Women at Armory," *Pittsburgh Courier*, Jan. 29, 1949. For more on the migration, see Louis Lautier, "Negro Role in Inaugural Events Bigger Than Ever," *Cleveland Call and Post*, Jan. 24, 1953, p. 1A.

    In Washington, Eunice stayed at the home of John and Mercedes Rector, where the other house guest for the festivities was Lena Horne. Mercedes was the queen of Washington sassiety. Her husband, John, would die the following year, and she would later marry Frank Horne, Lena Horne's uncle.

249 **pretended no Negroes** See, for example, Mary McNair, "Thousands Crowd Armory for Brilliant Inaugural Ball," *Washington Post*, Jan. 21, 1949, p. 2; and Annette Culler Ward, "Capital Scene Galaxy of Color: Inauguration Ball in Washington, Climaxing Week of Social Activities, Reaffirms Elegance for Evening, Emphasizing Satins, Tulles, Taffeta—Black Afternoon Dresses, Cocktail Suits in Crisp Fabrics at Truman's Reception," *Women's Wear Daily*, vol. 78, no. 15 (Jan. 21, 1949), p. 1.

249 **when the post office received** See Lillian Scott, "Along Celebrity Row," *Chicago Defender*, July 24, 1948, p. 17.

250 **probably Chester Williams** This is the implication of Eunice H. Carter to Mary McLeod Bethune, Feb. 17, 1948, Bethune Papers: "I sat in a long, private conference this morning with Chester Williams concerning a matter of most importance to us, but which, at this time, I do not dare put on paper. As soon as I see you, I shall apprise you of the matter and its significance." When a controversy arose over the invitation, Eunice would at first deny that she had made the initial contact through Williams, but later on she would insist that she had.

250 **She was annoyed** See, for example, Mary McLeod Bethune to Eunice Hunton Carter, Oct. 14, 1946, Bethune Papers, complaining about how Vivian Carter Mason represented herself abroad.

250 **selected instead Edith Sampson** The precise reason for Mrs. Bethune's decision to leave the matter to the board is not clear. Christine Lutz suggests that Sampson had repeated to Bethune a disparaging remark made by Eunice after the founder's health forced her to miss the 1948 convention of the National Council of Negro Women. Christine Lutz, "Another Post-War Settlement: Eunice Hunton Carter and Mary McLeod Bethune," *Selected Annual Proceeding of the Florida Conference of Historians*, vol. 16 (March 2009), p. 74. Another possibility (not at all inconsistent with Lutz's idea) is that Bethune had come to resent her protégée, who got the public credit for much of the NCNW's work. (Remember the Capra film and the union threat in 1947.) Then there was the trip to Geneva that Eunice practically stole from under Bethune's nose. And, of course, it was Eunice who, as chairman of the board, kept pressing Bethune to make budget cuts.

    Sampson's presence on the Town Hall tour was a rousing success. So effective was she that the other members chose her as president. When the tour ended, Sampson was much in demand as a speaker. That, too, must have rankled Eunice. For an account of Sampson's considerable achievements as part of the Town Hall, see Helen Laville and Scott Lucas, "The

American Way: Edith Sampson, the NAACP, and African American Identity in the Cold War," *Diplomatic History*, vol. 20, no. 4 (1996), p. 565.

250 **fired off a handwritten note** Eunice H. Carter to Mary McLeod Bethune, undated but clearly April 1949, Bethune Papers.

250 **"I had stabbed you"** Mary McLeod Bethune to Eunice H. Carter, April 14, 1949, Bethune Papers.

250 **more straightforward but still cool** Eunice H. Carter to Mary McLeod Bethune, April 20, 1949, Bethune Papers. The coverage of Sampson's work on the tour by the Negro press was predictably fawning. See, for example, "Town Meeting of the Air Is Ringing Freedom's Bell Around the World," *Chicago Defender*, July 16, 1949, p. 9. When a contretemps arose in Washington, D.C., when the Carlton Hotel refused to serve the Town Hall group because of Sampson's presence, coverage in the Negro press made Sampson the hero of the story. See "Town Hall Group Hits Racial Snag in Capital at End of World Tour," *Chicago Defender*, Oct. 29, 1949, p. 1.

250 **In early June she resigned** Eunice H. Carter to Mary McLeod Bethune, June 10, 1949, Bethune Papers.

251 **"At [first] the whole affair"** Eunice H. Carter to Mary McLeod Bethune, June 16, 1949, Bethune Papers.

251 **"right up there"** Toki Schalk Johnson, "Toki Types," *Pittsburgh Courier*, Oct. 1, 1949, p. 8.

251 **"see Sampson in hell"** Smith, "Mary McLeod Bethune and the National Council of Negro Women," pp. 278–79.

251 **She insisted that the minutes reflect** See Minutes of Nov. 13, 1949, meeting of the board of directors, NCNW, Bethune Papers.

252 **Members explained later** In particular, the delegates seemed to be moved by a speech by another leading candidate, Arenia Mallory, who argued that it was time for the NCNW to end the governance of the "select few." See "Dr. Ferebee Is Winner of Mrs. Bethune's Post: Edith Sampson, Third in Hot Ballot Fight," *Chicago Defender*, Nov. 26, 1949, p. 1.

252 **Bethune sent a curt note** See Mary McLeod Bethune to Eunice H. Carter, Oct. 31, 1949; Eunice H. Carter to Mary McLeod Bethune, Oct. 19, 1949; Mary McLeod Bethune to Eunice H. Carter, Oct. 12, 1949; and Eunice H. Carter to Mary McLeod Bethune, Oct. 10, 1949 (all at the Bethune Papers). The two letters from the second half of the month are particularly frosty.

253 **According to the historian** Lutz's thesis runs roughly as follows: The previous year, Bethune's health had kept her from attending the annual meeting of the NCNW. Eunice supposedly joked that the young people at the meeting had much to teach the older women who were unable to attend. Eunice could be clever and cruel, so it is possible that she said these words. It is also possible that Edith Sampson made them up or exaggerated them. For it was Sampson, "sometimes a chum and sometimes a rival," who repeated the remark to Bethune. In response, writes Lutz, "Mrs. Bethune had an asthma attack and blamed Mrs. Carter who, apart from political party choice, had been her loyal dogsbody for over a decade." Christine Lutz, "Another Post-War Settlement: Eunice Hunton Carter and Mary McLeod Bethune," *Selected Annual Proceedings of the Florida Conference of Historians*, vol. 16 (March 2009), p. 74.

In support of her argument, Lutz cites two letters from Eunice on April 20, 1948, one to Edith Sampson and one to Mr. Bethune. I do not read the correspondence the same way Lutz does. The letter to Bethune makes no mention of any dispute between the women, although one might be implied by this line: "There is not much more that I can say at this point, except I shall continue to work as I always have for what I consider the best interest of the Council and for you." Eunice also apologizes for any pain caused by "our attitude"— that is, in context, hers and Sampson's. Eunice H. Carter to Mary McLeod Bethune, April 20, 1948, Bethune Papers.

The letter to Sampson implies a different source of trouble than the one Lutz suggests: "Mrs. Bethune told me that you telephoned her. She said, however, that the manner in which you spoke upset her considerably. In fact, she had an attack of asthma and sat in a chair for the rest of the night." Eunice H. Carter to Edith Sampson, April 20, 1948, Bethune Papers. Thus in Eunice's telling, Bethune blamed Sampson for her asthma attack. Moreover, Bethune's subsequent letters to Eunice are as warm as ever. See, for example, Mary McLeod Bethune to Eunice H. Carter, April 23, 1948, and Mary McLeod Bethune to Eunice H. Carter, June 30, 1948, Bethune Papers.

253 **Bethune was busy putting distance** See Joyce Ann Hanson, *Mary McLeod Bethune and Black Women's Political Activism* (Columbia: University of Missouri Press, 2003), pp. 187–90. In particular, Bethune distanced herself entirely from another protégée, Vivian Carter Mason, who held a doctorate and was also once touted as a potential successor. Mason had moved too far left.

253 **increasingly wild political stances** Scant weeks later, as if to prove the point, Alphaeus was openly seeking signatures for a letter sending best wishes to Stalin on the occasion of his seventieth birthday. See Alphaeus Hunton, George B. Murphy Jr., and Doxey A. Wilkerson to W. E. B. Du Bois, Dec. 16, 1949, Du Bois Papers.

253 **spoke highly of each other** Eunice and Edith Sampson, on the other hand, remained at loggerheads for a while longer. For evidence, see, for example, "Backwash," *Chicago Defender*, Dec. 2, 1950, p. 6.

253 **Eunice was not among them** See "Funeral Rites Scheduled Today for Famed Negro Leader," *Orlando Sentinel*, May 23, 1955, p. 25.

21. The Reinvention

255 **hugely successful November gala** Lillian Scott, "Along Celebrity Row," *Chicago Defender*, Dec. 3, 1949, p. 9.

255 **In 1948 she had framed** See "Eunice Carter Frames Covenant," *Afro-American* (Baltimore), July 10, 1948, p. 11.

255 **would soon appear** See "Television," *Brooklyn Daily Eagle*, May 14, 1950, p. 12.

256 **at a hearing before the Senate Foreign Relations Committee** See "Bar Leaders Score Genocide Compact," *New York Times*, Jan. 25, 1950, p. 9.

256 **"The situation of the Negro"** *The Genocide Convention: Hearings Before a Subcommittee of the Committee on Foreign Relations, United States Senate, Eighty-first Congress, Second Session, on the International Convention on the Prevention and Punishment of the Crime of Genocide* (Washington, D.C.: U.S. Government Printing Office, 1950), p. 131 (testimony of Eunice H. Carter).

257 **Ronald Reagan managed** See Herbert Hirsch, *Genocide and the Politics of Memory: Studying Death to Preserve Life* (Chapel Hill: University of North Carolina Press, 1995), pp. 199–200.

258 **Papers as far away** See, for example, "NAACP Tea Party Backfires!: Mrs. (Judge) Waring Didn't Show, 'Cause Walter and Poppy Were Ignored," *Pittsburgh Courier*, March 11, 1950, p. 1; "Snub Mrs. White, So Mrs. Waring Cuts NAACP Tea," *Chicago Defender*, March 11, 1950, p. 1. Even the *New York Age*, in most cases reliably in Eunice's corner, called the event "the major social faux pas of the season." "NAACP 'Tea Party' Blowup Reveals Fight for Power," *New York Age*, March 18, 1950, pp. 1, 3. (Notice that all three papers put the story on the front page: a sign of the esteem in which Eunice was held, and also of a certain journalistic glee in seeing her fall.) A letter to the editor even proclaimed the refusal to invite Poppy as no less than "an attempt to discredit Walter White," adding pointedly, "I wonder if there wasn't a bit of 'she-cat' politics in this tea party incident." "That New York Tea Party? 'Cat Politics' to Writer" (letter to the editor), *Pittsburgh Courier*, April 8, 1950, p. 16.

259 **she traveled to Philadelphia** "'YW' Group Hears Eunice H. Carter," *Philadelphia Tribune*, May 9, 1950, p. 7.

259 **benefit luncheon at the Waldorf-Astoria** "A.W.V.S. Presents Style Show Today," *New York Times*, Oct. 18, 1950, p. 41.

259 **Once more she lost out** In the early 1950s, when Sampson's term expired, there was talk once more that the post might go to Eunice. See "New UN Delegate," *Jet*, Nov. 27, 1952, p. 13. But once again she was passed over.

260 **To compound the insult** "Predict Edith Sampson Will Do Excellent Job as Delegate to UN," *Chicago Defender*, Sept. 30, 1950, p. 7. Actually, Sampson's tenure at the United Nations would prove controversial, and she wound up disappointing civil rights leaders. In particular, she was sharply criticized for suggesting in a Helsinki speech in 1952 that Jim Crow was all but over and the Ku Klux Klan had been defeated. She also attacked the 1951 *We Charge Genocide* petition in the creation of which Alphaeus would later have a hand. All of this was apparently at the behest of the State Department. See the discussion in Carol Anderson, "Bleached Souls and Red Negroes: The NAACP and Black Communists in the Early Cold War, 1948–1952," in *Window on Freedom: Race, Civil Rights, and Foreign Affairs, 1945–1988*, ed. Brenda Gayle Plummer (Chapel Hill: University of North Carolina Press, 2003), pp. 93, 103–5.

260 **And Eunice must have writhed** See, for example, "Woman Attorney to UN: Significant Appointment by Truman; Mrs. Edith Sampson of Chicago Joins UN Delegation," *New Journal and Guide* (Norfolk, Va.), Aug. 26, 1950, p. B1 (black press); "Negro Woman Lawyer Slated to Be a U.S. Delegate to U.N.: Edith Sampson of Chicago First of Her Race in Post; Counter-Blow to Red Propaganda," *New York Herald Tribune*, Aug. 19, 1950, p. 1 (white press).

260 **"We understand that"** "A Knife Here and a Hand Grenade There," *Chicago Defender*, Sept. 16, 1950, p. 6.

260 **"to promote public observance"** See "Dewey Names Group to Promote U.N. Day," *New York Times*, Oct. 21, 1950, p. 4.

260 **she delivered one of the principal addresses** See "National Council of Women to Gather in D.C., Nov. 16–18," *Pittsburgh Courier*, Nov. 11, 1950, p. 10.

260 **did not even make the cut** "Women Move Forward in Many Walks of Life: Round-up of Social Activities for Women Ends '50," *Pittsburgh Courier*, Dec. 30, 1950, p. 8.

22. The Siblings

261 **In his 1958 book** J. Edgar Hoover, *Masters of Deceit: The Story of Communism in America and How to Fight It* (New York: Henry Holt, 1958), p. 86.

261 **was almost certainly fabricated** See Robert M. Lichtman, "Louis Budenz, the FBI, and the 'List of 400 Concealed Communists': An Extended Tale of McCarthy-Era Informing," *American Communist History*, vol. 3, no. 1 (2004), p. 25.

262 **Budenz specifically recalled** See Director, FBI [J. Edgar Hoover] to SAC [Special Agent in Charge], New York, July 7, 1950 (Hunton FBI file); and memorandum, SAC, New York, to Director, FBI, July 27, 1950, and attachments (Hunton FBI file). Budenz described Alphaeus as "a light-skinned negro," and recalled that in their "several conferences at the Daily Worker," Alphaeus "revealed himself as a thorough Communist" and "remained so until I left the Party."

262 **only a small one** The FBI, at this time, had a catechism for interrogating witnesses who made such allegations. Standard questions included, for example, whether the supposed Communist had traveled to Russia for training and whether he worked either for the United States government or in a "vital" industry. As answers to these queries do not appear in the summary of Budenz's statement about Alphaeus, we can assume that his replies were negative. Nevertheless, a request went to the Bureau's New York field office for "a report bringing subject's activities up to date." Agents in New York dutifully filed yet another memorandum, largely cobbled together from earlier reports. No further action was taken.

263 **A reception for the Ladies** Lucille Cromer, "Conversation Piece," *New York Age*, Sept. 23, 1950, p. 8.

263 **A speech in Philadelphia** "Mesdames Carter, Waring to Feature 'YW' Programs," *Philadelphia Tribune*, April 11, 1950, p. 5. See also "Prominent Women Preside at YWCA Public Meetings," *Philadelphia Tribune*, April 18, 1950, p. 7.

263 **A committee to support** "Political Notes," *Brooklyn Daily Eagle*, Oct. 20, 1950, p. 4.

263 **A reception for her rival** Lucille Cromer, "Conversation Piece," *New York Age*, Oct. 28, 1950, p. 14.

263 **Eunice took charge of organizing** See Earl Brown, "About the Friends of the NAACP," *New York Amsterdam News*, June 24, 1950, p. 10. See also Lucille Cromer, "Conversation Piece," *New York Age*, June 17, 1950, p. 7.

263 **found themselves in Wonder Lake** Lucille Cromer, "Conversation Piece," *New York Age*, July 22, 1950, p. 10. Also present was Julius Gikonyo Kiano, who would soon after become the first Kenyan to earn a Ph.D. Several other Africans listed as attending could not be traced; evidently their surnames were misspelled in the column.

264 **"brilliant gathering"** Lucille Cromer, "Conversation Piece," *New York Age*, Aug. 26, 1950, p. 10.

265 **misspelled the names** See Gerri Major, "Town Topics," *New York Amsterdam News*, Jan. 6, 1951, p. 16. The celebrant was the Reverend C. A. Nero. The article misidentifies Emily's parents as Mrs. George House (should be Howze) and Robert Ellis (should be David Ellis).

265 **That very December** See, for example, "Harlemites Celebrate Xmas in Four-Day Whirl of Gay Parties," *New York Amsterdam News*, Dec. 30, 1950, p. 17, and "NAACP Branch Committee, National Employees Give Sat. Parties," *New York Amsterdam News*, Dec. 16, 1950, p. 23.

265 **"attractive Westchesterite"** Lucille Cromer, "Conversation Piece," *New York Age*, Jan. 20, 1951, p. 8.

267 **she was replaced** "Back-Wash," *Chicago Defender*, March 10, 1951, p. 6.

267 **she traveled to Athens** "Federated Clubs: American Women of Color Are Traveling Abroad," *Chicago Defender*, April 21, 1951, p. 10.

267 **Eunice was back home** See, for example, "Dr. Dorothy Ferebee, Mrs. Carter Feted," *Afro-American* (Baltimore), June 30, 1951, p. 11; "Nurses' Party," *New York Amsterdam News*, June 16, 1951, p. 19; and "Local Women's Group Honors Two Delegates," *New York Amsterdam News*, June 23, 1951, p. 21. See also "Social Calendar," *New York Age*, June 9, 1951, p. 7.

268 *Dennis v. United States* Dennis v. United States, 341 U.S. 494 (1951). There is little dispute among contemporary scholars about the government's motive in the case: "The prosecution was essentially an attempt to destroy the Communist Party of the United States by convicting and imprisoning all its leaders." Lackland H. Bloom Jr., *Do Great Cases Make Bad Law?* (New York: Oxford University Press, 2014), p. 186.

268 **The case was headline news** See, for example, "11 Reds Lose in Supreme Court," *New York Herald Tribune*, June 5, 1951, p. 1; "Communist Leaders Convictions Upheld by Supreme Court," *Atlanta Daily World*, June 5, 1951, p. 1; "Supreme Court Spurs Further Trials of Reds," *Austin Statesman*, June 5, 1951, p. 1; and "U.S. Flashed Green Light for Prosecuting Communists," *Christian Science Monitor*, June 5, 1951, p. 6.

268 **she was the guest speaker** "Nurses' Party," *New York Amsterdam News*, June 16, 1951, p. 19. Eunice had played an advisory role with the organization for years. But as nursing schools began to integrate, it soon dissolved.

268 **she was up in Harlem** "Social Calendar," *New York Age*, June 9, 1951, p. 7. Dorothy Ferebee, president of the Council, was a co-honoree.

268 **she collected another award** "Dorothy Ferebee Talks at Awards Banquet," *Philadelphia Tribune*, June 19, 1951, p. 6.

269 **Dorothy Hunton writes** Dorothy Hunton, *Unsung Valiant*, p. 83. The friend was Nellie Stanly. I have not been able to discover much information about her. A woman of that name is listed in the Harrison, New Jersey, city directory for 1952, married to a bookbinder named Edward Stanly. This may be the same Nellie Stanly whom the 1940 census gives as white and born in Passaic, New Jersey, in about 1902, making her close to fifty years old at the time of these events, which seems the right age to be a close friend of Dorothy's.

269 **biggest sassiety event of the summer** "Aaron Douglases Celebrate Silver Anniversary," *New York Amsterdam News*, Aug. 18, 1951, p. 20.

269 **reminded its readers in the very first sentence** "Red Probers Jail Hunton," *New York Amsterdam News*, July 14, 1951, p. 5. See also Cliff Mackay, "The Week's News in Tabloid," *Afro-American* (Baltimore), July 21, 1951, p. 4.

270 **While at West Street** See, for example, "U.S. Jury Questions 2 Bail Fund Aides," *New York Times*, July 21, 1952, p. 22.

270 **They were in the grand jury** "3 Bail Trustees Questioned on 4 Missing Reds," *New York Herald Tribune*, July 19, 1951, p. 19.

270 **"frequent interruptions"** Frederick Vanderbilt Field, *From Right to Left: An Autobiography* (Westport, Conn.: Lawrence Hill, 1983), p. 227.

270 **Hunton and the other trustees** See "Red Leader Nears Removal to Coast," *New York Times*, Aug. 7, 1951, p. 6, and "Schneiderman Bail Reduced to $75,000," *New York Herald Tribune*, Aug. 7, 1951, p. 18.

270 **Once more they refused** "Red Bail Trustees Also Defy State," *New York Times*, Aug. 1, 1951, p. 4.

270 **Alphaeus and his fellow trustees** "Hammett Being Moved to Kentucky Prison," *Washington Post*, Sept. 20, 1951, p. B13.

271 **even jobs on Capitol Hill** In fairness, the reason Eunice did not take a job on Capitol Hill with the newly elected Senator Kenneth Keating in 1958 may have been her husband's illness. See "They Helped Rockefeller Win," *New York Age*, Nov. 15, 1958, p. 20. The article speculated nevertheless that appointment to a state board would be Eunice's "for the asking." Yet, once again, it didn't happen.

272 **There were several more** See "Women Pass Resolution to Back Civil Rights," *Atlanta Daily World*, Nov. 8, 1951, p. 2.

272 **"Corporation Counsel"** "Women's World," *Philadelphia Tribune*, Nov. 24, 1951, p. 6. Eunice, who once would have led off the column, is not mentioned until the very end. See also "Women Agree to Let Men Handle World," *New Journal and Guide* (Norfolk, Va.), Nov. 24, 1951, p. 3. Both papers reprinted the same article from the Associated Negro Press.

272 **A surviving photograph shows** In David Levering Lewis's splendid biography of Du Bois, this photograph is incorrectly dated 1954.

Epilogue

275 **adopted by the General Assembly** A good summary is David Owen, "The United Nations Program of Technical Assistance," *Annals of the American Academy of Political and Social Science*, vol. 270 (July 1950), p. 109.

275 **And Eunice did discuss** Mrs. Eunice Hunton Carter, "Women in the Technical Assistance Program," typescript, prepared for delivery in January 1951.

278 **"was in the process"** Federal Bureau of Investigation, Confidential Memorandum, "William Alphaeus Hunton," December 11, 1967 (Hunton FBI file).

279 **the end of America** Bernard Taper, "A Meeting in Atlanta," *New Yorker*, March 17, 1956, p. 93.

INDEX

ABOUT THE AUTHOR

STEPHEN L. CARTER is the bestselling author of six novels—including *The Emperor of Ocean Park* and *New England White*—and eight works of nonfiction. Formerly a law clerk for Supreme Court Justice Thurgood Marshall, he is the William Nelson Cromwell Professor of Law at Yale University, where he has taught for more than thirty-five years. He and his wife live in Connecticut.